Studying the Novel

Studying the Novel

7th Edition

Jeremy Hawthorn

Bloomsbury Academic
An imprint of Bloomsbury Publishing Plc

B L O O M S B U R Y
LONDON · OXFORD · NEW YORK · NEW DELHI · SYDNEY

Bloomsbury Academic

An imprint of Bloomsbury Publishing Plc

50 Bedford Square	1385 Broadway
London	New York
WC1B 3DP	NY 10018
UK	USA

www.bloomsbury.com

BLOOMSBURY and the Diana logo are trademarks of Bloomsbury Publishing Plc

First published in Great Britain in 1985
Second edition published in 1992
Third edition published in 1997
Fourth edition published in 2001
Fifth edition published in 2005
Sixth edition published in 2010
Seventh edition published in 2017 by Bloomsbury Academic

British Library Cataloguing-in-Publication Data
A catalogue record for this book is available from the British Library.

ISBN:	HB:	978-1-4725-7510-4
	PB:	978-1-4725-7511-1
	ePDF:	978-1-4725-7513-5
	ePub:	978-1-4725-7512-8

Library of Congress Cataloging-in-Publication Data
A catalog record for this book is available from the Library of Congress.

Series: Studying...

Cover design: Liron Gilenberg
Cover image © Getty Images

Typeset by Integra Software Services Pvt. Ltd.
Printed and bound in India

Contents

Introduction to the Seventh Edition

The seventh edition of this book includes new material and a certain amount of restructuring. There is now discussion of issues associated with reading novels in translation (Chapter 7) and inclusion of a new chapter (Chapter 9) on World Literature. Chapter 9 contains material on the novel and travel, the novel and cultural imperialism, and on fiction and the Holocaust, which in previous editions was located in other chapters.

The material on "Fiction and the electronic media" that had a chapter to itself in the sixth edition has been updated and repositioned in Chapter 4, and the section on "Using computers" in Chapter 6 has been thoroughly updated.

Four anonymous readers made valuable suggestions, and I am grateful to them for their advice. One reader pointed out that "the canon" is a contested and controversial term, and I have tried to make this clearer than I did in previous editions.

I thank Camilla Ulleland Hoel, for introducing me to the pleasures of *The Lizzie Bennet Diaries*, and Frode Lerum Boasson, for pointing me in the direction of useful material on the publishing history of Knut Hamsun's *Hunger*. I owe an especial debt to Jakob Lothe, who has read and commented on some of the new sections in this book. All errors and inadequacies in the published version are, of course, my sole responsibility.

Since my retirement in May 2012, the Norwegian University of Science and Technology has made it possible for me to continue to have a work space on campus, along with access to e-mail, computer, and library facilities. This has been of great benefit to me and I am very grateful.

Jeremy Hawthorn
Trondheim, Norway, January 2016

1

Fiction and the Novel

Preview

This chapter deals with:

- Some preliminary definitions: novel, fiction, narrative
- The universality of fiction and the distinctiveness of literary fiction
- Imaginary characters and real life
- Prose and narrative
- Showing and telling
- Characters, action, plot
- Novel, short story, novella: some preliminary comments

According to the *Oxford English Dictionary*, a novel is "a fictitious prose narrative or tale of considerable length (now usually one long enough to fill one or more volumes) in which characters and actions representative of the real life of past or present times are portrayed in a plot of more or less complexity." This may sound a bit like stating the obvious, but there are some important points contained in this very concise definition. Let us consider some of its component parts.

The universality and the distinctiveness of fiction

"Telling stories" is an activity that is so central to our culture that we pay it little analytical attention. From a very early age, we learn to distinguish not just between true and untrue reports but also between different sorts of untrue reports—"lies" and "stories," for example. Fiction is much wider than the novel or, indeed, than prose fiction: jokes, imitations and parodies, and songs and narrative poems can all be described as fictions—and wider, non-literary usages include such things as legal fictions and (perhaps) folktales and urban myths (fictions do not have to take the form of a story or a narrative). However, if fiction seems to be universally present in the lives of all human beings, it nevertheless assumes different forms in different ages and different societies. Not all fictions are novels, then, but the specific tradition or set of traditions which we refer to as "the novel" is made possible by a far more widespread and fundamental reliance upon fiction in human society.

We can start with a number of seeming paradoxes: fictions are not true, but they are not lies; they typically describe that which is not real but which is nonetheless not totally unreal; they can include references to real people and events without jeopardizing their fictional status; they are designed to get readers or listeners to respond "as if," but not (normally) to deceive them; even though readers are aware that fictions describe people who do not exist or events which have not happened, they may nonetheless produce real emotions, important reflections, and even altered behavior in the real world.

If fiction is in one sense universal, those fictions that we call novels and short stories are arguably possessed of certain unique features. In her book *The Distinction of Fiction* (1999), Dorrit Cohn makes an impressively energetic case for the distinctiveness of *literary* fiction. Cohn suggests that literary fictions can be distinguished from other non-fictional narratives in three ways. First, the distinction between *story* and *plot* (in her terminology *story* and *discourse*) does not have the same validity for "texts that refer to events that have occurred prior to their narrative embodiment." You will find this point easier to understand after having read the discussion of story and plot on p. 134. Second, only in fictional narratives can narrators enter the consciousness of persons apart from themselves. Third, in non-fictional narratives the distinction between author and narrator does not make the same sort of sense as it does when applied to fictional texts (1999, 130). I take up some of the issues raised by fictional accounts of actual events in Chapter 9 in a discussion of stories written by survivors of the Nazi Holocaust (see p. 252).

In the 1950s the London *Evening Standard* ran a regular feature entitled "Did It Happen?" The newspaper would publish an account of a striking experience, then ask readers to decide whether the experience really did happen, with the truth being revealed the following day. The authors ranged from Stevie Smith and Angus Wilson to Gerard Hoffnung and Benny Hill, and their contributions were gathered together and published as a book in 1956 (*Did It Happen?: Stories*). Reading through the contributions it is interesting to see what a writer has to do to leave the reader in doubt as to whether he or she is reading fact or fiction. All of the accounts are in the first person, and in no case does the narrator enter the consciousness of another person. No account suggests a distinction between author and narrator. Once we know whether the account is fact or fiction we can indeed recognize, as Cohn suggests, that the distinction between author and narrator and that between story and plot make a different sort of sense for the two types of account. But these are retrospective judgments. It is the entering of the consciousness of a person other than the narrator that seems to suggest most strongly that a narrative is fictional, and the authors of the "fictional" accounts seem instinctively to have recognized this.

Fiction, play, fantasy

Anyone who has watched a child grow and mature will know that he or she attempts to understand and master the world and his or her relation to it through modeled performances that we call play. However much we may like to think of play as sharply distinguished from the real, workaday world, relegated to "free time" or "relaxation," there seems little doubt that the rules of games can function as a model of the social and material restraints which we meet with in the world, and that play can help us to internalize these aspects of the world and of our operating within it. A number of recent theorists have developed this analogy in discussing the role that fiction plays in ordinary people's lives. In her book *Why We Read Fiction: Theory of Mind and the Novel* (2006), Lisa Zunshine writes as follows:

> The cognitive rewards of reading fiction might thus be aligned with the cognitive rewards of pretend play through a shared capacity to stimulate and develop the imagination. It may mean that our enjoyment of fiction is predicated—at least in part—upon our *awareness* of our "trying on" mental states *potentially available* to us but at a given moment *differing* from our own. (Zunshine 2006, 17)

In his book *The Rhetoric of Fictionality: Narrative Theory and the Idea of Fiction*, Richard Walsh introduces another helpful analogy—that between fiction and "exercise." As he notes, "When you go for a jog, you may not be trying to get anywhere in particular, but you are certainly not pretending to run" (Walsh 2007, 45). The comment is clearly aimed at those who believe that when, for example, Charles Dickens wrote *David Copperfield* as a first-person narrative, he was pretending to be David Copperfield, and he wanted the reader to pretend that his novel really was written by the character. Both Zunshine and Walsh agree that reading fiction does not require an abandonment of a sense of who we are or who the author is. Indeed they suggest that retaining such a sense is crucial to the reading of fiction.

Fictional stories present us with models of (especially) the social world with which we can empathize, but which we can observe because we are not constrained to act. According to Peter Lamarque and Stein Haugom Olsen (1994), readers "often fantasize with fictive content, 'filling in' as the whim takes them, and no doubt some genres of fantasy actively encourage this kind of whimsical response." This is rather stern, and it becomes more so as the two authors then insist upon the need to distinguish between authorized and non-authorized responses—with "the content itself and its presentation" as the source of this authority (89). Although academic discussion of literature has to insist upon such standards in order to establish ground rules for discussion and debate, I do not think that readers (as against students or critics) of novels are—or ever have been—obliged to remain within the boundaries of the academically authorized. Indeed, were it possible to render "whimsical responses" impossible, then I suspect that novel-reading would be a lot less popular than it is today. Remember, however, that "response" is not the same as "interpretation"; my response may be different from yours, but we can try to reach agreement about our interpretation of a given work through discussion of the text.

Imaginary characters and real life

The novel typically depicts imaginary characters and situations. A novel may include reference to real places, people, and events, but a narrative that contained *only* such references would have to establish its fictional credentials by imagining the thoughts of characters. Even though its characters and actions are imaginary, they are in some sense "representative of real life," as the dictionary definition has it; although fictional, they bear an important resemblance to the real. What exactly this resemblance is has been a matter of much discussion and dispute among literary critics, and it is arguable that it varies in kind from novel to novel. Even so, this resemblance to *real* life is one of the features that distinguishes the novel from other forms such as the epic and the romance (see the Glossary and also the discussion on p. 14), however much we recognize that "real life" is a problematic concept. Later on in Chapter 4 we will see that the term "realism" is one that, although arguably indispensable to discussion of the novel, requires careful definition and use.

The Russian critic Mikhail Bakhtin points out that "[t]he world of the epic is the national heroic past," it is based upon a "national tradition (not personal experience and the free thought that grows out of it)," and "an absolute epic distance separates the epic world from contemporary reality." The novel, "by contrast, is determined by experience, knowledge and practice (the future)" (Bakhtin 1981, 13, 15). The novel presents us with stories, experiences that are new; whereas those who experienced the epic knew what was to occur, when we pick up a novel we hope that our curiosity will be aroused by our wanting to know "what happens." As I will argue in Chapter 2, this difference has a lot to do with the different sorts of society from which these two genres emerge.

Prose

The novel is in prose rather than verse, although the language of novels may often strike us as very "poetic" on occasions. It would nonetheless be a serious mistake to assume that the language of a novel—and especially the speech of characters—is identical to that of ordinary speech or of most non-literary writing, and I discuss this more on p. 150. Even so, the fact that the novel is in prose helps to establish that sense of "real life"— of recognizable, everyday, "prosaic" existence—that is the preserve of the genre. Generalization is dangerous, but prose has the potentiality of being a more transparent medium than, for example, verse. Reading a novel, our attention is not naturally drawn to considering the language as language. The tendency is more for us to "look through" the language of the novel at what it describes and evokes than to "look at" it—although novelists can write prose that arrests our attention as language, and many novelists are known for the manner in which they draw the reader's attention to their use of language. In the course of studying novels, we must learn to pay more overt attention to their language than does the average casual reader.

Narrative

Novels and shorter works of literary fiction are *narratives*: in other words they all in some sense present readers with a "telling" rather than an "enacting," and this distinguishes them in an important sense from the drama. One useful way to define narrative involves reference to what Seymour Chatman has called "double chronology" (1990, 114): the things that happen in a novel happen in a particular order, and the telling of what happens also takes place in a particular order. Importantly, these two "orders" or chronologies are not necessarily the same, and the interaction between them constitutes a fundamentally important aspect of the novel and the short story. Double chronology entails that built into the very fact of narrative is an act of looking back, of *recounting*. As the first-person narrator of Javier Marías's novel *Tomorrow in the Battle Think on Me* remarks, "in fact, the person telling the story always tells it later on, which allows him to add things if he wants, to distance himself: 'I have turned away my former self, I am not the thing I was nor the person I was, I neither know nor recognize myself'" (Marías 1997, 308).

You will find more about narrative's double chronology in the discussion of story and plot on p. 134. Double chronology is a necessary but not a sufficient condition of a narrative, as it may apply also to plays and films. (*Citizen Kane* opens with the depiction of events which take place after the events that are recounted in the bulk of the film have taken place: the order-in-which-things-take-place is not the same as the order-in-which-we-witness-what-takes-place.) What is, I would argue, central to narration is the element of telling: events in a piece of prose fiction come to us mediated through an organizing consciousness that puts them into words.

Here I should note that not all narrative theorists would agree with my exclusion of film and drama from the category of narrative. In the previous paragraph, for example, I quote from Seymour Chatman, and the book from which his comment is drawn is entitled *Story and Discourse: Narrative Structure in Fiction and Film*. Those who argue that a film is as much a narrative as a novel generally base their view on the fact that the events and actions depicted in a film are (at least metaphorically) "told" to us through the organizing work of a director. Even so, watching a film or a play, we observe things as they happen. Reading a novel, we are told that things happen, have happened, or will happen.

Of course, novels can contain very dramatic scenes, scenes that grip us with their immediacy. Reading such scenes, we may forget that what we learn of character and event is not experienced directly through a presentation or an enactment (as in the theater or the cinema) but mediated through a particular telling, coming from a narrative source. Take the opening of Henry James's short story "The Lesson of the Master" (1888):

> He had been told the ladies were at church, but this was corrected by what he saw from the top of the steps—they descended from a great height in two arms, with a circular sweep of the most charming effect—at the threshold of the door which, from the long bright gallery, overlooked the immense lawn. (James 1970, 3)

If our first impression is that we are witnessing a scene directly, a second glance will confirm that we are actually being *told about* the scene, which is presented as one character experiences it. The telling is such that we can visualize what is described—that is often the mark of an accomplished narrative—but we see what is first selected and then pointed out to us by a narrator or a narrative voice or source. Of course, this selection and presentation are fictional: the author is actually *creating* rather than selecting what we see. Nevertheless, as we read we are given the sense that the scene's potentially infinite complexity is reduced, ordered, and explained to us through the organizing and filtering consciousness of a narrator. Could any filmed version of the above scene lead us to think of the steps as forming "two arms"? Would we find the effect of the "circular sweep" "most charming" unless a character used these words? Would we know that we saw the scene as a given character was seeing it? I will say more about the difference between film and prose narrative in Chapter 7.

An additional word of caution is needed at this point. You should be aware that there is a further way in which the term "narrative" can be used both with a narrow and specific meaning and also with a rather wider one. This sense has nothing to do with such questions as whether films are narratives, but with the issues raised by calling a long novel a narrative when it contains passages that are not strictly speaking narratives but may be lyric interludes or philosophical discussions. From a more restrictive perspective only parts of such a long novel would, then, qualify as examples of narrative: those involving the telling of events, the recounting of things that happen. (Clearly events can just as well be mental as physical: a sudden dawning of insight is as much an event as is the outbreak of the First World War.)

The words "tell" and "recount" are both related to the action of counting, or enumerating (think of a bank teller, who counts money). As "tell" is etymologically related to "tale," we can say that behind the act of narrative itself lies the idea of communicating things that can be counted. (Compare the French *conte*, for which a brief definition is provided in the Glossary.) If we limit ourselves to a restrictive definition of narrative, therefore, we must remember that neither *description* (of a beautiful scene) nor *argument* (about, say, the existence of God) are examples of narrative in this strict sense; they do not involve the telling or enumerating of discrete events or countable entities. However, the term "narrative" is also conventionally used in a less restrictive sense to include everything that comes within the purview of a particular telling or recounting. From this perspective a novel is a narrative even though it contains passages of description and argument. If you think about it, much the same is true of our use of the word "fiction." After all, many statements in novels are literally true, yet we do not restrict use of the word "fiction" to only those parts of novels that are untrue.

In Chapter 8 I will say more about *narratology*—a body of theory that has emerged in the past four decades out of attempts to generalize about different types of narrative, and to develop concepts and methods that can be used to classify and analyze narratives.

Characters, action, plot

The novel has *characters*, *action(s)*, and a *plot*: it presents the reader with individuals who do things in a defining context or "secondary world" (see p. 19) ruled over by some sort of connective logic: chronology, cause and effect, or whatever. In most novels we also find a connection between these three elements such that they form some sort of unity. A poem does not have to contain characters or a plot—or, indeed, any action—but it is only very rare novels which dispense with one of these elements, and in such unusual cases it is often a matter of dispute as to whether the net result is recognizable as a novel. Some recent narrative theorists have preferred to talk of "actors" rather than characters, pointing out that a work of science fiction might be based on roles filled by non-human participants. I return to the relationship between literary characterizations and the emergence of ideas of human individuality on page 27.

We have of course to give the term "action" a relatively broad meaning in the present context. Much recent fiction involves significant concentration upon what has been termed "inner action," that is, events taking place in a character's consciousness rather than in the social and physical worlds outside. It is nevertheless revealing that there are few novels that consist only, or mainly, of inner action. It is as if our view of the novel requires that it contain a significant amount of action more traditionally defined.

Ian Watt has argued that the novel is distinguished by the fact that unlike the works of the great English and Classical poets and dramatists, its plots are generally not taken from traditional sources (Watt 1963, 14). If we compare the modern novel with the prose fictions of antiquity, or the medieval romance, Watt's point is certainly justifiable. On the other hand, even the modern novel has recourse to certain recurrent plots and story lines (see the more extended discussion of plot on p. 134). As a result, many modern novels manifest an important and productive *tension* between their fidelity to the random and unpredictable nature of everyday life and their patterning according to the demands of certain predetermined but widely different structures, from "tragedy" to "repetition" or "the journey." Novels can be written within traditions that are highly *formulaic*—that is, written to conform to a particular, pre-existing pattern. The popular romance of today with its shy blonde heroine who is finally appreciated by the good-looking hero after he has seen through the strikingly attractive but treacherous dark anti-heroine is but one in a long line of formulaic sub-genres that can be traced back to the folk tales of oral cultures.

Novel, short story, novella

Finally, the novel is of a certain length. A poem can be anything from a couplet to a thousand pages or more, but we feel unhappy about bestowing the term "novel" on a tale of some forty or fifty pages. Of course it is not just a question of length: we feel that a novel should involve an investigation of an issue of human significance in such a manner as allows for complexity of treatment, and by common consent a certain length is necessary to allow for such complexity. In practice, therefore, we now usually refer to a prose narrative of some twenty or thirty pages or fewer as a short story, while a work that seems to hover on the awkward boundary between "short story" and "novel," having a length of between forty or fifty and a hundred pages, is conventionally described as a novella (plural: novelle or novellas). I say "now," because some of these conventional categorizations are relatively recent, particularly so far as the short story and the novella are concerned, and some of the issues raised by dividing prose fiction into three main categories in this way are discussed in-depth in Chapter 3.

Topics for discussion

- What elements must a literary work contain to be considered a novel? Does the answer change as the novel changes?
- Is literary fiction different from other fictions? If so, in what ways?
- Do you read novels to escape from "the real world" or to learn more about it? Or both?
- Can reading a novel change your life?
- Why do we classify novels and short stories as narratives?

2

History, Genre, Culture

Preview

This chapter deals with:

- The problem of deciding when (and if) the novel was born
- The relationship between the novel and the romance
- The contribution of literacy, printing, a market economy, and individualism to the novel
- The novel, secularism, and urban experience

When was the novel born?

In her *The True Story of the Novel* (1996), Margaret Anne Doody reminds her readers that the distinction between novel and romance (see below, p. 14) is one that is not reflected in all languages in the way that it is in English, and she proposes that it "has outworn its usefulness, and that at its most useful it created limitations and encouraged blind spots" (1996, xvii). Resisting a common view that the novel emerges as a new literary form in the late seventeenth or early eighteenth century, she claims that the novel "as a form of literature in the West has a continuous history of about two thousand years," a fact that, she argues, recent scholarship has denied or obscured (1996, 1). In order to press her case, she advances a rather wider and more all-embracing definition of the novel from that which I quoted from the *OED* at the start of my first chapter; for her, a work is a novel if "it is fictional, if it is in prose, and if it is of a certain length" (1996, 16).

A less comprehensive attack on the conventional view that the novel emerges with Defoe, Richardson, and Fielding is provided by J.A. Downie, who draws attention to the fact that "writings calling themselves novels had been appearing in print in English for about a hundred and fifty years before the publication of *Robinson Crusoe* [in 1719]," and that while Richardson's *Pamela* did indeed lead to a sustained increase in the demand for fiction, Defoe's work did not (Downie 2000, 311, 325).

There is no doubt that, if one defines the novel as Doody recommends, then it is quite correct to see it as a literary form with a continuous history of two thousand years, and it is certainly the case that the term "novel" did not emerge for the first time in the eighteenth century. It is also the case that we should avoid falling into the trap of believing that the works on modern literature syllabuses were the only ones read by and exerting influence on readers and writers, and we need further to be aware that there are continuities and lines of tradition that cut across the sharp dividing lines posited by talk of "the birth of the novel."

Critics other than Margaret Doody have also engaged in debate about the extent to which those "novel" works produced by writers such as Defoe, Richardson, and Fielding in the first half of the eighteenth century were or were not in direct line of descent from the chapbooks and the French fiction of the late seventeenth century, hundreds of which were translated into English and published in England at this time (Novak 1991, 8). Even those who concur with the view that the modern novel emerges as a new literary genre in the eighteenth century concede that it still owes much to traditions and works, literary and non-literary, from earlier times. No serious student of the novel would deny, for example, that its development in the eighteenth century was profoundly influenced by works such as François Rabelais's *Pantagruel* and *Gargantua* (1532 and 1534) and Miguel de Cervantes's *Don Quixote* (1605–15)—whether or not one agrees to classify these works as novels.

These views notwithstanding, my own view is that what happened to prose fiction in the course of the eighteenth century in Europe represents such a radical change that what, to sidestep debate, we can call "the modern novel" merits and repays separate study. As Michael McKeon points out, it was the first modern "novelists" themselves who affirmed that "a distinct new form" had emerged: Richardson believed he had introduced a new "species" of writing while Fielding claimed a new "kind" or "province" (McKeon 1987, 410). (See too Samuel Johnson's comments on "[t]he works of fiction, with which the present generation seems more particularly delighted," on p. 17 later in this chapter.)

Ancestors and close relations

It would be a serious mistake to assume that to trace the novel's descent we need to examine only a sequence of written forms, or of oral and written narratives. We should rather picture a family tree in which certain lines of descent involve various written forms, certain involve a succession of oral narrative forms, but others involve a wide range of very different elements. I have already suggested that fiction has an analogue in play, but other relatives are equally important: introspective self-analyses, both in diary and in unrecorded form; joke-telling; sermons; travel accounts; letters. What distinguishes the novel is, among other things, the heterogeneity of its ancestry, a heterogeneity that Mikhail Bakhtin has argued is mirrored in the variety of different "voices" to be found in any single novel. He claims (and this is by no means uncontroversial) that, however many contradictions and conflicts are developed in a poem, the world of poetry is always illuminated by "one unitary and indisputable discourse." The novel, in contrast, is he argues characterized by that "variety of individualized voices" that is "the prerequisite for authentic novelistic prose" (Bakhtin 1981, 286). It should be noted that the term "voice" has more than a physical reference for Bakhtin, and includes ideological and existential elements too.

One of the impulses that often moves those who compile family trees is a desire to prove that all the discovered ancestors were respectable and legitimate. In the case of the novel, we have to be prepared to accept that many of its ancestors were neither. As J. Paul Hunter has put it,

> I join the debate here by arguing that the emerging novel must be placed in a broader context of cultural history, insisting that popular thought and materials of everyday print—journalism, didactic materials with all kinds of religious and ideological directions, and private papers and histories—need to be seen as contributors to the social and intellectual world in which the novel emerged. (Hunter 1990, 5)

Even though it be true that fictional narratives can be found almost as far back as we have written records, those produced before the emergence of the modern novel lack many of the characteristics that today we associate with the novel. First, they are often in verse rather than prose. Second, they rarely concern themselves with "the real life of past or present times" but portray the experiences of those whose existences can be said to resemble "real life," however it is defined, only in extremely convention-governed and indirect ways (gods or mythical heroes, for example). Third, their characters tend not to be individualized—to the extent that even the use of our familiar term "character" is problematic. We do not feel too comfortable calling a purely stereotyped or conventionally portrayed individual a character precisely because today the term "character" is associated with *distinctive* traits, with some particularity or individuality. (For further discussion of literary character, see p. 126.)

The etymology of "character" is very revealing: the word comes from a Greek word for an instrument used for marking or engraving, just as "style" is etymologically related to the word stylus and is also associated with a cutting instrument. As a result, the word's literal meanings—as the *OED* will confirm— are related to marks that distinguish and represent individuality (think of the obsolescent use of the word "character" to mean a person's handwriting). From this we get the familiar *OED* definition: "A personality invested with distinctive attributes and qualities, by a novelist or dramatist." Our sense of human individuality, this etymology suggests, is closely related to making marks—to *writing*. Writing allows human beings to develop individualities, to be and to know themselves to be different, particular, unique.

Novel and romance

There is no better example of the problems attendant upon generic classification than those connected with the romance, universally agreed to represent one of the most important traditions contributing to the emergence of the modern novel. (The term "roman," as Margaret Anne Doody reminds us [see p. 11], is the equivalent of "novel" in many modern European languages. Etymologically the two terms tell different stories; while the word "novel" comes from the Italian "novella"—"small new thing"—the word "romance" evolves from a word denoting a concern with the Romans. Even in modern usage this sense of the novel looking forward to the new and the romance looking back to the old can be detected.)

The traditional chivalric romance that developed in twelfth-century France depicted not epic heroes but a highly stylized and idealized courtly life founded upon rigid but sophisticated conventions of behavior. Like the epic (which it displaced) it often involved supernatural elements— another factor that in general terms distinguishes it from the modern novel. The distinction with which we are familiar is first commented upon in the eighteenth century, the century in which, I have argued, the novel appears in its recognizable modern form in Britain. Geoffrey Day quotes the following from a review of Frances Burney's novel *Camilla*, which appeared in *The British Critic* of November 1796:

> To the old romance, which exhibited exalted personages, and displayed their sentiments in improbable or impossible situations, has succeeded the more reasonable, modern novel; which delineates characters drawn from actual observation, and, when ably executed, presents an accurate and captivating view of real life. (Day 1987, 6)

As Day notes, "throughout the eighteenth century 'romance' was seen by many as a term suggesting excessive flights of fancy" (1987, 6). However as Day adds, this neat definition, one which served to distinguish the "romance" from the "novel," was not universally accepted: many writers tended to lump the two terms together relatively uncritically.

> [T]hough there is a tradition of clarity of definition, there is vastly more evidence to show that those works now commonly referred to as "eighteenth-century novels" were not perceived as such by the readers or indeed by the major writers of the period, and that, far from being ready to accept the various works as "novels," they do not appear to have arrived at a consensus that works such as *Robinson Crusoe*, *Pamela*, *Joseph Andrews*, *Clarissa*, *Tom Jones*, *Peregrine Pickle* and *Tristram Shandy* were even all of the same species. (1987, 7)

(In case we should be tempted to feel superior to these dull individuals who were incapable of recognizing the birth of a new genre, it is salutary to stop and think about the enormous formal variety that this short list of works represents.)

In an extract from a letter written by the eighteenth-century man of politics Lord Chesterfield to his son, we can detect both the familiar novel–romance distinction and also a sense that the two categories overlap to a considerable extent.

> I am in doubt whether you know what a Novel is: it is a little gallant history, which must contain a great deal of love, and not exceed one or two small volumes. The subject must be a love affair; the lovers are to meet with many difficulties and obstacles, to oppose the accomplishment of their wishes, but at last overcome them all; and the conclusion or catastrophe must leave them happy. A Novel is a kind of abbreviation of a Romance; for a Romance generally consists of twelve volumes, all filled with insipid love nonsense, and most incredible adventures.

...

In short, the reading of Romances is a most frivolous occupation, and time merely thrown away. The old Romances, written two or three hundred years ago, such as Amadis of Gaul, Orlando the Furious, and others, were stuffed with enchantments, magicians, giants, and such sort of impossibilities, whereas the more modern Romances keep within the bounds of possibility, but not of probability. (Carey 1912, 90; the original letter is in French, and is probably written 1740–1)

Geoffrey Day points out that in his *Dictionary* (1755), Samuel Johnson also insisted on the importance of length, defining a novel as "A small tale, generally of love." Today Samuel Richardson's *Clarissa* (1747–8) is uncontroversially defined as a novel, but it is certainly not a "small tale"; at the same time, Johnson's own small tale *Rasselas* (1759) cannot comfortably be assimilated into what we now think of as a novel. It is arguably only in the early years of the nineteenth century that our present understanding of what a novel is starts to emerge as a consensus view.

Although the development of the English novel is generally associated with a concern with the everyday and a rejection of the supernatural, those aspects of the romance that were repressed as the novel defined itself did not disappear from fiction altogether. Freudians claim that the repressed always returns, and the history of prose fiction would seem to confirm this: the fantastic, the supernatural, the other-worldly (whether defined in religious or in astronomical terms) constitute the novel's dogged shadow. Sometimes this family of repressed elements emerges within what we can call mainstream fiction in hints and suggestions (madness, dreams, and fevered hallucinations are a favored way of introducing the supernatural into fiction without directly challenging a realistic framework). At the same time, this family of excluded romance components also survives in what we can call sub-genres such as the modern romance or the ghost story. As I will argue later on, it is noticeable how many of the elements excluded from what I have termed mainstream fiction suddenly reappear in forms associated with the electronic media. There are clear and, I think, undeniable lines of descent from the medieval romance through the gothic novel to fantasy games such as "Dungeons and Dragons" and computer games such as *Tomb Raider* (for more discussion of this, see Chapter 4, p. 86).

However, even if fantastic and romance elements survive in the novel, there is no doubt that an emphasis upon the this-worldly is fundamental to the novel's emergence as a major genre, and at the time of the birth of the modern novel in the early and mid-eighteenth century, this emphasis was widely believed by contemporary readers to distinguish the novel from the romance. Geoffrey Day cites another useful contemporary definition that again defines the novel by contrasting it to the romance, from Samuel Johnson's fourth *Rambler* essay (1750). Johnson clearly has in mind what we now call the novel in these comments, but he designates it "the comedy of romance."

> The works of fiction, with which the present generation seems more particularly delighted, are such as exhibit life in its true state, diversified only by accidents that daily happen in the world, and influenced by passions and qualities which are really to be found in conversing with mankind.
>
> This kind of writing may be termed not improperly the comedy of romance, and is to be conducted nearly by the rules of comic poetry. Its province is to bring about natural events by easy means, and to keep up curiosity without the help of wonder: it is therefore precluded from the machines and expedients of the heroic romance, and can neither employ giants to snatch away a lady from the nuptial rites, nor knights to bring her back from captivity; it can neither bewilder its personages in desarts, nor lodge them in imaginary castles.
>
> …
>
> The task of our present writers is very different; it requires, together with that learning which is to be gained from books, that experience which can never be attained by solitary diligence, but must arise from general converse, and accurate observation of the living world. (Johnson 1958, 60, 61)

This is what was seen to be new about the fictional narratives written by Defoe, Richardson, and Fielding, whether or not these works were called novels. "Life in its true state," "accurate observation of the living world": these narratives have a relationship with *ordinary* life, with the *detail* of *contemporary experience*, both social and individual, which sets them apart from the romance. Michael Seidel sums up these characteristics as follows: "a concentration on daily life in particularized settings; a sense of information and immediacy; conventions of behaviour that would appear, at least to a reading audience, as part of its recognizable world" (Seidel 2000, 194). It is worth noting that Johnson thought that this characteristic of the emerging genre carried with it specific *dangers*. He observed that novels were

> written chiefly to the young, the ignorant, and the idle, to whom they serve as lectures of conduct, and introductions into life. They are the entertainment of minds unfurnished with ideas, and therefore easily susceptible of impressions; not fixed by principles, and therefore easily following the current of fancy; not informed by experience, and consequently open to every false suggestion and partial account. (61)

These new and vulnerable readers would not have been tempted to model their behavior on the old romances because these depicted transactions and sentiments "remote from all that passes among men," but, fears Johnson, they may be so tempted by depictions of a world similar to their own.

> [W]hen an adventurer is levelled with the rest of the world, and acts in such scenes of the universal drama, as may be the lot of any other man; young spectators fix their eyes upon him with closer attention, and hope, by observing his behaviour and success, to regulate their own practices, when they shall be engaged in the like part. (62)

Thus whereas nowadays our cultural guardians are most worried that fantastic or unrealistic fiction or film may corrupt readers (think of the worries about the Harry Potter books!), for Johnson it is fiction that depicts our own familiar world that is most likely to corrupt its impressionable readers.

Michael McKeon points out that "even though Defoe, Richardson, and Fielding explicitly subvert the idea and ethos of romance, they nonetheless draw upon many of its stock situations and conventions," and he suggests that the "general problem of romance in all three novelists is related to the particular problem of spirituality, equally antithetical to the secularizing premises of formal realism, in Defoe." In addition, McKeon draws attention to the fact that the romance exhibits certain characteristics of formal realism, and that it continues to coexist with the novel during the period of the latter's emergence (McKeon 1987, 2–3). J. Paul Hunter too warns against drawing too absolute a distinction between the novel and the romance.

> We do the novel—and not only the early novel—a disservice if we fail to notice, once we have defined the different world from romance that novels represent, how fully it engages the unusual, the uncertain, and the unexplainable …
>
> A closely related feature involves the novel's engagement with taboos. Operating from a position of semi-respectability from the start, the novel has always been self-conscious about appearing to be pornographic, erotic, or obscene. (Hunter 1990, 35)

Michael Seidel again has a useful comment, noting that while it is true that paradigms of romance such as victimage, forbearance, and rescue remain entrenched in the realist fiction that emerges in the form of the modern novel, "what is removed are those generic parts of romance that define causality and circumstance by forces inapplicable to the world of conventional experience" (Seidel 2000, 196).

Before moving on, I would like to draw your attention to Hunter's use of the term "different world." In the course of a discussion of fiction and the electronic media later on in this book, I will consider the concepts of "textual world" and "simulated world" provided by commentators on "electronic fiction" (see p. 89). What readers seem always to require of a work of fiction is that it provide such a "world," a distinct *space* within which characters can move that is governed by a clear, coherent, and consistent set of rules and conventions. In realistic fiction the world concerned is very much like the reader's, even though it may be removed in time, space, or culture from his or hers. In works of fantasy, the ghost story, science fiction, or cyberfiction, the world we encounter is very different from that of the reader—although the two may share certain important common elements. But, however different, it must offer the reader some sense of inner consistency. Neil Cornwell provides a useful comment taken from T.E. Little's *The Fantasts*:

> All writers of creative fiction are subcreators of Secondary Worlds. The secondary world of a non-fantastic writer will be as close to the Primary World as his talents and the needs of his art will allow … A licence is granted to writers of "normal" creative fiction to change the Primary World for the purpose of their art. Fantasy begins when an author's Secondary World goes beyond that license and becomes "other" … Such a creation should be called a *Tertiary World*. (Cornwell 1990, 16, quoting from Little 1984, 9–10)

Cornwell himself notes that Mary Shelley's *Frankenstein* (1818) can be seen as a key text, because in it religion has been replaced by science as the basis of a reality different from the everyday, a suggestion worth thinking about when you read my later comments on the novel and secularism (p. 29). Cornwell also suggests that we should see fiction in terms of a continuum that can be split into two. The first half-continuum is "mimesis dominated." It moves from *nonfiction* to *faction* to realism to *uncanny realism* to the *fantastic–uncanny* and ends in the *pure fantastic*. The second half-continuum takes up from the *pure fantastic* and moves through the *fantastic-marvelous* to the *marvelous* and ends up in *mythology* (Cornwell 1990, 39). (You will find many of these terms defined in the Glossary. The term *mimesis* means "imitation" or "copying," but it is associated with theories of realism that see the job of the artist as that of copying nature and human beings accurately.) At points on Cornwell's continuum we will find many novels that mix realistic and—say—supernatural elements. Think for example how many suggestions of the supernatural there are in Emily Brontë's *Wuthering*

Heights, a novel that is also full of very specific references to a world of concrete objects and social realities.

At this point I am conscious of the voice of an imaginary reader of this book, a student of literature who makes the following complaint. "During my study of the novel and shorter fiction I have read Horace Walpole's *The Castle of Otranto* (1765), in which a key role is played by a ghost; Fyodor Dostoyevsky's 'The Double' (1846), in which the hero Golyadkin encounters his double, who takes over his life bit by bit; Robert Louis Stevenson's *Dr Jekyll and Mr Hyde* (1886), in which the hero alternates between a good and a bad identity; Oscar Wilde's *The Picture of Dorian Gray* (1891), in which a man escapes the ageing process while his picture depicts a representation of an older and older man; Henry James's *The Turn of the Screw* (1898), in which the ghosts of two dead servants (may) seduce two young children; Franz Kafka's 'Metamorphosis' (1912), which opens with the hero discovering that he has turned into a giant insect; C.S. Lewis's *The Lion, The Witch and the Wardrobe* (1950), in which children go through their wardrobe into a magic world and meet a talking lion who is sacrificed but who returns to life; Philip K. Dick's 'We Can Remember It for You Wholesale' (1966), which is set in a future world in which false memories can be purchased and implanted in the mind so that they are believed to be real; and Angela Carter's *The Bloody Chamber* (1979), which contains short stories that blend fairy-tale elements with real-world settings. How can you claim that the novel is to be distinguished from medieval romance because it presents us with our familiar, everyday world rather than impossible situations and enchanted worlds?"

I think that my response to this challenge would go something like this.

- Some of the works cited are generally categorized in a way that draws attention to their divergence from mainstream fiction—for example: "the gothic novel," "the ghost story," "science fiction," "magic realism" (see the Glossary for more on some of these terms). The very need so to categorize them suggests that we do not expect such elements in the mainstream novel.
- Many of the works referred to are short stories or novellas, and shorter fiction does seem more likely to contain fantastic or non-realistic elements (See Chapter 3, "Shorter Fiction," for more discussion of this topic.).
- *The Lion, The Witch and the Wardrobe* is a story written for children, and romance and fantastic elements have survived in much stronger

form in children's literature. Fairy stories, for example, are nowadays told mainly to children.

- In a number of the works named, the supernatural or fantastic occurrence is hinted at or presented as a possibility, but alternative, realistic explanations are possible (Golyadkin is actually going mad and imagining his double, just as the governess imagines the ghosts in *The Turn of the Screw*; Dr. Jekyll's transformation is caused by science not magic; the implantation of memories could be possible in a future, technologically advanced world).

- Finally, even where the events are fantastic, they may cause us to think about very this-worldly things. "Metamorphosis" shows how people respond to chronic illness; "We Can Remember It for You Wholesale" causes us to consider whether illusions can be as satisfying as reality; the stories in *The Bloody Chamber* remind us how many attitudes to gender are based on the highly stereotyped and discriminatory models found in the traditional fairy stories that are told to children. These stories thus still refer back to the everyday, rather than constituting an escape from the everyday in the manner of the medieval romance.

Life and pattern

Arnold Kettle has suggested that most novelists show a bias toward either "life" or "pattern" in their approach to writing: toward, in other words, either the aim to convey the vividness, the particularized sensations and experiences of living, or that of conveying some interpretation of the significance of life. According to Kettle, the novelist who starts with pattern often tries to "inject" life into it, while the novelist who starts with life tries to make a pattern emerge out of it. He relates these two very general tendencies to, on the one hand, such sources and influences as the parables of the Bible, the morality plays of the Middle Ages, and the sermons that common people listened to every Sunday ("pattern") and, on the other hand, the seventeenth- and early eighteenth-century prose journalism and pamphleteering of writers such as Thomas Nashe and Daniel Defoe (who, we should remember, was a political journalist before he wrote prose fiction). As Kettle says of such writers, the germ of their books is never an idea, never an abstract concept; they are "less consciously concerned with the moral significance of life than with its surface texture" (Kettle 1967, 20).

In her essay "Phases of Fiction," Virginia Woolf uses similar terms to explain what she too believes is a fundamental tension within the genre of the novel:

> For the most characteristic qualities of the novel—that it registers the slow growth and development of feeling, that it follows many lives and traces their unions and fortunes over a long stretch of time—are the very qualities that are most incompatible with design and order. It is the gift of style, arrangement, construction, to put us at a distance from the special life and to obliterate its features; while it is the gift of the novel to bring us into close touch with life. The two powers fight if they are brought into combination. The most complete novelist must be the novelist who can balance the two powers so that the one enhances the other. (Woolf 1966b, 101)

It is perhaps the mark of the greatest novels that with them it is most difficult to say whether or not the novelist has tried more to convey what Kettle calls "pattern" and "life" and Woolf calls "design and order" and "life," for both seem so consummately present.

The "rise of the novel"

Let us return to the issue of that disputed birth date. Most of those concerned to map and to explain the development of the modern novel are agreed in singling out certain factors crucial to this development. Of these the following are perhaps the most important.

Literacy

The modern novel emerged, and has developed, as a written form—unlike poetry, which existed for centuries prior to the development of writing and still flourishes in oral cultures today. There have been cases of illiterate people gathering to hear novels read; part of Dickens's audience was of this sort. It is also the case that many novels and short stories are presented as if they were written transpositions of oral deliveries, of spoken tellings (see the discussion of the term *skaz* in the Glossary). Nonetheless, the novel is typically *written* by one individual in private and *read silently* by another individual who has no personal relationship with the author. In contrast, listening to someone reading or watching an actor acting are social or collective activities. Thus writing brings with it a change in the relationship between reader and writer:

the relationship is more indirect, but one that, paradoxically, allows him or her to feel that the reading of a novel is a personal, even intimate experience. J. Paul Hunter has noted the novel's liking for the confessional and the exhibitionistic (Hunter 1990, 37); the problem pages of popular magazines will remind us that confession and self-exposure are often easier through the impersonal medium of print than in person-to-person contact.

There was a rapid growth of literacy in the English-speaking world from 1600 to 1800, and whereas it is estimated that in 1600 about 25 percent of adult males in England and Wales could read, by 1800 the figure is probably between 60 and 70 percent (Hunter 1990, 65–6). Although the figures for female literacy lag behind those for male literacy, more and more women too could read during this period.

Printing

The modern novel is the child of the printing press, which was needed to produce the vast numbers of copies required to satisfy a literate public at a price that it could afford. Note the two-way process here: more people are literate so that the market for books is bigger and publishers and printers have a reason to produce more books, while more books are produced so that more people have an incentive to learn to read. Michael McKeon points out that a number of different factors—technological, social, and legal— conspire to assist the development of printing:

> By the close of the seventeenth century England had become a major producer of paper, type, and various kinds of publication, a development that could not have occurred without the abolition of protectionist printing legislation. By the middle of the eighteenth, licensing laws had been replaced by copyright laws; the commodification of the book market as a mass-production industry had become organized around the mediating figure of the bookseller; and the idea that a writer should get paid for his work was gaining currency on the strength of the perception that there was a growing mass of consumers willing to foot the bill. On the other hand, these new consumers of print were also produced by print—most obviously by the early modern "educational revolution," which received a great stimulus from the invention of the press and played the central role in raising the levels of literacy in England. (McKeon 1987, 51)

J. Paul Hunter sums up as follows: "From the beginning, moreover, novels were artifacts of the world of print. They had been conceived that way, and they lent themselves readily to the physical, social, and psychological circumstances that affected potential readers of printed books" (Hunter 1990, 41). Later on in this book I shall consider the argument that it is the design of the physical book that imposes linear narrative on the novel, and that it is only with the birth of the electronic media that the dominance of this linearity is challenged (see p. 96).

Print did not succeed oral delivery in one fell swoop; David Margolies points out that the manuscript circulation of written work represented a sort of in-between stage and "provided a model for the literary relationships of the early novelists" (Margolies 1985, 23). Margolies notes that writing for anonymous readers presented writers with a new set of problems, and he quotes from Austen Saker's *Narbonus* (1580):

> and he must write well that shall please all minds: but he that planteth trees in a Forest, knoweth not how many shall taste the Fruit, and he that soweth in his garden divers Seeds, knoweth not who shall eat of his Sallets. He that planteth a Vine, knoweth not who shall taste his Wine: and he that putteth any thing in Print, must think that all will peruse it: If then amongst many blossoms, some prove blasts, no marvel if amongst many Readers, some prove Riders. (Margolies 1985, 24)

Compare this to the opening words of Chapter 1 of Henry Fielding's *Tom Jones* (1749): "An author ought to consider himself, not as a gentleman who gives a private or eleemosynary [i.e. charitable] treat, but rather as one who keeps a public ordinary [i.e. a public house], at which all persons are welcome for their money." The relationship between the writer of a novel and its reader is, then, typically impersonal and commercial, rather than based on personal acquaintance and friendship. This is such a familiar state of affairs for us today that we pay no attention to it: for us, it is a matter of note if we *do* know the author of a book we are reading. We should remember that this situation is historically new and is associated with the development of printing. With prose fiction the issue of the relationship between *writer and reader* is complicated by the fact that the reader's immediate relationship is with a *narrator* rather than an *author*, and I will have more to say about this in Chapter 5. What I can say here, however, is that novelists had to learn how to become adept at convincing their readers that they were in intimate contact with a narrator who was interested in them as individuals. As J. Paul Hunter argues:

> [The novel's] rejection of familiar plots, conventional mythic settings, and recognizable character types represents a recognition that its future lies in developing a new kind of relationship with new combinations of readers.

...

One audience-related feature involves the novel's tendency both to probe and promote loneliness and solitariness, rather ironic in view of the novel's expressed design to portray people in their societal context. If the tendency to expose secrets of personal life points one way, the tendency to enclose the self, to treat the self as somehow inviolable and insistently separate in spite of the publication of secrets once thought too personal to articulate, points the other. (Hunter 1990, 39)

Hunter makes the astute point that this may well be why the novel, although born in another time, is so well placed to represent some central experiences that emerge in a more widespread and dominant form in the twentieth century: a concern with subjectivity, isolation, and loneliness (Hunter 1990, 41–2).

As David Margolies claims, writers did not necessarily learn the new ways of writing that we associate with print without difficulty; early printed works often show signs of a still-flourishing oral tradition, and J. Paul Hunter has argued that the first modern novels "had their relevant contexts—ultimately even their origins—in a culture that was partly oral and partly written, where functions traditionally performed in communal and family rituals and by oral tradition more and more fell to the impersonal processes of print" (Hunter 1990, xvii). We should not look upon this as a disadvantage: the novel still owes much of its richness to the importation of techniques and perspectives from oral delivery. From its earliest days the novel has been able to make readers think that they are hearing a voice when they are actually reading print, and the gains of verisimilitude and dramatic immediacy that this has enabled are considerable. One of the striking characteristics of many novels written in the twentieth and twenty-first centuries by writers from the working class of industrialized societies and by writers from newly independent ex-colonies is that oral rhythms and structures are taken from a rich heritage of non-literary traditions. Take the opening of Jack Common's semiautobiographical novel, *Kiddar's Luck* (1951):

She was a fool, of course, my mother. Her mother said so: "Bella is a fool, I'm afraid, a weak fool. Here she is marrying a common workman, one who drinks and is not a good Christian. She will never know happiness now." You would think the old lady was great shakes herself to hear her. And she was in her way. Not that she had any money ever, but she made poverty respectable.

The intimate relationship established here between narrator and reader feeds off a living tradition of oral storytelling at the same time as it exploits the potentialities inherent in the privacy and anonymity central to the narrator–reader relationship associated with the novel.

Market economy

Most commentators agree that crucial to the "sociology of the modern novel" is a *market relationship* between author and reader mediated through publishers. In contrast to earlier methods of financing publication or supporting authors such as *patronage* (a rich patron would support a writer while a book was being written) or *subscription* (wealthy potential readers would subscribe money to support a writer while he or she was writing), a market economy increases the relative freedom and isolation of the writer and decreases his or her immediate dependence upon particular individuals, groups, or interests (although, of course, it makes him or her *more* dependent upon publishers and, especially, sales). The growth of a market economy is an integral aspect of the rise of capitalism—the socioeconomic system that had displaced feudalism in Britain by the eighteenth century. In his book *The Rise of the Novel* (1957), Ian Watt argued that there is a close relationship between the rise of the novel and the rise of the middle class—the class most involved in the triumph of capitalism in Britain. In different ways literacy, printing, and a market economy can all be related to the growing dominance of capitalism in the period during which the novel emerges.

Michael McKeon draws attention to the debate in Cervantes's *Don Quixote* between Don Quixote and Sancho Panza about whether the latter should receive "favours" or "wages," suggesting that the relationship between these two characters thus "mediates the historical transition from feudalism to capitalism" (McKeon 1987, 283). J. Paul Hunter has gone further and suggests that crucial to the development of the new genre in England is the confrontation between "a Protestant, capitalistic, imperial, insecure, restless, bold, and self-conscious culture" and "a constrictive, authoritarian, hierarchical, and too-neatly-sorted past" (Hunter 1990, 7).

Capitalism is founded on competition, and from its earliest days the novel is concerned with conflict. The novel's portrayal of confrontations between individuals very often has a representative quality, pointing in the direction of larger social, historical, or cultural rivalries. This is significant in terms not just of the content of novels but also (and this of course is not a separate issue) of their readership. Novels appealed to groups of individuals who were emerging into new prominence and increased power: women and young people, for example. Hunter points out that from its earliest days the novel has been particularly concerned with "the crises of the decisive moments in adolescence and early adulthood" (Hunter 1990, 43). A novel such as Jane Rule's splendid *Memory Board* (1987), which focuses on characters who are old and tackling senility, has few parallels with novels written before the twentieth century.

The novel and the individual

Ian Watt sees as typical of the novel that it includes "individualization of … characters and … the detailed presentation of their environment." Unlike many of the narratives that precede it, the novel does not just present us with "type" characters; we are interested in Tom Jones, David Copperfield, Maggie Tulliver, and Paul Morel as distinct individuals with personal qualities and idiosyncrasies. As Ralph Fox puts it, "The novel deals with the individual, it is the epic of the struggle of the individual against society, against nature, and it could only develop in a society where the balance between man and society was lost, where man was at war with his fellows or with nature. Such a society is capitalist society" (Fox 1979, 44). Fox contrasts the *Odyssey* with *Robinson Crusoe* (1719), pointing out that whereas Odysseus lives in a society without history and knows that his fate is in the hands of the gods, Robinson Crusoe is prepared to make his own history. Furthermore, whereas Odysseus's efforts are directed toward returning *home*, for Crusoe it is the outward and not the homeward trip that is important; he is "the man who challenges nature and wins." Crusoe is thus, for Fox, representative of that spirit of expansionism, self-reliance, and experimentation that characterizes early capitalist man.

It certainly seems to be the case that the new spirit that accompanies the early development of capitalism infuses the emerging novel. Along with a stress on individualism goes, too, a growing concern with the inner self, the private life, subjective experience. As the individual *feels* himself or herself a unique individual rather than just a member of a static feudal community with duties and characteristics that are endowed at birth and shared with others, then he or she starts more to think in terms of having certain personal rather than shared communal interests. This gives the individual something to *hide*. Without wishing to oversimplify an extremely complex and far from uniform historical development, we can say that in a certain sense the private life as we know it today is if not born with then certainly revolutionized by capitalist society, and that the novel both responds and contributes to this development.

It doubtless seems very odd to many readers to claim that people have not always felt themselves to be individuals in the way that modern men and women from developed societies do, and indeed this assertion has been challenged by a number of recent writers, including Margaret Anne Doody in her *The True Story of the Novel*. Other commentators have detected Eurocentric and even racist attitudes behind the assumption that those from non-literate cultures are not "individuals" in the way that those from modern developed cultures are. Fictional works do nevertheless offer strong evidence to support the view that people from non-literate cultures perceive themselves and their individuality rather differently from the way in which those from literate cultures do. A classic case for this view is made by A.R. Luria in his book *Cognitive Development* (1976). Focusing specifically on the novel, in *Form, Individuality and the Novel* (1990) Clemens Lugowski examines a number of fictional works dating from the sixteenth and early seventeenth centuries, including the anonymous *Eine schöne Historie von den vier Heymonskindern*, Georg Wickram's *Amadis*, the stories known as *Thyl Ulenspiegel*, and the novellas of the *Decameron*. He concludes that these works contain nothing that might be referred to as an "individual."

This conclusion prompts the question: "What is an individual?" Nowadays there is a common assumption that all adult human beings are persons, and that they are individuals. But our sense of what an individual is—our sense of what it means to be a specific human being—is not necessarily one that we share with all other human beings. Moreover we need to pause and ask ourselves who are "we"? A complicating but fascinating factor here is that how modern people understand individuality is something to which the novel has undoubtedly both responded and contributed. For example, one of the things that the novel both reflects and helps to establish—in the form that it assumes from Defoe onwards—is a fundamental belief that what a person *is* goes beyond what that person *says or does*. We believe, today, that our identity exceeds what is observable to others. According to both Lugowski and Luria, not all human beings share or have shared this belief, and Lugowski argues that prior to the emergence of the modern novel, a view of fictional characters as more "components of a whole" (what we might call types rather than characters) than "genuinely autonomous individuals" means that fictional characters as we understand them did not exist (Lugowski 1990, 83). Lugowski's argument assumes that the ability to distinguish oneself from the world in which one lives is not universal, and that its gradual emergence encourages and takes support from the emergence of the novel in its modern form. He argues that "when the autobiographer explicitly *wishes* to describe his own life, and yet then describes the world outside, then what this means is that his life really *is* the world" (Lugowski 1990, 155; compare Luria 1976, Chapter 7: "Self-Analysis and Self-Awareness"). Moreover, Lugowski suggests that it is when human beings begin to question their "position in and profound commitment to the world" that an individuality that involves seeing oneself as separate from the world can emerge (Lugowski 1990, 176).

Similarly, in his essay "Forms of Time and of the Chronotope in the Novel," Mikhail Bakhtin says of the work of Rabelais (which he much admires), that in it "life has absolutely no *individual* aspect. A human being is completely external." He continues: "For indeed, there is not a single instance in the entire expanse of Rabelais' huge novel where we are shown what a character is thinking, what he is experiencing, his internal dialogue. In this sense there is in Rabelais' novel no world of interiority" (Bakhtin 1981, 239). Characteristic of the modern novel, in contrast, is its exploration of *both* the subjective and the social, *both* the private and the collective. It is this combination of the broadest social and historical sweep with the most acute and penetrating visions of the hidden, private life, *and their interconnections*, that is characteristic of the modern novel and at the heart of its power and continuing life. Paradoxically, although the novel is both written and read in private, it relies upon a highly organized society and industry to produce and circulate it. Even in its sociology it combines the personal and the social—that combination that is at the heart of its aesthetic.

This is not to say that the novel is able critically and analytically to portray all human organizations and groups as well as it can represent and explore the individual. Brook Thomas has, indeed, suggested that "the generic demands of the novel seem to guarantee that novelistic representations of corporations will lag behind the way in which other forms of discourse have been able to respond to the rise of corporations" (Thomas 1991, 150), implying that the novel is generically unfitted to portray and examine human beings in certain of their collectivities.

The novel and secularism

When we say that *secularism* is crucial to the development of the novel, this is not to imply that a novel may not explore religious themes or be underpinned by a religious imperative. It does mean, though, that the modern novel emerges in a world in which people were more and more likely to try to find non-supernatural explanations for the problems that they faced, and that this cast of mind is reflected in the novel. Milan Kundera remarks thus: "As God slowly departed from the seat whence he had directed the universe and its order of values, distinguished good from evil, and endowed each thing with meaning, Don Quixote set forth from his house into a world he could no longer recognize" (Kundera 1988, 6).

Even today, when a novelist wishes to make a religious point, he or she is typically encouraged by the conventions of the genre to set it in a context of secular explanation. Thus when a character in David Lodge's *Small World* (1984) prays for help in confronting the imminent task of delivering a conference paper that he has not yet written, his prayer is answered by a sudden outbreak of Legionnaires' Disease that requires that the conference be abandoned. The reader is allowed to read this as either divine intervention or a fortunate coincidence. It is true that there are novels that encourage the reader to imagine supernatural occurrences and fantastic worlds different from our own (the gothic novel, science fiction, magic realism— see the definitions in the Glossary), but it is striking how consistently such novels hedge their bets by allowing for non-supernatural explanations or interpretations of what happens. It is for this reason, among others, that modern readers tend to find the novels of Ann Radcliffe more acceptable than her near-contemporary William Beckford's *Vathek* (1787), in which the supernatural interventions allow for no natural explanation.

The novel and urban experience

Franco Moretti has argued that with the exception of Dickens, "English narrative draws its rhythms and problems from the countryside, and its masterpiece—*Middlemarch*—bears the name of a mediocre provincial town" (Moretti 2013b, 22). Here I part company with Moretti. There are many English novels set in the country, of course, but for me, from its earliest days the novel appears to have had a special relationship with town life, and in the eighteenth century both the readers and the writers of novels were more likely to be town-dwellers than country-dwellers. If we look at what has a fair claim to be one of the first modern novels—Daniel Defoe's *Moll Flanders* (1722)—we can see that the town and the novel form have much in common. Both involve large numbers of people leading interdependent lives, influencing and relying upon one another, but each possessing, nevertheless, a core of private thoughts and personal goals. Modern readers may need to be reminded that the growth of large towns and of urban life ushers in new forms of loneliness and privacy at the same time that, paradoxically, these large collectivities depend upon and bear witness to collective planning and human cooperation.

Consider the following four passages, each written in a different century. The first is from *Moll Flanders*, and it concludes the scene in which Moll robs a young child of a necklace:

> Here, I say, the Devil put me upon killing the Child in the dark Alley, that it might not Cry; but the very thought frighted me so that I was ready to drop down, but I turn'd the Child about and bad it go back again, for that was not its way home; the Child said so she would, and I went thro' into *Bartholomew Close*, and then turn'd round to another Passage that goes into *Long-lane*, so away into *Charterhouse-Yard* and out into *St. John's-street*, then crossing into *Smithfield*, went down *Chick-lane* and into *Field-lane* to *Holbourn-bridge*, when mixing with the Crowd of People usually passing there, it was not possible to have been found out; and thus I enterpriz'd my second Sally into the World. (Defoe 1971, 194)

The second is from Charles Dickens's *Oliver Twist* (1837–9), which describes Oliver's entry into London in the company of the Artful Dodger ("John Dawkins"):

> They crossed from the Angel into St. John's Road; struck down the small street which terminates at Sadler's Wells Theatre; through Exmouth Street and Coppice Row; down the little court by the side of the workhouse; across the classic ground which once bore the name of Hockley-in-the-Hole; thence into Little Saffron Hill; and so into Saffron Hill the Great: along which the Dodger scudded at a rapid pace, directing Oliver to follow close at his heels. (Dickens 1966, 102–3)

The third is from Samuel Beckett's *Murphy*, which was first published in 1938.

> She took the Piccadilly tube from Caledonian Road to Hyde Park Corner and walked along the grass north of the Serpentine. Each leaf as it fell had an access of new life, a sudden frenzy of freedom at contact with the earth, before it lay down with the others. She had meant to cross the water by Rennie's Bridge and enter Kensington Gardens by one of the wickets in the eastern boundary, but remembering the dahlias at Victoria Gate she changed her mind and bore off to the right into the north, round the accident house of the Royal Humane Society. (Beckett 1957, 150–1)

Finally, the following passage is taken from W.G. Sebald's *Austerlitz* (first published in German in 2001):

> For over a year, I think, said Austerlitz, I would leave my house as darkness fell, walking on and on, down the Mile End Road and Bow Road to Stratford, then to Chigwell and Romford, right across Bethnal Green and Canonbury, through Holloway and Kentish Town and thus to Hampstead Heath, or else south over the river to Peckham and Dulwich or westward to Richmond Park. (Sebald 2001, 178)

How well the world of London—rendered "real" by the detailing of actual streets—and the world we now associate with the novel fit! In all four passages we observe rapid mobility in a well-known world, that everyday world with which so many readers are familiar, alongside a sense of one's private self that, even in the place where so very many people live, is one's own alone. Moll Flanders's comment that by mixing with a crowd of people "it was not possible to have been found out" may be less true in an age of electronic surveillance, but it remains the case that sometimes we are most alone when surrounded by other people (this odd fact of urban life is much exploited in modernist fiction). *Secrecy* and *movement* in a location crammed with other people: this mixture has remained central to the novel for over three hundred years. (See also the discussion of travel on p. 240.)

Public world and private life

From its earliest days the novel seems often to split not just between novels where the author starts with "life" and those in which the author starts with "pattern"—to use Arnold Kettle's terms—but also between novels in which the author is more interested in the public world and novels in which the author is more interested in private life. Again, it is only the very greatest novels that seem to combine the two such that we feel no sense of subordination of either. Henry Fielding's *Tom Jones* (1749) and Samuel Richardson's *Clarissa* (1747–8) can be taken as representative here, with the former's greater interest in a masculine, public life of movement, action, and life in the larger social world in sharp contrast to the latter's concentration upon a feminine, more inward life of feeling, personal relationships, and personal moral decision. This is not to deny that Fielding's novel includes a concern with feeling and moral duty and Richardson's with the larger social context of the inner world. Nonetheless there is a very significant difference between the two writers and their respective fictional works, one of which their contemporaries were well aware. J.A. Downie has agreed that the creative dialogue between Richardson and Fielding was a significant factor in the growing popularity of "the novel" (Downie 2000, 325), and in his *The Life of Samuel Johnson*, which was first published in 1791, James Boswell shows how attitudes toward these two writers could cause serious dissension. Talking to Johnson and Thomas Erskine, Boswell expressed surprise at Johnson's calling Fielding a "blockhead" and "a barren rascal," and continued:

> "Will you not allow, Sir, that he draws very natural pictures of human life?" JOHNSON. "Why, Sir, it is of very low life." Richardson used to say, that had he not known who Fielding was, he should have believed he was an ostler. Sir, there is more knowledge of the heart in one letter of Richardson's, than in all Tom Jones ... ERSKINE. "Surely, Sir, Richardson is very tedious." JOHNSON. "Why, Sir, if you were to read Richardson for the story, your impatience would be so much fretted that you would hang yourself. But you must read him for the sentiment, and consider the story as only giving occasion to the sentiment." (anecdote from 1772)

We do not need to accept Johnson's value judgments to feel the force of the distinction made here, between a primary interest in drawing very natural pictures of life—albeit low life—and in revealing knowledge of the human heart.

The female voice

I refer above to Fielding's interest in the masculine and Richardson's in the feminine sphere, and I should make it clear that this is a historical rather than a universal judgment; "masculine" and "feminine" as they were defined by eighteenth-century English middle-class society, in which men alone were able to live a public life—of travel, work, exploration, and adventure— as well as a domestic life. As I have already indicated, the relationship of women to the novel is a very important one. This importance is both as writers and as readers (and, of course, as characters). Toward the end of the eighteenth century in England, more and more women were writing novels, and even male novelists recognized the importance of female readers. The anonymous but probably male author of *The Amicable Quixote; or, The Enthusiasm of Friendship*, published in London in 1788, mentions in his preface "the commendations of the ladies, *for whom works of this kind are generally written.*" Because of the market economy on which novel production depended, the increasing importance of female readers inevitably had an appreciable effect upon the sorts of novels that were written, and there is evidence that some male authors experienced this as an unwelcome pressure. Here, for example, is a comment from the narrator of Richard Graves's *The Spiritual Quixote or The Summer's Ramble of Mr. Geoffry Wildgoose. A Comic Romance*, which was published in 1773:

> Should any of my amiable country-women, I say, smit with the love of novelty, carry home this trifling volume from some Circulating-library; and throwing herself negligently upon her settee or sopha—or even on the feet of her truckle-bed—have patience to attend two such odd fellows thus far; she will probably be disgusted that she has not been entertained with a single love-tale, which are generally looked upon as essential to works of this kind; and not only make a principal part of every episode, but are usually interwoven with the body of the fable. (Graves 1967, 77)

This felt tension between what male authors wanted to write and what they perceived that female readers wanted to read clearly alters in important ways as more and more women themselves write novels. But even though women were a dominant force not just as readers but also as writers of the novel by the nineteenth century, this does not mean that within the world of the novel all the inequalities of the time miraculously disappear. No novel can totally escape the ideological bounds of its time. Interestingly, it is often the experience of colonialism and imperialism that throws up issues of gender in sharp relief in the modern novel. I will return to this issue below (p. 241).

It is arguable that the novel's success in exploring the private world, the subjective self, could never have been accomplished without the contribution to the genre of that introspective self-knowledge and sensitive perception of interpersonal relations that women's domestic imprisonment had trained them to be so expert in. No man could have written Jane Austen's novels.

Topics for discussion

- If the novel rises with the middle class, is it a middle-class genre?
- To what extent do romance traditions survive in the novel?
- Must the novelist choose between "life" and "pattern"?
- How does silent, private consumption condition novel-reading?

3
Shorter Fiction

Preview

This chapter deals with:

- The short story and the novella as fuzzy categories
- The taint of commercialism and "definition by length"
- The "anecdotal" and the "epiphanic" short story
- Compression, suggestiveness, and the short story
- The distinctiveness of the novella

I have already suggested that our familiar tripartite division of prose fiction into the novel, the short story, and the novella is one that simplifies a more complex and varied reality, and it is as well to start this chapter with a warning against allowing a use of these categories (more popular perhaps with academics than with writers or the common reader) to obscure the variety of forms open to the writer of prose fiction—both today and in the past. Moreover the terms "short story" and "novella" are by no means as widely used or as unambiguous as is the term "novel." Although the term "novella," from which the English "novel" descends, can be traced back to the Italian, use of this term today to designate a prose fiction that is shorter than a novel but longer than a short story descends from nineteenth-century German usage. The term is little used outside schools and universities. The term "short story" is more widely understood, but it too is problematic in ways that—for all of the issues of definition that I have discussed in the previous chapter—the term "novel" is not. Graham Good provides a useful summary of these terminological problems:

> Short fiction terminology is extremely varied and often inconsistent. The
> word "novella" is gradually gaining acceptance in English among publishers,

writers, and latterly critics, to denote a fictional prose narrative of "medium" length. This usage is supplementing rather than supplanting "short story," which has been firmly established since the turn of the century. The older terms "tale" and simply "story" were still employed by writers like [Henry] James and [Joseph] Conrad to refer to any narrative shorter than a novel, from about five to a hundred or more pages. (Good 1994, 148)

In fact, Conrad used the term "tale" rather more promiscuously than this suggests: his longest novel, *Nostromo*, is sub-titled "A Tale of the Seaboard." One of the reasons why the terms "short story" and "novella" were pressed into use by writers and critics from (especially) the early days of the twentieth century is probably that alternative terms such as "tale" were just too elastic.

Behind the search for terms is a sense that length does make a difference, and that although the cake of fiction can be cut into slices of varying sizes, a tripartite division accords well with our experience of reading fictional works varying from (say) the 1,824 words of James Joyce's "Eveline" through the 42,700 words of Henry James's *The Turn of the Screw* to the 168,000 words of *Nostromo* (and there are many novels that are longer by far than *Nostromo*). Although not all commentators are happy with these terms or the categories they propose, I will use them in what follows to structure my comments since the tripartite division between novel, novella, and short story possesses a certain utility and convenience.

Most if not all of the novels written since 1800 that you are asked to study will have been written by authors who had a relatively clear sense of what a novel was. But the same cannot be said of the short story or, especially, the novella. It can be helpful to think of works such as D.H. Lawrence's *The Fox* (1922) and Joseph Conrad's *Heart of Darkness* (1899) as novellas, but to the best of my knowledge neither of these writers actually used the term "novella," certainly not to describe these works. Mary Doyle Springer has suggested that "[t]he kinds of works which are now recognized as novellas began to arise in the nineteenth century" (1975, 8), but the application of the term "novella" to these works only becomes common in English-speaking cultures in the 1970s.

A letter written on January 7, 1902, by Conrad to his publisher illustrates some of these terminological issues. In the letter Conrad outlines a plan for a new piece and comments: "Of course it shall be 'fiction' in the same sense that *Youth* is fiction. Some critics, at the time, called it a short story!" (Karl and Davies 1986, 368). "Youth" is only about 13,400 words long, and my guess is that when it is included on a school or university reading list today it is categorized unproblematically as a short story. Conrad clearly views this term with disdain, and the titles of his shorter works are given a range of other sub-headings: "a tale," "a story," "a narrative," "a sketch," "a memory," "an episode"—but never "a short story." It is very likely that Conrad liked the term "tale" because it linked works of shorter fiction with a tradition of oral narrative (many of his works are presented as oral tellings), and that he disliked the term "short story" because of its association with the commercial and the popular.

Mr Voyt, a character in Henry James's evocatively entitled story "The Story in it," comments to two female conversational partners: "Behind these words we use—the adventure, the novel, the drama, the romance, the situation, in short, as we most comprehensively say—behind them all stands the same sharp fact that they all, in their different ways, represent" (Edel 1964, 319). Voyt may not be the voice of Henry James, but he does seem to reflect his creator's view that what these different sub-genres have in common is more important than what distinguishes them from one another. According to Dieter Meindl, James generally preferred the greater length of the novella (which he termed the nouvelle) to the short story, but he adds the following:

> James did not care for the designations now commonly used for the intermediary narrative genre: long short story, novella, or novelette. For him, a short novel would be something still longer, an affair of some 200 pages like *The Spoils of Poynton* (1897). As witnessed by the title of the New York Edition, he used the term "tale" for all his short fiction, including several texts exceeding one hundred pages, such as "The Turn of the Screw." A really short story or short story proper—for example his darkly comic, Boston-based "Europe" (1899; 19 pages nevertheless)—would be called an "anecdote" by James. For James, however, the anecdote is nonetheless generally entwined with the nouvelle, as the latter has for him an anecdotal basis. (Meindl 2008, 32)

Not surprisingly, the idiosyncratic (although not thereby uninteresting) terminology preferred by Conrad and James has not been generally accepted. We have to be aware that behind the simplicity of our tripartite division many other distinctions and divisions can be found.

The short story

Commercialism and size

Two specters haunt the short story. The first of these involves a reaction against what the critic Norman Friedman, in an article entitled "What

Makes a Short Story Short?" (first published in 1958), has called the taint of commercialism—the belief that the short story is a debased form to which writers descended only in order to earn money (Friedman 1976, 131). (Short works of fiction published in magazines in the late nineteenth and early twentieth centuries generally earned far more per word for their authors than did long novels.) The second involves the fear that perhaps all that distinguishes the short story from longer works of prose fiction *is* its shortness, rather than any more aesthetically interesting characteristic. Both of these specters have made serious writers and serious critics— those who share an interest in raising the status and the dignity of short fiction—suspicious of the term. The now celebrated short-story writer Elizabeth Bowen, introducing a new edition of her first collection *Encounters*, which was first published in 1923, makes a representative comment.

> Decision to fall back upon the short story, on the part of a poet *manquée*, would today seem obvious. In those days, the retreat was more uncertain; the position of the short story was anomalous. It was not yet—I think I am right in saying—recognised as "a form." There had appeared so far, that is to say, little constructive-critical interest in the short story's possibilities and problems. (Bowen 1949, viii)

Behind such attitudes lies a strong tradition of usage that links the short story with more unambiguously commercial works of the sort associated with the American writer O. Henry, works that appealed to a popular market and that were characterized by, among other things, unexpected endings of an ironic or whimsical variety. One recent commentator—William O'Rourke— has commented on the revealing fact that "as fewer commercial magazines publish it and the general public continues to avoid it, the short story rises in critical favor, not only among professors but among literary reviewers" (O'Rourke 1989, 199).

However, beyond such debates about terminology there are other arguments about types of shorter fiction, and I would now like to turn to some of these.

Oral or written? Traditional or modern?

Arguments as to whether the short story is the product of a long tradition of oral storytelling or a modern form associated with magazine publication are clearly intertwined with arguments about whether it is a very old or a very modern genre. In a commentary entitled "Writing Short Stories," Flannery O'Connor suggests that "[l]ike a river fed by countless small streams, the modern short story derives from a multiplicity of sources" (Martin 2006, 1563), and the fact that some of these sources are very old and others more recent may make it hard to fix the short story's date of birth unequivocally.

If, as I have claimed, the novel is very much the child of print, one might assume that at least superficial resemblances between the short story and oral narratives—tales, anecdotes, and so on—might suggest that the short story has much older parents, which is in part what Mulk Raj Anand implies (see Chapter 9, p. 246). The length of the typical short story makes it possible to associate it with a single oral telling, and many writers have seized upon this possibility. (Note that this also means that the typical short story can be *read* without pause.)

In an essay entitled "A Theory of the Short Story," which was first published in 1917, James Cooper Lawrence confidently asserts that "[t]he more we look into the matter the more evident it becomes that the limits and distinguishing characteristics of the short story as we know it today are the limits and distinguishing characteristics of the spoken story as it has existed from the beginning of time" (Lawrence 1976, 61). Certainly the man or woman talking to a group of listeners, the individual reminiscing to friends, the *speaker* rather than the *writer*, the tale as heard rather than the tale as read—all of these admittedly fictional narrative devices have appealed to writers wishing to conceal or qualify the situation of the lonely writer reaching out through the mediation of print to a similarly lonely reader. An ostensibly spoken narrative allows the writer access to colloquial speech, to those hesitations and unwilling disclosures that writing conceals, to the collectivity of a listening group, and to exchanges between teller and (fictional) listeners (see the discussion of *skaz* in the Glossary). Longer novels can be presented as spoken rather than written, but the conventions start to creak as the pages mount up. Joseph Conrad reacted to criticism of the impossibility of most of *Lord Jim* being delivered as one continuous oral account, but his protestations are not wholly convincing.

Many recent commentators have, however, argued that the short story is a modern form rather than one with a venerable history. Introducing *The Faber Book of Modern Short Stories* in 1936, Elizabeth Bowen states bluntly that the short story "is a young art: as we know it, it is the child of this century. Poetic tautness and clarity are so essential to it that it may be said to stand at the edge of prose; in its use of action it is nearer to drama than to the novel" (Bowen 1976, 152). Frank O'Connor, one of the most influential theorists of the short story, also resists associating the short story with the centuries-long tradition of the spoken tale. He argues that the short story, like the novel, "is a modern art form; that is to say, it represents, better than poetry or drama, our own attitude to life."

This is not to say that O'Connor believes the short story to be merely a truncated novel: "even from its beginnings, the short story has functioned in a quite different way from the novel" (O'Connor 1963, 13). In his attempt to describe the nature of this difference, O'Connor is thought-provoking if, on occasions, eccentric. He suggests that, unlike the novel, the short story does not encourage identification between the reader and a character, claiming that the short story has never had a hero but has, instead, had "a submerged population group." He further claims that there is always in the short story a "sense of outlawed figures wandering about the fringes of society" along with "an intense awareness of human loneliness" (1963, 17–18, 19). This argument implicitly extends the claim that the short story is a modern form, as the outlaw figure and a concentration on human loneliness are both very typical elements in modernist literature (about which I will talk more in the next chapter).

Fragments and wholes

Another Irish critic, Sean O'Faolain, has argued in a book on the short story first published in 1948 that there can be no development of character in the short story. Of course, characters in a short story may undergo shocking experiences and they may experience dramatic illuminations, but these are, nonetheless, different from that gradual development of character that we can observe in a full-length novel. For O'Faolain, at the heart of the short story has to reside the writer's ability to make fragments of experience speak for the whole of life (185). The suggestion is an interesting one, and it again associates the short story with the development of literary modernism, from let us say around the start of the twentieth century. Valerie Shaw links "the rise of the short story in England" with "the emergence of the characteristic figure of the modern artist, and with anti-Victorianism in its widest sense" (Shaw 1983, 4), while Suzanne Ferguson, in an article entitled "The Rise of the Short Story in the Hierarchy of Genres," argues that "the preeminence of the short story as a modernist genre grew out of the modern, highbrow audience's acceptance of fragmentation as an accurate model of the world, with a concomitant focus on 'being'—as in Woolf's 'moments of being'—

rather than the 'becoming' that characterizes the plot of the Romantic and the Victorian novel" (Ferguson 1989, 191).

Discussion of such Woolfian "moments" very often involves use of the word "epiphany." In the Christian tradition this word has been used to signify the manifestation of God to humanity: the feast of the Epiphany on 6 January celebrates the manifestation of Christ to the Gentiles. The term developed a specific literary sense in the course of the nineteenth century, and in his initial version of *A Portrait of the Artist as a Young Man*, then named *Stephen Hero*, James Joyce used the term in a secular sense to denote those experiences in which the full identity of the commonest object is displayed suddenly and completely.

For a writer such as James Joyce, for example, the depiction of an "epiphany" can be as effectively achieved in one of the short stories collected in *Dubliners* (1914) as in the over 700 pages of *Ulysses* (1922). The economy of the epiphany inevitably makes it attractive to the writer with limited space at his or her disposal. But do *all* short stories have this intimate relationship with the epiphany?

The "anecdotal" and the "epiphanic" short story

In an essay entitled "The Debunking Rhythm of the American Short Story," Thomas M. Leitch reports that short-story theorists have continued to distinguish between two different kinds of—or structures for—the short story, which he terms the "anecdotal" and the "epiphanic":

> The anecdotal story, typified by Hawthorne's "The Birthmark," Poe's "The Gold-Bug," and the Sherlock Holmes stories of Arthur Conan Doyle, presents an Aristotelian action with a beginning, middle and end; the epiphanic story, represented by Chekhov's "The Lady with the Dog," Joyce's "Ivy Day in the Committee Room," and Crane's Civil War stories, adumbrates a fictional world not by developing a plot involving purposive agents but by unfolding particular sensations or emotions and proceeding to a climactic revelation that does not necessarily take the form of a complete overt action. (Leitch 1989, 130–1)

So far as Leitch's two sorts of story are concerned, the much-praised American short-story writer Flannery O'Connor, again in the essay entitled "Writing Short Stories," makes it clear that her preference is for what Leitch terms the anecdotal short story.

> A good short story should not have less meaning than a novel, nor should its action be less complete. Nothing essential to the main experience can be left out of a short story. All the action has to be satisfactorily accounted for in terms of motivation, and there has to be a beginning, a middle, and an end, though not necessarily in that order. (Martin 2006, 1558)

As can be seen, however, there is a kick in the tail of this comment: the short story, O'Connor agrees, must have what Leitch dubs "an Aristotelian action" with its standard tripartite division, but O'Connor reserves the right to juggle the order of the standard and conventionally successive components.

It is worth thinking about O'Connor's witty (but fundamentally serious) point in relation to one of the examples cited by Leitch—Arthur Conan Doyle's Sherlock Holmes stories. In one of the classic stories, "Silver Blaze," we do indeed move through a number of apparently conventional stages. The story opens *in medias res* (see the Glossary).

> "I am afraid, Watson, that I shall have to go," said Holmes, as we sat down to our breakfast one morning.
> "Go!—Where to?"
> "To Dartmoor—to King's Pyland."
> I was not surprised. (Doyle 1974, 13)

Holmes has read in the newspapers of a mysterious affair involving the apparent abduction of a top racing horse (Silver Blaze) and the murder of the trainer of the stables, John Straker. As Holmes and Watson travel by train to Devonshire, they recapitulate the known facts of the case (thus conveniently informing the reader of these). On arrival they talk to the police officer in charge as they travel with him from the station, and to those connected to the stables when they arrive there. Holmes inspects the localities associated with the crime, and visits an unpleasant neighbor, Silas Brown, who is cowed by something that Holmes whispers to him. At this point Holmes announces that he and Watson will travel back to London, thereby convincing the victims of the crime that he has failed to solve it, even though he assures the owner that the horse will run four days later in the Wessex Cup. Before they leave, however, he provides a response to a question from Watson that has become famous.

> "Is there any other point to which you would wish to draw my attention?"
> "To the curious incident of the dog in the night-time."
> "The dog did nothing in the night-time."
> "That was the curious incident," remarked Sherlock Holmes. (34)

Note how this celebrated exchange focuses the reader's attention not primarily on what is happening *in the characters*, but more on what happened in terms of *actions* the night of the assumed murder.

A short line break in the text announces a shift of scene, and we are at the Wessex Cup. Colonel Ross the owner has been prevailed upon not to withdraw his horse from the race, and indeed it appears and wins, although the colonel is not at first convinced that it *is* his horse as its familiar markings have been obscured. After a further line break we find ourselves with Holmes and Watson in the Pullman car back to London, and Holmes explains all, revealing the significance of clues that have been available earlier on to the reader.

Let's go back to Flannery O'Connor. If my summary of Doyle's story does indeed give us a beginning (Holmes's inability to ignore a fascinating case), a middle (his investigation of the scene of the crime), and an end (his successful production of the missing horse and explanation of the trainer's death), it also gives us the same sequence in reverse order: first an end (the unsolved crime); then a middle (the events that occurred immediately before the crime, about which Holmes learns on Dartmoor, next the crime itself, described by Holmes in the Pullman car); and finally a beginning (the personal situation of John Straker that generated the whole sequence of events). Like all classic detective stories, then, "Silver Blaze" makes a particular sort of use of the double chronology of prose narrative (see p. 6); it consists of *two* sequences—the one involving the solution of a mystery, and the other involving the sequence of events that constitute the mystery.

Crime scene → Investigation → Solution
Motivation → Planning and crime → Crime scene

It is the laminating of these two sequences in an intriguing manner that constitutes the skill of the writer of detective stories. What satisfies the reader at the end of the story is a sense of having followed a set of cause-and-effect relationships such that everything clicks together, like a successfully assembled furniture flatpack. Indeed, at the end of the story we are able to combine these two sequences into a single, linear sequence.

Motivation → Planning and crime → Crime scene → Investigation → Solution

But actually *telling* the story in such a sequence would furnish the reader with no fun at all. O'Connor is right, that even in the "anecdotal" short story "beginning, middle, and end" do not necessarily have to be in that order.

Thomas M. Leitch is also correct to point out that this sort of story creates a fictional world for the reader "by developing a plot involving purposive agents." These purposive agents do not, as in the "epiphanic" short story, unfold "particular sensations or emotions," proceeding then "to a climactic revelation that does not necessarily take the form of a complete overt action." Holmes and Watson are the same throughout the story; indeed they are more or less the same throughout all of Doyle's Sherlock Holmes stories. The stories are *formulaic* to the extent that, admittedly with small twists and variations, they present the reader with a pattern that is repeated again and again. And this pattern has little concern with changes or subtleties in the inner lives of the characters.

Not all "anecdotal" stories are equally formulaic, and I should add that those of Flannery O'Connor are certainly not. But they do tend to present a sharp contrast to the sorts of story that Leitch dubs "epiphanic." Significantly, of the examples Leitch gives, two (James Joyce and Stephen Crane) are leading figures in the movement known as *modernism* (see p. 59), while the third, Anton Chekhov, can be seen as a precursor of modernism. Martin Seymour-Smith has noted that as a story-writer Chekhov "depends not on plot or surprise … but on atmosphere and the captivation of the sense of a whole life in just a single of its moments" (Seymour-Smith 1973, 937)—precisely what we can term an epiphanic focus. In my discussion of modernism in the chapter following I devote some time to analyzing a classic modernist story, James Joyce's "Eveline," a work that exemplifies the epiphanic short story and also typifies certain key qualities of modernist prose fiction. After you have read this analysis, you can consider to what extent Leitch's division between the anecdotal and the epiphanic short story is worth maintaining.

The short-story cycle

Not all short stories are published in magazines—or at least, not only in magazines. Some of the most important examples of the short story owe part of their force to publication in single-volume collections. The title of James Joyce's *Dubliners* (1914), for example, signals that the different stories contained in the volume have something in common, and that the volume as a whole says something about a city and its inhabitants. As many commentators have pointed out, the first paragraph of "The Sisters," the opening story of *Dubliners*, has the youthful first-person narrator musing over three words that prepare the reader for themes that recur throughout the collection as a whole. All of the stories collected in Angela Carter's *The Bloody Chamber* (1979) offer disturbing blendings of traditional fairy tales and modern settings and issues. The cycle or collection allows the short-story writer to obtain that sense of an extended investigation into a particular issue or topic that the novelist can achieve in the course of a single work, and authors often plan individual short works as component parts of a larger whole.

Informing and suggesting

If the modernist short-story writer is interested in making a fragment or epiphany imply or display a larger whole, then he or she, according to Sean O'Faolain, must become adept at replacing direct *informing* by *suggesting*:

> Telling by means of suggestion or implication is one of the most important of all the modern short-story's shorthand conventions. It means that a short-story writer does not directly tell us things so much as let us guess or know them by implying them. The technical advantage is obvious. It takes a long time to tell anything directly and explicitly, it is a rather heavy-handed way of conveying information, and it does not arrest our imagination or hold our attention so firmly as when we get a subtle hint. Telling never dilates the mind with suggestion as implication does. (O'Faolain 1972, 177)

To make his point, O'Faolain presents his readers with a splendid analysis of the opening sentence of Anton Chekhov's short story "The Lady with the Little Dog" (in his account granted a slightly different title in English translation from the one used by Thomas M. Leitch). O'Faolain concentrates upon this opening sentence because he believes that the openings of short stories in particular demand of the author that he or she be adept at influencing the reader by means of suggestion and implication. The sentence in question reads as follows: "It was reported that a new face had been seen on the quay; a lady with a little dog." Here is O'Faolain's commentary:

> The amount of information conveyed in that sentence is an interesting example of the shorthand of the modern short-story. What do we gather from it? ... We gather, altogether by implication, that the scene is laid in a port. We gather that this port is a seaside resort, for ladies with little dogs

do not perambulate on commercial docks. We gather that the season is fine weather—probably summer or autumn. We gather that this seaside resort is a sleepy, unfrequented little place: for one does not observe new faces at big, crowded places like Brighton or Deauville. Furthermore, the phrase "it was reported" implies that gossip circulates in a friendly way at this sleepy resort. We gather still more. We gather that somebody has been bored and wakes up at this bit of gossip; and that we shall presently hear about him. I say "him," because one again guesses, when it is a question of a lady, that the person most likely to be interested is a man. (O'Faolain 1972, 177–8)

As he adds (perhaps redundantly, in view of the contrast between the length of his commentary and that of the sentence in question!), "we may imagine how much time it would take, and how boring it would be, to have all that told at length."

Much of the skill of the short-story writer has to be devoted to making characters appear three-dimensional in spite of the fact that we see them for only a very short period of time. In addition, care has to be taken to render atmosphere and situation convincingly. Very often the short-story writer will use something akin to shock tactics to make the reader think and respond: an unexpected ending, a dramatic unveiling, a surprising twist of plot. Many consider these to be artistically inferior techniques, less sophisticated than other means of creating depth and body in the short story. What are these alternative methods?

We have already mentioned *suggestion*, and clearly there are a number of techniques whereby we get people's imaginations racing. We should probably remember that there are two sorts of suggestion: the first when we know exactly what it is that we want the target person to think (as when Iago gets Othello to imagine that Desdemona has been unfaithful without actually stating as much), and the second when a person's imagination is stimulated to be innovative and to think of things that the suggester him- or herself may never have intended. A much-quoted example of this second sort is to be found in Henry James's comment in his "New York" Preface to a collection of tales including *The Turn of the Screw*:

Only make the reader's general vision of evil intense enough, I said to myself—and that already is a charming job—and his own experience, his own imagination, his own sympathy (with the children) and horror (of their false friends) will supply him quite sufficiently with all the particulars. Make him *think* the evil, make him think it for himself, and you are released from weak specifications. (James 1999, 128)

There seems little doubt that the second of these alternatives is potentially richer and more aesthetically rewarding, as it gives the reader's imagination a genuinely creative function.

A classic example of such suggestiveness used to full aesthetic effect is to be found at the end of James Joyce's "The Dead" (started 1907, published 1914), the final story in *Dubliners*. At this point of the story, the character Gabriel, in a hotel room with his sleeping wife after the annual dance held by Gabriel's aunts, is sinking into sleep. The final lines of the story read:

> A few light taps against the pane made him turn to the window. It had begun to snow again. He watched sleepily the flakes, silver and dark, falling obliquely against the lamplight. The time had come for him to set out on his journey westward. Yes, the newspapers were right: snow was general all over Ireland. It was falling on every part of the dark central plain, on the treeless hills, falling softly upon the Bog of Allen and, farther westward, softly falling into the dark mutinous Shannon waves. It was falling, too, upon, every part of the lonely churchyard on the hill where Michael Furey lay buried. It lay thickly drifted on the crooked crosses and headstones, on the spears of the little gate, on the barren thorns. His soul swooned slowly as he heard the snow falling faintly through the universe and faintly falling, like the descent of their last end, upon all the living and the dead. (Joyce 2000, 225)

The suggestiveness of this very rich passage is partly a matter of inexplicitness: what, for example, does "The time had come for him to set out on his journey westward" mean? We have earlier learned that Gabriel does not want to accompany his wife on a visit to the west of Ireland. Has he changed his mind, or is the reader supposed to recall that the idiom "to go west" means to die, and to associate this with sleep as proleptic of death? This is my second sort of suggestiveness, one that is creative and open-ended rather than closed and with a single, fixed objective.

Those who have read "The Dead" will recognize that in this final paragraph a shift to what we can call a different mode takes place; the language becomes more poetic, and the more literal meanings of certain statements are hard to determine, while at the same time there is uncertainty as to who is making them. The ending makes extremely difficult demands on the reader, and is suggestive in a number of different ways (to take a simple example, the mention of "crosses," "spears," and "barren thorns" inevitably calls the Passion of Christ to mind, a very different passion from the one experienced by Michael Furey, although one which also ended in death and which thus fixes a certain association between passion and death that has already been implied).

In addition to being suggestive, the ending is also evocative. It calls up particular states of mind and forms of experience, very often in their concrete particularity. Having said this, it is less easy to say exactly what it is that is evoked. There is a general movement in the paragraph from a focus on particulars to a universal perspective, fixed in the actual mention of the word "universe" in the last sentence. It is as if we leave Gabriel (whose consciousness we abandon as the vision becomes more and more general), and take more and more in our view. As this shift coincides with Gabriel's falling asleep, one of the experiences evoked is precisely that of falling asleep, leaving more rational, specific topics of thought and entering into a dream-state that deals with more general and universal topics. Note that what I have written about this passage is necessarily tentative; if one is dealing with suggestion then interpretive certainty is no longer possible.

The final paragraph of "The Dead" illustrates other important techniques. The use of poetic devices such as repetition and chiasmus (reversal involving the pattern "ab ba," as in the opposition of "falling faintly" and "faintly falling"), symbolism (see the discussion of symbol and image starting on p. 146, which pays particular attention to the repeated references to snow in "The Dead"), and other techniques is not limited to the short story, but such techniques very often have to carry a heavier weight in this genre to compensate for the limitations that a restriction of length places on the development of plot and character.

The novella

The novella has had less theoretical attention devoted to it than has the short story, and this is especially so in its modern and its Anglo-Saxon manifestations. In my first chapter I suggested that the novella was typically between about forty or fifty and a hundred pages long, and Mary Doyle Springer proposes a word-count between 15,000 and 50,000 (Springer 1975, 8).

D.H. Lawrence's *The Fox* is just over 27,000 words long—sixty-two printed pages in a standard edition of Lawrence's *Collected Stories*. It offers us a good test-case for the need for a third generic term in addition to "novel" and "short story." A sixty-two-page work of fiction seems too short to be dubbed a novel, and of those characteristics that we associate with the short story—a lack of character development, a focus on epiphanic enlightenment or revelation rather than slow change, coverage of a very limited time span—only the moment of epiphany is to be found in *The Fox*. There is restriction: there are essentially only three characters involved in Lawrence's story, and their interaction takes place exclusively in one place. But to call *The Fox* a short story seems as misleading as to call it a novel.

In *The Fox* we meet two women in their late twenties—Banford and March—who are trying to make a success of running a farm in the years immediately following the First World War. They are not well equipped for this task, and the farm is going badly.

> One evil there was greater than any other. Bailey Farm was a little homestead, with ancient wooden barn and low-gabled farm-house, lying just one field removed from the edge of the wood. Since the war the fox was a demon. He carried off the hens under the very noses of March and Banford. Banford would start and stare through her big spectacles with all her eyes, as another squawk and flutter took place at her heels. Too late! Another white Leghorn gone. It was disheartening. (Lawrence 1994, 651)

Early on in the work, March, who we have been told in the second paragraph of the tale "would be the man about the place," goes out with a gun and falls into a sort of musing trance.

> The trees on the wood-edge were a darkish, brownish green in the full light—for it was the end of August. Beyond, the naked, copper-like shafts and limbs of the pine trees shone in the air. Nearer the rough grass, with its long, brownish stalks all agleam, was full of light. The fowls were round about—the ducks were still swimming on the pond under the pine trees. March looked at it all, saw it all, and did not see it. She heard Banford speaking to the fowls in the distance—and she did not hear. What was she thinking about? Heaven knows. Her consciousness was, as it were, held back.
>
> She lowered her eyes, and suddenly saw the fox. He was looking up at her. Her chin was pressed down, and his eyes were looking up. They met her eyes. And he knew her. She was spellbound—she knew he knew her. So he looked into her eyes, and her soul failed her. He knew her, he was not daunted.
>
> She struggled, confusedly she came to herself, and saw him making off, with slow leaps over some fallen boughs, slow, impudent jumps. Then he glanced over his shoulder, and ran smoothly away. She saw his brush held smooth like a feather, she saw his white buttocks twinkle. And he was gone, softly, soft as the wind. (652)

Soon after this epiphanic, revelatory episode occurs, a young man—Henry Grenfel—chances upon the farm and ends up staying to work for the women. As soon as she encounters him, March sees him in a particular way.

> The youth stared at them without changing colour or expression. If he had any expression, besides a slight baffled look of wonder, it was one of sharp curiosity concerning the two girls; sharp, impersonal curiosity, the curiosity of that round young head.
>
> But to March he was the fox. Whether it was the thrusting forward of his head, or the glisten of fine whitish hairs on the ruddy cheek-bones, or the bright, keen eyes, that can never be said: but the boy was to her the fox, and she could not see him otherwise. (656)

As this identification is strengthened, so too is another one: "Meanwhile he was talking softly and smoothly to Banford, who loved nothing so much as gossip, and who was full of perky interest, like a bird" (658).

I will stop at this point, and suggest that if my account has whetted your appetite then you get hold of Lawrence's tale and read it. The desire to read on is aroused less by what any of the characters has said or done overtly and more by the sense Lawrence's narrative creates of a parallel plot taking place below the surface of the work's realistic detail. Our impression of a mystical or supernatural identification of human characters with animals—fox, bird— creates a sense of profundity, as if the realistic plot detail is but the visible part of the iceberg. And in this way, if I can extend my spatial metaphor, the very limited *length* of the work is supplemented by a sense of greater *depth*. The critic Mary Rohrberger, incidentally, suggests that "perhaps more than any other narrative structure, the short story veers toward what Joseph Frank calls 'spatial form,' a set of narrative techniques and processes of aesthetic perception that works to impede linearity" (Rohrberger 2004, 6). (For discussion of linearity, see p. 96.) We can extend the scope of this observation to the novella.

Although the typical novella is more limited in its concerns than the novel, often restricting itself to a single state of affairs, collection of relationships, or setting, it characteristically compensates for this limitation by means of a greater reliance on implied or suggested secondary meanings. Hence it has some of the concentrated power of the short story, but without the frequent one-dimensionality that characterizes many short stories.

Writers of short stories and novellas do not just produce truncated novels. These different fictional genres require a different use of the resources of prose, and they should not be read or judged in the way that we read or judge a 500-page novel.

Topics for discussion

- Does the short story have any other distinctive characteristics apart from its length?

- Imagine what a favorite short story would be like extended to novel length—or a novel compressed into a short story. What are the gains and losses? Does the novel have all the advantages?

- A short story, unlike a novel, can be read in one session. Does this impact on our reading experience?

- "Neither one thing nor another." Is the novella more than a failed novel or a short story that has got too long?

4

Realism, Modernism, Postmodernism—and Beyond

Preview

This chapter deals with:

- The problems of defining realism, modernism, and postmodernism
- Realism as content, or realism as effect on the reader
- Modernism and postmodernism as periodizations and as generic classifiers
- Fiction in the electronic age

The three "isms" mentioned in the title of this chapter occur so frequently in discussion of the novel that they merit separate consideration at this point. So far as prose fiction is concerned, the use of all three terms is complicated by the fact that each can be used to indicate *a historical period of literature*, *a trans-historical type of literature*, and *a specific set of literary characteristics*. But a further complication is that very often the terms are invoked to specify a particular philosophical outlook or position, or to indicate aspects of a given society or culture. Thus you might well take a course on "The modernist short story," but you might also come across Fredric Jameson's 1991 book *Postmodernism: Or, The Cultural Logic of Late Capitalism*—a title that seems to locate postmodernism in a specific political or economic system rather than in the realm of literature.

In some respects the problems associated with the use of these terms are not dissimilar to those attached to the use of the term "romanticism"— another word that can also be used to denote a tightly delimited historical period of literature, a more general variety of literature with its associated conventions, or a set of trans-historical cultural attitudes or beliefs. And just as not all literature written during the Romantic Period is necessarily romantic in a generic or philosophical sense, so too not all fiction written in the early twentieth century is modernist, and neither is all the fiction written today necessarily postmodernist.

"Enough!" you may feel like saying: "given all these complications let us agree to avoid using any of these terms." This tempting solution is not, alas, a viable one. The history of the novel is so intimately bound up with the issue of realism that we can hardly talk about the novel without addressing it. Moreover, that there is a family of new characteristics to be found in significant works of art and literature produced at the end of the nineteenth century and the beginning of the twentieth century can scarcely be disputed, and the term "modernism" helps us to isolate these characteristics and to distinguish between radically different lines of development in the art and literature of the twentieth and twenty-first centuries. Finally, although theories of the postmodern have come into prominence only during the last four decades, so many works of fiction from the post–Second World War period are regularly described as "postmodern" that some consideration of what the term may denote is needed. So we have to grit our teeth and engage with the difficult task of producing at least working definitions of these three terms.

Realism

We saw in our earlier discussion of the emergence and development of the novel that the genre is distinguished by what we can call its "formal realism": it is stocked with people and places that *seem real* or *evoke the real* even if they are imagined, whereas genres such as the romance or the epic were peopled with people and places that seem (and were meant to seem) unreal, and that turned attention not to everyday reality but to an imagined, alternative world. We can note, furthermore, that "realism" is a term which a large number of novelists have felt the need to use in connection with their work.

On a simple level it can be said that something—a character, an event, or a setting—is "realistic" if it resembles a model in everyday life. The matter becomes more complex, however, when we remember that a novelist can make us think seriously and critically about the real world by creating characters, events, and settings that in many ways diverge from what we would expect in everyday life—in "reality." Peter Lamarque has noted that a "fiction is realistic if it describes characters with combinations of properties that would not be strange or out of place if exemplified in individuals in the real world," but he goes on to discuss the problems raised by a novel such as George Orwell's *Animal Farm* (1945), which, in spite of the fact that it contains farmyard animals that speak, think, and reason exactly like human beings, also strikes us as "realistic" or "true to life." He suggests that what we need in order to explain this apparent contradiction "is an appeal to levels of interpretation or understanding" (Lamarque 1996, 38). In other words, it is difficult to arrive at a concept of realism which is not trivial unless one goes beyond a concern with simple one-to-one resemblance and proceeds to consider not just the ways in which characters and events in a novel may be like characters and events in the real world but also *how a reader responds* to these characters and events and to their presentation.

This is a shift of emphasis that opens up a set of new problems. William B. Warner, for example, has argued that because what he calls "the realist effect" can be provoked by a given novel at one time and not at another, the whole association of the novel with realism is thus rendered suspect: "Because history undermines the naturalness and self-evidence of received modes of representing the real, it has proved difficult to sustain any 'realist claim' made by or for a novel" (1998, 35). This I feel casts out the baby with the bathwater, for even though readers may find the same novel more, or less, "realistic" at different periods of history, as conventions become stale and apparent rather than invisible, such changes seem to me to involve relative rather than absolute shifts of response. We still find Dickens's novels more realistic than William Beckford's *Vathek*, even though we are perhaps more conscious of many conventional elements in them than were Dickens's first readers.

Warner's point does serve to remind us that a novel seems realistic to readers even when it charts events and describes characters that are far from typical or everyday: think how many unusual coincidences and extraordinary events there are in those novels which are normally described as highly realistic. George Eliot's *Middlemarch* (1871–2) is a good example.

Lamarque's mention of *Animal Farm* should also draw our attention to the issues raised by parody and satire, both of which can be used by the novelist to make us think about the real world we inhabit. A parody is often very unrealistic in one sense, depending upon such extremes of exaggeration and such pointed selection that it cannot be said to give us anything that can be compared to our everyday world *in terms of direct, one-to-one resemblance.*

Even so, parodies and satires clearly *do* cause us to see our everyday world very differently—otherwise their targets and victims would not be annoyed by them. The paradox, then, is that sometimes that which distorts what the real world is like may actually lead us to see the real world more accurately.

Brecht, Lukács, and the realism debate

One of the most influential debates about the nature of realism in the twentieth century involved a critic very much associated with the novel—the Hungarian Marxist Georg Lukács. For Lukács, who saw realism as the contemporary artist's necessary, even ultimate, aim, the artist was required to represent the totality of reality at any given point in history, to penetrate between surface appearances, and to reveal processes of change. This sounds a tall order, and of course Lukács accepted that "the totality of reality" could only be displayed by the writer through representative selection. For Lukács, the artist's task was similar to that set for himself by Marx: to understand world history as a complex and dynamic totality through the uncovering of certain underlying laws. In practice this led Lukács to place a supreme value upon certain works of classical realism (see p. 58) in the novel—the names of Tolstoy, Balzac, and Thomas Mann are frequently on his lips or at the tip of his pen—and to wage an unceasing campaign against different aspects of what he classified as modernism (see below). At the end of his *The Historical Novel* (written 1936–7), Lukács referred to the "misunderstanding" of his position as one entailing "a formal revival, an artistic imitation of the classical historical novel" (Lukács 1969, 422), but in spite of this disclaimer many commentators have seen his opposition to modernism as so all-embracing that this is actually what would have been required in order to satisfy his requirement that a literary work be realistic.

When the German dramatist Bertolt Brecht, writing about the concept of realism, stated that we "must not derive realism as such from particular existing works" (Brecht 1977, 81), the unstated target was clearly Lukács (especially as Brecht goes on to refer to Balzac and Tolstoy). Brecht's argument is, in a nutshell, an anti-essentialist one. In other words, realism for him is not intrinsic to a literary work, born with it like a genetic code and remaining unchanged through all its vicissitudes, but a function of the role the work plays or can play—the effect it has on a reader's (and not necessarily *all* readers') view of the world. Brecht's realism focuses on questions not of form or content, but of function.

Lukács and Brecht exemplify the two fundamentally different ways of understanding realism that I have already outlined—as a quality that is *innate* in a text or as one that is measured in terms of a text's changing *effect* on its readers or audiences. From Lukács's perspective a text either is, or is not, realistic; from Brecht's perspective it may be realistic at one time, but not at another. The important point to bear in mind is that when a critic discusses whether or not a novel is realistic, he or she can be referring either to what it contains or to what it does. Think of it this way: if what we read in a novel seems just like the world we experience every day, it may be unlikely to encourage us to examine that world critically, to see it in a new light, to ask whether its appearance is deceptive. In contrast, if a novel presents us with a world that seems extremely unusual, it *may* encourage us to ask to what extent our familiar world perhaps really *is* like this, in ways we have not previously considered.

The term "realism" very often implies that the artist (and not just the literary artist) has tried to include a wider and more representative coverage of social life in his or her work, and in particular that he or she has extended the coverage of the work to include "low life" and the experiences of those deemed unworthy of artistic portrayal by other artists. The apparent realism of the early novel was intimately related in the public mind to the fact that it often concerned itself with the lives of the sort of human being who would not only never have been portrayed by the romance but whose depiction was clearly out of bounds too for the genteel eighteenth-century poet. Fielding's Joseph Andrews, Defoe's Moll Flanders, Smollett's Humphry Clinker—none of these characters or their real-life equivalents could have entered into the polite world of Alexander Pope except in certain forms of satire or burlesque. This is one of the reasons why *Joseph Andrews* (1742), *Moll Flanders* (1722), and *Humphry Clinker* (1771) are generally taken to be more realistic works than Pope's mock-heroic poem *The Rape of the Lock* (1711).

"Realism" also has a specific reference to a particular literary movement which started in France in the early nineteenth century, and flourished in the latter part of the century. The novelists most associated with this movement are Balzac, Stendhal, and Flaubert. These writers made enormous efforts to ensure that "factual details" in their works were "correct"—that is to say, capable of being checked against an external reality by empirical investigations. They achieved this accuracy by lengthy and painstaking research. "Realism" in connection with these writers is thus both a term denoting a group of novelists and also a term referring to a particular method of composition. (See also the comments on "naturalism" in the Glossary.)

One conclusion that can be drawn from the foregoing is that the term "realistic" should be used only with extreme care in connection with a novel; it is a problematic rather than a self-obvious term and raises complex questions about what "reality" is (our fantasies are after all real in the sense that they really exist and are related to our experiences in the real world), and about the means whereby a novelist explores the real. Having said all this it remains important to be able to distinguish between novels that—in however complex and indirect a way—cause us to think about reality critically and those that encourage us rather to escape from our everyday reality into a world of illusory imaginings.

The "classical realist novel"

A term that you may encounter in discussion of fiction is "the classical realist novel" (sometimes rendered as just "the classical novel"). What is meant by this term, and how is it used?

Generally speaking we can say that this term is used to denote and classify "canonical" (see the entry for "Canon" in the Glossary) novels of the nineteenth century, such as those by the Brontë sisters, Elizabeth Gaskell, Charles Dickens, William Makepeace Thackeray, Leo Tolstoy, Nathaniel Hawthorne, Herman Melville, (the early) Henry James, and others. What is it that these works are seen to have in common? A short list in answer to this question might include the following elements:

- A belief in the knowability of a unified world, which, however many secrets it contains, can be explored and studied.
- A similar belief in the knowability of the self, which, like the external world, is conceived as unitary except in certain significant exceptional cases (doubles, split selves).
- A plot based on cause-and-effect that has a clear beginning and normally an even clearer ending.
- A commitment to "the reality illusion"—in other words, a "contract" with the reader that the world of the novel will be treated as real, and that the reader's immersion in this world will not be broken by the author's or narrator's admission that it is only make-believe (see the quotation from Henry James below, p. 68).

A crude but helpful test here is the ease with which one can respond to the unacademic question: "What's this novel about?" Asked this question of, say, Charlotte Brontë's *Jane Eyre*, one could reply as follows: "It's a story about Jane Eyre, told by herself, that traces her growth and development from a deprived childhood through her attempts to build a life for herself in spite of her poverty. In particular it traces her relationship with two potential husbands, who offer her the prospect of very different sorts of married life. After many complications (including her finding out that the second of these men is married), Jane is able to find contentment with this man, Rochester."

Now if your response to such a summary is: "So what?," imagine how you would respond to this inquiry were the novel in question Virginia Woolf's *The Waves* (1931). If I had to answer the question with regard to Woolf's novel, I might end up saying something like this: "It's a novel that traces the lives of seven characters, six of whom become known to the reader through monologues that represent their thoughts and their sense of the world and of themselves. These monologues are interlaced with sections printed in italics that represent not the perceptions of any individuals but a reality that is, paradoxically, not observed by anyone."

Even at this point it's possible to make two observations concerning what I have written. First, that it is not uncontroversial, especially with regard to the italicized sections in Woolf's work. But second, that while the summary I gave of *Jane Eyre* could have been said of a real person, or an autobiography, in order to explain what *The Waves* is "about" I have to engage with its fictional and conventional characteristics, even in a short two-sentence summary.

This is not to imply that any classical realist novel could be mistaken for a biography, autobiography, or a work of history if the cover and title page did not announce it as a novel. As I note on p. 55, there are certain aspects of even the most realist novel that announce the work as fictional. But it does mean that the classical realist novel typically presents its characters and events according to conventions that may not coincide, but that certainly overlap, with those conventions that we apply to the telling of stories about real people and events. When the novel stops presenting characters and events in such a way—as in the case of *The Waves*—a new term is needed to indicate the importance of this shift.

Modernism

"Modernism" is a term that (at least so far as its general acceptance is concerned) is younger than the works that it describes. During five years as a student of English at a British university in the 1960s, I cannot recall having come across it once. It is now widely used to refer to those art works (or the principles behind their creation), produced since the end of the nineteenth century, that decisively reject many of the key artistic conventions of the previous age. Foremost among such rejected conventions are those associated with realism in a generic sense. In particular, modernist works tend to be *self-conscious* in ways that vary according to the genre or art form in question; in different ways they deliberately remind the reader or observer that they are art works, rather than seeking to serve as "windows on reality." Whereas one may forget that one is reading a novel when immersed in, say, Tolstoy's *War and Peace* (1865–8)—responding to characters and events as if they were "real"—this is not a reading position invited by a modernist work such as Virginia Woolf's *The Waves*. Thus Picasso's rejection of representational art and of the conventions of perspective in his early paintings can be compared with the rejection of the "tyranny of plot" by novelists such as Joyce, Woolf, and Marcel Proust. This shift in attitudes from realism to modernism can be witnessed in the work of Joseph Conrad. In 1898 Conrad wrote to his friend R.B. Cunninghame Graham, "You must have a *plot*! If you haven't, every fool reviewer will kick you because there can't be literature without plot" (Karl and Davies 1986, 5). Four years later, in 1902, he wrote to Arnold Bennett (one of those Virginia Woolf criticized as a "materialist" [see below p. 81] and thus far from what we now call modernism), "You just stop short of being absolutely real because you are faithful to your dogmas of realism. Now realism in art will never approach reality" (Karl and Davies 1986, 390). What we see here is a writer beginning to question "dogmas of realism" and to search for alternatives to the well-made plot, the rounded and lifelike character, the knowable world wholly accessible to reasoned and rational inquiry.

Modernism and the inner self

The modernist novel typically pays proportionally greater attention to the states and processes *inside* the consciousness of the main character(s) than to public events in the outside world. If the twentieth century was the century of Sigmund Freud and Karl Marx, then we can say that the modernist novel has much more in common with the outlook of the former than that of the latter (which explains, incidentally, why an orthodox Marxist critic such as Georg Lukács argued so bitterly for realism and against modernism during his long life). Moreover, as I will go on to argue in greater detail in

Chapter 5, the emergence of modernism involves profound changes with regard to novelists' conception of *character*. Michael Levenson opens his book *Modernism and the Fate of Individuality* as follows:

> This thing we name the individual, this piece of matter, this length of memory, this bearer of a proper name, this block in space, this whisper in time, this self-delighting, self-condemning oddity—what is it? who made it? Ours may be the age of narcissism, but it is also the century in which ego suffered unprecedented attacks upon its great pretensions, to be self-transparent and self-authorized. (Levenson 1991, xi)

For the great modernist novelists (Levenson pays particular attention to Conrad, James, Forster, Ford Madox Ford, Wyndham Lewis, D.H. Lawrence, and Woolf), character can no longer be taken to be self-transparent—more than one character in a modernist novel asks "Who am I?" without receiving a clear answer. Nor is the self any longer its own source of authority—which does not necessarily mean that any alternative source of authority is readily available.

This focusing upon the problems of the self and of the inner life has encouraged the development of new *methods* of fictional expression. If modernism can be defined negatively in terms of its rejection of realist conventions and assumptions, its positive side can be seen in its remarkable development of techniques such as *stream of consciousness* and *internal monologue*, its challenging of traditional conceptions of story and plot, its markedly greater emphasis upon what Joyce calls "epiphanies" and Virginia Woolf "moments" (see p. 41), and its revolutionary use of various forms of what we can call "poetic expression" in the novel (witness my earlier discussion of the final paragraph of Joyce's "The Dead" on p. 47). Such techniques will be discussed in Chapter 5.

A brief comment should be added concerning the philosophical underpinnings of modernism. These are very often implicit rather than overt, but frequently we find that modernist novels are pessimistic in tone, unsure about the sense or logic of the world, and look on human beings as isolated and alienated. The philosophical corollary of the rejection of perspective in art, and of an omniscient view of a knowable world obeying certain laws in fiction, seems to be a view of reality as lacking any unifying logic, to the extent that one should perhaps talk rather of "realities" than of reality. (Again risking a generalization, we can say that modernists have a monist view of reality but accept that complete knowledge of this reality is impossible, while postmodernists adhere to a pluralist view and suspect that it may make little sense to talk of a single reality.) Thus, for the modernist, different perspectives have to be combined because although what they reveal may appear contradictory, there is no "super-perspective" by means of which to rank their validity.

A modernist short story: James Joyce's "Eveline"

The Irishman James Joyce wrote one of the longest works of modernist fiction—*Ulysses*—and also one of the shortest, the 1,824-word-long story "Eveline," which appeared in his collection *Dubliners* (first published in 1914, but started in 1905). What the Irish critic Vivian Mercer said of a later central modernist work—Samuel Beckett's play *Waiting for Godot* (1953)— could also be applied to "Eveline": in it, "nothing happens, twice." The entire story is limited to two scenes. In the first of these the reader meets the title character Eveline sitting at the window of her home, musing about the past and looking forward to her forthcoming elopement with her young man Frank, who is to take her away from Ireland to Buenos Ayres. In the final, even shorter scene she is waiting on the quay for the ship that is to take both of them to a new life, but it appears that Eveline is, when the point of decision comes, unable to break her ties with her family and her past.

The story thus exemplifies well two of the characteristics that I have suggested are typical of modernist fiction: its focus on the inner self, and its abjuration of a traditional plot in which characters interact through involvement in events that succeed one another in a cause-and-effect manner. The important things that "happen" in "Eveline" happen *inside* Eveline, although they are related to things that have previously happened around and outside her. Interaction between characters occurs only in retrospect, in Eveline's memory, and the events that are planned for the future seem doomed not to occur.

This is how "Eveline" opens.

> She sat at the window watching the evening invade the avenue. Her head was leaned against the window curtains and in her nostrils was the odour of dusty cretonne. She was tired.
>
> Few people passed. The man out of the last house passed on his way home; she heard his footsteps clacking along the concrete pavement and afterwards crunching on the cinder path before the new red houses. One time there used to be a field there in which they used to play every evening with other

people's children. Then a man from Belfast bought the field and built houses in it—not like their little brown houses but bright brick houses with shining roofs. The children of the avenue used to play together in that field—the Devines, the Waters, the Dunns, little Keogh the cripple, she and her brothers and sisters. Ernest, however, never played: he was too grown up. Her father used often to hunt them in out of the field with his blackthorn stick; but usually little Keogh used to keep *nix* and call out when he saw her father coming. Still they seemed to have been rather happy then. Her father was not so bad then; and besides, her mother was alive. That was a long time ago; she and her brothers and sisters were all grown up; her mother was dead. Tizzie Dunn was dead, too, and the Waters had gone back to England. Everything changes. Now she was going to go away like the others, to leave her home. (Joyce 2000, 29)

Initially the reader is introduced to Eveline, and told certain things about her that may represent her conscious thoughts but may well not (she may not be aware of the smell or of her tiredness). But in the second paragraph we are taken into Eveline's mind and we follow her perceptions and thoughts, both those that are prompted by what she observes and those that she retrieves from her memory. The movement in these two paragraphs is almost cinematic: it is as if the camera moves nearer and nearer to Eveline, until we stop looking *at* her and start looking—and thinking—*with* her.

Fixing the reader as it were inside Eveline's head, the head of a person who is on her own and who seems to be better at communicating with herself than with other people, has the effect of forcing the reader to experience and share the character's isolation. Speaking personally, I find the experience of reading this story to be one that merits the adjective "claustrophobic"; it is as if, for the duration of one's reading, one is imprisoned in Eveline, in her mind and in her alienated life, and unable to escape.

This sense of alienation is very typical of much modernist literature. A lonely person reading a Jane Austen novel might well find relief in the sense of belonging to a world in which characters interact and engage with one another—not always successfully or in a positive manner, of course, but in a way that confirms their existence in a social world of connections and influence. The same lonely person reading "Eveline" might find some comfort in the sense that others had been there before, but the story engenders a pessimistic and depressing sense in the reader, one that suggests, perhaps, that our lives are more cut off from the lives of others than we would like to admit. Even the memories of human contact in the past are qualified: "they *seemed* to have been rather happy then": "Her father was *not so bad* then."

And those with whom Eveline shared a childhood vitality are either dead or have left Ireland for England.

A couple of words of warning are necessary here. First, the fact that Joyce locates the reader so firmly in the isolated consciousness of Eveline should not be taken to imply a lack of interest in the outside world, or in the specific social and historical characteristics of the Dublin setting of the collection of stories to which "Eveline" belongs. Indeed, if *Dubliners* is read from cover to cover the reader builds up a sense from story to story that the characteristics of inertia, alienation, and non-communication are very intimately related to this setting. In *Ulysses* the character Stephen Dedalus expresses his frustration at being the servant of two masters, the imperial British state and the holy Roman catholic and apostolic church, and this sense of political and ideological enslavement forms too a constant background in the stories that make up *Dubliners*. Second, the fact that the reader is imprisoned so securely in Eveline's consciousness in this story does not mean that Joyce is unable to insert levels of meaning in the story that are independent of her understanding.

Even in the second of the two paragraphs I quote, for example, the name "Waters" is unlikely to have been chosen at random given the motifs of aridity that run through the story: at the end of "Eveline" the title character feels that "All the seas of the world tumbled about her heart. He [Frank] was drawing her into them: he would drown her," and this fear of water and of drowning is, in the context of *Dubliners* as a whole, symptomatic of what Joyce saw as the inability of the people of early twentieth century Dublin to renew themselves and throw off their oppressors. (That this fear of renewal was not limited to either Ireland or to modernist fiction can be confirmed by its centrality to another classic modernist text: T.S. Eliot's poem "The Waste Land" [1922].) The other names listed in this paragraph may also have a specific resonance: "the Devines, the Waters" has a half-suggestion of water-diviners, so that Eveline's choice is between searching for something new, some new source of life, and admitting that her life is "Dunn" and dead.

In the previous chapter I referred to Thomas M. Leitch's report that commentators on the short story continued to distinguish between the "anecdotal" and the "epiphanic" story, and I noted that the use of the term "epiphany" with reference to modernist literature was particularly associated with James Joyce's writing. According to Leitch, the "epiphanic" short story "adumbrates a fictional world … by unfolding particular sensations or emotions and proceeding to a climactic revelation that does not necessarily take the form of a complete overt action" (Leitch 1989, 130–1). This definition fits the end of "Eveline" perfectly. In the story's short final scene Eveline waits on the quay to board the ship that will take her and Frank to Buenos Ayres. But although he calls to her, she seems frozen—paralysed.

> —Come!
> All the seas of the world tumbled about her heart. He was drawing her into them: he would drown her. She gripped with both hands at the iron railing.
> —Come!
> No! No! No! It was impossible. Her hands clutched the iron in frenzy. Amid the seas she sent a cry of anguish. (Joyce 2000, 34)

The waters that at the start of the story seem to hold out the promise of life and renewal are here experienced as a threat, the danger of existential drowning. As in Leitch's comment, we are not given "a complete overt action"—rather the reverse: an inability to act, a panic-filled paralysis on Eveline's part. But nonetheless we are given a "climactic revelation": Eveline's life has been invaded by the paralysis of her surroundings. She and we perceive that she is lost. In this final epiphany we see the full extent of her inner hopelessness.

Postmodernism

Although one commentator has traced the term "postmodernism" back to the mid 1930s (Hassan 1985, 119–31), it has only really come into more common use in Europe and the United States in the last four or five decades. Thus works which before this time were categorized as either "experimental" or "modernist" have in some cases received a new, often disputed, categorization as postmodernist. The term is more associated with controversy than is "modernism": Andreas Huyssen notes that, "one critic's postmodernism is another critic's modernism" (Huyssen 1988, 59), while John Frow claims that while it may be used to denote a specific period, theorists are unable to agree on what this period is (Frow 1997, 26–8).

Other commentators make what amounts to a political gesture by pointedly referring to "late modernism" rather than "postmodernism": behind the debate is the issue of whether we now inhabit a new sort of reality—the "postmodern world"—which is fundamentally different from the world, or social systems, that produced the great modernist art. This political edge to the debate is worth noting, as the term "postmodernism" is often used in a rather wider sense than is "modernism," referring to a general human condition, or society at large, as much as to art or culture (a usage which was encouraged by Jean-François Lyotard's book *The Postmodern Condition: A Report on Knowledge*, the English translation of which was published in 1984).

Postmodernism, then, can be used today in a number of different ways: (i) to refer to the non-realist and non-traditional literature and art of the post–Second World War period; (ii) to refer to literature and art that take certain modernist characteristics to an extreme stage; and (iii) to refer to aspects of a more general human condition in what is tendentiously referred to as the "late capitalist" world of the post-1950s which have an all-embracing effect on life, culture, ideology, and art, as well as (in some but not all usages) to a generally welcoming, celebratory attitude toward these aspects.

As a result, the label "postmodern" when applied to a work of fiction may refer primarily to technical and formal characteristics, or to the depiction of aspects of recent social and cultural change, or to both.

Those modernist characteristics which may produce postmodernism when taken to their most extreme forms include the rejection of representation in favor of self-reference—especially of a "playful" and non-serious, non-constructive sort; the willing, even relieved, rejection of artistic "aura" (sense of "holiness") and of a view of the work of art as organic whole; the substitution of confrontation and teasing of the reader for collaboration with him or her; the rejection of "character" and "plot" as meaningful or artistically defensible concepts or conventions; even the rejection of meaning itself along with the belief that it is worth trying to understand the world (or that there is a world to understand).

Postmodernism often takes the subjective idealism of modernism to the point of solipsism, while rejecting its tragic and pessimistic elements. It has been argued that there are affinities between postmodernism and the philosophical positions to be found in the work of various post-structuralist and deconstructive critics such as Jacques Derrida, Michel Foucault, Jean Baudrillard, and Jacques Lacan (for post-structuralism see p. 222).

Postmodernism is characterized in some but not all accounts by a more welcoming, celebratory attitude toward the modern world. That this world is one of increasing fragmentation, of the dominance of commercial pressures, and of human powerlessness in the face of a blind technology is not a point of dispute with modernism. Even so, whereas the major modernists reacted with horror or despair to their perception of these facts, some (but by no means all) postmodernists react in a far more accepting manner to them. The extent to which postmodernism is mimetic of recent and new social, economic, and political practices in the societies in which it appears is a matter of some debate. Thus the different but uncommunicating worlds with which many a postmodern novel faces the reader reflect, it has been claimed, the fact that more and more people in the modern world live in self-contained ghettoes about which outsiders know little or nothing. Moreover in the developed ("late capitalist") countries the advances of the communications and electronics industries have, it is argued, revolutionized human society. Instead of reacting to these changes in what is characterized as a Luddite manner, the postmodernist may instead counsel celebration of the present: enjoyment of that loss of artistic aura or "holiness" which follows what Walter Benjamin (one of the most important theorists of modernism and to a certain extent also a prophet of postmodernism) called "mechanical reproduction." In common with some much earlier avant-gardists, many postmodernists are fascinated with rather than repelled by technology, do not reject "the popular" or the commercial as beneath them, and are very much concerned with the immediate effect of their works: publication is for them (allegedly) more a strategic act than a bid for immortality.

David Harvey's *The Condition of Postmodernity* (1989) initiated much discussion around such issues, and subsequent debates involving (among others) Terry Eagleton and Fredric Jameson further helped to create a wider awareness of the issues involved. It should be added that the adjective "postmodern" is often applied to works of fiction in a relatively promiscuous manner. Thus I have seen Paul Auster's *Timbuktu* (1999) described as a postmodern novel, apparently primarily on the basis that the narrative follows the consciousness of a dog. But so does Virginia Woolf's *Flush* (1933), and Talbot Baines Reed's *The Adventures of a Three-Guinea Watch* (1883) has the eponymous watch as its narrator, and neither of these novels has been described as postmodern.

The legacy of World War

In Chapter 9, in the context of a discussion of World Literature, I include a discussion of what I term the literature of atrocity, focusing especially on examples of fiction written by those who experienced the horrors of Nazi concentration camp life, and who took this as their subject. The seriousness of this topic and of its treatment make me unwilling to use the term "postmodernism" in discussing it because of the frequent association of fantasy and playfulness with this term. And yet some works of fiction published in the decades that followed the Second World War that are very frequently seen as influential examples of postmodernist fiction do treat their authors' terrible wartime experiences in ways that blend the horrific, the fantastic, and even the comic. If this seems an odd combination of characteristics, we can surmise that soldiers experiencing long periods of boredom but with the threat of violent death never far from their minds may be naturally impelled toward a sort of dark humor. The British comedian Spike Milligan's five-volume war memoirs are full of jokes, surrealist humor, and irreverent fantasies, but he was much offended when the critic Clive James described a volume as "an unreliable history of the war," responding: "Well, this makes him a thoroughly unreliable critic, because I spend more time on getting my dates and facts right than I did in actual writing" (Milligan 1980, 5).

Milligan's memoir is, at base, a work of genuine history; in contrast Joseph Heller's *Catch 22* (1961) and Kurt Vonnegut Jr's *Slaughterhouse 5* (1969) are works of fiction. But they have in common with Milligan's work a blending of the horrific and the laughable and a concern with a world in which the surreal has become everyday reality. Both works achieved considerable popularity during the Vietnam war, as their portrayal of the insanity of war was taken particularly by younger readers as comment on the immorality of American engagement in Vietnam, and indeed a scene early on in *Slaughterhouse 5* moves suddenly from describing the capture of the novel's hero by German troops in 1945 to attending a Lions Club luncheon in 1967, at which the speaker is a major in the marines who insists that Americans had no choice but to keep fighting in Vietnam until they achieved victory, and who "was in favor of increased bombings, of bombing North Vietnam back into the Stone Age, if it refused to see reason" (1972, 45).

Elsewhere in this book I have argued that it is important for the reader to be able to experience the "world" of a work of fiction as consistent and in a sense self-enclosed. In a very influential essay on the novel entitled "The Art of Fiction" (1888), the novelist Henry James insisted that the novelist-as-real-person should never appear within the pages of his or her creation and expose its fictionality to the reader.

> Certain accomplished novelists have a habit of giving themselves away which must often bring tears to the eyes of people who take their fiction seriously. I was lately struck, in reading over many pages of Anthony Trollope, with his want of discretion in this particular. In a digression, a parenthesis or an aside, he concedes to the reader that he and this trusting friend are only "making believe." He admits that the events he narrates have not really happened, and that he can give his narrative any turn the reader may like best. Such

a betrayal of a sacred office seems to me, I confess, a terrible crime. (James 1984, 46–7)

Much postmodernist fiction challenges James's position head-on, and *Slaughterhouse 5*, like Jeanette Winterson's *Lighthousekeeping*, which I discuss below, deliberately and even defiantly breaks the unspoken rule that the author should not reveal his or her real-world identity within the world of the fiction.

Thus what might in a more traditional novel have constituted a Foreword or Preface is, in *Slaughterhouse 5*, the novel's first chapter. This is how this chapter opens.

> All this happened, more or less. The war parts, anyway, are pretty much true. One guy I knew really *was* shot in Dresden for taking a teapot that wasn't his. Another guy I knew really *did* threaten to have his personal enemies killed by hired gunmen after the war. And so on. I've changed all the names. (Vonnegut 1972, 9)

About two-thirds of the way through *Slaughterhouse 5*, we can read about a group of American prisoners of war who, early 1945, have reached a camp and have been fed by British troops there. The food causes a violent reaction in them.

> An American near Billy wailed that he had excreted everything but his brains. Moments later he said, "There they go, there they go." He meant his brains.
> That was I. That was me. That was the author of this book. (1972, 86)

Such a "betrayal of the sacred office" of the novelist by allowing the author to appear in the pages of a work of fiction as his non-fictional self is a characteristic typical of the postmodern novel.

"Billy" is Billy Pilgrim, the main character in *Slaughterhouse 5*, who has the ability to travel in time and space, although he "has no control over where he is going next" (23). At one time he is in the Ilium School of Optometry prior to being drafted for war service, at another he is serving in the infantry, is captured, and is in Dresden at the time it is firebombed in early 1945, at another time he is on the planet Tralfamadore after having been abducted, and is put on display with a pornographic actress named Montana Wildhack in a Tralfamadorian zoo. That Billy's interplanetary experiences seem if anything less remarkable than what he witnesses in Dresden has the effect of defamiliarizing (see the Glossary) war for the reader of the novel, forcing us to see that what has become known and familiar is outrageous, and impossible to assimilate to a view of human society as sane and rational.

Billy's time- and space-traveling allow Vonnegut to make sudden shifts in time and space in the narrative, shifts that force the reader to confront similarities between, say, Dresden in 1945 and Vietnam in the 1960s. Although it is possible to read Billy's time-travels as delusional episodes caused by his war experiences, the novel also allows us to take them as real.

A much-quoted passage from *Slaughterhouse 5* has Billy, the night after his daughter's wedding in 1966, waiting for the abduction by a Tralfamadorian flying saucer that he knows is coming and killing time by watching a movie on TV. Coming "slightly unstuck in time" he watches the movie (about American bombers in the Second World War) both backwards and forwards.

Seen backwards by Billy, the story went like this:

> American planes, full of holes and wounded men and corpses took off backwards from an airfield in England. Over France, a few German fighter planes flew at them backwards, sucked bullets and shell fragments from some of the planes and crewmen. They did the same for wrecked American bombers on the ground, and those planes flew up backwards to join the formation. (1972, 54)

The planes then fly backwards over a German city, open their bomb bay doors, and by a "miraculous magnetism" shrink the fires below, gather them into cylindrical containers, and lift these containers into the bellies of the planes. Then over France "German fighters came up again, made everything and everybody as good as new" (1972, 54). The conceit is extended, with the steel cylinders being shipped back to the United States, dismantled, and the dangerous contents separated into minerals which are hidden in the ground "so they would never hurt anybody ever again" (1972, 54). It is impossible for the reader to escape the message that the reversed chronology described in this passage, far from being absurd, pictures a world that seems to make much better sense than does the world that Billy Pilgrim and we inhabit.

In his non-fictional account of life as an inmate in the Auschwitz concentration camp, Primo Levi includes a chilling vignette.

> Driven by thirst, I eyed a fine icicle outside the window, within hand's reach. I opened the window and broke off the icicle but at once a large, heavy guard prowling outside brutally snatched it away from me. "*Warum?*" I asked him in my poor German. "*Hier ist kein warum*" (there is no why here), he replied, pushing me inside with a shove. (Levi 1996, 29)

Slaughterhouse 5 includes a scene from 1945 in which an American prisoner mutters something that a guard does not like, gets hauled out of ranks, and knocked down, losing two teeth. The American is astonished.

"Why me?" he asked the guard.

The guard shoved him back into ranks. "Vy you? Vy anybody?" he said. (1972, 64)

The question "why?" asks for an explanation based on cause and effect, but in the mad world of war and genocide such logic has been abandoned. The postmodernist exploration of worlds in which logical progression from beginning to end, and cause to effect, and the possibility of explanation do not exist is not something that emerges in the heads of writers from nothing; it is prompted by experience of a real world from which reason appears to have been banished.

Late capitalism as postmodernism

More recently many works of postmodernist fiction have explored lives that seem hardly to make direct, or even any, contact with a real world, lives that encounter reality primarily or even exclusively through the medium of electronic screens of one sort or another. For certain individuals the electronic display *is* their reality. In Don DeLillo's *Cosmopolis* (first published 2003), most of the novel follows the twenty-eight-year-old billionaire currency trader Eric Packer around in his limousine, following the stock market and other sources of information on screens.

> He looked past China toward streams of numbers running in opposite directions. He understood how much it meant to him, the roll and flip of data on a screen. He studied the figural diagrams that brought organic patterns into play, birdwing and chambered shell. It was shallow thinking to maintain that numbers and charts were the cold compression of unruly human energies, every sort of yearning and midnight sweat reduced to lucid units in the financial markets. In fact data itself was soulful and glowing, a dynamic aspect of the life process. This was the eloquence of alphabets and numeric systems, now fully realized in electronic form, in the zero-oneness of the world, the digital imperative that defined every breath of the planet's living billions. Here was the heave of the biosphere. Our bodies and oceans were here, knowable and whole. (DeLillo 2004, 24)

The extent to which passages such as this in DeLillo's work are to be taken as celebration or satire, or both, has formed the subject of debate. DeLillo uses Free Indirect Discourse (see p. 122) to display Packer's sensations and beliefs, but in such a way as to leave open the possibility that some of the character's judgments are indeed accurate. What is clear in this particular sequence is that Packer's experience of this world of representations is a pleasurable one, providing him with a sense of power and control: if DeLillo is giving us a dystopia, it is one in which at least some of the inhabitants are, perhaps only temporarily, happy. It is also one in which representations mediated electronically are described not as artificial, but in terms of the natural world: "organic patterns," "birdwing and shell," "the life process." Electronic images have replaced direct contact with living things.

If we agree that *Cosmopolis* is a postmodern work, then its postmodernity resides not in the use of striking new narrative techniques or in the mixing of the fantastic with the realistic—in formal and technical terms the novel is more conventional than one written by Virginia Woolf or James Joyce—but in its portrayal of a *world* that is in some way postmodern. This world—in many respects *our* world—has characters living in ways that a few short decades earlier could be found only in works of science fiction. Michael Frayn's novel *A Very Private Life* (1968), for example, depicts a world in which the privileged class make contact with those outside their family circle exclusively through electronic displays, and control their emotions, including those associated with sex, through medications. Frayn wrote the novel shortly after visiting the United States, and it can be seen as a European's projection of the shock of a first encounter with a world of limousines, all-day TV, and air-conditioning. But no one in 1968 called Frayn's novel postmodern. What was science fiction in 1968 is postmodern in 2003.

DeLillo's portrayal of a world of simulacra has been related to the ideas of the French philosopher Jean Baudrillard, who claimed—most dramatically in a work entitled *The Gulf War Did Not Take Place* (1991)—that we now construct an image of the world from media images that fictionalize what is actually taking place. In this postmodern world, signs lead a life of their own, detached from what in previous societies they represented. Here is Eric Packer talking in his limousine to his "chief of theory" Vija Kinski.

> "We want to think about the art of money-making," she said.
> She was sitting in the rear seat, his seat, the club chair, and he looked at her and waited.
> "The Greeks have a word for it."
> He waited.
> "*Chrimatistikós*," she said. "But we have to give the word a little leeway. Adapt it to the current situation. Because money has taken a turn. All wealth has become wealth for its own sake. There's no other kind of enormous wealth. Money has lost its narrative quality the way painting did once upon a time. Money is talking to itself." (77)

Again, whether this is DeLillo parodying philosophers such as Baudrillard or exploring the extent to which their ideas really do describe something about the postmodern world can be debated, but it is hard to avoid the sense that for DeLillo, Vija Kinski is not altogether wrong. Standing behind her and pointing at the information screens, Packer "knew what she was thinking."

> Never mind the urgent and endless replenishment, the way data dissolves at one end of the series just as it takes shape at the other. This is the point, the thrust, the future. We are not witnessing the flow of information so much as pure spectacle, or information made sacred, ritually unreadable. The small monitors of the office, home and car become a kind of idolatry here, where crowds might gather in astonishment. (80)

If the belief that this is the future suggests that human beings really are starting to live in a world of Baudrillardian pure spectacle, the word "idolatry" leaves open the possibility that what we are witnessing is only the latest form that human self-delusion is taking.

The world of *Cosmopolis* is a world in which everything has been commodified. As his limousine drives through a demonstration and is attacked by protesters who are swept off the car by his bodyguards, Packer thinks briefly about the partition behind the driver: "It had a cedar frame with an inlaid fragment of ornamental Kufic script on parchment, late tenth century, Baghdad, priceless" (90). Here the cultural treasures of humanity are reduced to items of automobile *décor*. But if the reader's first response may be to feel that such passages cry out to be parodied, the second may be a worried recognition that they are not wholly inaccurate depictions of aspects of the debased world in which we live. As the limousine leaves the demonstrators, Packer "thought there was something theatrical about the protest"—rather than being focused on those they are attacking, the demonstrators are performing for the media. DeLillo's postmodern world is one in which people no longer act: they perform for the media.

Postmodernism as technique: Jeanette Winterson's *Lighthousekeeping*

The British author Jeanette Winterson has been, as Sonya Andermahr puts it, "resistant to postmodernism … believing it to be a faddish phenomenon compared to the gravitas of the modernist canon" (Andermahr 2009, 17; for "canon," see the Glossary). Andermahr agrees that we must take seriously the view that Winterson is a modernist writer, not least because this is how Winterson views her own work.

> However, she is also indubitably a postmodernist engaged in a playful and parodic rescripting of popular and canonical genres, and in the construction of reality as precisely an intricate web of fictional worlds, of endless stories. Winterson's novels clearly exemplify a postmodern aesthetics, demonstrating high levels of temporal dislocation, self-reflexivity, intertextuality and pastiche. (19)

Andermahr's comments, while reminding us that there is no Berlin Wall between modernism and postmodernism, also I think legitimize my using *Lighthousekeeping*—which is by no means the most obviously postmodernist of Winterson's novels—in the context of a discussion of postmodern fiction.

Lighthousekeeping was first published in 2004. In 2005 the novel was reissued in paperback under the HarperPerennial imprint, and I would like to focus on this particular "textual manifestation" of Winterson's novel in the comments that follow. Note that this is the only time in this book that I direct attention toward one particular *edition* of a work of fiction, and this unusual focus has something to do with the postmodernist features of the work in question. (Readers using other editions of the novel, including the 2006 Harvest edition of this book published in the United States, will not have access to the additional material I discuss below, but I hope that this will not prevent consideration of the issues I discuss.)

There are a number of unusual features about the actual text of the novel, but let us skip over these for the time being. After the novel's final page (p. 232), a new section follows entitled *P.S. Ideas, Interviews and Features*. I suspect that had the novel been published ten years later, this section might well have been moved to a Web page dedicated to *Lighthousekeeping*, but having it in the book itself makes it easier to explore its significance.

The section is repaginated—in other words, its first page is numbered 1. It is divided into three subsections: "About the author," "About the book," and "Read on." Some of the material in these sections is written by journalists and others, some is written by Jeanette Winterson herself. There is even a final sub-subsection entitled "Find out more" that provides information about books and Web pages, ranging from Virginia Woolf's novel *To the Lighthouse* to Web pages on the (actual) Cape Wrath Lighthouse, about Jeanette Winterson, and about holidays in a Scottish lighthouse.

None of this, I admit, is earth-shattering. Indeed, it is to a large extent the sort of material that we have come to *expect* in "academic" issues of older works of literature—that is, editions aimed at the student market. But it marks a substantial change from the way in which a *new* novel would have been packaged a couple of decades ago. In particular, devoting attention to the figure of the *author,* to *actual places* mentioned in the novel, and to *writers* whose lives and works are alluded to in the novel may seem to weaken that conventional boundary between "the world of the fiction" and "our normal, everyday world" that we saw crossed by Kurt Vonnegut in *Slaughterhouse 5.*

All of the "surrounding material" in *Lighthousekeeping* to which I have referred has been given a descriptive name: "paratext." The term is a coinage of the French narrative theorist Gérard Genette, used in his work *Seuils* (1987; English translation *Paratexts: Thresholds of Interpretation* [1997]). According to Genette, "Paratext" refers to "those liminal devices and conventions … that mediate the book to the reader: titles and subtitles, pseudonyms, forewords, dedications, epigraphs, prefaces, intertitles, notes, epilogues, and afterwords." Genette even distinguishes between such material found within the text, which he calls *peritext,* and material found outside it, which he calls *epitext.* In the former category in our case might come such things as the section headings that we find in the novel.

We might say that the bits of paratext that come at the front of *Lighthousekeeping*—a list of other works by the author and extracts from reviews of the novel—detail the novel's *effects*—while many of the bits of paratext at the end of the book detail the materials used to *create* the book— historical characters, geographical locations and events (the Great Exhibition of 1851), and works of fiction and their characters. So, what comes first in the book is what came last in time, and some of what comes at the end of the book is what preceded the writing of the novel.

My point in detailing all this is to draw attention to the fact that this is a book constructed in a manner that actively encourages the reader to link the world depicted in the novel with the real world of places, events, individuals, reviews—and author. Instead of the sharp division between the world of the real-life author and the created world of the fictional text recommended by Henry James, we have very blurred boundaries between these two worlds— so blurred, in fact, that we may wonder whether the world of the novel *is* separate from the everyday world of author (and reader). Reading this book, then, is almost like watching a film or a TV play in which the director and cameras are in constant view. If in Don DeLillo's *Cosmopolis* representations appear to have displaced or replaced reality, here the world of the novel and the world outside the novel flow into each other. What is more, the world of *Lighthousekeeping* is a strange, surrealistic one, in which bits of our real world coexist with fantastic people and events.

Fictional and real people and places

In the actual text of *Lighthousekeeping* we find the same encouragement to the reader to link the people, places, and events of the fiction with both real people, places, and events and people, places, and events taken from other novels mentioned in the book's "peritext." Like many novels—realist and modernist, as well as postmodernist—*Lighthousekeeping* is populated with both fictional and real people and places. Thus there really is a lighthouse at Cape Wrath, and it really was built by the father of the novelist and traveler Robert Louis Stevenson, who appears as a character in Winterson's novel. Moreover, Robert Louis Stevenson's novels *Treasure Island* and *The Strange Case of Dr Jekyll and Mr Hyde* are referred to both directly and indirectly throughout *Lighthousekeeping*.

Dr Jekyll and Mr Hyde is named in the text, initially when the protagonist Silver finds a copy of the book.

> I took them out. Two first editions: Charles Darwin, *On the Origin of Species*, 1859, and *The Strange Case of Dr Jekyll and Mr Hyde*, 1886. The other books were the notebooks and letters that had belonged to Babel Dark. (Winterson 2005, 124)

Note here the move from the historically real to the fictional: Darwin and Stevenson and their books existed in the everyday world, Babel Dark exists only as a character in this novel. So far as *Treasure Island* is concerned, there are many allusions to this work in *Lighthousekeeping*. The novel opens with two characters: a lighthouse-keeper named Pew, and his helper, the narrator Silver. One of the characters in *Treasure Island* is named Blind Pew, while the hero is the boy named Jim—the name of Silver's dog. And the villain of *Treasure Island* is a Pirate named Long John Silver—thus hinting that Silver is herself descended from him. References such as this are called *intertextual* references (see the Glossary), and the topic of intertextuality is raised explicitly on the second page of the P.S. section of the book, in an interview with Winterson.

Now at this point you may protest that many novels contain passing allusions to other works (Scott and Cowper are discussed by the characters early on in Jane Austen's *Sense and Sensibility*, for example). But *Lighthousekeeping* is packed full of intertextual references to which the reader's attention is drawn by both the characters and the narrator— and, in the peritext, by the author. Thus in case we might not have realized that in reading the novel we need to bear in mind Virginia Woolf's *To the Lighthouse*, this novel is listed in the additional material in the subsection "Find Out More" in the P.S. section of the book. It is almost as if Winterson is acting as her own critic. Let me pause here in order to make some provisional summarizing points.

We can, I hope, agree that *Lighthousekeeping* is possessed of many *formal* characteristics that are frequently described as typical of postmodern fiction.

- self-reference
- "ludic" or playful games with the reader; teasing the reader
- the rejection of artistic "aura" or seriousness
- the rejection of conventional ideas of character and plot
- blurring the boundaries between the factual and the fictional

Let me consider these features one at a time.

- So far as self-reference is concerned, I will come back below to the way in which a discussion about the nature of stories and storytelling—of *narrative*—threads its way through the whole novel.
- So far as the novel's ludic qualities are concerned, we can trace a jokey quality throughout the work.

> I lived in a house cut steep into the bank. The chairs had to be nailed to the floor, and we were never allowed to eat spaghetti. We ate food that stuck to the plate—shepherd's pie, goulash, risotto, scrambled egg. (3)

> My mother was a single parent and she had conceived out of wedlock. There had been no lock on her door that night when my father came to call. So she was sent up the hill, away from the town, with the curious result that she looked down on it. (4–5)

> Pew—why didn't my mother marry my father?

> She never had time. He came and went. (85)

This ludic quality has the effect, among other things, of undermining artistic seriousness and "aura"—although, importantly, there are moments of passion, intensity, and insight that are powerful and moving in the novel.

- It is clear, too, that it is hard to find a conventional plot in the novel—not least because it spans such a long period of time. The characters in it too are sometimes strange—like the succession of Pews, all blind, who pass the job of lighthouse keeper on from generation to generation. Furthermore the intertextual references to *Dr Jekyll and Mr Hyde* undercut the idea that a character—either fictional or real—

is consistent and integrated, and what is called "self-transparent," because the two characters named in the title are two personalities or identities that are contained in a single individual. (You may note, however, that because Stevenson's novel was first published in 1886, this means that in the history of the novel, the attack on a belief in the unity of the individual and of the individual character is something that predates postmodernism by a long stretch.)

- So far as blurring the boundaries between the factual and the fictional is concerned, consider these two quotations:

> Storytelling is a way of establishing connections, imaginative connections for ourselves, a way of joining up disparate material and making sense of the world.

> The continuous narrative of existence is a lie. There is no continuous narrative, there are lit-up moments, and the rest is dark. (134)

The first quotation comes from the P.S. section of the book, and represents Winterson talking in her own voice in an interview; the second comes from the text of the novel, and it is given to us as delivered by Silver. It is hard, surely, to say that the first belongs to a world of fact and the second to an enclosed world of fiction.

Text and peritext

In my comments above I note that the section headings in the novel could be considered to be an aspect of what Gérard Genette terms the work's *peritext*—that is, of paratextual material "inside" the novel proper which is not strictly part of the fictional world of the novel, but material that represents structurally ordering and categorizing information that we attribute to either the narrator or the author. It is important to remember that many of the most realist of nineteenth-century novels include such material, even if it is just limited to chapter divisions and numbering. But if we look at such peritextual material as it appears in what we now consider to be standard nineteenth-century novels, we can see that it is different from what we encounter in *Lighthousekeeping*.

Here are a couple of examples from nineteenth-century novels.

CHAPTER XXVI
I fall into Captivity

XI
THE ARCHED WINDOW

The first of these is from Charles Dickens's *David Copperfield* (1849–50), while the second is from Nathaniel Hawthorne's *The House of the Seven Gables* (1851). The two chapter-headings are representative of the novels in which they appear, as those in Dickens's novel are presented as if they were written by the character-narrator David Copperfield himself, while those in Hawthorne's novel seem to emanate from a categorizing intelligence that is apart from the world in which the characters live. Henry James, we should not be surprised to discover, had a preference for minimalist chapter- and part-headings that consisted merely of a number, and many of his modernist successors reduced chapter-division markers to textless space. Virginia Woolf's *The Waves*, for example, reduces such markers to page-breaks—although the novel's alternation between roman and italic typeface also plays an important role in denoting perspectival shifts and thus divisions between sections, as it does too in Winterson's novel. In Woolf's last-published novel, *Between the Acts*, there are no conventional part- or chapter-divisions, but occasional line spaces are used to suggest a movement from one scene to another.

Now even though it seems to make sense to attribute the chapter heading from *David Copperfield* to David himself, it is a David who is as it were standing back from the action, separated from what is told both by time and by tone. If we return to *Lighthousekeeping* we become immediately aware that the neat division between (to use Genette's terms) text and peritext is hard to maintain. For example, the normal division between a chapter or section heading and the text that follows is often omitted in a manner that draws attention to this challenging of conventions. Note that if the headings that Winterson puts in bold in the examples below were set in roman and closed up with the text that follows them, we would be hard put to see the shift from heading to text.

A beginning, a middle and an end is the proper way to tell a story. But I have difficulty with that method.
   Already I could choose the year of my birth—1959. (23)

As an apprentice to lighthousekeeping my duties were as follows:
   1) Brew a pot of Full Strength Samson and take it to Pew.
   2) 8 am. Take DogJim for a walk. (37)

Dark was looking at the moon.
   If the earth's history was fossil-written, why not the universe? The moon, bone-white, bleached of life, was the relic of a solar system once planeted with earths.

He thought the whole of the sky must have been alive once, and some stupidity or carelessness had brought it to this burnt-out, warmless place. (147)

In the first two of these examples, the headings appear to be written by the narrator Silver and to merge into the subsequent first-person text. (And the year in which Silver is born is also the year in which her creator, Jeanette Winterson, was born.) But the third example details actions that took place years before Silver's reported birth, and so both the heading and the following text have to be attributed to a source other than that of Silver herself.

The postmodernist novel: Some observations

It is tempting to suggest that a neat way of answering the question, "What is postmodernism?" is by means of the reply: "Everything that Henry James would have disapproved of!" For James, maintaining the reading illusion that characters and events are in some sense real is fundamental to the success of a novel. If the novelist intrudes as him- or herself in the pages of the created work, reminding the reader that characters are his or her creation, and events could have been decided otherwise, then the reader can no longer take what is read seriously, can no longer become involved with characters and their fates in a manner resembling the way in which we get involved with real people and their fates.

So it is worth asking whether novels such as Kurt Vonnegut's *Slaughterhouse 5* and Jeanette Winterson's *Lighthousekeeping* can serve as a sort of Jamesian Awful Warning. Does the intermingling of real-world and fictional-world people and events cause us to lose interest in the writer's creation? When the writer suddenly appears in the text as him- or herself, do we stop believing in the story narrated? If we can see the strings and the puppet-master or mistress, do we lose interest in the puppets? Each reader will have to answer these questions themselves, but I have to say this is not how I respond to these novels. What is very striking and not a little strange to me is that in spite of all their postmodernist characteristics, I find myself as much gripped by both novels as by a novel by Henry James, just as much involved with the lives of the characters and as concerned with what happens to them.

In *Lighthousekeeping*, even the recurrent references to storytelling, to what we can call theories of narrative, do not lead me to disengage from the characters and events about which I am reading. Here are a few short examples.

> It was a long story, and like most of the stories in the world, never finished. There was an ending—there always is—but the story went on past the ending—it always does. (11)
> "Why can't you just tell me the story without starting with another story?"
> "Because there's no story that's the start of itself, any more than a child comes into the world without parents." (27)

It seems to me that comments like these perform a sort of double function: on the one hand, their self-referential nature has a sort of "alienating" effect on the reader, who is reminded that the neat conventions of the novel beginning on the first page and ending on the last page may simplify the complex reality of life. But, on the other hand, they make perfectly good sense as utterances delivered by a narrator who is forced to make choices about—for example—where to start her story.

In the material included in the P.S. section of *Lighthousekeeping* Winterson includes a comment that suggests that her interest in narrative does not just come from books: "Our mental processes are more like a maze than a motorway. We do not remember our lives chronologically, nor do we reflect on them in neat order." The comment provides a useful reminder that while some aspects of postmodernism are taken from their predecessors the modernists—and even from their predecessors, the "classic realist" novelists—others are the result of introspection. Virginia Woolf's essay "Modern Fiction" has long been recognized as one of the key theoretical texts of modernist fiction, written by one of its leading practitioners. In this essay, Woolf takes issue with what she calls "materialist" writers such as H.G. Wells, Arnold Bennett, and John Galsworthy, and, having provided an unsympathetic account of their fiction (from which, in the case of Arnold Bennett, she claims "life escapes"), she outlines an alternative. Instead of a concern with the objects of the outer world she proposes that we "look within." If we do, she suggests, we will see that the mind "receives a myriad impressions," and that

> as they fall, as they shape themselves into the life of Monday or Tuesday, the accent falls differently from of old; the moment of importance came not here but there; so that, if a writer were a free man and not a slave, if he could write what he chose, not what he must, if he could base his work upon his own feeling and not upon convention, there would be no plot, no comedy, no tragedy, no love interest or catastrophe in the accepted style, and perhaps not

a single button sewn on as the Bond Street tailors would have it. Life is not a series of gig lamps symmetrically arranged; life is a luminous halo, a semi-transparent envelope surrounding us from the beginning of consciousness to the end. (Woolf 1966b, 106)

Note that although Woolf's essay represents a key statement of modernist principles, it also reveals the extent to which Woolf aims to represent life more realistically than her predecessors. If "life escapes" from their accounts, she clearly hopes that life does not escape from hers; if there is more "life" in her fiction, then it is, arguably, more realistic than fiction from which life has, to a greater extent, escaped.

All new movements in fiction seem to involve a rebellion on the part of writers against conventions that have become so fixed that they end up almost as templates to which the novelist must conform, templates that push the novel in the direction of stereotype, cliché, and the formulaic. It is perhaps ironic, in view of the use I have made of it, that Henry James's essay "The Art of Fiction" was itself a polemic against precisely such a template—a guide to the writing of fiction by Walter Besant. But for Virginia Woolf there is a different template to be rejected, and although postmodernist writers may sympathize with and learn from her rebellion, they also see the need to push further.

The electronic revolution

This section clearly involves something of a category shift. After discussing three different "isms," suddenly we have a shift of focus away from the formal qualities of fictional works and the characteristics of the worlds they represent to the new technologies underlying the ways in which fiction is composed, published, accessed, and read. I have previously discussed how technological change, interlocking with social and political changes, has over many centuries enabled and influenced the writing and reading of fiction. The development of more and more efficient forms of printing, the rise of literacy, the availability of leisure time in which to read—all of these played a crucial role in the "rise of the novel" and the development of new forms of fiction (see p. 22). Most of us are aware that although we have little difficulty reading books from the eighteenth century onwards, behind a relatively similar end-product reside many technological revolutions. From an author who writes with a quill pen and whose work is set in moveable type on a flat-bed printing press, through an author who writes with a steel pen whose work is printed on a rotary printing press, through an author who writes on a typewriter and whose work is printed on a hot-metal printing press, to an author who writes on a computer and whose work is printed offset from electronically set and corrected copy, enormous variations lie behind the black-and-white pages of a printed novel. These changes are not without their effects: handwritten manuscripts can be misread, alterations to hot-metal set copy are complicated and costly, and so on.

But these technical advances seem minor when compared to the ways in which the electronic revolution of the last three decades has affected the writing, circulation, and reading of fiction. Most novels may still be produced in relatively traditionally ways: an author slaves away at a text, the text is submitted to various publishers, perhaps one of these publishers gets professional readers to assess the text and make suggestions, the author revises the text in light of these suggestions, the novel is published in printed form, people buy the book after having read reviews or marketing copy, and they read it—a process that in broad outline has remained relatively unchanged for over two centuries. But even in such cases the novel concerned is likely to be available electronically as well as in print form, readable on a tablet or a Kindle or even listened to, as a computer program transforms printed into spoken words.

However, the real revolution that the digital age has brought to fiction lies alongside such traditional survivals. As the readership of this book probably consists primarily of those about fifty years younger than the author, many of the examples that follow are likely to be familiar, but I want to focus on the ways in which they have changed our understanding of what fiction is—on the potentialities of fiction. To start with, however, let me provide some specific examples.

In the previous edition of this book I reported that according to an online newspaper article accessed on August 3, 2004, up to four million players worldwide regularly visit make-believe lands to fight, hunt for treasure, or just chat (Meek 2004, 1). All of these individuals are participants in online fantasy games known by the acronym MMORPG ("Massively multiplayer online role-playing games"). Eleven years later I learn from various internet sources that a single such game—*World of Warcraft*—had in November 2014 over ten million subscribers. In such games each player adopts an online identity and, using this identity, is able to enter virtual worlds and to interact with other players (who also, of course, have entered the game by means of other adopted identities). Here there is no single plot, no shared beginning and—the companies who earn vast amounts of money from these games earnestly wish—no ending. MMORPGs represent only one of the new fictional experiences currently on offer to those with a personal computer and (ideally but not essentially) an internet connection.

Such games represent just one of the ways in which fiction has escaped from the confines of the printed page in recent decades. Here are some others, chosen from a very large range of possible examples.

Elizabeth Bennet goes digital

The Lizzie Bennet Diaries is, as its Web page announces, "the groundbreaking multiplatform adaptation of *Pride and Prejudice*. It became the first YouTube series to win a Primetime Emmy, receiving the 2013 Primetime Emmy Award for Outstanding Creative Achievement in Interactive Media-Original Interactive Program," and "reimagines Austen's classic around a fictional vlog filmed in the bedroom of a 24 year-old grad student, living at home and burdened with a mountain of student debt" (<http://www.pemberleydigital.com/the-lizzie-bennet-diaries/). A "vlog" is a video blog (and, for the benefit of the really ancient, a "blog" is a Web log—a diary or regularly updated report posted on the internet). This particular vlog is fictional, and consists of a hundred separate episodes, in which a modern-day version of Jane Austen's *Pride and Prejudice* unrolls, narrated through the spoken-to-camera accounts of an actor playing "Lizzie Bennet" and various other contributing actors. The titles of these episodes display a relentless cultural updating of Austen's novel: "Bing" is neither a search engine nor a 1930s crooner but a modern reincarnation of Jane Austen's Mr Bingley, Kitty Bennet is on Twitter, and American festivals such as Thanksgiving and the Superbowl are woven into the plot. On one level this is clearly an example of an adaptation, and might well have been included in the section on this topic (p. 185). Although it gestures toward interactive contact with viewers through question-and-answer sessions, it is not genuinely interactive.

A million Penguins

"A million Penguins" is, or was, what is known as a "networked book"—otherwise known as "collaborative fiction." There is a long history of works of fiction being written by two or more collaborating authors—Joseph Conrad and Ford Madox Ford produced three such jointly written works—but recent examples involving collaboration through the internet can be written by hundreds or thousands of "authors." "A million Penguins" was begun in February 2007 through collaboration between Penguin Books and Kate Pullinger on behalf of the Institute of Creative Technologies at De Montfort University, in the United Kingdom. It was created on MediaWiki, using the same software as Wikipedia. During the five weeks that it was active, any visitor could contribute to it, but contributions were moderated by a team of students from De Montfort University. Those accepted were incorporated into the text at regular intervals, but there were periods when the text remained fixed so as to allow readers to get their heads around developments in stages (this attempt to impose some textual fixity on the growing work is revealing, and I will comment more on readers' need for textual fixity below).

No commentator appears to have found the end result of anything other than academic interest. You can find a research report on the whole project written by Bruce Mason and Sue Thomas at <http://www.ioct.dmu.ac.uk/documents/amillionpenguinsreport.pdf>. The report is frank, and quotes one reaction to the final result as "the worst book I've ever read," while finding the process (rather than the result) of the experiment of some interest.

In search of Oldton

"In search of Oldton" (<http://www.oldton.com/>) describes itself as a 90 percent true story by Tim Wright. It consists of fifty-two electronically displayed cards "that locate all the people, events and emotions that have been lost until now" superimposed on a map of the (semi-)fictional Oldton, each of which can be clicked to reveal aspects of the place. The map and other details are based on "texts, photos and artefacts" sent to Wright by those accessing the site. Associated with the site are a road show (the author visiting various towns), a radio play, published "memories" from contributors who have sent them in, and comments which are moderated by Wright. The material on the site seems to be, as Wright describes it, "90% true," but which elements fall into the 10 percent untrue (or fictional) is not easy to determine, and the site offers a curious mixture of a semi-voyeuristic view into the private life of the author and of contributors, and the more traditional imaginative pleasures of fiction.

At this point I want to step back and, rather than looking at further specific examples of "digital fiction," attempt to group the most significant of these new developments into some dominant categories.

The computer game

In his book *More Than a Game: The Computer Game as Fictional Form*, Barry Atkins argues that "computer game-fiction is a form of popular fiction" (Atkins 2003, 9). For Atkins, many of the most popular computer games available today can be linked directly to forms of traditional narrative. Discussing one of these games—the now-dated *Tomb Raider*—he argues that in many ways it "conforms to the generic conventions of the folk tale, and particularly the quest narrative, and wears many of its folk tale credentials on its sleeve" (42). He explains:

> As in *Tomb Raider* there are few extraneous or irrelevant encounters within the folk tale quest narrative: anyone or anything encountered will prove to be either an adversary or a helper. Overcoming adversaries through violence is virtually mandatory and, as in *Tomb Raider* or any amount of contemporary *Rambo*esque versions of the quest narrative, there is no ethical or moral problem with such violence.
>
> …
>
> The occasional riddle must be solved. Often an object must be retrieved. (43)

Of course, the riddles to be solved differ in nature from those in the traditional folk tale, and the player of the game must solve problems correctly before being allowed to proceed through the narrative, but the parallels between the computer game and, say, the picaresque novel (see the Glossary) are striking. One important difference, however, is that although the reader of a picaresque novel is able to empathize with the picaro, some of the experiences of the *hero* in the earlier form become the experiences of the *reader/player* in the new one. I should add that many computer games do allow players to shift their point of view—to experience events at one moment through an active "hero" or "heroine" and at another moment from a more detached and contemplative perspective.

As Atkins points out, the computer game is only "interactive" in a very limited way: one cannot stray too far from the "correct," and circumscribed, path and generally one can only perform actions that have been predicted or allowed for by the game-fiction's designers (41). But then much the same can be said of the experiences offered by different varieties of popular fiction to which the label "formulaic" has been attached—the folk tale, the picaresque novel, the detective novel, and the romance, for example. However formulaic and restricted the choices offered by the computer game may be, they do show how very traditional elements from narrative fiction can be married to the resources of the electronic media in ways that will inevitably become more sophisticated (and perhaps, although not necessarily, more aesthetically productive) as time goes by.

Interactive fiction

It is not a long jump from computer games to what is known as interactive fiction, or IF. Indeed, deciding where the frontier between the two forms is to be drawn is by no means a straightforward matter. According to Nick Montfort, "IF works are often, among other things, games, with an optimal outcome that the interactor, acting as a player, tries to attain" (Montfort 2003, 13). Like Barry Atkins, Montfort also comments on the presence of the old in the new, noting that the narratives generated by IF "are often more trivial and repetitive than even the bluntest folktale" (14). Montfort explains that a work of IF is not itself a narrative: "it is an interactive computer program" that can, when "played," generate narratives (25). When we start such a program our initial experience is that we are much more active than we are when we read the printed text of a traditional novel. We have to respond, to make decisions, to *interact* with the program. Should we take this route or that route, should we do this or do that? My choice of words is deliberate here, because IF programs typically present us with a finite—indeed a small—number of pre-decided options to choose from rather than asking us to come up with a totally new and original plot movement. The experience of IF is thus closer to the experience of finding our way through a maze than to sitting down and reading a novel from scratch—something strongly suggested by the title of Montfort's book: *Twisty Little Passages: An Approach to Interactive Fiction.* This is why I wrote that our *initial* experience is that we are much more active than we are when we read the printed text of a traditional novel— because the sort of activity in which we engage when we play a computer game is actually rather less sophisticated, and less artistically satisfying, than the sort of mental activity generated in us when we read a major novel. When we read *Bleak House* or *The Waves* we do not interact with the text by choosing between or among specific proffered plot alternatives, although we certainly do wonder about how the plot will develop. Our reading experiences are by no means purely passive, and this is one of the reasons why no two readings of an important novel, whether by the same reader or by two different readers, are identical. This is an important point and I would like to suggest that the reader pause here and consider the sorts of interaction that take place when we read a challenging novel, and how these differ from the interaction offered by IF.

As is the case with the computer game, the artistic or aesthetic worth of such generated narratives is not generally deemed to be high, but interactive fiction is worth commenting on for a couple of reasons. The first is that it is striking how useful the conceptual tools of modern narratology (see p. 212) have been found in describing elements in the IF world. Thus, for example, Montfort distinguishes between the *commands* keyed in by the IF "reader"— which are "diegetic" (that is, they refer to an action in the IF world)—and *directives*, which are keyed-in instructions "such as those that save, restore, quit, restart, change the level of detail in the room descriptions, or address some entity that is not part of the IF world—for instance, to ask for hints" (26), and which are by implication "extradiegetic." Why is this significant? Because it perhaps demonstrates that however modern IF may appear, in narrative terms it is relatively old-fashioned and (to coin a horrific term) "pre-postmodernist." By this I mean that, as insisted upon by Henry James (see p. 68), IF involves fictional worlds that are insulated from direct contact with our everyday world, worlds that have their own laws, constraints, and conventions.

In her excellent study *Narrative as Virtual Reality: Immersion and Interactivity in Literature and Electronic Media* (2001), Marie-Laure Ryan discusses the tension and the interplay between "immersion" and "interactivity" in the reading of fiction. Her discussion has points of contact with my contention in this book that both when reading and when studying the novel we have to alternate between treating the characters and events as in some way real and treating them as creations of the writer's craft (see, for example, p. 180). Ryan suggests, correctly I think, that "immersion" in a fictional work of any sort is only possible by means of "an imaginative relationship to a *textual world*" (Ryan 2001, 14), and she suggests that our concept of a textual world assumes four features: "connected set of objects and individuals; habitable environment; reasonably intelligible totality for external observers; field of activity for its members" (91). The word "external" is important here: it only makes sense to talk about *immersing* ourselves in the world of a fiction if that world is in some way fenced off from our own world. One further important point argued by Ryan is that when we assess the viability of a work of fiction "as a document of real-world events," we are no longer reading it as fiction but as non-fiction (105). In other words, immersion in a fictional world requires some sort of abandonment of our own "real world." Readers must decide to what extent such a position is undercut by my comments on postmodernist fiction earlier in this chapter.

This very sharp distinction between the extrafictional world, in which the real-life reader lives in his or her everyday life, and the realized world of the fiction, that can only be entered imaginatively and interacted with by him or her if its rules are adhered to, is one that is familiar to readers of conventional fiction, although once again it is important to underline that we are talking about two very different sorts of interaction here. Nothing that goes on in my head while I am reading *Wuthering Heights*, or after I have finished reading it, will change the text of that work, although— and this is an important point—it *will* change my perception of that text. Nevertheless, one of the things that traditional print-based novels from *Moll Flanders* to *The Hours* have in common with various modes of electronic fiction is that they offer what Montfort calls "simulated worlds" that are possessed of an internal coherence and logic that may mimic the coherence and logic of the extrafictional world but that are nevertheless distinct.

The second reason why IF is worthy of consideration, then, is precisely because it reminds us that a fiction is only of interest to the extent that it offers the reader some *resistance*. A generated IF fiction in which the reader-player can change the rules of the fictional world at will is merely boring; however much we may want certain things to happen when we are reading a novel, a fiction that allows us to realize and enact any desired outcome is neither stimulating nor satisfying. Imagine reading a work of fiction on the screen of an electronic book, and coming across the following message:

> Final chapter: press 1 for happy ending, 2 for tragic ending, 3 for ambiguous ending (advanced users only)

After the fifth edition of this book was published I discovered that Julian Barnes had got there before me in his novel *Flaubert's Parrot*, although as the novel was published in 1984 the choices offered were not electronic.

> After all, if novelists really wanted to simulate the delta of life's possibilities, this is what they'd do. At the back of the book would be a set of sealed

envelopes in various colours. Each would be clearly marked on the outside: Traditional Happy Ending; Traditional Unhappy Ending; Traditional Half-and-half Ending; Deus ex Machina; Modernist Arbitrary Ending; End of the World Ending; Cliffhanger Ending; Dream Ending; Opaque Ending; Surrealist Ending; and so on. You would be allowed only one, and would have to destroy the envelopes you didn't select. *That's* what I call offering the reader a choice of endings; but you may find me quite unreasonably literal-minded. (Barnes 1985, 89)

Note again, however, that even in this example there is a limited choice between predetermined alternatives: the reader cannot write a new ending to suit him- or herself.

Since 1984 it has become clear that the technological capacity to offer readers such options at the click of a computer mouse is already with us—and electronic texts offering a succession of such choice-points may soon be on offer (if they are not already). But one of the aspects of the extrafictional world that is simulated by fiction is that reality is not something that we can mold at will and to our will. Marie-Laure Ryan expresses the matter with telling economy:

If the reader or spectator can choose whether Jack will be a hero or a coward, this means that Jack's behavior, and by extension the fate of the entire fictional world, is determined not by any kind of internal necessity but by the decisions of an omnipotent creator located in the real world. Yet the loss of the sense of the autonomy of the fictional world that occurs at every decision point is not compensated by a gain of creative power, because the choices are all prescribed paths. (2001, 283)

If then the fictional world is one into which we can enter, which we can observe, and to which we can emotionally respond, but which we cannot act within or change, does not this turn the reader into a sort of voyeur? Ryan would not be dismayed by the question: "Whether or not we like to admit it, voyeurism has a lot to do with the pleasures we take in narrative fiction: where else but in a novel can we penetrate into the most guarded and the most fascinating of realms, the inner workings of a foreign consciousness?" (149).

Modes such as the computer game and IF may thus teach us a negative lesson: the fixity of print-based fiction, the unalterability of a novel published in book form, may actually contribute to its artistic force. Our ability to change the physical and social world is significantly limited in real life; perhaps the unchangeability of the printed text mirrors and models this aspect of our experience of the world.

Fan fiction

From an academic perspective, fan fiction (otherwise "fanfic") may perhaps be almost the least respectable form of fiction being written today, but it too is not without its points of interest for the serious student of fiction. Fan fiction is very much a child of the internet, and publication is almost exclusively in electronic format. Its authors are the fans of particular books, films, or TV series who use the characters from these sources to create their own extensions of the stories in the originals. Some fan fiction also involves the creation of stories in which real celebrities appear as characters. Fan-fiction stories generally involve accounts of activities barred to the original outlets, especially ones involving sexual activity. Authorship can be individual or collaborative (as in IF—see p. 87). The anonymity of internet publication may be an essential aspect of this form of writing, and it may also make contact between fan-fiction writers less problematic than it would otherwise be. Although it is a disregarded form of writing so far as academics are concerned, it is widespread and fast-expanding.

Fan fiction makes visible an activity in which many readers of conventionally published fiction engage: imagining new scenes involving the characters, including scenes in which the reader him- or herself is involved. Beyond this, fan-fiction writing is a very democratic affair, lacking the usual distinction between the few (authors) and the many (readers). It thus serves to remind us how central fiction is to ordinary lives, and how closely related to the everyday exercise of our ability to imagine and to fantasize, and how bound up with our private and secret lives. It offers a relevant example of the way in which a new technology may offer new possibilities for satisfying some very ancient human impulses and capacities.

Hypertext fiction

Nick Montfort, to whose book *Twisty Little Passages* I have already referred, provides a neat definition of hypertext fiction:

> A hypertext fiction (as it is most commonly defined and discussed) is a system of fictional interconnected texts traversed using links. An interconnected text is referred to by George Landow (1992) and others as a *lexia*, a term borrowed from Barthes (1974), who applied it differently as a block of signification or unit of reading that was empirically determined, during a reading … There is, however, nothing in the nature of the lexia or the link, those fundamental

elements of hypertext, that allows the reader to type and contribute text or provides the computer with the means to parse or understand natural language. (2003, 12)

The definition does not state whether these varied "lexia" are written by the same person or by a number of individuals, or whether the "fiction" is produced with all of its lexia available from the start, or whether it can be added to as time goes on. These are presumably details that vary from fiction to fiction.

Marie-Laure Ryan notes that for some commentators:

Hypertext thus becomes a metaphor for a Lyotardian "postmodern condition" in which grand narratives have been replaced by "little stories," or perhaps by no stories at all—just by a discourse reveling in the Derridanean performance of an endless deferral of signification. (2001, 7)

This short comment needs some unpacking. One of the characteristics attributed to our "postmodern condition" by the French theorist Jean-François Lyotard is the replacement of "grand narratives" by "little narratives." "Grand narratives" are ideological systems of belief such as Marxism or religious beliefs such as Christianity, and for Lyotard the postmodern world is characterized by the loss of such all-embracing and comprehensive stories that provide meaning. Instead, we live in a world and at a time when sense and meaning are not all-embracing but have only a local purchase—"little narratives." Ryan's reference to the French philosopher Jacques Derrida deals especially with Derrida's concept of "différance," a term that in French combines the meanings "to differ" and "to defer." The concept is part of a much more complex argument on Derrida's part, but the important point for our purposes is that it builds upon a vision that also rejects some of the formal characteristics of the traditional narratives that we use to make sense of our lives, especially fixity of meaning, cause and effect, and completion (what is often referred to as "closure").

From Ryan's perspective, hypertext fiction thus shares a philosophical position with postmodernism; the technical possibilities displayed by hypertext actualize already existing elements in the postmodern world. These include: a loss of totalizing systems of meaning, a concern with local, self-contained explanations rather than final answers, and an individually chosen and potentially never-ending route through a maze of possibilities rather than a walk along a broad single highway of meaning in the company of everyone else, until the end of the road is reached. Ryan calls such new modes of organization "rhizomic," picking up on ideas taken from another French theorist, Gilles Deleuze. The potato plant exemplifies such a connective system, with each potato (in botanical terms a rhizome) connected to other potatoes not in one long linear string, but in a network of interconnections. As Ryan puts it:

> In a rhizomic organization, in opposition to the hierarchical tree structures of rhetorical argumentation, the imagination is not constrained by the need to prove a point or to progress toward a goal, and the writer never needs to sacrifice those bursts of inspiration that cannot be integrated into a linear argument. (2001, 8)

So what?

Let us, in conclusion, remind ourselves of certain characteristics of the novel that extend from the early eighteenth century to the present day. When we pick up a printed novel we know that we are expected to start reading from the beginning and continue sequentially through to the end, following the single track of what is known as a "(uni)linear narrative" (a telling that follows a single line of written text). Note that even if the narrative is progressively unveiling two or more separate threads in the plot, the actual *telling* still has this quality of "one thing at a time"—in contrast to a film, which can (and generally must) depict a number of different things going on at the same time. The conventional generic requirements associated with the novel sanction pauses to contemplate what we have read, and the reader is also permitted to flick back to pages that have already been read so as to review their content. A reader can also choose his or her own speed of reading, and can vary this from chapter to chapter or paragraph to paragraph. Note that this gives the individual reader a control over his or her own reading experience that the members of the audience of a play or a publicly shown film do not enjoy. Such actions as peering at a novel's conclusion before we have read all the pages that precede it, omitting chapters, or even deciding to ignore the final chapter printed in the book and write our own conclusion, are in contrast not sanctioned by the unstated but universally agreed conventions of novel-reading; it breaks the established and understood codes that all novel readers have to a greater or lesser extent internalized. Moreover, the fact that a novel is still usually contained in a physical object—a book—means that we have a very clear sense of how much more there is to read as the right-hand collection of pages gets thinner and thinner or the text at the bottom of our Kindle screen informs us what percentage of the work is still unread.

We expect, furthermore, that excepting a few rare and unrepresentative cases, what we read will be the responsibility of a single author, however much he or she may have been influenced by others. (Interestingly, in a number of cases of joint authorship the writers conceal their plurality behind a single pseudonym.) We also assume that this single person is ultimately both author and authority: he or she alone can decide what happens in the world of the novel. We do not expect to open a newspaper and to read a headline that states: "Readers Reject Conclusion of New Harry Potter Novel: Publisher Sacks Author and Starts Search for a Replacement." If that seems a merely silly example, we should remember that this sort of thing actually happens all the time in the world of television soaps and comedies—usually without millions of viewers knowing that it has happened. The high status, visibility, and legal authority possessed by the writers of novels are not enjoyed by all writers of fiction.

It is often assumed that such conventions were faithfully and uncomplainingly adhered to until suddenly the possibilities offered by the new electronic media presented writers and readers with the chance to subvert or ignore them. But in *The Anthology and the Rise of the Novel: From Richardson to George Eliot*, Leah Price shows that subversions were there from the start, and sometimes encouraged by the authors themselves. Thus Samuel Richardson himself published an anthology of "sentiments, cautions, aphorisms, reflections and observations" taken from his novel *Clarissa* (and published only three years after the novel), which were arranged in alphabetical order. By 1760 Richardson was responsible for a "set of entertaining Cards, neatly engraved on Copper-Plates, Consisting of moral and diverting Sentiments, extracted wholly from the much admired Histories of PAMELA, CLARISSA, and SIR CHARLES GRANDISON" (Price 2000, 17). So much for the modernity of the subversion of linear narrative! But Price also reports that Lady Bradshaigh

> accepted Richardson's invitation for friends to write a sequel to Grandison which he himself would merely edit, so "that every one of my Correspondents, at his or her own Choice, assume one of the surviving Characters in the Story, and write in it; and that … I shall pick and choose, alter, connect, and accommodate, till I have completed from [the contributions], the requested Volume." (38)

So much too, then, for the view that interactive fiction was born in and with the necessary help of the electronic age—although it is noticeable here that Richardson does retain for himself the power to decide what to include and what to alter or omit (he may thereby deserve the title of the world's first moderator of interactive fiction). While these "subversions" are interesting, what I find more telling is the fact that today we still read *Clarissa* but the entertaining cards and the anthology of sentiments are to be found only in dusty library vaults.

From the start of the modern novel, then, there have been sporadic if not widespread attempts to subvert, expose, or submit to pressure some of the most established of fictional conventions: linearity and fixed sequential progression through the text of the novel (which does not, of course, entail a fixed chronological progression through the events of the story; see the discussion of story and plot on p. 134), a fixed text determined by a single author who cannot be interacted with directly by the reader, and a coherent and unitary story-world within which certain laws of irreversibility generally apply ("generally," because genres such as fantasy and science fiction do complicate this last element somewhat). Granted that such precedents can be found, however, it is certainly the case that the electronic media have opened up new possibilities for such subversion—or, to avoid prejudgment, let us say for rewriting the ground rules of fiction. What possibilities in particular do the electronic media offer? Let us consider the most important ones.

Textual fluidity

A book once printed cannot be significantly altered. Misprints and mistakes can be indicated in an "erratum" slip, and new, corrected, editions can always be produced, but there is a very powerful tendency in print culture to consider printed texts as complete, unalterable, and sacrosanct. The dramatist Joe Orton ended up in prison after being caught defacing library books, and even if this is an extreme example, it does show how alterations to written texts have tended to be seen not as creative additions but as violations. In the days of hot-metal typesetting (which only really disappeared in the book trade in the 1970s), publishers used to send out instructions to authors along with proofs warning them that the addition of a single comma could necessitate the re-setting of several pages of print, at very great cost. Today an electronic typesetter is able to make such an adjustment in a fraction of a second, and everyone knows how very easy it is to alter electronic text. But even with electronic typesetting, once a book has been printed it cannot be changed in the way that an electronic text on a computer screen (or an electronic book display unit) can. It is thus hard to treat an electronic text as "finished," as complete and unalterable, in the way that a book appears to us to be. Even a text written by someone else can be imported and changed on a computer. One result of these new possibilities is that whereas traditional books have beginnings and ends, the beginnings and ends of electronic texts tend to have a much more provisional quality to them. When the final page of a book is read, there is no more. With an electronic text, what is the final word today may be followed by additional text tomorrow.

From linearity to random links

According to Milan Kundera, "since its very beginnings, the novel has tried to escape the unilinear, to open rifts in the continuous narration of a story," and he notes that although Cervantes's Don Quixote travels on a linear journey, he meets other characters who tell their own stories and thus the reader is able to step outside the novel's linear framework (Kundera 1988, 74). However, even if the line of Quixote's journey may be interrupted, the reader has to follow Cervantes's line of prose wherever it takes him or her.

No one who has surfed the net can be unaware that by clicking on a succession of links one can take a path through a variety of texts that may well be unique to oneself. It is typical of the reading experiences offered by the electronic media that they do not conform to a strict linear pattern. This does seem to represent a fundamental shift in reading habits. Of course, we can always say that the person who read a novel and who stopped every now and then to look up a word in a dictionary, or to consult an entry in an encyclopedia, or even to check what happened in another novel by the same author was exploring "links" in just the same way as a person who clicks on a link on a computer screen. However, although there is arguably a parallel here, it is a weak and a very restricted one, and cannot obscure the fact that while linear progression characterized most reading experiences—and especially the reading of fiction—from the eighteenth century to about 1990, the growth of the World Wide Web means that nowadays this is no longer the case. We have even coined a new verb to reflect this: "to surf." Readers in the past could skim or skip or browse or "dip into" books (strange that so many of these metaphors are connected to water!), but surfing is arguably different from all of these slightly shameful ways of dealing with printed texts.

Interaction and collective authorship

Generally speaking, although the reader can tell an author what he or she thinks of a novel after having read it, actually influencing how it is written *while* it is being written has until recently been possible only for a few intimate friends of the author. We have two endings for Charles Dickens's *Great Expectations* because Edward Bulwer-Lytton, who read the novel in proof, persuaded Dickens to write a happier ending. And to remain with Dickens: the special circumstances of serial publication meant that readers could plead with him concerning the fate of favored characters. However, this example is perhaps as well known as it is precisely because it is so unusual and atypical. As the discussion of IF above has shown, the electronic media have undermined both the fixity of the text and the absolute authority of the single author.

The great electronic novel?

Discussing some of these new fictional forms, Marie-Laure Ryan provides a useful distinction between *multilinear* texts, which are those that offer the reader a choice among many well-charted sequences, and *nonlinear* texts, which are those "that allow the reader to break her own trail" (209). From such a perspective the traditional novel with its linear narrative, single fictional world, story line linked by laws of cause and effect, and an overall meaning relating to a plot with a beginning, middle, and end is based upon assumptions that no longer match our experience of, or beliefs about, the world. In contrast, the infant mode of hypertext fiction reflects more accurately the world in which we live, and the ways in which we live in the world.

In very general terms such a view can be said to be sociological in essence. It argues a broad similarity between the dominant characteristics of an age (both how the age "works" and how people living at that time perceive reality) and the dominant characteristics of fiction. The argument goes something like this: In the nineteenth century the fiction produced in developed countries was realist because it reflected the way people made sense of the world (a shared sense of what was real, explanatory narratives based on strict rules of cause and effect, unitary characters with an understanding of themselves and their identities, and a commitment to "grand narratives" that were "teleological," that is, that were moving toward a predetermined and meaning-conferring goal). In the modern age (that is, for the first three-quarters of the twentieth century), in contrast, people yearned to live in this same world but could not, and thus modernist fiction contrasts the tragic gap between the need for a comprehensive system of belief that explained the individual's place in the world and the recognition that actual experience is meaningless, personality is fragmented, and communication between human beings is at best partial. Then, in the postmodern world of the late twentieth century, an acceptance that meaning can be at best local, and that the movement from experience to experience is largely or completely random and fortuitous, finds expression in postmodernist fiction. And finally, in the present day, postmodernist fiction is able to be most completely itself when granted the resources of the electronic media, resources that at last allow it to shrug off the fetters of the single linear plot, the fixed text, and the passive reader.

It should be clear that although I find such arguments interesting, I strongly suspect that they are at best half-truths (among other things, the proposed periodization strikes me as too crude). But I will allow myself just two comments that reiterate points that I have made earlier in this discussion. The first is that when one considers the ways in which fictional composition and reading habits have been adapted to the electronic media, one cannot but be struck by the blending of the very old and the very new. Modes such as the computer game and IF, as a succession of commentators have pointed out, wed advanced computer technology to some of the most traditional (and among the lowest-status) narrative and fictional conventions.

The second (and perhaps related) comment is that even sympathetic commentators on the various modes of electronic fiction generally concede that, so far, the great work of electronic fiction remains unwritten. This may of course be because the modes I have been considering do not produce single texts. But it may also be, as Marie-Laure Ryan concludes, that there is something about linear narrative that makes it indispensable to Western culture and, arguably, to culture in general (2001, 270).

This is not just, I hope, cultural snobbery or a fuddy-duddy refusal to grant that new forms are possessed of artistic importance. There is a useful contrast to draw here with the graphic novel, a form that had to struggle to gain recognition. Early examples of graphic novels were typically dismissed by academics as comics for the immature—like the "Classics Illustrated" series of comic-book versions of "canonical" literary texts that were published between 1941 and 1971 and were aimed at those for whom texts without pictures were too boring to read. But the genre is now taken very seriously, and has its recognized masterpieces (there are many competing internet listings of the best graphic novels). Interactive fiction, fan fiction, and the rest are still waiting for theirs.

Topics for discussion

- Do you like novels to be "true to life"? Explain why (or why not). What does "true to life" mean?
- Why do governments often fear "unrealistic" parodies and satires?
- Is modernism "the realism of the age of Freud"?
- What technical innovations are associated with modernism and postmodernism? Why are they needed?
- Do any of the new works of interactive fiction or hypertext fiction have any artistic merit?
- Have computers finally liberated fiction?

5

Analyzing Fiction

Preview

This chapter deals with:

- The different ways in which a work of fiction can be narrated
- Different sorts of narrator; different relationships between narrator and story
- Stream of consciousness, interior monologue, Free Indirect Discourse
- Types of character and methods of characterization
- Story and plot; setting and theme
- Symbol and image
- Representing speech and dialogue in the novel

Prose fiction and formal analysis

The association of the novel with realism has meant that there has always been a strong temptation to discuss it as one would discuss reality—however defined—and ignore the art (especially the verbal art) that is a necessary part of its existence. Poetry typically calls attention to its verbal art and formal techniques, while performance arts such as drama require the discussion of verbal detail as a part of the planning of performance. There are venerable traditions of theoretical discussion of the art of the dramatist and the poet, starting with Aristotle, that have bequeathed a vocabulary and a set of principles to the critic. In contrast, the very popularity of the novel—something that has often been found regrettable by various guardians of culture—has meant that it has seemed inappropriate or unnecessary to devote the same analytical attention to novels as has been paid to plays and poems.

I do not want to suggest that detailed analytical concern with prose fiction (as against a scholarly interest in its texts and its history) cannot be found in the eighteenth and nineteenth centuries. However, it is the case that such a concern emerged in its recognizably contemporary form in the late nineteenth century, and developed via a number of routes. First, early modernists such as Henry James, Joseph Conrad, Virginia Woolf, and James Joyce—and their contemporaries writing in languages other than English—took their art seriously and often wrote about it, and, by frustrating the expectations of the reader in their fiction, they drew attention to the changing conventions on which it was based. Second, colleges and universities began to provide for the study of literatures other than those of Classical antiquity. Third, particular schools of criticism such as the Russian and Czech Formalists and the New Critics (see Chapter 8) significantly extended our understanding of the art of the novelist by means of detailed analyses. Fourth, the recent development of *narratology* as an academic and intellectual discipline (see again Chapter 8) has helped to build up a far more precise vocabulary and conceptual basis for the analysis of narratives in general and prose fiction in particular.

Much of what follows in this chapter is indebted to these sources. This chapter focuses not on the novel's history and its changing historical identity, but rather on those techniques and skills—the craft of the novel—that can be found in novels and shorter works of prose fiction from various cultures and historical periods, and on the methods, concepts, and approaches that have been developed to analyze works of prose fiction by critics and theorists. The reader should, however, remember that the craft of the novel has its own history, and different techniques emerge at different times, often in response to changes in the way people live and think, although they typically outlive the circumstances of their birth and the forces behind their creation.

Narrative technique

In my opening chapter I drew attention to the fact that everything we read in a novel comes to us via some sort of "telling." We are told what happens in a novel; no matter how successful the novelist is in making a scene seem dramatic, it is never dramatic in the way that a play or a film is. We may feel that we "see," but we see as a result of what we visualize in response to a telling, not through witnessing an enactment. Even in those relatively rare cases in which a novelist makes extended use of the present tense, a technique which gives an added sense of immediacy to the narrative, we are still *told* what is happening rather than observing it directly as we can with a play or a film. The fact that when reading a novel we know that we can flip forward a page or a chapter, or look at the last page, is thus worth thinking about: it explains that sense we have that in reading a novel we are going through what *has already happened*, that which is being recounted to us. Whereas the last page of a novel is already printed and waiting there for us, the final scene in a play has not yet been performed as we watch the first scene, even if it has been written long ago and perhaps performed the night before.

In one respect, however, the writing of a novel is comparable to the making of a film. When we watch a film we seem to be seeing "things as they are"—"reality." We need to remember that a director has *chosen how* we see these things, this reality; he or she has decided whether the camera will be placed high or low, whether or not there will be rapid cuts from one camera angle to another, whether a camera will follow one character as he or she walks along a street, and so on. One scene in a film could be shot in innumerable ways, and each of these ways would produce a different effect upon the audience. Even with a simple conversation between two characters the audience's attitude toward each character can be affected by different camera angles, cutting, and so forth.

The novelist has a far greater range of choices open to him or her than does the film director, and we conventionally refer to that particular selection which he or she makes as the *narrative technique* of a particular work. Narrative technique includes such matters as the choice of *narrator* and *narrative situation*, the creation of a *plot* with its implied underlying *story*, selection and variation of *perspective and voice* (or "point of view"), implied *narrative medium*, linguistic *register* (e.g. the choice between colloquial or formal language), and techniques such as *Free Indirect Discourse* (FID). All of these I will discuss below. The Glossary can also be consulted for definitions of many of these terms.

Let us start with narrators, with the individuals or voices who (or which!) *tell us* the story. And let us start with two sets of alternatives:

- personified narrator or unpersonified narrator
- character narrator or non-character narrator

If this looks like two ways of describing the same distinction, remember that a narrator may seem to have many of the attributes of a human being without being a character in the story that he or she narrates. In other words, it is possible to have a personified, non-character narrator.

Let us turn first to the issue of personification.

Narrators: Impersonal or personified

An author may choose to have the story told through the mediation of a *personified narrator*, a "teller" recognized by the reader as a distinct person with well-defined individual human characteristics. Alternatively, the narrative source can seem so undefined as to make it doubtful whether or not we are dealing with an individualized human source which comes between the author and the reader. (There is no ideal term to describe such a narrator: *authorial*, *impersonal*, and *third-person* all have their drawbacks. The first suggests identification with the real-life author, the second suggests a lack of intimacy which may be misleading, and the third excludes those first-person narrators on whom we are unhappy to bestow full "personhood.")

Consider the narrator of Laurence Sterne's *Tristram Shandy*, whose distinct personality is thrust at us in the opening words of the novel: "I wish either my father or my mother, or indeed both of them, as they were in duty both equally bound to it, had minded what they were about when they begot me." The opening of D.H. Lawrence's *Sons and Lovers* (1913), in contrast, strikes us as far more impersonal; whereas the opening of Sterne's novel draws our attention to the narrator, who is talking about himself, the narrative of *Sons and Lovers* focuses our attention on *what* is told rather than *who* tells or how: "'The Bottoms' succeeded to 'Hell Row'. Hell Row was a block of thatched, bulging cottages that stood by the brookside on Greenhill Lane. There lived the colliers who worked in the little gin-pits two fields away."

Some narrators may even have names and detailed personal histories, as does Nick Carraway, the narrator of F. Scott Fitzgerald's *The Great Gatsby* (1925). Other narrators merely suggest to us that they are persons—perhaps by the occasional use of "I" in their narrative—but tell us no more about themselves than this. We thus have a continuum of possibility: (i) personified, named, and with a full human identity; (ii) human but anonymous; (iii) not corresponding to any recognizable human entity.

Narrators: Character or non-character

One obvious distinction between the narrative of *Tristram Shandy* and that of *Sons and Lovers* is that the first of these novels is narrated in the first person, while the second is what is often referred to as a third-person narrative—it is a narrative told from a source external to the world of the novel by a narrator who is not one of the characters in the novel. As I suggest above, two different issues are involved here: (i) Is the narrator personified? (ii) Is the narrator presented as an individual who lives in the same world as the characters? While it is the case that there is a conventional association of personified narrators with life inside the world of the novel, and of third-person narrators with a perspective on characters and events from outside the world of the novel, there are exceptions. The narrator of Henry Fielding's *Tom Jones*, for example, is personified and makes first-person comments but he appears to live in a different world from Tom and the other characters, and he is able to comment upon their fictionality. He is thus outside of this world even though he can see into it, like God looking down on (and into the hearts and minds of) humankind.

The standard technical terms used by structuralist narratologists (see Chapter 8) to define narrators get at some of these distinctions, but they can also be somewhat frightening. Let me provide some examples. The basic term here is that of *diegesis*, which is used to refer to the "story level" of a narrative as against its "narrating level." This basic distinction is refined in a set of more specific terms.

An extradiegetic narrator is in some sense or other "superior to," or on a higher level from, the story he or she narrates—like the narrator of D.H. Lawrence's *Sons and Lovers*. But as Shlomith Rimmon-Kenan puts it, further explicating a terminology that stems from the work of structuralist narratologist Gérard Genette, "if the narrator is also a character in the first narrative told by the extradiegetic narrator, then he is a second-degree, or intradiegetic narrator" (1983, 94), and she cites Marlow in *Heart of Darkness* as an example.

Note that an extradiegetic narrator may, or may not, be a frame narrator. In Joseph Conrad's *Heart of Darkness* the extradiegetic narrator is a character who listens to Marlow's narrative and transmits it to the reader. He is thus also a frame narrator. But in Conrad's *Lord Jim*, in which the first four chapters are told by a non-personified and (on occasions) omniscient narrator, this narrator is extradiegetic but he is not a frame narrator and neither, in this case, is the Marlow who takes over the mantle of narrator in the fifth chapter a framed narrator.

Rimmon Kenan further notes that a narrator who does not participate in the story is called heterodiegetic, whereas one who does so participate, "at least in some manifestation of his 'self,' is 'homodiegetic'" (1983, 95). Finally, an autodiegetic narrator is him- or herself the main character in the story he or she tells, thus (in her own narrative but not in the narrative of the anonymous frame narrator) the governess in *The Turn of the Screw* plays an autodiegetic role. These basic terms can then be combined to produce a range of compounds:

- extra-heterodiegetic narrator: a "first level" narrator who narrates a story in which he or she is not present
- extra-homodiegetic narrator: a "first level" narrator who narrates a story in which he or she is present
- intra-heterodiegetic narrator: a "second level" narrator who narrates a story in which he or she is not present
- intra-homodiegetic: a "second level" narrator who narrates a story in which he or she is present

You will doubtless be relieved to hear that in recent years a more self-explanatory set of terms have been proposed by rhetorical narratologists (again see Chapter 8) to mark some of these distinctions—for example "character narrator" and "non-character narrator." There seems every chance that these more user-friendly terms for English speakers will replace the hard-to-remember terms used by structuralist narratologists, even if they do not so precisely specify all the distinctions covered in Genette's terminology. As I suggest in Chapter 8, if even academics confronted with such terms have on occasions to reach surreptitiously for their dictionaries and glossaries, then it may be simpler just to spell out what the terms mean. (Try innocently asking your lecturer what the difference between intra-heterodiegetic and intra-homodiegetic is!)

"Omniscient" is also a term about which many recent commentators have expressed reservations (see the entry for *omniscience* in the Glossary). "Omniscient" means "all-knowing," and the word implies that the narrator knows everything: what has happened and what will happen, what the characters are thinking, and so on. One objection to the term is that it has been applied rather loosely to any non-character narrator, many of whom actually profess ignorance about their characters and the events with which they are involved. Another objection is that it seems odd to talk about some narrators knowing "everything" when there is nothing more to know in a work of fiction than that which is created by the author. Such objections are unlikely to get rid of the term, and indeed many sophisticated narratologists still have recourse to it, and to handy if illogical compounds such as "semi-omniscient."

As human beings are not generally all-knowing it is conventional for omniscient narrators to be unpersonified, although this convention is sometimes broken. The term "omniscient" is often used in a loose way to indicate any work in which the narrative has access to that which—like a character's secret thoughts—is normally concealed to observers in the real world. However a so-called omniscient narrator may not, actually, be completely all-knowing. The first sentence of Joseph Conrad's *Lord Jim* reads: "He was an inch, perhaps two, under six feet, powerfully built, and he advanced straight at you with a slight stoop of the shoulders, head forward, and a fixed from-under stare which made you think of a charging bull." The word "perhaps" reveals that however much this narrator may later on appear to "see all," it is not quite all that is seen—maybe because Conrad wants the reader to respond to the narrator more as a personified individual than as an omniscient source of information at this stage of the novel.

Unnatural narrators

Some narratives are delivered in ways that go beyond the alternatives that I have outlined above. Brian Richardson's study *Unnatural Voices: Extreme Narration in Modern and Contemporary Fiction* (2006) concentrates on twentieth-century examples of what he calls "unnatural" narrators and narratives. These include "narration by animals, small children, corpses, machines, and a Minotaur" (2006, x), and also such formal oddities as second-person narrative, and self-erasing narratives that deny statements previously uttered. Of particular interest is Richardson's discussion of the "permeable narrator"—that is to say a narrator who or which slips "into other minds and discourses and speaks what should be impossible for it to know" (2006, xi).

Why?

What leads an author in his or her choice between personified and non-personified narrator, and between character and non-character narrator?

Dieter Meindl makes some interesting points about the relative advantages of the first set of choices, although in his terminology the choice is between a first-person and a third-person narrator.

> First-person narration is limited in scope: the narrator cannot simply state the inner world (thoughts, feelings) of others. Conversely, the first-person narrator—a real person or subject—is unlimited in manner, commanding as s/he does the whole range of subject discourses—erring, deceiving oneself and/or others, etc., as well as telling the truth: s/he is (un-)reliable. The narrative agency ("narrator") of third-person narrative is not a person or subject; hence, third-person narrative can hardly be subjective or unreliable, but is basically reliable in the sense of being authorial. (Meindl 2008, 35)

You may notice that this goes against what I argued above when talking about the narrator of Henry Fielding's *Tom Jones*, in which novel I claimed that we had a personified narrator who did have access to the inner lives of other characters: Meindl is here talking about the most usual variants of these alternative types of narrator, but as the example of *Tom Jones* shows, there are exceptions. His comments are, nonetheless, useful. Reading the account of a personified narrator we react in some ways as we do to the account of a real person telling a true story (or a false one!), whereas when reading the account of an unpersonified narrator we have a sense of reliability that we can rarely attach so fully to the stories told by human individuals. However, the human characteristics that attach easily to a personified narrator—self-deceptions, boastings, humility, and so on—are much harder to associate with an unpersonified "agency."

Framed narratives

One classic technique for combining the advantages of different sorts of narrator is by means of a "framed narrative." Examples of this technique can be found in both Henry James's *The Turn of the Screw* and Joseph Conrad's *Heart of Darkness*. Both of these works start with a group of people talking, and then one of the conversationalists starts to deliver the "framed" narrative, the main telling contained in the work. In both cases the "outer" narrator is unnamed, while in Conrad's novella but not James's the inner narrator is named. I shall have more to say about the narrative of *The Turn of the Screw* in Chapter 7 when I discuss film adaptations of works of fiction. Although many film adaptations of framed narratives—including those mentioned by Conrad and James—often drop the framing device, it is possible to retain it even in a film. (Woody Allen's film *Broadway Danny Rose* [1984] is remarkably like *Heart of Darkness* with respect to its use of the framing device of a man telling a story to a group of companions that the film then dramatizes.)

Narrative medium and language

In addition to choosing a narrator or narrative source, the novelist can (but need not) select a stated or implied *medium* for his or her narrative. Leaving aside graphic novels, and the issue of illustrations (a fascinating topic in its own right), all novels consist of words. Traditionally these were read from a printed book; nowadays they may well be read on the screen of a tablet. A novel may, however, be presented to the reader as if it were spoken or thought rather than written, or it may even be presented in such a way as to suggest that it is a sort of medium-less narrative—something impossible outside the realms of literature.

Thus, to take two very different examples, Agatha Christie's *The Murder of Roger Ackroyd* (1926) and Fyodor Dostoyevsky's *Notes from Underground* (1864) are both presented to the reader as *written* documents. We learn this only toward the end of Christie's story, when the narrator explains how he came to write his account (and that should make us pause for thought: think of the oddness of reading a story and not knowing until the end of the story whether it is a written document we are reading: that is because the written text *we* see stands for another text, about the precise nature of which we can be left in the dark by the novelist). In Dostoyevsky's story we find the following interpolated comment on the first page:

> (That's a rotten joke, but I don't intend striking it out. I wrote it down thinking it would come across very witty, but now that I've seen that I only wanted to do a spot of vulgar bragging I shall let it stand on purpose!) (Dostoyevsky 2009, 4)

We may well ask: why should one author want to reveal the implied narrative medium of the story on the first page, and another only toward the end? What difference does it make to the reader's response to the story? (Compare Philip Roth's *Portnoy's Complaint* [1969], in which the fact that the narrative is a spoken one is revealed on the last page along with the precise circumstances of its delivery.)

Now in one sense language is the medium of a novel just as paint is the medium of a painting, but this is a misleading comparison as painters do not generally represent paint, whereas novelists often represent language: *Heart of Darkness*, for example, is not just *in* language, it *represents* language—the language uttered by Marlow and used by the novella's frame narrator. Thus in one sense the *actual* medium of this novel—language—is also its *implied* medium (although the implied medium of most of *Heart of Darkness* is spoken, not written, language). A novel may well have no stated narrative medium: Joseph Conrad's *The Shadow-Line* (1916–17) can be read as if written, spoken, or thought in origin.

Where a novelist does not state his or her implied narrative medium, all sorts of variations are possible. Emily Brontë's *Wuthering Heights* opens as if it might be some sort of diary entry: "1801.—I have just returned from a visit to my landlord—the solitary neighbour that I shall be troubled with. This is certainly a beautiful country!" Other parts of the novel, told by Mr Lockwood, as is this opening passage, read more like thought processes than writing. This is the third paragraph of Chapter 10:

> This is quite an easy interval. I am too weak to read, yet I feel as if I could enjoy something interesting. Why not have up Mrs Dean to finish her tale? I can recollect its chief incidents, as far as she had gone. Yes, I remember her hero had run off, and never been heard of for three years: and the heroine was married: I'll ring; she'll be delighted to find me capable of talking cheerfully.
>   Mrs Dean came. (Brontë 2003, 95)

There is, I think, a slight clumsiness here. Novelists following Brontë perfected techniques for making such transitions between narrative viewpoints and media less obtrusive.

Closely related to the foregoing issues is the matter of *linguistic register*. ("Register" here means a particular sort of language-use that is appropriate to a given circumstance.) Whether a narrative is formal or colloquial, for example, depends a lot on whether it is told by a personified or unpersonified narrator, and on whether we are to assume that it is spoken, written, or thought. (Conversely, of course, the degree of informality of a novel's language may lead us to infer that a narrative is, for example, a spoken tale by a personified narrator.)

Narrative and representation

The previous comment may seem to contradict what I said earlier about all narrative being a telling: does not a telling necessarily require a medium by means of which the telling takes place? It should be said that this question touches upon a number of very complex disputes within the theory of narrative. Some theorists prefer to distinguish between *representation* and *telling*, and claim that the novelist can represent—say—a character's consciousness in such a way as gives the reader knowledge of this consciousness without any sense of this information being told or transmitted—something that is, of course, impossible outside the realms of written narrative.

Thus the narrative theorist Ann Banfield has argued that representation is, as the name suggests, a "re-presentation" which makes "present" what is either absent or past, and which is thus unlike narration, having only a single point of reference with respect to time and place (Banfield 1982, 268). (A narration has two: the time and place of the narrated events, and the time and place of their narrating—compare my earlier remarks on the novel's double chronology on p. 6.) Banfield accordingly argues that some thoughts, events, and so on may be represented in a novel but are not told or narrated to us by anyone—hence the title of the book in which she argues this case: *Unspeakable Sentences*. In Banfield's view, the novelist may give us sentences which are not and cannot be delivered by anyone; their function is that of representation, not telling or narrating.

Ways of telling

Let us pause for a moment and ask why all this is important. What difference does it make? Well, in everyday life the fact of *who* tells us a story, and *how*, makes a very big difference. Telling someone that you want to end a relationship in person has a rather different force from telling them in the form of a text message or a Twitter announcement. Source and medium affect the *selection*, the *authority*, and the *attitude toward what is recounted* of the narrative—and thus, of course, the effect on the reader or listener. (One of the problems involved in Banfield's view of representation is, it seems to me, that even such representation involves selection by someone, if only the author, and the act of selection implies some form of mediation.)

The same is true with the novel: different narrators, different narrative media *change* a story; they affect not just how we are told something but what we are told, and what attitude we take toward what we are told. Nobody knows this better than novelists themselves, and different novelists have given us some revealing accounts of the problematic processes that deciding upon a narrative technique involves. There is, for example, a fascinating entry in Virginia Woolf's diary dated September 25, 1929, outlining her plans for her novel *The Waves*, which at this stage of her work on it she had provisionally entitled *The Moths*. She writes as follows:

> Yesterday morning I made another start on *The Moths*, but that won't be its title; and several problems cry out at once to be solved. Who thinks it? And am I outside the thinker? One wants some device which is not a trick. (Leonard Woolf 1972, 146)

Note how the choosing of a particular perspective, a particular center of perception for the telling, presents itself as a *problem* right at the start of Woolf's work on this novel. Note too her distinction between "I" and "the thinker"—in other words, between the creative-moral center of authority and the perceiving-observing-telling situation, in the novel. It is very important to recognize the fact that these two are not necessarily identical, either in *The Waves* or in any other novel or short story. Finally, that comment that she "wants some device which is not a trick" also underlines the fact that this sort of choice is not a purely technical one, but has aesthetic and ethical implications which demand careful consideration.

Jean Rhys also struggled with the right way to tell what was to become *Wide Sargasso Sea*. Writing to her daughter, in 1959, she noted:

> It can be done 3 ways. (1) Straight. Childhood, Marriage, Finale told in 1st person. Or it can be done (2) Man's point of view (3) Woman's ditto both 1st person. Or it can be told in the third person with the writer as the Almighty. Well that is hard for me. I prefer direct thoughts and actions.
> I am doing (2). (Wyndham and Melly 1984, 162)

Later on in the same year she wrote to Francis Wyndham and admitted that the novel had already been written three times, first told by the heroine in the first person, second told by the housekeeper Mrs Poole as the "I," and finally using two "I"s: "Mr Rochester and his first wife." According to Rhys it was unsatisfactory to have the heroine tell all the story herself because the result was obscure and "all on one note," and it was also unsatisfactory to have the housekeeper Grace Poole tell the whole story because although technically this was the best solution, the character "wouldn't come to life" (172). Before we leave this example, you should think a bit about the phrase "Man's point of view." This has both a technical and an ideological or "sexual political" meaning: a writer's choice of "point of view" is rarely just a technical matter.

Another such example involves Franz Kafka's novel *The Castle* (1926), which Kafka started writing with a first-person narrator. The early part of the manuscript of the novel has "I," crossed out and replaced by "K." If you have read this work you will appreciate how very significant this change is;

it alters the reader's whole relationship with the main character. Like Jean Rhys, Kafka clearly found the right voice and perspective (see below) for his novel only after having started writing the work—when he could perhaps more easily put himself into the position of a potential reader.

What difference does this make? Well, a good way to demonstrate this is by means of what we can call the *transposition test*: transposing a novel (in one's imagination) from one "camera angle" to another. Imagine *Middlemarch* told in the first person by Dorothea, or by Dorothea and Lydgate in successive sections. What would *Wuthering Heights* be like as an epistolary novel, with Isabella's letter about her marriage to Heathcliff as only one of a whole sequence of letters describing the events and developments of the work—or with the events of the novel seen exclusively through Heathcliff's eyes? It can be an extremely revealing exercise to take a brief passage from a novel and to rewrite it in this manner. There is some evidence that Jane Austen's *Sense and Sensibility* was started as an epistolary novel, although in its published version it is told by an omniscient narrator, and it is worth considering the reasons Austen might have had for making such a change.

One term which has, I think, a useful summarizing function here is *narrative situation*. We can indicate what this term covers by asking about the relationship *between the telling and what is told*. Is the narrator personified? If so, is he or she a character involved in the action of the work? Is the narrative dramatic and immediate or distanced?—and so on. Narrative situation thus includes both perspective and voice, and also a range of other matters such as tone and frequency (see below for discussion of these terms, and also the separate Glossary entries).

Perspective and voice

A disadvantage with the traditional term "point of view" is that it obscures what recent theorists have identified as an extremely important distinction, that between *perspective* and *voice*. We can sum up what these terms cover in two questions: "Who speaks?" and "Who sees?" In Katherine Mansfield's short story "The Voyage" (1922), for instance, the voice is essentially that of a third-person, non-character-narrator who is semi-omniscient and extradiegetic or "outside the story." The reader is, nevertheless, encouraged to see everything through the eyes of the main character of the story, the little girl Fenella. We experience through her senses, even though what we know of these experiences comes to us via a third-person narrative. As hers is the only consciousness we enter, it is as if we *are* her as we read the story.

It is always worth asking to whose thoughts we are made privy in a novel or a short story, as the answer gives us significant information about the author's focus of concern. In "The Voyage," then, the *voice* is that of a semi-omniscient third-person narrator, but the *perspective* is Fenella's.

Reliable and unreliable narrators

Following Wayne C. Booth's *The Rhetoric of Fiction* (1961), many critics have found it useful to distinguish between *reliable* and *unreliable* narrators. Reliability apart, we associate some narrative choices more with the views and position of actual authors, and some not at all (or far less) with their creators. In general we can say that a single, consistent, unpersonified voice is more likely to be associated with authorial beliefs than is a personified narrator in a novel with many narrators, although of course in both cases this depends upon the attitudes expressed in and revealed by the narrative. Thus it is easier to assume that the opinions expressed by the anonymous narrator of Conrad's *The Secret Agent* (1907) are close to those of Conrad himself than it is in the case of his personified narrator Marlow, who appears in four of his works. Moreover, even if Marlow is a generally reliable narrator, we do not take everything he says on quite the same trust as we do what the narrator of *The Secret Agent* tells us, simply because we see Marlow from the outside and treat him as we would treat another person, whereas we adopt the perspective of the narrator of *The Secret Agent* and, as we read, think ourselves fully into his position from the inside.

Consistency is a crucial issue here. An inconsistent narrator cannot, logically, be wholly reliable, although we may recognize in fiction as in life that inconsistency may be the result of a continued and painful attempt to be truthful and accurate. The fact that Gulliver in Swift's *Gulliver's Travels* seems alternatively percipient and obtuse, blindly patriotic and unchauvinistically humanistic, warns us that we cannot relax into unguarded acceptance of his statements or opinions. On the other hand, although few if any readers of *Wuthering Heights* can identify totally with Mr Lockwood, he is consistently portrayed, and so we feel more and more confident in assessing his opinions in light of our view of his personality and character.

In addition to choosing a narrator and (perhaps) an implied narrative medium, the novelist has to select a *form of address* for his narrator. In so doing, he or she normally helps to define what has been termed a *narratee*: the person to whom the narrative is addressed (see the Glossary). Note that the narratee may be the actual reader, but is not necessarily so. The narrative can, for instance, be directly addressed to the "Dear Reader," or it can be spoken or written to another intradiegetic (or "intra-fictional") target or destination, or it can be projected into a void. In *Tom Jones*, Henry Fielding uses "interchapters" in which the reader is addressed directly, while the remainder of the novel is less overtly pointed at any reader or listener.

What, for example, do we make of the opening lines of Albert Camus's *The Outsider* (1942)? "Mother died today. Or maybe yesterday, I don't know. I had a telegram from the home: 'Mother passed away. Funeral tomorrow. Yours sincerely.' That doesn't mean anything. It might have been yesterday" (Camus 1983, 9). In a previous edition of this book I wrote of this passage: "Clearly this could be addressed to someone (would there be any sense in saying it to oneself?), but the narrative might represent a state of mind and a sequence of events which the reader is not meant to think are actually aimed at any recipient in particular." A correspondent has suggested that this could indeed be Meursault talking or thinking to himself. A general problem here is that because our mental statements or questions to ourselves are not necessarily verbalized, or at least not rendered in formally correct sentences, when such processes are depicted in fiction the writer has the choice either to help the reader and use formally correct sentences (thus making the processes appear unlike the way we actually think) or to try to capture the nature of non-linguistic or semi-linguistic thoughts in unconventional language (thus making the reader work harder to interpret them).

As this suggests, a fictional character who talks to him- or herself can be both narrator and narratee. In the final section of James Joyce's *Ulysses*, Molly Bloom is both narrator and narratee.

Recent writers associated with *rhetorical narratology* (see p. 215) have stressed the importance of the *occasion* on which a narrative is delivered. Is the narrator at ease, or under pressure? Has he or she one narratee or many? Is the narrative delivered long after the events it recounts took place, or a few days later? Such elements of the narrative situation are used by readers to interpret the significance of what they read.

Complicity and intrusion; intimacy and involvement

Narratives can also involve such elements as *complicity*, *intrusion*, and *intimacy*—all of which are normally instantly recognized by readers while remaining tricky to analyze.

Take for example the following brief extract from Chapter 3 of E.M. Forster's *Howards End* (1910), in which Mrs Munt is talking at cross purposes to Charles Wilcox, believing him to be engaged to her niece Helen:

> "This is very good of you," said Mrs Munt, as she settled into a luxurious cavern of red leather, and suffered her person to be padded with rugs and shawls. She was more civil than she had intended, but really this young man was very kind. Moreover, she was a little afraid of him: his self-possession was extraordinary. "Very good indeed," she repeated, adding: "It is just what I should have wished."
>
> "Very good of you to say so," he replied, with a slight look of surprise, which, like most slight looks, escaped Mrs Munt's attention. (Forster 1975, 31)

That final narrative comment is the culminating stroke in a process whereby the reader is sucked into complicity with the narrator. We share the narrator's slightly contemptuous amusement at Mrs Munt's obtuseness and self-importance, and as a result of such passages we are likely to be far more malleable in the hands of the narrator, far more willing to accept his value-judgments and assessments of characters. It should perhaps be added that at this and other points many readers feel that it is the author himself with whom we become complicit, and although this view has become unfashionable in recent decades, it should not be dismissed. (It is perhaps for this reason that it seems natural to refer to this particular narrator as "he.")

The line between complicity and intrusion can be difficult to draw. For many readers, the last paragraph of Thomas Hardy's *Tess of the d'Urbervilles* (1891) starts with an annoyingly intrusive and heavy-handed comment from the narrator, a comment which such readers feel detracts from the power of the scene depicted at this point of the novel: "Justice was done, and the President of the Immortals, in Aeschylean phrase, had ended his sport with Tess." In contrast, at the end of the first chapter of Jane Austen's *Mansfield Park* (1814), we find this concluding sentence about Mrs Price (Fanny's mother): "Poor woman! she probably thought change of air might agree with many of her children." Although technically intrusive, this seems less to break in upon an established tone or perspective than does Hardy's comment, and so seems to have offended fewer readers than has that final paragraph of *Tess of the d'Urbervilles*. Note, incidentally, the force of the word "probably" here, which is similar to Conrad's use of "perhaps" in the first sentence of *Lord Jim*. At this point in the novel the reader responds to Austen's narrator as to a human observer of Mrs Price, rather than an all-seeing non-human narrator.

A narrative can be either *recollective* or *dramatic*. Of course, *any* narrative involves recollection; to be told a story is to be informed of something which has already happened, something which is being remembered, *recounted* (see the comments on double chronology on p. 6). We should probably exclude those rare examples of future narrative, although even here, because we are given the impression that the narrative *knows* what events are to happen, in a sense they exist already in completed form. In Margaret Atwood's short story "Weight" (1991), for example, the present-tense, first-person narrative gives way in the four final paragraphs to the future tense. In these paragraphs the speaker is thinking about what she will do the next day and what will happen then, and so the emphasis is still on the present thinking rather than the future happening.

Present-tense narrative is more problematic, but it can be argued that this technique at least implies a gap between the happening and the recounting, although in English the use of the present continuous can give a sense of immediacy. Thus on the penultimate page of Atwood's "Weight" we can read the following paragraph:

> Charles is walking me to the door, past white tablecloth after white tablecloth, each one held in place by at least four pin-striped elbows. It's like the *Titanic* just before the iceberg: power and influence disporting themselves, not a care in the world. What do they know about the serfs down in steerage? Piss all, and pass the port. (Atwood 1991, 192)

There is no doubt that the reader is given a sense of being present as things happen here, although I think that probably this is the female narrator's retrospective imagining-what-it-was-like-when-it-took-place: the things that have happened unfold in her head as she remembers the events in the restaurant. What is narrated is the retrospective unfolding in the head rather than the actual events.

Such subtleties and marginal cases should not obscure what every sensitive reader of fiction knows: some ways of telling a story can have far more dramatic effect than others (as is clear from Samuel Richardson's character's comment on the epistolary technique, quoted in the entry on "Epistolary novel" in the Glossary). Note how in the following passage Jean Rhys changes tense in order to create dramatic immediacy in her novel *Good Morning, Midnight* (1939):

> The lavatory at the station—that was the next time I cried. I had just been sick. I was so afraid I might be going to have a baby …

Although I have been so sick, I don't feel any better. I lean up against the wall, icy cold and sweating. Someone tries the door, and I pull myself together, stop crying and powder my face. (Rhys 1969, 101; ellipsis in original)

Compare a passage from a much-quoted scene in Chapter 4 of Charles Dickens's *Great Expectations*. The young Pip has robbed the pantry of food, which he has given to the escaped convict, and is eating Christmas dinner with his family in fear and trembling:

Among this good company I should have felt myself, even if I hadn't robbed the pantry, in a false position. Not because I was squeezed in at an acute angle of the table-cloth, with the table in my chest, and the Pumblechookian elbow in my eye, nor because I was not allowed to speak (I didn't want to speak), nor because I was regaled with the scaly tips of the drumsticks of the fowls, and with those obscure corners of pork of which the pig, when living, had had the least reason to be vain. No; I should not have minded that, if they would only have left me alone. But they wouldn't leave me alone. (Dickens 1965, 56)

Here the author does all in his power to reduce immediacy and emotionally to disengage the reader from Pip's experiences. In reading this passage we do not feel with the young Pip, we watch amusedly with the older, narrating Pip. We observe from a distance, with narrator-Pip, rather than experiencing with character-Pip. Note how different this is from our intimate relationship with Joyce's Eveline (see p. 62). To indicate such variations in intimacy the term *distance* is used by narratologists and critics. Such narrative distancing does not necessarily prevent the reader from experiencing with a character; it can sometimes involve deliberate understatement which allows the reader to imagine for him- or herself what the experience involved must have been like. A novelist can control the extent to which a reader empathizes with a character by means of the manipulation of narrative distance. The more "here and now" the narrative is—both spatially and temporally—the more likely the reader is to enter into the character's experiences.

Narrative technique and history

The craft of the novel has its history, and different narrative techniques emerge at different times, often in response to changes in the way people live and think. Thus the rise of the epistolary novel (see the Glossary) in the eighteenth century, for example, cannot be understood apart from the great importance of letter-writing at that time, while the emergence of the stream-of-consciousness novel in the twentieth century has to be related to the development of modern psychology and the increasing interest in mental operations that accompanies it. There is no doubt that we are bang in the middle of another such shift now, with large parts of our lives spent staring at electronic screens on devices that were unknown a few short decades ago.

The following factors are all important in assessing the significance of a particular narrative technique:

- Changes in the dominant modes of human communication (think of the substantial effect that the telephone had on human communication during the first three-quarters of the twentieth century, and of the enormous and continuing reverberations of the computer revolution—including those of the internet—since the late 1980s).
- The effect of different worldviews, philosophies, and ideologies (there is clearly a parallel between a belief in a God who sees everything and novelists' use of omniscient narrators—witness Jean Rhys's phrase "told in the third person with the writer as the Almighty" (p. 112). The weakening of a universal belief in such a God seems to have been paralleled by a disenchantment with the possibilities of narrative omniscience).
- Changes in readership patterns and habits (it is perhaps harder for an author to feel intimate with a larger, more amorphous, and anonymous set of readers, but, paradoxically, it may be easier to be open with unknown readers and to give them a sense of intimate closeness to a narrator).
- Significant changes in the way people live, and in the modes of consciousness attendant upon these changes (think of the growth of urban living, of mass communication, of modern science, and politics).

The impact of such factors is typically indirect and diffused when it comes to formal or technical revolutions in the novel, rather than one-to-one. George Butte has commented on one such revolution that occurred at the close of the eighteenth century.

> A sea change in the representation of consciousness in narratives in English becomes visible in the time of Jane Austen. It is a change so subtle and fundamental that it has been difficult to conceive and describe ... One aspect

of the change has received careful attention in recent years: the move into the interior of the self. (Butte 2004, 25)

What causes such a change? A neat, all-embracing response to such a question is unlikely ever to be forthcoming, but it seems highly unlikely that the revolution was utterly unconnected to changes in the world at large—social, intellectual, and ideological. If this sea change can, as Butte argues, be dated from the very start of the nineteenth century, the exploitation of techniques allowing access to the inner self intensifies throughout the nineteenth and, especially, the early years of the twentieth century (see the discussion of modernism on p. 59).

Stream of consciousness and interior monologue

Let me at this point say a few words about *stream-of-consciousness* technique and the *internal* (or *interior*) *monologue* (terms also defined in the Glossary). The two need carefully to be distinguished. Strictly speaking, an internal monologue implies the use of *language*, and if an individual is "talking to himself or herself," then that in turn presupposes a certain amount of consciousness of what is going on in that person's mind. (If you think about your own mental processes, you will probably find that some of these involve words, and some do not.) Milan Kundera, talking about "the fantastic espionage of interior monologue," claims that James Joyce set a microphone within his character Leopold Bloom's head (Kundera 1988, 28). The famous closing section of James Joyce's *Ulysses* gives us, essentially, the stream of Molly Bloom's consciousness, but in internal monologue; she is (I think) thinking to herself in words and is conscious of what she is thinking. I say "I think" because novelists can transpose unverbalized thoughts and sensations into verbal statements which are attributed to the character in question, and it is possible that at least part of this chapter should be read in this way. The chapter opens as follows:

> Yes because he never did a thing like that before as ask to get his breakfast in bed with a couple of eggs since the *City Arms* hotel when he used to be pretending to be laid up with a sick voice … (Joyce 1993, 690)

It is possible that the reader is meant to imagine Molly experiencing a primarily sensuous (visual/tactile) memory of the previous recumbent breakfast, and that the words we read are to be taken as a token of this set of sensuous, non-verbal memories. This seems unlikely though—first because the chapter in spite of its lack of punctuation has a logical structure and presents us with Molly's *arguments*, and it is difficult if not impossible to argue non-verbally, and second because Joyce typically presents thought processes as verbalized.

Now consider the following passage—the first two paragraphs of D.H. Lawrence's short story "Fanny and Annie" (1922):

> Flame-lurid his face as he turned among the throng of flame-lit and dark faces upon the platform. In the light of the furnace she caught sight of his drifting countenance, like a piece of floating fire. And the nostalgia, the doom of home-coming went through her veins like a drug. His eternal face, flame-lit now! The pulse and darkness of red fire from the furnace towers in the sky, lighting the desultory, industrial crowd on the wayside station, lit him and went out.
>
> Of course he did not see her. Flame-lit and unseeing! Always the same, with his meeting eyebrows, his common cap, and his red-and-black scarf knotted round his throat. Not even a collar to meet her! The flames had sunk, there was shadow. (Lawrence 1994, 573)

The passage is extremely complex, in part because it mixes what the narrator tells us and what Fanny is thinking, so that at several points it is hard if not impossible to tell whether what we are reading represents a narrative comment or Fanny's thoughts. I would like to draw attention to the fourth sentence ("His eternal face, flame-lit now!") and the whole of the second paragraph down to the end of the penultimate sentence quoted ("to meet her!"). It seems to me highly likely that these sentences represent Fanny's stream of consciousness rather than the narrator's commentary, although some parts could be both or either. However, what seems almost certain is that Fanny is not thinking by means of the actual words we read. She is not thinking to herself "His eternal face, flame-lit now! Of course he does not see me, flame-lit and unseeing! Always the same, with his meeting eyebrows, his common cap, and his red-and-black scarf knotted round his throat. Not even a collar to meet me!," although the reader may assume that she verbalizes *some* of these thoughts by means of the words we read. What Lawrence's words do is to give us Fanny's stream of consciousness rather than her internal monologue. We can summarize and say that an internal monologue gives us a character's stream of consciousness (or at least part of it, if we imagine images accompanying words), but not every stream of consciousness is an internal monologue.

Free Indirect Discourse

The difficulty I mentioned above of distinguishing between what a narrator says and what a character thinks or verbalizes may become particularly acute with the use of a technique which is known by a number of different terms: "Free Indirect Discourse (or speech)," "represented speech and thought," "narrated monologue," or the German and French terms *erlebte Rede* and *style indirect libre*. The complications of terminology are worth wading through, for the technique itself is arguably one of the most important in the novel since Jane Austen. Indeed, the "sea change in the representation of consciousness in narratives in English" that George Butte dates to the time of Jane Austen (see above, p. 119), a change that he claims allowed access to characters' inner lives without risking solipsism (or imprisonment in the self), seems to have involved a much greater, and more sophisticated, use of this technique.

Look again at the opening of "Fanny and Annie." Who is it who says "Of course he did not see her?" The grammatical structure of the sentence, with Fanny referred to as "her," might suggest that it is the narrator (it cannot be Harry, the man, precisely because he has not seen her). Is it not rather odd for the narrator to utter this comment, as if Harry's behavior were expected but nonetheless irritating, and as if the reader knew enough about Harry to legitimize that "of course"? The same can be said of "Always the same, with his meeting eyebrows, his common cap, and his red-and-black scarf knotted round his throat. Not even a collar to meet her!" Is it not odd for the narrator to say this, first because we do not expect an omniscient narrator to get so quickly irritated by a character, and second because the statement assumes that whoever hears this comment will be familiar with poor Harry's shortcomings? How do we know that Harry is always the same? This is the first time that we have encountered him!

In fact, as most readers have no difficulty in working out, it is not Lawrence's narrator, but Fanny, whose irritation at Harry's familiar inadequacies is thereby expressed. Typical of "Free Indirect Discourse"—to use what is now generally accepted as the best term in English to describe this technique—is the use of the grammar of third-person utterance (with certain modifications) to present us with a character's speech or (verbal or non-verbal) thoughts. (As will be understood, terms such as "Free Indirect Speech," "represented speech," and "represented thought" have a more specific and limited application than does the blanket term "Free Indirect Discourse.")

The traditional way of defining what we can refer to as FID makes use of grammatical or linguistic evidence. This involves seeing FID as a midway point between direct and indirect (or reported) discourse (DD and ID), or as a combination of the two which blends their grammatical characteristics in a distinctive mix. Thus we can use the following simple illustration, in which one can note that the third example retains the third-person "he" and past tense from ID, but in its truncation resembles the words in inverted commas in the DD example.

DD: He said, "I love her"
ID: He said that he loved her
FID: He loved her
(example from Rimmon-Kenan 1983, 111)

What should strike us immediately about the third example ("He loved her") is that, in common with the sentences in the passage from "Fanny and Annie" at which we have already looked, in the context of a passage from a novel it could be ambiguous. It could either give us from within the consciousness of the "he" referred to, his realization that he loves a woman, or it could give the reader a statement by a narrator about a character (who might not even realize, yet, that he loves the person concerned). This ambiguity is exploited by the most skilled writers of prose fiction, and very often allows them to move backward and forward between narrative comment and character consciousness, often with no apparent seams. Look once again at the opening of Lawrence's story. It clearly gives us both (i) comment that comes from a narrator or source outside the depicted characters and events and also (ii) what Fanny is thinking. It is nevertheless impossible to make a sharp distinction between the two such that one ends up with two neat piles, one labeled "narrator's comment" and the other "Fanny's thoughts." This, I would argue, is a strength rather than a weakness of the passage; if you disagree, try rewriting it so as to exclude any ambiguity as to whom statements should be attributed.

Let me return to the issue of the ambiguity associated with the technique, an ambiguity which may make it impossible definitively to attribute a statement either to narrator or character. Take this passage from Virginia Woolf's *Mrs Dalloway*:

Elizabeth rather wondered whether Miss Kilman could be hungry. It was her way of eating, eating with intensity, then looking, again and again, at a plate of sugared cakes on the table next them; then, when a lady and a child sat down and the child took the cake, could Miss Kilman really mind it?

> Yes, Miss Kilman did mind it. She had wanted that cake—the pink one. The pleasure of eating was almost the only pure pleasure left her, and then to be baffled even in that! (Woolf 1992, 142)

Whose consciousness is represented in the last three sentences? Is it (1) narrator (2) narrator (3) narrator? Or (1) narrator (2) narrator (3) Miss Kilman? Or (1) narrator (2) Miss Kilman (3) Miss Kilman? It is even possible that these sentences give us Elizabeth's thoughts as she imagines what Miss Kilman is thinking. As with the opening of "Fanny and Annie," these ambiguities do not constitute a flaw in the passage but quite the reverse: we know what Miss Kilman is thinking and we understand the narrator's attitude toward her and her desires without having to attribute a form of words either to the narrator or to the character. Note that a "principle of inertia" operates in our response to such passages: unless we are given good reason for changing the way we ascribe statements to a particular source or consciousness, we tend to go on attributing them to the one already established as the operative one. The technical term for this "principle of inertia" in narrative theory is *obstination* (see also the Glossary).

Katherine Mansfield's "The Daughters of the Late Colonel" includes a striking exploitation of the possibilities of FID. The two daughters of the title, Josephine and Constantia, have lived in the shadow of their tyrannical father all their lives, and are extremely close. In the immediate aftermath of his death, they find themselves in a strange and unfamiliar world. A visiting clergyman suggests that he could arrange a communion for them at home.

> But the idea of a little Communion terrified them. What! In the drawing-room by themselves—with no—no altar or anything! The piano would be much too high, thought Constantia, and Mr. Farolles could not possibly lean over it with the chalice. And Kate would be sure to come bursting in and interrupt them, thought Josephine. And supposing the bell rang in the middle? It might be somebody important—about their mourning. Would they get up reverently and go out, or would they have to wait … in torture? (Ellipsis in original) (Mansfield 1951, 96)

If we follow these sentences in order, we see that (1) describes their reaction from a perspective detached from both of them, (2) gives their shared response in FID, (3) gives Constantia's thoughts in indirect or reported speech, while (4) seems to show Josephine responding mentally to what her sister has thought, again using indirect or reported speech. But (5),

(6), and (7) give us the shared thoughts of the two sisters, using FID. Thus the passage leaves open the possibility that the sisters can read each others' minds, but without actually stating this unambiguously. This is a culmination of the achievement of the revolution of which George Butte speaks—giving us access to the inwardness of (in this case two) characters, while retaining an external, distanced perspective on them.

Yet another technique, one which has something in common with Free Indirect Discourse without having quite the grammatical specificity of this technique, is that of *colored* discourse or narrative. This involves the "coloring" of a piece of (normally but not necessarily) third-person narrative with words, phrases, expressions that the reader associates with the verbal habits of a particular character. The technique is closely related to techniques used to mock, mimic, or satirize others in speech. The fiction of Dickens contains innumerable examples of it, from which the following (the opening of Chapter 25, "Book the Second," of *Little Dorrit* [1857–8]) will serve as illustration:

> The dinner-party was at the great Physician's. Bar was there, and in full force. Ferdinand Barnacle was there, and in his most engaging state. Few ways of life were hidden from Physician, and he was oftener in its darkest places than even Bishop. There were brilliant ladies about London who perfectly doted on him, my dear, as the most charming creature and the most delightful person. (Dickens 1953, 702)

The whole of this chapter is characterized by bitter and ironic mockery of the pretensions of those involved, but in this passage we see Dickens actually incorporating a verbal "signature" from those he is mocking; "my dear" is, we take it, the sort of frequent hypocrisy to be found in the conversation of the ladies being ridiculed, and its inclusion colors the narrative around it. Richard Walsh has suggested that "[m]imicry is a reasonably good model for how FID works" (2007, 97); here we see mimicry providing the model for colored discourse (see also the entry for coloring in the Glossary).

Tone

Mimicry carries with it the idea of *tone*, or the way in which a particular utterance is coded to communicate a particular attitude on the part of the speaker with regard either to what is being spoken about or to whoever is addressed. In real life, when a person says "I'm so sorry to hear about your accident," this can be said in a way that suggests genuine sympathy or in a way that suggests that the person speaking is just repeating a conventional phrase. Narrators too can tell stories in ways that suggest different attitudes. The means available to them are very varied and hard to summarize, but careful reading can often reveal what they are. One fails to understand *Gulliver's Travels*, for example, if one does not perceive the satirical tone that pervades the whole work. In like manner, although it is true that a work like Kafka's *The Castle* suggests that life is meaningless and that communication between human beings is impossible, this aspect of the work has to be seen in consort with the tone of deep pity and sympathy for humanity which pervades the novel.

Character

Character and individuality

I suggested in Chapter 2 that it was a moot point whether much fiction from before the time of the modern novel could be said to contain characters as we understand the word. For us, "character" is intimately bound up with individualism: a character is unique, not just the property of a person but somehow simultaneously both the person and the sign or token of the person. According to Clemens Lugowski, so long as human existence is dominated by myth (which is timeless and collective) rather than by history, "there can be no individual characters," for instead of being autonomous individuals "they are no more than components of a whole" (Lugowski 1990, 83). No literary or artistic form has a closer relationship to what we now know and understand as character than does the novel.

Many readers will doubtless feel unable to accept Lugowski's denial of full individuality to those who lived before the modern age. But if we are prepared to concede that individuality takes different forms in different cultures, and that literacy in particular changes it radically, then we may be open to other possibilities. First: how human individuals are represented in books has some connection with how they are conceived by themselves and by others in real life. Second: as our view of human individuality in the real world changes, so too may our view of fictional character. Third: just as there are conventions that govern (or at least influence) how speech is represented in the novel (see p. 150), so too there are comparable and changing conventions that govern the depiction of character in the novel. Thus in her influential essay "Mr Bennett and Mrs Brown" (1924), Virginia Woolf claims (doubtless part tongue-in-cheek) that "in or about December, 1910, human character changed" (Woolf 1966a, 320). Woolf is of course exaggerating for humorous and other purposes, but it is clear that she is serious in the main point that she makes in the essay, that changes in human beings have taken place, and thus changes in the ways novelists represent human beings must also occur.

My earlier discussion of modernism and postmodernism should have suggested that recent fiction to which the labels "modernist" or "postmodernist" can be attached will be likely to portray the human individual in ways different from those to be found in the classic realist fiction of the previous century. This is indeed the case. What often seem to disappear in the characters we find in modernist fiction are individual coherence, comprehensive self-knowledge, and autonomy. Virginia Woolf's *The Waves* is a textbook example of this sort of change. Woolf's character Bernard repeatedly utters statements such as "I am not one and simple, but complex and many"; "I am more selves than Neville thinks"; "We exist not only separately but in undifferentiated blobs of matter." Not surprisingly, Bernard repeatedly asks "Who am I?" and even describes himself as a man without a self. Other modernist novelists have also portrayed character as complex and problematic rather than simple and self-evident. Think of Klamm in Kafka's *The Castle*, who appears to be different to everyone who sees him and each time that he is seen. It is true that we can find doubles and split selves in the fiction of the nineteenth century—in Dostoyevsky's "The Double" and Stevenson's *Dr Jekyll and Mr Hyde*, for example—but these are portrayed as extreme cases, whereas Woolf's Bernard is characterized by his normality.

Postmodernist fiction generally takes this disintegration of character a stage further, playing with the conventions governing the representation of character in works of fiction so as to expose these to the reader's scrutiny. Thus a *cancelled character* (sometimes called an *erased character*) is a character in a postmodernist work who (or which) is introduced in order to make the reader accept him or her as a human individual, but who is later cancelled or erased and revealed to be only the creation of the novelist, a construct who (or, again, which!) has existence only in the pages of the work. Cyberfiction takes some of these elements even further, imagining futures in which the grafting together of organic and non-organic materials is able to produce cyborgs, beings part-human and part-machine (see the entry for Cyberpunk/cyberfiction in the Glossary).

Types of literary character

These rather extended introductory comments are necessary because "character" may well appear to be one of the least problematic terms with which you have to deal in studying the novel. The proper names we encounter in a novel—Tom Jones, Anna Karenina, Daisy Miller, Huck Finn, Captain John Yossarian—seem very much like the proper names we meet in everyday life and by which we designate individual human beings.

Yet even if we stop at names we may realize that characters in novels are not quite like real people. In everyday life we sometimes meet a person with an unusually appropriate name: the very tall person called Long, for example. In novels it is different. The peculiar appropriateness of a name such as Heathcliff is surely hardly ever met with in real life. What about Dickens's Esther Summerson—who acts like a "summer sun" in *Bleak House*, dispelling the shadows with which the work is, initially, filled? Even "Tom Jones" with its resolute lack of connotations or associations seems extraordinarily appropriate a name for the non-aristocratic, normally healthy hero of Fielding's novel.

"Tom Jones" is a rather different name from "M'Choakunchild"—the name given by Dickens to one of his characters, however, which reminds us of an important point: there are different *sorts* of literary character. Of course there are different sorts of people in ordinary life, but it is not this sort of variation that I have in mind. Think of Meursault in Albert Camus's *The Outsider* and Mr Guppy in Charles Dickens's *Bleak House*. Both are young men who have problems communicating with others and who have an odd relation to their mothers. There are also important differences between them, however, and if we were asked to explain these differences we would have to talk about them not just as if they were ordinary human beings but also in a way that recognizes that they are different *types* of literary character, existing within very unlike sorts of novel, very varied *narrative situations*.

A good test here is to ask to what extent a character from one literary work could be transplanted to another. We have little difficulty in imagining a meeting between, for example, the title character from Jane Austen's *Emma* (1816) and Mr Darcy from her *Pride and Prejudice* (1813). This is because the fictional worlds of these two novels are so similar that such a meeting, which is as much a meeting of fictional worlds as it is of characters, does not seem absurd. If we go back to *The Outsider* and compare the narrator with Mr Guppy from Charles Dickens's *Bleak House*, we realize that Mr Guppy could not be transported to the fictional world of *The Outsider*; he could not survive in that novel as we know him in *Bleak House*. My concept of "fictional world" is not just a matter of setting (about which I talk below). After all, the settings of *Moll Flanders* and *Robinson Crusoe* are very different, but their fictional worlds are much less so. The concept refers, in other words, not just to the real-world elements (places, events, history) depicted in the works but also to the representational conventions governing the portrayal of these and other things. *Bleak House* and *The Outsider* are held together in part by philosophical and ideological elements: views of the nature of the world which enter into the very fabric and texture of the novels. Meursault lives in a world defined by the preoccupations of existentialist philosophy, a world from which Mr Guppy is very far removed. (Note that the important thing is not whether the *individual character* has certain philosophical or other concerns but whether their *fictional presentation* accords with these concerns.) That is why we have films with titles like *Godzilla Meets King Kong*, but not, outside the realms of parody, with titles such as *Bambi Meets Godzilla*. (There is actually a very short film with this title—you can find it through a Google search on the internet—but even without watching it you will be able to guess that it has to be a parody!)

Subsequent to my writing the previous paragraph I discovered Christine Brooke-Rose's novel *Textermination* (1991), in which a conference of characters out of the great works of literature is convened at the San Francisco Hilton, to pray for their own continued survival in readers' minds. It is not exactly *Bambi Meets Godzilla*, but it does have Emma Bovary sharing a carriage with Jane Austen's Mr Elton. Of course, the characters' knowledge of themselves as literary characters gives them something in common and something which their originals lack; thus the fictional world of *Textermination* is one colored and formed by the post-structuralist interests of its author. It is not in any way a simple mixing of the fictional worlds of the different characters—and nor could it be.

Let us try to explore some of the differences that exist between literary characters. We have some well-established terms to draw on initially: "major and minor characters," "flat and round characters," "stock characters," "types," and so on.

We can sum up one important distinction that has a bearing upon all of the above terms: is the writer primarily concerned to develop a character in order to *represent something*, or in order to present a *particular individuality*? The distinction is related to that between novels of "life" and novels of "pattern," to which I referred on p. 21, for it is in novels of pattern that one is likely to find characters who stand for something (a giveaway feature is often the names) and in the novel of life that one finds characters possessed of a distinctive, idiosyncratic, and unique individuality. However, even in the latter case we have to face the paradox that a highly individualized character may also stand for something: Mr Toots in Dickens's *Dombey and Son* and Prince Myshkin in Dostoyevsky's *The Idiot* (1869) are "originals," yet they also stand for certain valuable qualities which contribute importantly to the themes of the two novels mentioned. Moreover, just because a character is a recognizable *type* (another of Dickens's grotesques, one of Dostoyevsky's eccentrics) does not necessarily mean that he or she cannot also be a realized individual personality in the work.

In his book *Aspects of the Novel* (1927), E.M. Forster uses Dickens's Mrs Micawber (from *David Copperfield*) as an example of what he calls a "flat" (as against a "round") character: "The really flat character can be expressed in one sentence such as 'I never will desert Mr Micawber.' There is Mrs Micawber—she says she won't desert Mr Micawber; she doesn't, and there she is." James Phelan proposes a rather more sophisticated division:

> (1) Character consists of three components—the mimetic (character as person), the thematic (character as idea), and the synthetic (character as artificial construct). (2) The relationship between these components varies from narrative to narrative. (Phelan 1996, 29)

We can surmise that Mrs Micawber exists primarily as artificial construct, and not really at all as person or idea.

The term *synonymous character* has been applied to recent, especially experimental, novels; synonymous characters are those which are possessed of essentially the same characteristics and functions in a piece of prose fiction, and are thus to all intents interchangeable. The term is very close to the more old-fashioned "stock character."

Functions and types

The word "function" also deserves some attention at this stage. Its literary-critical usage is most associated with the analyses of folktales carried out by the Russian Vladimir Propp, who argued that all folktales consist of a selection from a finite number of functions, a function being "an act of a character, defined from the point of view of its significance for the course of the action" (Propp 1968, 21). Not all the available functions would be selected in any given tale, but those that were selected had to appear in a strict order. Such a description seems foreign to those of us more familiar with the novel than with the sort of work with which Propp was concerned. However, although *in general terms* we can distinguish the novel from other fictional forms which represent human individuals but are less interested in their particularity and individuality than in what they do or stand for (the type-characters of the fable or parable, for example), we should recall that even those novelists most renowned and admired for their creation of living characters utilize recognizable types: think, for example, of the minor characters created by Jane Austen and Charles Dickens.

In recent years a number of critics have developed the concept of *projection characters*, that is characters into whom the novelist projects aspects of him- or herself—often aspects which cannot be acknowledged either to others or to the author him- or herself. (Psychoanalytic theories of projection lie behind the term, the idea being that what we cannot accept in ourselves we often project onto others.) In Charles Dickens's *Great Expectations*, for example, the character Orlick is like a dark shadow of the hero Pip and seems almost a personification of Pip's repressed desires. He stands up to Mrs Joe (who treats Pip so unfeelingly) and eventually strikes her down, and he openly lusts after Biddy, for whom Pip eventually acknowledges his own desire. In a late, climactic scene he announces his intention of murdering Pip himself, thus dramatizing what otherwise would be a purely internal struggle in Pip. If we take into account the considerable extent to which Pip's portrayal (like that of David Copperfield) is modeled by Dickens on his own character and experiences, then we can understand that Orlick can be described as a projection character: whereas the similarities between Dickens and Pip are open and overt, those between Orlick and Dickens are concealed and even denied.

"Telling" and "showing"

A classic but still useful distinction between two fundamental ways of creating (or "revealing") character is one that we owe to Percy Lubbock's *The Craft of Fiction* (1921). When Jane Austen opens her novel *Emma* in the following way, she is *telling* rather than showing us what Emma is like:

> Emma Woodhouse, handsome, clever, and rich, with a comfortable home and happy disposition, seemed to unite some of the best blessings of existence; and had lived nearly twenty-one years in the world with very little to distress or vex her.

Later on in the novel, however, when Mr Knightley criticizes Emma's rudeness to Miss Bates, we are *shown* an aspect of Emma's personality through her behavior and her responses to him. It may be worth adding that Austen's use of the word "seemed" in the above passage encourages the alert reader to wonder whether Emma's happy situation may turn out to contain some less positive elements.

So far as the creation of lifelike characters is concerned, it is very often the interplay between "shown" and "told" attributes that makes them fascinating. Think of Heathcliff in *Wuthering Heights*; we partly understand why he is as he is because we have witnessed key events in his upbringing. However, some of his attributes seem to be beyond such an explanation; they are presented as givens rather than as effects or results.

Methods of characterization

What are the most important methods of characterization available to the novelist? I would suggest four that are worth thinking about. First is *description* or *report*. In Conrad's *Heart of Darkness*, we know a very large amount about Mr Kurtz before ever he appears before us; other characters in the novella have talked about him so much, reporting his actions and beliefs, that we feel almost as if we had met him ourselves.

The description of physical characteristics—and especially of physiognomy—is a very traditional means whereby the writer can suggest what sort of character we are encountering. Here is a description taken from the second paragraph of Philip Larkin's novel *Jill* (1946). The novel's main male character, John Kemp, is traveling by train to Oxford:

> It looked cold and deserted. The windows of the carriages were bluish with the swirls of the cleaner's leather still showing on the glass, and he confined his eyes to the compartment. It was a third-class carriage, and the crimson seats smelt of dust and engines and tobacco, but the air was warm. Pictures of Dartmouth Castle and Portmadoc looked at him from the opposite wall. He was an undersized boy, eighteen years old, with a pale face and soft pale hair brushed childishly from left to right. Lying back against the seat, he stretched his legs out and pushed his hands to the bottom of the pockets of his cheap blue overcoat. The lapels of it curled outwards and creases dragged from the buttons. His face was thin, and perhaps strained; the expression round his mouth was ready to become taut, and a small frown lingered on his forehead. His whole appearance lacked luxuriance. Only his silky hair, as soft as seeding thistle, gave him an air of beauty. (Larkin 1975, 21)

Just imagine that you have met someone on a train, and when discussing this meeting with someone you know, later on, you start to describe him. You would, I venture to suggest, hardly come out with something along the lines of the above paragraph. If you did, it would probably be because you were a student of literature indulging in a little parodic behavior. To put the matter another way, we can say that Larkin's description of John Kemp depends upon certain fictional conventions that regulate the depiction of character, conventions that require that physical characteristics be seen to have a much more reliable function as indicators of non-physical qualities (and even, perhaps, of past or future events and experiences) than they do in real life.

Thus from this passage we can detect that John Kemp is not rich, and is not a thrusting, self-confident youth ready and eager for heroic exploits. We assume that the journey he is making has not been made by him before; otherwise he would not notice so many details about his surroundings. (We are not told that it is he who sees and smells these details, but we are encouraged to assume this.) We deduce too that behind his lack of position and self-confidence there reside qualities which now are apparent only to the discriminating and which will allow him to deal well (finally, perhaps) with whatever trials he has to face. It is almost unthinkable that this is a description of a man who will turn into a pompous and conforming hypocrite, who the reader will end up hating. Behind his portrayal we may, even at this stage, recognize what can be called a mythic element: the unregarded person who has a potentiality that, when revealed, may surprise those who take him at face value. That silky hair of John Kemp's along with the expression round the mouth and the frown on his forehead, betoken much more on the first page of a novel than they would in real life: they stand for that unregarded quality or virtue which exists only *in potentia*, whose emergence the novel will trace. As the description also insists on the shabby cheapness of Kemp's clothes and of the third-class compartment, we can feel reasonably confident, too, that the novel will pay particular attention to the problems raised by his background and by issues of social class—especially as the first paragraph of the novel has informed us that the train he is on is heading for Oxford. Notice how much we know of Kemp and how much we are already expecting—and he has said nothing and done nothing so far!

Second, character can be established in fiction as in life: by *action*. When Insarov in Turgenev's *On the Eve* (1859) throws the insolent German into the water—an action of which his effete Russian companions are palpably incapable—then we learn something about him which pages of description could not give us.

Third is through a character's *thought* or *conversation*. Dialogue in particular is a wonderful way of revealing character: think how much we learn about Miss Bates in *Emma* merely through her conversation—so much so that comment from Austen's narrator is really superfluous. Modern novelists have shown how much we can learn about a character merely by following his or her thoughts; in Virginia Woolf's *Mrs Dalloway* (1925), Clarissa Dalloway and Peter Walsh actually *do* very little, but by the end of the novel we feel that we know them quite well just by having followed so many of their thoughts (and through their thoughts Woolf is able to retrieve actions and encounters from their pasts, shared and private).

Finally, the novelist can use *symbol* or *image* to reveal and develop a character. In Jean Rhys's novel *After Leaving Mr Mackenzie* (1930), the heroine, Julia, has just been to see a Mr James, shortly after visiting her dying mother and her spinsterish sister Norah:

> She wanted to cry as he went down the stairs with her. She thought: "That wasn't what I wanted." She had hoped that he would say something or look something that would make her feel less lonely.
>
> There was a vase of flame-coloured tulips in the hall—surely the most graceful of flowers. Some thrust their heads forward like snakes, and some were very erect, stiff, virginal, rather prim. Some were dying, with curved grace in their death. (Rhys 1971, 84)

The tulips present us symbolically with the varied fates of the different women in the novel: snake-like cunning and self-interested behavior; prim and virginal lifelessness (like Norah); and death—like Julia's mother. Such a passage contributes to our knowledge of and attitudes to characters in the novel even though nothing is said directly about any character.

Plot

In ordinary, non-academic discussion, the terms "plot" and "story" are often used loosely and interchangeably, but in academic discussion of fiction the distinction between the two is important. For narrative theorists a plot is an ordered, organized presentation of events and actions. Plots in this sense are found in novels rather than in ordinary life; life has stories, but novels have plots and stories (see the earlier comments on the double chronology of literary fiction on p. 6). E.M. Forster claimed that a story was a narrative of events arranged in their time-sequence, whereas a plot was a narrative of events with the emphasis falling on causality. Not all commentators would agree that causality is the distinguishing feature, but all would agree that there is a necessary distinction to be made between the incidents about which we are told in a novel arranged in their chronological order, and the actual narrating of these events in either the same or a different order. I prefer the terms "story" and "plot" to make this distinction, but some critics use terms created by a group of theorists known as the Russian Formalists (see p. 221), the terms *sjužet* ("plot") and *fabula* ("story").

Narratologists (see p. 212) have performed a useful function in providing terms and concepts such that we can more accurately analyze how and why the plot of a novel deviates from strict and simple chronological progression. We owe many of the terms I discuss below to structuralist narratologists, especially Gérard Genette.

Order

First of all are a number of terms connected to what is termed *order*. The plot of a novel may move backward and forward in time, instead of proceeding steadily forward in chronological order. If life always goes ABCDE, novels often go DEACB (compare my comments on Conan Doyle's "Silver Blaze" on p. 42). Any deviation from such strict chronological progression is termed an *anachrony*, and there are a large number of such deviations possible. The most frequent are *analepsis* (or flashback) and *prolepsis* (or flashforward). The italicized terms are perhaps to be preferred, as "flash" suggests a rather short movement backward or forward in time, whereas an analepsis or a prolepsis may be of very considerable duration.

Ellipses

Second, a novel's plot may include gaps, omissions, absences. These can be referred to collectively as *ellipses*—the same term that is used to refer to the succession of dots in a text that indicates that something has been left out. Thus in *Wuthering Heights* we never get to know what Heathcliff does after his sudden disappearance and up to the time of his reappearance. This is what can be termed a (relatively) *unmarked* ellipsis—in other words, the text does not ostentatiously display the fact that something is not there. But when in the second paragraph of Chapter 30 of Charles Dickens's *Bleak House* Esther Summerson seeks to explain why she finds Mrs Woodcourt irksome, and breaks off with the words, "I don't know what it was. Or at least if I do, now, I thought I did not then. Or at least—but it don't matter" (Dickens 1971, 467), then we have a clearly *marked* (or explicit) ellipsis: the reader's attention is drawn to the fact that something that is known to the narrator is being withheld. A novelist typically uses a marked ellipsis to get the reader's imagination working: What has happened here? Why are we not told? An unmarked ellipsis may turn out to be of great importance later on—especially in sub-genres such as the detective story.

Duration

Third, the element of duration is also of great significance. Nearly all works of prose fiction vary the relationship between narrating and narrated time. (The term *tense* is sometimes used to refer to this relationship, although this usage, taken from structuralist narratology, has not achieved general acceptance among Anglo-American critics.)

Whatever term we use, the essential characteristic involved is crucial to how novels work. A novelist can spend fifty pages to tell us about one day in the life of a heroine and then ten further pages to cover fifty years. Such extremes are sometimes referred by means of the linked terms *scene* (a passage in which there is a sort of equivalence between narrated and narrating time—for example, a dialogue in which all the words exchanged are given) and *summary* (where it is clear that the narrative is reducing all the potentially available material to a descriptive outline). Within a single novel the ratio of narrated to narrating time can alter very substantially, and it is worth paying careful attention to such shifts.

In *Tristram Shandy*, for example, Laurence Sterne makes frequent jokes about the relationship between narrated and narrating time. At the start of Chapter 21 the text breaks off into a digression in the middle of a sentence uttered by uncle Toby, to utter which he has had to take his pipe out of his mouth. The digression finished, the text continues: "But I forget my uncle Toby, whom all this while we have left knocking the ashes out of his tobacco pipe."

Frequency

Fourth, narrative theorists also isolate the important topic of *frequency*, and note the following fundamental possibilities:

(i)   one event narrated once (*singulative frequency*)
(ii) a repeated event narrated the same number of times that it occurs (*multiple frequency*)
(iii) one event narrated many times (*repetitive frequency*)
(iv) many events narrated once (*iterative frequency*)

Probably the most usual of these is (i): many unique events that are depicted in a novel are recounted only once. The same event can, however, be recounted many times, as in (iii). Sometimes this has the effect of sharpening our understanding: the detective novel typically recounts the same events more than once, so that what was unclear the first time becomes comprehensible in the detective's final version. In Joseph Heller's novel *Catch-22* (1961), as Snowden's death in the bombing raid is as it were "replayed" repetitively through the anti-hero Yossarian's consciousness while the novel unfolds, the reader is reminded of a psychoanalytic patient recalling more and more of a repressed event, and the repetition conveys the traumatic effect that the event has had on Yossarian. Sometimes clarity is not the intended result: the repeated but incompatible depictions of the same events in Alain Robbe-Grillet's *The Voyeur* (1955) lead the reader to lose confidence in the existence of a single, isolable series of events.

Many similar events may, as in (iv), be recounted as one. In Conrad's *Lord Jim*, Marlow's narrative is introduced as an iterative narrative—in other words, we are told that what we are about to read is an account that has been given many times. (The word "would" often confirms that the account is an iterative one, as can be seen in the extract below from Guy de Maupassant's novel *Bel-Ami*.) By the time Marlow's account ends it has become a single, particular act of recounting. In the same novelist's *Nostromo*, the shifts between the singulative and iterative modes are technically contradictory, but they draw attention to important thematic concerns about the uniqueness of events and the repetitions of history. Conrad deliberately and repetitively frustrates his readers' expectations: passages change unexpectedly from singulative to iterative mode, and from iterative to singulative mode (I have written more on this elsewhere: see Hawthorn 1998).

Gérard Genette has isolated a variation on the above alternatives which he calls the "pseudo-iterative." According to his definition, the pseudo-iterative occurs when "scenes presented, particularly by their wording in the imperfect, as iterative," are possessed of a "richness and precision of detail [which] ensure that no reader can seriously believe they occur and reoccur in that manner, several times, without any variation" (Genette 1980, 121). Consider the following passage from Guy de Maupassant's novel *Bel-Ami*:

> So they would go into low dives and sit down at the end of the squalid murky room on rickety chairs at decrepit wooden tables. An acrid cloud of smoke and the smell of fried fish filled the room; men in their working clothes were shouting at each other as they downed their glasses of raw spirits; and the waiter would stare at the strange couple as he put the two cherries-in-brandy down in front of them.
>
> Scared and trembling, but blissfully happy, she would begin sipping the red fruity liquid, looking around her, bright-eyed but uneasy: each time she swallowed a cherry she felt she was doing something wrong, every drop of the spicy, burning liquid that slipped down her throat gave her a sharp pleasure, the pleasure of forbidden fruit, of being naughty.
>
> Then she would whisper: "Let's go." And so they would leave. She slipped away hastily, tripping along and holding her head down, like an actress leaving the stage, between the drinkers sitting with their elbows on the table, who looked up with a suspicious, surly air as she went by. And when she was through the door, she gave a big gasp as if she had just escaped from some terrible danger.
>
> Sometimes, with a shudder, she asked Duroy:
>
> "What would you do if they insulted me in a place like that?"
>
> He said airily:
>
> "Defend you, of course!" (Maupassant 1975, 124–5)

It seems clear that the detailed dialogue provided here is not fully reconcilable with the suggestion that it represents what was said again and again on different occasions. Maupassant wants to give the reader a sense of repeated—even obsessively repeated—actions, while giving them enough individualized flavor to dramatize them and to prevent the reader from getting bored. Note that technically there is a change of frequency at the end of this passage from "Sometimes … she asked Duroy" (*iterative*—she asked more than once) to "He said" (*singulative*—he replied only once; we are not told "he would say"). This oscillation between the iterative and singulative modes is often a sign of the pseudo-iterative.

Chronology and coherence

If a novelist abandons strict chronology, how else can he or she retain coherence, make the novel hang together? Well, as Forster points out, *causality* is one important possible way: even if we know *what* happened, we read on to discover *why*.

Another technique is for a novelist to draw *parallels* and *resemblances* between characters, situations, and events such that the novel has coherence even if it plots neither chronological sequences nor causal relationships. It is only to a limited degree that we believe that the experiences of the second-generation characters in *Wuthering Heights* are actually caused by the lives and actions of the first-generation characters. Even so, the parallels (with variations) and resemblances between the younger Cathy, Linton Heathcliff, and Hareton Earnshaw and their parents suggest that this latter part of the novel continues themes and inquiries from the first part of the novel. It is important for the reader first to encounter the mature and embittered Heathcliff; this means that we see the young Heathcliff in the context of what we know he will later become, and thus our attention is focused in very particular ways as Nelly Dean starts to tell Lockwood of the childhood and young adulthood of Heathcliff and Catherine.

Alternatively, a novel can be held together by a common character or event. The picaresque novel and the *Bildungsroman* (see the Glossary), for instance, are held together by the personality of the central figure. The extent to which this provides a sophisticated or a crude unity depends to a certain degree upon the complexity of the central character. The work of major modernist and postmodernist writers has led many to question whether it is desirable that a novel should compose a unity: in her essay "Modern Fiction" (1919), Virginia Woolf represented the traditional, well-structured, realist plot as one of a number of distorting conventions in need of being discarded.

Types of plot

We can categorize plots in two ways: either in terms of the dominant human activities which form the motivating principle in them or which are induced in the reader by them, or in more technical ways. In the first category we can include plots structured around *conflict* as in many ways the plot of *Nostromo* is; around *mystery* as are many of Dickens's novels; around *pursuit* or *search* as is *The Castle*; around a journey as is *Gulliver's Travels*; or, finally, around a test as is Joseph Conrad's *The Shadow-Line*. Now of course these are very simplistic descriptions and we would want to say that all of these novels engage with far more complex issues than the single topics mentioned. Even so, it is worthwhile remembering that a novel is often given force and coherence by a dominating element such as one of these plot types provides. *The Shadow-Line* is structured around a journey as well as a test, but the theme of the test is a sort of archetypal bedrock within the organizing logic of the plot.

A more technical classification of plots will provide us with terms such as "picaresque/episodic," "well-made" (the traditional nineteenth-century realist plot), "multiple" (many novels have two or more lines of plot, sometimes interconnecting and sometimes not). It is very often important to be able to single out a *main plot* from its attendant *subplot(s)* for the purpose of analysis.

You may recall that much earlier on in this book I quoted Johnson's remark that if one were to read Richardson "for the story," one would be so fretted one would hang oneself (p. 33). Plot and story fulfill different sorts of functions in different novels. According to Johnson, the story in a novel by Richardson is there only to give occasion to the sentiment; in other novels the tension and suspense relative to our desire to know "what happens next" are an integral part of the appeal of the work. When the "outer" or "frame" narrator of *Heart of Darkness* warns us (indirectly) that we are about to hear "about one of Marlow's inconclusive experiences," we need to adjust our expectations with regard to the plot of the novella. Modernist works of fiction very often have inconclusive endings, endings which leave the reader perhaps puzzled and unsatisfied, but puzzled and unsatisfied in ways that are productive of further thought. You should, again, remember that such matters go beyond the merely technical. Novels without omniscient narrators and with inconclusive endings are perhaps less likely to betoken an optimistically conventionally Christian worldview in which everything is concluded in the manner in which God wishes; a novelist whose novels all have happy endings is unlikely to suffer from very much existential doubt. (See the entry for *closure* in the Glossary.)

Structure

Structure and plot are closely related to each other, and it might have made sense to include this section as a sub-section of "Plot." However, critics often use "structure" in a rather wider sense than such a placing might suggest. If we can think of the plot of a novel as the way in which its story is arranged, its structure involves more than its story, encompassing the work's total organization as a piece of literature, a work of art. "Structure" is perhaps the most comprehensive of these terms; as we will see below, unlike plot it includes things such as patterns of imagery and symbolism. In previous editions of this book I argued for a distinction between "structure" and "form," but I now concede that in practice these terms are often treated as equivalents, and both are used to refer to our sense of a novel's overall organization and patterning, the way in which its component parts fit together to produce a totality, a satisfying whole—or, of course, the way in which they fail so to do.

Let us start by observing that different novels have very different sorts of structure. We feel, for example, that some parts of *Moll Flanders* or *Huckleberry Finn* (1884) could be shifted around in position without making too great a difference to the works in question: how many readers of the former work remember clearly whether Moll robbed the little girl of her necklace before or after she robbed the drunken man in the coach? But to shuffle around the parts of *Wuthering Heights*, or of Henry James's *What Maisie Knew* (1897), would, we feel, seriously damage the works in question. Clearly the fact that a novel has an *episodic* structure has an important bearing upon such issues; if a work is structured around a series of relatively self-contained episodes, then these can be assembled in different orders without making too much difference—just as on a modular degree scheme with self-contained modules one can often take different courses in any order one chooses.

The matter goes beyond plot, as I have suggested. In *Moll Flanders* there is very little alteration in Moll's character, or in the values the narrative underwrites, or in the symbolic meanings contained in the work (if there are any worth noting in this novel!). In short, *Moll Flanders* is consistently structured on the principle of "repetition-with-slight-variation." There is somewhat more development and change in *Huckleberry Finn*—in the characters and relationship of Huck and Jim, in the general tone of the novel before and after the return of Huck and Jim to "civilization," and so on. Thus, although some of the scenes in this novel might be switched around without too much effect, such alteration would have to be more limited than with *Moll Flanders* if we wished to avoid damaging the work. The intricate patterning of a novel such as *What Maisie Knew* would, surely, be completely destroyed if we started to move sections of it from place to place.

Very often the *chapter* and *section* divisions made by the author impose a structure upon a work—or bring out one that is implicit but not overt in it already. (My earlier comments on *paratextual* elements in a novel are relevant here: see p. 75.) It is interesting to read Conrad's *The Shadow-Line* in his manuscript version, in which there are no section divisions, and then to see how differently the first edition of the novel reads with these divisions included. (There is evidence that Conrad himself was not responsible for introducing the divisions, and the recent scholarly edition of the work published by Cambridge University Press omits them.) Very often such divisions perform the useful function of telling the reader when he or she can pause and put the book down for a bit, and, as it is at these points of time that we think backward over what we have read and forward to what we hope for or expect, such divisions can be very significant.

As I have argued, structure involves thematic elements too. Note how the repetition of thematic elements in Charles Dickens's *Bleak House* helps to structure that work. Just to take one example: Esther Summerson, like her mother Lady Dedlock, has to choose between two suitors: a rich, older, "safe" one and a younger, less wealthy, more "risky" match with more passionate potential. Whereas Lady Dedlock makes what we are led to see as the wrong choice in marrying the older man, Esther—after an initial false decision—makes what is clearly the right decision for her. Now this produces an element of *pattern* in the work which contributes to our sense of its structure, a pattern which blends in with other things in *Bleak House* to produce a satisfying work of art.

Take a different example. In Katherine Mansfield's short story "The Voyage" we have a very simple story: a little girl leaves her father at a New Zealand port and travels by boat with her grandmother to the south island of New Zealand, to her grandparents' home. In the course of the voyage we discover that her mother has died, and the reader comes to understand what Fenella—the girl—has not yet realized: that henceforth she is to be brought up by her grandparents. What is striking about the story is that, whereas images of darkness and cold dominate the opening of the story, these gradually give way to images of light and warmth which (especially the images of light) dominate the close of the story. Now clearly this shift of images contributes to the structure of the story: without actually being told it directly, we realize that Fenella is moving out of an unhappy period of her life into a potentially much happier one. The physical voyage is from one *place* to another, but this is complemented structurally by travel from one *emotional state* to another.

Structure involves ideas and sensations of some sort of pattern: *completion, reiteration, contrast, repetition, complementarity*—all of these and others can be invoked by a work's structure. We should note too that the *frame* of a narrative—what constitutes its outer limits—can contribute importantly to our sense of structure. Consider the narrative framing of the "tale within a tale" of *Heart of Darkness* and *The Turn of the Screw*. Think of the importance of the fact that the events recounted in James Joyce's *Ulysses* and Virginia Woolf's *Mrs Dalloway* take place within twenty-four hours. Note the thematic framing effect of our being told in E.M. Forster's novel *Howards End* that the work is not to be concerned with the very poor, who are "unthinkable." In each case our view of what is "in" the novel is given structure by our sense of what is excluded from it.

Setting

"Setting" is one of those terms about which recent literary critics have tended to feel a little uneasy. Does the term not suggest a perhaps too-simple relationship between characters and action, on the one hand, and the context within which these take place, on the other? Does it not sound rather unsatisfactory to talk about the Nottinghamshire "setting" of D.H. Lawrence's *Sons and Lovers* or the Yorkshire "setting" of *Wuthering Heights*, as if the same actions might conceivably have taken place elsewhere—in Tunbridge Wells or Minnesota? The fact that so many characters in Emily Brontë's novel have names that are also the place-names of towns and villages around her native Haworth suggests a relationship between character and environment too organic, we feel, to be described with the term "setting."

"Setting" may also suggest too neat a parallel between places in a work of fiction and places in the world at large, a parallel that even in the special case of the regional novel is never more than partial. Many modernist novelists present the reader with settings whose unfamiliarity and unwelcoming aspect is frequently generalized or universalized. If all large towns are unwelcoming and dehumanizing, then does it matter which large town one is in? It is surely an essential part of the force of Franz Kafka's *The Trial* (1925) that the setting is not specified in real-world or real-time terms. The point is that in our age the events depicted could take place in many different locations: our time is the time of universal human experiences.

Yet even today it is important to be aware of the context within which the action of a novel takes place—and this does not just mean its geographical setting; social and historical factors are also important. It is just as important to ask why the author has chosen the setting he has chosen when it is generalized (as in the case of *The Trial*) as when it is highly specific (as with, say, Walter Greenwood's *Love on the Dole* [1933]).

To start with, we need to distinguish between realistic and conventional or stylized settings. The famous country house of the classic detective story is obviously a highly *conventional* setting; we are not interested in the particularity of such country houses and their environments—they serve, rather, the function of providing a stylized and familiar setting within which a conventional set of happenings can unfold. Many detective stories actually choose relatively artificial settings that have the function of isolating the characters (or suspects) from the outside world: the closed world of Agatha Christie's *Orient Express* stuck in the snow is a paradigm case.

At the other extreme we can cite highly realistic settings like that of the tuberculosis sanatorium that dominates Thomas Mann's *The Magic Mountain* (1924). Here, however, we need to tread carefully, for although this may be a realistic setting, it is also a very *symbolic* one. It is not hard to see the sanatorium full of sick people as representative of pre–First World War Europe with its sicknesses and fatal illnesses.

Sometimes the choice of a suitable setting helps an author to avoid the need to write about things that he or she is not good at, or interested in, writing about. A setting in the historical past can often help an author to avoid contemporary issues about which he or she feels confused; the setting that E.M. Forster chose for *Howards End* enabled him, as he admitted, to avoid writing about the very poor. Dickens's frequent choice of London as the setting for his novels was convenient in other ways: the mass of concealed relationships, indirect forms of human communication and innumerable secrets to be found in London offered a perfect opportunity to a novelist whose plots contain all of these elements in abundance. (See my comments on the four passages detailing a character's movement through London streets on p. 31.)

Just as there are conventions relating to the description of individual human appearance and the representation of speech (see p. 132 and p. 150), so too descriptions of places and environments are conventionally seen to denote something about the people associated with them. Think of the symbolic force of the descriptions of Wuthering Heights and Thrushcross Grange in *Wuthering Heights*, or the contrast between Mansfield Park and the Portsmouth home in Jane Austen's novel.

A setting can also be a crucial factor in the creation of *mood* or *moral environment*. If we think of *The Great Gatsby*, we can see, I think, how a setting can make an essential contribution to a work's mood. This example reminds us that theme and subject and setting can be inextricably intertwined: you could no more set *The Great Gatsby* in the England of the 1930s than you could set *Love on the Dole* anywhere else.

Remember that there is a difference, in this context, between "mood" and "tone," although these two terms are frequently used in ways that overlap. Correctly speaking, tone involves narrative *attitudes toward* what is recounted and described, while mood is what is created for and in the reader by such things as setting, narrative treatment, and so on. This said, clearly tone impacts upon mood, although it does not determine it. Thus a narrator's frivolous presentation of a tragic story may, for example, shock the reader into a pessimistic mood as he or she takes this as representative of the human capacity to treat the suffering of others lightly.

Theme

"Theme" is a much-used word in the literary criticism of the novel, and a favorite word for use by lecturers and teachers in essay and examination questions: "Discuss the treatment of the theme of evil in *Crime and Punishment*"; "Write about the theme of escape in *Huckleberry Finn*"; "Examine the theme of alienation in *The Castle*"; and so on. A fundamental distinction used in literary criticism is that between the *formal* and the *thematic*. "Sin and Retribution in *Bleak House*" clearly indicates an interest in one of the novel's supposed themes, whereas "The Unreliable Narrator of *The Good Soldier*" promises the reader a more formal or technical reading of the novel in question. In practice, of course, it is hard to write about themes without taking account of formal matters, and although it may be easier to write about formal issues without confronting thematic questions, few studies of the novel are flushed clean of all interest in matters thematic.

Theme and thesis

Some critics find it useful to distinguish between theme and thesis. The simple distinction here is that although both pose questions, a thesis also suggests or argues for answers. A theme, in contrast, can involve establishing a set of issues, problems, or questions without any attempt to provide a rationale or answer to satisfy the demands these make of the reader. Traditionally, novels dominated by a thesis have been valued less highly than those in which certain themes are raised or treated: in contrast to earlier generations of readers perhaps, some recent critics have preferred our novels not to be overtly didactic, to be open-ended rather than pointed toward solutions at which the author has already arrived.

One problem with distinguishing between theme and thesis is that for some commentators "theme" is something of an umbrella concept and includes what we have just termed "thesis." If we define theme in the former, weaker sense (distinguishing it from thesis), then we will not be surprised to discover that a large and complex novel can have a range of varied themes attributed to it. Charles Dickens's *Bleak House*, for instance, has been variously interpreted as containing the themes of "parental responsibility," "the heartlessness of the law," "the evil of 'causes,'" "the destructiveness of choosing money and position rather than love," "the centrality of writing to Victorian society," and many more. It needs to be remembered that a complex novel is likely to be susceptible to analysis in terms of numerous different—perhaps interlocking—themes.

Overt and covert themes

A theme may be overt or covert. That is to say it can be either consciously intended and indicated as such by the author or, alternatively, discovered by the reader/critic as an element in the novel of which perhaps even the author was unaware. (If we retain the distinction between theme and thesis, then it will be understood that a thesis is much more likely to be consciously intended than a theme.) Thus although we can be pretty certain that Saul Bellow had the *carpe diem* theme ("Live today, while you can") consciously in mind in his novella *Seize the Day* (1956)—because the title makes this much clear—we cannot be so sure that Alan Sillitoe had the theme of working-class socialization equally in mind with regard to the writing of his *Saturday Night and Sunday Morning* (1958). (We should also bear in mind the possibility that Bellow recognized his theme and chose his title after he had completed his story.)

Symbol and image

Symbol

In E.M. Forster's *Howards End* the motor-car plays an important role. "Not surprising," someone might comment, "the car had not been around for very long at the time that the novel was written, and Forster was merely incorporating a piece of contemporary reality into his novel for the purpose of increased verisimilitude."

Few readers of the work would find this an adequate response. The motor-car in *Howards End* clearly *stands for* or *represents* something; it is not merely a means of transport but a *symbol* in the novel. By this we mean that it carries with it various ideas, associations, forms of significance that in ordinary life it might not have in people's minds: "innovation and the destruction of tradition"; "the mechanical as against the organic"; "unfeeling social change"; "violence and death"; "the selfish pursuit of personal comfort by the rich"; and so on.

Notice that I have not suggested that the car in *Howards End* stands for just one, fixed thing; it is characteristic of symbols that they do not have a simple one-to-one relationship with what they stand for or suggest. In this respect a symbol can clearly be distinguished from an *allegory*, the secondary meaning of which is usually single and distinct. Thus the allegorical meaning of John Bunyan's *Pilgrim's Progress* (1676) is that life as a Christian brings problems comparable to those experienced by the pilgrim. In contrast to such a one-to-one relationship, the lighthouse in Virginia Woolf's *To the Lighthouse* (1927) has obvious symbolic force in the novel, but it would be an unwise critic who stated definitively the one thing that it stood for. Perhaps the lighthouse does stand for the unfulfilled dreams of youth, or masculine aggressiveness—but part of its power comes from its multiple suggestiveness and indirect significance. Note that Forster's car and Woolf's lighthouse can be said to exist on two planes: on the realistic level they are what they are in the real world—a car and a lighthouse—while on the symbolic level they have meanings that cars and lighthouses do not necessarily have outside of fiction.

In James Joyce's story "The Dead," we feel that the repeated references to snow have a symbolic force. This is partly because snow is referred to so repetitively and suggestively that the reader of the story cannot but feel that there is something significant in the function that it performs in the story. It is also, of course, because we naturally associate snow with some things rather than others—especially in Ireland, where extensive falls of snow are relatively rare. Put briefly, we can suggest that in "The Dead" snow stands for or suggests *death*: it is cold, it covers the graveyard, it affects the whole country just as death comes to us all, and so on. Now the justification for this interpretation is partly that snow is naturally associated with death, because it is cold like a dead body and because people lost in snow die. Moreover in

"The Dead" Joyce draws attention to certain of these qualities and associates them with other references in the story (not least with its title) so as to make these associations clear. If we think of the death of Gerald in the snow in D.H. Lawrence's *Women in Love* (1920), we will see, I think, that both Joyce and Lawrence are able to incorporate a public symbol into the private or internal world of meaning in their respective fictional works.

On occasions a writer will create a symbol that has the meaning and significance that it does have only in the context of one particular work. If we think of a green light, for instance, the natural symbolic associations that it has for most of us today are positive: advance, road clear, eco-friendliness—all of those extensions of meaning that have accrued from the greenness of nature and from our use of green lights in traffic regulation systems. It is arguable that none of these references or associations is active in our response to the repeated mention of the green light that marks out the quay by Daisy's house for Gatsby in Scott Fitzgerald's *The Great Gatsby*. What Fitzgerald succeeds in doing in this novel is to create a private symbol, something that has meaning only within the world of the novel.

A synonymous set of terms for public and private symbols is *motivated* and *unmotivated* symbols. In practice, of course, it is hard to find a completely public or a completely private symbol. I suggested, for example, that Forster's use of the motor-car in *Howards End* developed associations that "motor-car" might not have in people's minds prior to their reading the novel. However, for some people the motor-car *might* have had these associations, and the symbolic force that the motor-car has in *Howards End* is, as it were, a potential force already implicit in the motor-car as it was experienced in Edwardian England. (Think of the role played by the motor-car in a work of fiction that is nearly contemporary to Forster's: Kenneth Grahame's *The Wind in the Willows* [1908]; Messrs Toad and Wilcox may belong to very different fictional worlds but they do have certain qualities in common.)

Actions and settings can also be possessed of symbolic force. When Hester in Nathaniel Hawthorne's *The Scarlet Letter* (1850) undoes her hair and lets it fall free, the action has an enormous symbolic charge: in a novel so concerned with repression and concealment it suggests a breaking of bonds, a triumph of natural and healthy impulse over artificial and corrupt restraint. Similarly, innumerable novels also make use of another symbolic potentiality involved in this scene in *The Scarlet Letter*: the contrast between indoors (representing society, the artificial, restraint) and outdoors—especially in a wild or undomesticated setting (representing pre-social impulses, the natural, the outpouring of feeling). Think of the role performed by windows as the dividing line between these two sets of associations in both Brontë's *Wuthering Heights* and Joyce's "The Dead."

Image

I referred earlier to Katherine Mansfield's short story "The Voyage," and commented upon the movement from dark and cold references at the start of the story to warm and—particularly—light images at the end. Let me quote a little from the close of the story:

> On the table a white cat, that had been folded up like a camel, rose, stretched itself, yawned, and then sprang on to the tips of its toes. Fenella buried one cold little hand in the white, warm fur, and smiled timidly while she stroked and listened to grandma's gentle voice and the rolling tones of grandpa.
>
> A door creaked. "Come in, dear." The old woman beckoned, Fenella followed. There, lying to one side of an immense bed, lay grandpa. Just his head with a white tuft, and his rosy face and long silver beard showed over the quilt. (Mansfield 1951, 183)

You will notice the recurrence of words that connote light and warmth here ("white," "warm," "silver," "rosy"). These I would dub images rather than symbols. The distinction is not an easy one to explain, and there are differences of usage that complicate matters, but the following points are probably worth remembering.

- Images are usually characterized by their evocation of concrete qualities rather than abstract meanings; they normally have a more sensuous quality than symbols—calling the taste, smell, feel, sound, or visual image of the referred-to object sharply to mind.
- Symbols, in contrast, because they stand for something other than themselves, bring to mind not so much their own concrete qualities but more the idea or abstraction that is associated with them.

Thus in the extract from Katherine Mansfield the feel of the cat's fur, its whiteness, and warmth are brought sharply to our minds in *themselves*—we do not automatically wonder what they "stand for" (note how this tactile sense is encouraged by the contrast with Fenella's cold hand). We do not experience sharp sensory responses to Gatsby's green light or Woolf's lighthouse: it is what these stand for or call to mind *apart from* themselves that is important. If we think of a continuum stretching from the sensuous to the intellectual, we can say that images are located toward the sensuous end while symbols are located toward the intellectual end. With Joyce's snow and Forster's motor-car we may pause: in these cases we think both of what they stand for and of their individual sensory qualities. In these two cases, therefore, we may guess that the references have an imagistic function alongside their primary symbolic purpose.

This is not to say that images never contribute to thematic elements in a work. Although it is true that an image is distinguished by its concrete qualities in an immediate sense, it sets up waves of association in the mind that have other than a purely concrete significance. Thus, as I have already suggested, the images in Mansfield's "The Voyage" contribute importantly to our sense of the multileveled nature of Fenella's voyage, away from unhappiness and suffering and cold to warmth and the promise of happiness.

Speech and dialogue

As modern readers we are fortunate in that we live in an age of recording devices. Although the earliest of these devices was developed in the mid-nineteenth century, it is only really with the portable tape recorder that the means to record ordinary, unrehearsed and unscripted conversations became available to the general public (rather than those interested in espionage!). Since the closing decades of the twentieth century, then, we have been able to study normal, unselfconscious conversation in a way that our ancestors could not—and can thereby discover that nobody actually talks quite as people are portrayed as talking in novels. The conventions that govern the speech that is represented in novels cover technical matters such as the syntax of the sentences that make up separate utterances. They also govern matters such as the sort of things that can be talked about and the sort of language that can be used in such discussions—which have, of course, a significant ideological dimension. There is an amusing exemplification of this point in Josef Skvorecky's novel *The Engineer of Human Souls* (first published in Czech in 1977), in which a character, Mrs Santner, tries to defend the "bad" language used in a novel by referring to how people in real life would actually speak if in the same circumstances as the novel-character in question:

> "You have to read it in context," she explains. "After all, those words are spoken by an anti-Nazi revolutionary who's afraid the Gestapo will catch him. When people are afraid, they use strong language. It's a well-known phenomenon."

Her defence is too scholarly for Mr Senka. "But this is a book, madame," he cries. "A book."

This time it is Mrs Santner's turn not to understand. For her the word "book" has none of the sanctimonious overtones it has for Mr Senka, for whom a book is a household object to be taken up only on very special occasions. Mrs Santner's husband leans over her shoulder and whispers, "Now, Betty, don't let's get into an argument," but this only goads her on.

"I can't help it. In context, language like that has a valid function. That's the way people actually talk in situations like that."

"But they don't talk like that in *books*."

Each is partly right, according to his experience. (Skvorecky 1985, 158–9)

This is the sort of conflict toward which the realist imperative almost inevitably impels novelists and their readers. We want the novel to give us our recognizable, everyday world, warts and all: but that world includes taboos, prescriptions, repressions to which the novel is not immune.

In his book *Art and Illusion* (1960), Ernst Gombrich has explored at length the paradox that the world does not look like a picture, but a picture can look like the world. In like manner, we do not talk like people in books, but the dialogues in books seem to us to be like the conversations we have in real life. People in novels tend, unlike real people, to talk in complete sentences, with few indicated hesitations, repetitions, mistakes of grammar, "ums" and "ers," and so on. As Skvorecky's narrator perceptively notes, both Mr and Mrs Santner are partly right. Why is this? The answer has to be that novelists follow conventions in the representation of speech and dialogue with which we are so familiar that we are unaware of any conventionality. (Just as individuals from Britain or the United States are unaware that they follow conventions governing the nodding and the shaking of heads to mean "yes" and "no"—until they travel to a country like Turkey or Bulgaria, where these conventions are reversed.)

The novelist has to convey exclusively in words what in ordinary conversation we convey by words, tone of voice, hesitations, facial expression, gesture, bodily posture, and by other means. Learning how to do so was not accomplished overnight, and we can note a great difference between the way novelists in most of the eighteenth century represented dialogue and the way later novelists have done so. If, for example, you open Henry Fielding's novel *Joseph Andrews* (1742) at Chapter 5, which is the chapter directly parodying Richardson's *Pamela* in which Lady Booby attempts to seduce her servant Joseph much as Mr B— in Richardson's novel had attempted to seduce Pamela, then you will notice something odd about the layout of the page. Although conversation takes place all through this short chapter, the prose is set out in one continuous unparagraphed stream. Thus Fielding has to keep including "tag-phrases" such as "he said" and "she replied." The result is not just that reading the chapter is rather hard work, but that the guiding presence of the narrator keeps intruding: we have narrative tag-phrases in addition to the actual words spoken by the characters.

By the time Jane Austen's *Pride and Prejudice* is published, a little over half a century later, we see a very different picture. Dialogue is presented in a recognizably modern form, with paragraph breaks indicating a change of speaker. Here the narrator may intrude or remain hidden at will. If necessary the characters can be left to speak for themselves with no interruption from anyone. This certainly increases the *dramatic* effectiveness of scenes involving dialogue; we feel that we are actually witnessing conversations taking place rather than being instructed by an intrusive stage-manager who keeps pointing out what we have to notice. Take the conversation between Mr Bennet and his wife that opens *Pride and Prejudice*:

> "My dear Mr Bennet," said his lady to him one day, "have you heard that Netherfield Park is let at last?"
>
> Mr Bennet replied that he had not.
>
> "But it is," returned she; "for Mrs Long has just been here, and she told me all about it."
>
> Mr Bennet made no answer.
>
> "Do not you want to know who has taken it?" cried his wife impatiently.
>
> "You want to tell me, and I have no objection to hearing it."
>
> This was invitation enough.

Note how Jane Austen wrings so much significance out of her use of direct and indirect speech here. "Mr Bennet replied that he had not" must be one of the most economically sarcastic lines in English literature: the shift to indirect speech somehow conjures up Mr Bennet's weary, long-suffering response to his wife's importuning. Even so, our sense of a narrator who shares Mr Bennet's weariness does not intrude on our impression that we are witnessing a real conversation. We are aware of the presence of an ironically observing narrator, but she is in the background with as it were a faint smile on her face. In the foreground are Mr and Mrs Bennet, who we observe directly.

Representing speech or reproducing speech

Recent narrative theorists have pointed out that the writer of fiction has at his or her disposal a range of more or less distanced means whereby characters' speech can be rendered. In her *Narrative Fiction: Contemporary Poetics*, Shlomith Rimmon-Kenan reproduces a useful seven-element model of the different ways in which speech may be presented in fiction.

At one extreme we have what she calls *diegetic summary* (in her usage "diegetic" means loosely "of or within the story"). This is where the reader is given the "bare report that a speech act has occurred, without any specification of what was said or how it was said." Second there is *summary, less purely diegetic*, which "to some degree represents, not merely mentions, a speech event in that it names the topics of conversation." Third is *indirect content paraphrase* (or: *indirect discourse*), "a paraphrase of the content of the speech event, ignoring the style or form of the supposed 'original' utterance." Fourth is *indirect discourse, mimetic to some degree*, which is a "form of indirect discourse which creates the illusion of 'preserving' or 'reproducing' aspects of the style of an utterance." Fifth comes *Free Indirect Discourse*, which I have already discussed on p. 122 (and which, we should remember, can be used to represent more than just speech). Sixth is *direct discourse*, in which the actual words spoken are "quoted," although, as Rimmon-Kenan points out, always with some degree of stylization. Finally there is *free direct discourse*, which is "direct discourse shorn of its conventional orthographic cues," a good example of which would be first-person interior monologue.

If these descriptions are hard to follow, the examples provided by Rimmon-Kenan may make the distinctions easier to comprehend. All are taken from John Dos Passos's trilogy *U.S.A.* (1938):

1. When Charley got a little gin inside him he started telling war yarns for the first time in his life.
2. He stayed late in the evening telling them about miraculous conversions of unbelievers, extreme unction on the firing line, a vision of the young Christ he'd seen walking among the wounded in a dressing station during a gas attack.
3. The waiter told him that Carranza's troops had lost Torréon and that Villa and Zapata were closing in on the Federal District.
4. When they came out Charley said by heck he thought he wanted to go up to Canada and enlist and go over and see the Great War.
5. Why the hell shouldn't they know, weren't they better off'n her and out to see the goddam town and he'd better come along.
6. Fred Summers said, "Fellers, this war's the most gigantic cockeyed graft of the century and me for it and the cross red nurses."
7. Fainy's head suddenly got very light. Bright boy, that's me, ambition and literary taste … Gee, I must finish *Looking Backward* … and jez, I like

reading fine, an' I could run a linotype or set up print if anybody'd let me. Fifteen bucks a week … pretty soft, ten dollars' raise.

(Rimmon-Kenan 1983, 109–10; examples taken from
McHale 1978, 249–87)

In one sense we are back to life and pattern here. At the number 7 end of the continuum, we have maximum life, and we are close to the actuality of a character's living use of language. At the number 1 end, we have at least maximum potentiality for pattern: the novelist can choose what lessons to draw, what moral to underline, as the character's speech is summarized. Here the novelist's or the narrator's view of the character predominates over the character's actual speech. You can probably think of many other reasons why a novelist may or may not wish to render a given character's use of slang, colloquialism, or dialect. These evoke ways of life, values, cultural specifics which may or may not be what the novelist wants to bring to mind at a given stage of a narrative.

As Mikhail Bakhtin has pointed out, a voice is not just a "medium" or a channel of communication; it involves complex ideological elements as well. Take the following passage from Lewis Grassic Gibbon's *Grey Granite* (1934), the final part of the trilogy *A Scots Quair*. Ewan Tavendale is talking to a number of other apprentices, and one of them, Norman, reveals that, while he can never be bothered to go to a trades-union meeting, his father has a more positive attitude:

> And he looked a bit shamed, *He's Labour, you see.*
>
> Tavendale said *There are lots of chaps that, my stepfather was,* and you all cheered up, sitting on buckets in the furnace room, a slack hour, and having a bit of a jaw, you were none of you Labour and knew nothing about politics, but all of you had thought that the Bulgars of toffs were aye Tory or Liberal or this National dirt. And somehow when a chap knew another had a father who'd been Labour you could speak to him plainer, like, say what you thought, not that you thought much, you wanted a job when apprenticeship was over and a decent bit time and maybe now and then a spare bob or so to take your quean to the Talkies—och, you spoke a lot of stite like the others did, about the queans that you'd like to lie with, and the booze you'd drink, what a devil you were, but if you got half a chance what you wanted was marriage and a house and a wife and a lum of your own. (Gibbon 1986, 389–90)

If we are not Scottish, then we may be sent to a specialist dictionary to discover the meaning of some of the dialect terms in the passage, but most of us can probably guess at their meaning without too much difficulty, and

British readers will probably work out that "Bulgar" is a euphemism for "Bugger"—a term that Gibbon's publisher would certainly have bridled at in 1934.

Beyond vocabulary, the language of this passage is crucial to certain other effects. We can say that it mimics the speech and thought patterns of a Scottish working man of the period, especially one talking among a group of his peers. The use of "you" is especially interesting. On the one hand, it represents an accurate piece of observation on Gibbon's part; in Britain people of this background will use "you" as a generalizer where a person from a middle-class background would use "one" (as Virginia Woolf does throughout her writing, and the British royal family do throughout their speech). On the other hand, it involves the reader in a process of collective sharing of attitudes: we feel as we read that we are part of the group that is thinking out its beliefs; it is as if these beliefs come out of a group to which we belong. We thus experience the ideology of the group from the inside while having it displayed in a manner that allows us to look at it more objectively. The natural form of the work-group conversation conceals what is actually quite an unnatural process—whereby a group is made to speak those taken-for-granted items of ideological positioning that, just because they *are* taken for granted, are normally not spoken. Virginia Woolf does something rather similar in *The Waves*, although revealingly the statements in this work are more individual and even individualistic; the class with which she is concerned lacks the collective voice and consciousness that Gibbon wishes to display. (Compare my comments on p. 249 about the ways in which in Ngũgĩ wa Thiong'o's *Weep Not Child* the narrative has to combine the consciousness of a character and the collective consciousness of a people.)

There is, in other words, a sort of sleight of hand in the above passage. Gibbon is actually in one sense telling us something about the working class from a vantage point outside of its typical self-knowledge. Because he dramatizes this telling in the form of a discourse that belongs to the class, however, the reader is given the impression that as we experience the ideology with the collectivity, so too we are simultaneously detached from it and allowed to look at it through its members' self-aware analysis of themselves. (One of the things that is being mimicked here is the style of a working-class anecdote. It is as if the reader is being addressed in an intimate way by the collective voice that is thus personified through the language that it speaks.) Gibbon could not have achieved such a complicated effect without having borrowed the language and habits of expression of the group, even if he uses these in a way that members of the group would not have done.

Topics for discussion

- Do you prefer a novel to be told by an "anonymous voice" or an identified character? Why?

- Take one or more novels you know, and imagine them as told in different ways by different narrators. Discuss the gains and losses of such changes.

- Why on earth should a novelist choose to use an unreliable narrator?

- Find examples of "flat" and "round" characters. Discuss their use.

- Find examples of "showing" and "telling." Is showing always preferable?

- "The essence of telling a story is to keep some information from the reader." Is it? Explain why.

- List the themes of a favorite novel. Are you sure that they were all intended by the novelist? Does it matter?

- Find examples of symbols and images in a work of fiction. How do they differ?

6

Studying the Novel

Preview

This chapter deals with:

- Studying the novel in the digital age
- Reading, responding, and note-taking
- Learning how to choose critics; how to assess the significance of their affiliations
- Using libraries and using computers
- Writing essays: analyzing topics, planning your response
- Preparing for examinations and taking them

Studying the novel in the digital age

The first edition of this book was published in 1985, before the internet existed, and before I had ever used a computer. My students, like me, read fiction and criticism from the printed page. They generally wrote their essays by hand, although some endeared themselves to their teachers by producing legible essays on a typewriter—but because typewriters are noisy, these were generally banned from public spaces such as in libraries. If the local library did not possess a book or subscribe to a particular journal, an inter-library loan request had to be made, and it could take many weeks before the physical copy was available.

Today, a student may quite possibly never touch a printed page when studying a specific novel and writing an essay about it. The digital age has brought with it the most profound revolution in reading and writing habits since the printing press, and the computer and the internet now offer to students of literature tools that really were beyond my wildest dreams in 1985. The MLA Commons webpage "Literary Studies in the Digital Age" (<https://dlsanthology.commons.mla.org/>) is a good place to start if you want to get a sense of what the computer and the internet can provide for the student of literature. The sub-section "Textual Analysis" by David L. Hoover is particularly relevant to the topics discussed in the present chapter, and is strongly recommended.

The tools offered to the student of literature by computers and the internet, to simplify, can be listed as follows:

- Finding texts
- Accessing texts
- Circulating texts
- Analyzing texts
- Discussing texts

I start with "finding texts," because not only does the internet offer sophisticated search engines to locate critical texts, it also offers students an easy way to find the least expensive—or indeed free—copies of primary texts. This is a possibility that should be used with great care. On the one hand, if you can find a used copy of the edition of a novel that your lecturer recommends for a fraction of the new price, by searching second-hand bookstores through AbeBooks (<www.abebooks.com>) or ViaLibri (<www.vialibri.net>), then do so (but check that the very cheap copy you are offered is not a different edition from the one recommended, and that it is not full of comments from previous readers). But don't just find the cheapest copy available irrespective of date or edition—and certainly don't just download a free copy because it is free. Why? Because the text may be unreliable—either taken from an unreliable edition or badly scanned from a paper copy, and because it will not contain the helpful introduction and invaluable notes that the edition your lecturer has chosen will probably contain. Many free electronic texts of novels have sections missing, a surprising number reproduce censored versions, and some are inaccurate in other ways (see p. 201 for my comments on the different editions of English translations of Knut Hamsun's novel *Hunger* that are available online and in print).

However, if a free electronic copy of a novel is available, then it is still worth downloading it even if you read the text in a more reliable edition, as the electronic text can be searched and analyzed in ways that a printed text cannot. I will say more on this below.

I will have more to say on the other possibilities given in the bulleted list above later on in this chapter, but I want now to turn to a key question for students of the novel: how do you combine the functions of reader and critic?

Reading, responding, criticizing

Whether you are reading a printed version of a novel or you are reading it on a Kindle or a tablet, given that studying a novel involves being conscious of many of those aspects of a work that operate on the "common reader" without their being conscious of the fact, there is always an element of tension and even incompatibility between the activities of reading for pleasure and reading for study. Moreover, because novels often invite readers to "lose themselves" in the story, maintaining an attitude of distanced observation and making note of formal and technical issues can involve reading against the grain of habit. On the other hand, most students of fiction find that, after a period of awkwardness, practice in analyzing technical issues can lead to an enrichment of their reading pleasures. Being made aware of, for example, complex shifts in the manipulation of perspective and voice in a novel can increase a reader's appreciation of a writer's skill without lessening those pleasures experienced by the common reader.

We may read a shortish novel in one sitting, while anything up to twenty or more sessions will be required for a long and complex novel such as Tolstoy's *War and Peace*. For those readers who read Victorian novels when they were first published in serial form, there was no choice: they *had* to stop and wait at certain stages in their reading. When we pause in our reading of a novel we go over what we have read and we think forward to what we guess will happen or what we would like to happen. Frequently, we will imagine ourselves in situations described in the novel; perhaps we will hold imaginary conversations with characters, or wonder what we might have done in their positions.

In other words, expectation, surprise, disappointment, foreboding, tension, suspense, imagination, and fantasy all form part of our reading of a novel. To read a novel is to be involved in a *cumulative process*.

The problem which this raises for the study of the novel is that there are certain reader-experiences, and certain events in the novel, which lodge far more permanently in the mind than do others. Indeed, it is part of the way that a novel works upon us—part of its power as a source of enjoyment—that some aspects of our reading experience should fade more quickly than others. If it is some time since you read *Wuthering Heights*, then try this test on yourself: at what stage in the novel does the older Catherine die? I suspect that unless you are an unusually retentive and conscientious reader you are likely to place this event far later in the novel than it actually occurs.

The issue is complicated by the fact that we often read a novel more than once. On a subsequent reading, we are normally less preoccupied with "what happens next" and so are able to read more carefully and notice many details that slipped our attention on first reading. To retain such details we need to take notes. Taking notes is actually a skilled operation and one that requires practice. It takes time to develop one's skill to the point at which it does not interfere with pleasurable reading.

How to take notes

Printed books

Notes can be written either in the novel itself or in a separate notebook. The advantage of the former method is that it does not disturb one's reading too much; the disadvantages are that it spoils a book, it affects one's second reading, there is not always sufficient room for notes on the page, and *retrieval* of the notes afterwards for purposes of study is difficult. One way round these problems is to write very brief notes in pencil in a novel as you are reading, and then to copy these up and expand them in a separate notebook or electronic folder later on. This also allows you to copy out brief extracts from the novel which strike you as important, and it means that you file for future reference only notes about which you have thought a second time after having finished reading the novel. Pencil marks can be erased once they have served their purpose.

If something in the text strikes you as important or significant but you do not want to puzzle over why, lest you break your train of thought, then mark or underline the passage in question, note the page reference on the inside back cover of the book, and come back to ponder the point once you have finished the novel. If you have both a printed and an electronic copy of a text, you can copy and paste extracts from the latter into your notes—but check that they are identical to the text of your printed copy.

Electronic texts

Different types of electronic text have their own advantages and disadvantages when it comes to taking notes. A text file read on a tablet or computer offers easy copy-and-paste options, so that extracts can be saved on a separate file along with your own comments. A text saved as a word-processing file can be annotated (using Word's Comment or Highlighter functions, for example). PDF files of texts have the advantage that they may reproduce the pagination of a printed text, which is useful if you want to reference passages quoted, and most modern word-processing programs have inbuilt OCR (optical character recognition) functions that will allow you to copy and paste text into a word-processing program. But even though OCR programs and functions are much more reliable than they were a decade ago, they still make mistakes, especially with older printed texts.

Passages in texts read on newer versions of the Kindle can be copied and pasted into a word-processing file, but the process is far from quick or straightforward, although with practice you will become more comfortable with it. The same is true of writing annotations on a Kindle text, although highlighting is straightforward. However, typing annotations on a reader such as a Kindle is much more fiddly than on a computer (or with pencil on a book). For academic work, a more serious problem with such devices is that unless you are using them to read PDF files that reproduce a printed text, they do not provide page numbers that can be used to reference specific passages. It is not at time of writing possible to copy and paste from a PDF file on a Kindle.

Annotations made on a tablet or a computer can be backed up to a flash drive or cloud storage facility, and those made on a Kindle can be backed up on Amazon. Such backups add a level of security that paper books cannot provide. Back in 1987, an IT consultant told me, "Remember that there are two sorts of hard drive: those that have failed, and those that will fail." Programs such as Dropbox offer free cloud storage up to a certain limit: even if the dog eats your essay, the unconsumed version will be safe on the cloud. When I had to copy files to a diskette or a flash drive, I often did not bother, but copying to Dropbox is so easy that now I always save files there when I take a break from the keyboard.

There are various e-book readers available. One I have found very useful is Calibre, "a free and open source e-book library management application" that you can download from <http://calibre-ebook.com/>. Not only does it allow you to read e-books published in a variety of formats on a computer or a tablet, but it also has advanced options for converting from one format to another. Remember that some conversions may go against the agreement you clicked when you downloaded a file, and some formats incorporate blocking mechanisms that prevent such conversions.

What to note

Learning what is of significance in a novel, and in your response to it, is a matter of practice. Teachers and lecturers often ask for analyses of selected passages from novels, and undertaking such analyses is an excellent way of sharpening your eye for important detail in the reading of fiction. Such close reading is, however, only part of what constitutes a full critical reading of a novel. In addition to responding to significant detail in the prose of a work of fiction, you need also to be able to perceive larger patterns and movements in the work as a whole, as well as connections to other works. The list that follows is intended to serve a double purpose. On the one hand, I hope that it will be useful to work from when you are engaged in the analysis of a particular passage from a novel or a short story. In addition, however, I hope that its perusal will serve as a reminder of the sort of points that can be noted in the process of reading or rereading a work of fiction. The golden rule here is: if in doubt, then make a note.

Checklist

Narrative technique All information relating to the manipulation of narrative in the work: clues about the values or personality of the narrator; voice and perspective; what the narrator does *not* know; changes of narrator or narrative perspective; narrative intrusion or comment. "Telling" and "showing."

Story and plot Sketch out what happens (i) in chronological order and (ii) as it is told. What differences are there? What is added, missed out, repeated? If more than one narrator is involved, who tells us what?

Action Any information that advances the plot, gives significant new developments in human relationships or new events.

Tone Is it familiar or formal, intimate or impersonal? Who (if anyone) is apparently being addressed? Does the vocabulary or syntax suggest a particular style of delivery? Does the tone vary over time, or from narrator to narrator?

Characterization Information about how we learn about characters; any indication that characters are changing or developing; significant new information about a character; views as to what the writer is trying to achieve in the presentation of character.

Speech and dialogue Use of direct, indirect, or Free Indirect Discourse. Do characters speak for themselves or does the narrator intrude, comment, or direct? Is the dialogue realistic or conventional? What functions does it perform? (Development of character, of plot, introduction of dramatic element, discussion of theme[s].)

Thoughts/mental processes Do we "get inside characters' heads?" If so, which heads, and how? Does a narrator have full, or only partial, access to a character's inner self?

Dramatic involvement Is the reader drawn into events as they happen, or rather encouraged to observe them dispassionately? How is this achieved? (Manipulation of distance.)

Setting and description What is significant about where the action takes place, and about descriptions of people and places? Do shifts of place correlate with other changes in characters?

Symbol or image Patterns of symbolism, repeated images. Do symbols/images relate to others used elsewhere in the work?

Theme(s) Any development of themes dealt with elsewhere in the work; introduction of new thematic elements. Moral problems/issues raised for the characters or for the reader.

Your own response Strong personal preferences/responses the work evokes in you—or dislikes/disapproval; strong identification with a character—or the opposite; tension, desire to know what happens; particular expectations (especially at the end of chapters/sections, or when a mystery or problem is presented). Any experience of bafflement or surprise; and points where you feel you disagree with or react against a narrative opinion (or the opinion of a character).

Note that all of the above relate to a single work of fiction and your responses to it. An additional level of commentary and analysis comes when and if you compare or contrast this work to others—either by the same author or by different authors. See below (p. 220) for more discussion of this.

Using critics

In the fifth edition of this book, I opened this sub-section as follows: "A glance at the library shelves may convince you that you will never even scratch the surface of what might be read: even for a single major novelist it seems that a good library can provide weeks or even months of reading. How should you proceed?" In the decade since I wrote those words, the digital revolution has continued to accelerate. Student essays today frequently contain only references to material accessed electronically, and none to material taken from a book or journal pulled off the library shelf ("What's a library?," as one of my students joked). So that the problem my opening sentence confronted has become even more acute for the poor student. How are you to select what to read from the enormous amount of material available?

The first thing to do is to heed the advice of your lecturers. Syllabuses and booklists generally contain advice on "secondary reading," and this advice is based upon your lecturers' knowledge of the set texts and of your needs and capacities. Lecturers rarely expect you just to plough through everything on such a list: you have to be selective. Remember that it is possible to talk to even busy lecturers, and to ask them about the secondary reading that they have (and have not) recommended. Explain what your interests are, what essay you want to write, and ask for suggestions.

Any good academic library should subscribe to certain journals that are particularly concerned with the novel. Titles such as *Novel: A Forum on Fiction* or *Eighteenth-century Fiction* speak for themselves. You will probably find very few of these on shelves nowadays, as it is more and more common for libraries to subscribe to electronic, rather than paper, editions of periodicals. Generally speaking, far more journals are available online in a typical university library than used to be available in printed versions, although on the negative side, academic libraries in the humanities today buy fewer and fewer books. Many electronic journal subscriptions allow you to download articles, and it is also possible legally to download other articles that are "open access" (see below). Of course, many important essays on the novel are published in periodicals with a less focused concern, and here electronic searches (again, see below) can be invaluable.

If you are not looking for help with a particular essay, but feel that you want to read some criticism on a novel or a novelist, then again it will probably be worth spending a bit of time planning. Remember that different "secondary works" will be concerned with very different aspects of a writer or a text. In Chapter 8, you will find a discussion of critical approaches to fiction, and this should help you to categorize the books and articles on your library shelves in a general way. A biography of Henry James might help you with material for your essay on *The Turn of the Screw*, but this material is likely to be very different from a recent psychoanalytic reading of James's novella, and both will differ from a New Critical essay on the tale written in the 1950s.

If you look at an edition of a novel published in a student edition by a respected publisher, you will note that normally the text of the novel comes right at the beginning of the book, preceded only in certain series by a brief note on the text. Material on "backgrounds," contemporary responses, critical essays and debates—all these follow the text of the novel. This order is chosen because almost every authority recommends that a relatively open-minded reading of the actual text should precede the reading of biographical, contextual, or critical material. My strong advice, then, is that you divide your search for secondary works up into two stages, following your reading of the "primary text"—the literary work itself.

So, you have read the novel. What next? *Stage 1* of your search for secondary material should involve two things: first, a listing of all the questions that your reading of the novel has raised, and, second, a general survey of the matters discussed and debated by critics. If, as I have recommended, you have taken notes while reading the novel, you should have a basis for constructing a list of issues arising from your own reading, especially those concerned with *problems* or *puzzles*—questions that you want answers to. Here, for example, are the issues about which I felt I wanted to read more when I had finished a first reading of Ford Madox Ford's novel *The Good Soldier* (1915). The points are adapted from notes I found scribbled in my copy of the work, and are listed in the order in which I found them.

- The narrator Dowell: how much are his shortcomings recognized or shared by Ford? How much does Ford expect the reader to be critical of him and his values (his leading the life of the idle rich), his violence (two physical assaults on others), his report (that "This is the saddest story I have ever heard")?
- Ditto the characters: I am not positively inclined toward any of them. Is that a comment on me, or is Ford writing a sort of social satire that requires the reader to be distanced from the characters being satirized?
- Religion: clearly crucial for certain characters (Catholicism and Protestantism). Is the reader free to situate him- or herself with regard

to religious/spiritual issues, or does the novel adopt a standpoint and impose this on the reader?

- Novel published at the start of the First World War. Easy to see it in terms of Ford's portrayal of a way of life that is now threatened or destroyed—but is this the effect of hindsight?
- Lots of references to "hearts"—thematic importance?
- American/English contrasts: Ford writing in the shadow of Henry James?

Now you may well not have read Ford's novel, but even so I think that you should be able to recognize that the issues raised for me by a first reading of this novel are of very different *sorts*. Some are what we can term *textual* or *interpretative*—for example, the issue of "hearts." In this case, I would be likely to receive help from more interpretative or analytical studies of the novel that pay detailed attention to elements in it that may well have thematic or symbolic significance (see the previous chapter).

My puzzlement concerning Ford's narrator is also in part a textual matter, but we can term it as much *technical* as thematic, and a study of Ford's *narrative technique* is likely to be of use to me here.

So far as the issue of religion is concerned, a good biography of Ford such as Max Saunders's *Ford Madox Ford: A Dual Life* (1996) helps to establish what Ford's own religious position was when he wrote the novel. A good biography may also help to fix Ford's attitude to the lives of the idle rich, and it may tell me something of the effect of the war on the novel's composition, although again it may not answer all the questions raised for the reader by these matters. (In Chapter 8, you can read about both the benefits and the problems associated with using biographical information to illuminate a literary work; see p. 227.)

Biographical information can be supplemented and often modified by more interpretative or analytical studies of a work that attempt to isolate themes and patterns of meaning. Thematic studies of *The Good Soldier* are thus likely to have much to say about the importance of religion in the novel—and about the significance of the fact that the novel defines characters not just in terms of their religion but also in terms of their nationality, their wealth, and their cultural traditions.

If you look at a modern scholarly edition of *The Good Soldier*, such as the Norton Critical Edition edited by Martin Stannard (1995), you will find, in addition to the text of the novel and commentary on textual issues, sections containing contemporary reviews of the work, a long section on literary impressionism, and a section containing biographical and critical commentary. My questions concerning the narrator and Ford's narrative are the easiest to find answers to: other readers of the novel have needed to investigate Ford's use of—and attitude toward—Dowell, and their discussion helps me to explore this matter. I also find discussion of the issue of "hearts," and some concern with issues of religion—although not as much as I feel the need for.

Surveying relevant criticism

Let us leave my reading at this stage, and ask how you can start to get a sense of the tradition of critical discussion associated with a particular novel. A good recent edition of a novel aimed at student use will reference important critical studies, and will give you a sense of what critics of a particular work have concentrated their attention on. Nowadays, the easiest way to extend and focus such a sense is by accessing the relevant critical work listed in an online database such as Literature Online (see below). If you generate hits so that they are presented in chronological order, you will be able not just to display the most important topics explored by critics, but also to see how critical topics relating to a single work have changed over time. If you don't have access to such a specialist database, more general and free search engines such as Google Scholar can be useful—and you can also find the relevant shelf in your library and look through the books available there. *The Year's Work in English Studies* (your library may subscribe to the printed or the electronic version, or both) provides useful summaries of critical responses to individual works.

Now you can move to *stage 2*. You have your two lists; compare them. To what extent will some of the sequences and traditions of critical discussion that you have uncovered help you with the questions that your own reading has thrown up? You are now better able to start looking for particular essays or books that you can use to deepen your involvement in the novel you have just finished reading. You should find that a brief survey of the critical debate around a particular writer or work will actually open your eyes to issues of which you have been unaware, issues which do not feature on the list you compiled on the basis of your reading notes, but which you recognize to be important once your attention is drawn to them.

Sometimes you may find that an issue raised for you by a novel or short story has been discussed little or not at all by critics. You should not assume that you should abandon such a potential line of enquiry: during my many years as a university academic, undergraduates have frequently raised issues about even well-known texts that I, and other critics and lecturers, have missed.

When I started to look at critical responses to Ford's *The Good Soldier*, I found discussion of some issues that my own reading of the novel had not raised for me: Ford as impressionist writer, for example, and articles which see *The Good Soldier* as comedy (in one case) and tragedy (in another). These articles sent me back to the novel to reconsider my reading, to look at certain scenes and passages again—and generated a checklist of issues to consider on a rereading of the work. Critics do not just provide answers to questions; they also provide questions for you to answer.

If you have been given an essay topic and a deadline for submitting the finished essay, then you will be under more pressure. But you should not just rush to your computer or the library with a list of words from the essay topic that you then attempt to find online or on the shelves. Spend some time *analyzing* your essay topic: this will help you in your literature search.

At the end of stage 2, you should have a shortlist of relevant books and articles that you can use for your essay. Find out which are available online or in the library. For hard-to-get items remember that sometimes buying a second-hand book online can provide a copy more speedily than interlibrary loan (and interlibrary loan is not always free); a librarian can usually tell you how long such an order will take. As you read criticism, you will refine your shortlist: some new references that you may want to consult are likely to be thrown up, and you may also be sent back to reread parts of the literary text with which you started.

Using computers

I mentioned above the very useful internet resource from MLA Commons entitled "Literary Studies in the Digital Age." Some of the sections in this resource go beyond what an undergraduate student of literature is likely to need, but even in such cases you may find browsing them interesting. "Digital Scholarly Editing," for example, is a topic more likely to be relevant at master's or doctoral level, but knowing some of the issues involved in such editing will do an undergraduate no harm, and will certainly help you to appreciate the problems of producing a reliable text of a standard work.

"Information Visualization for Humanities Scholars" by Stéfan Sinclair, Stan Ruecker, and Milena Radzikowska contains fascinating information on the possibilities of a GIS (graphic information system) for literary studies—imposing information about what happened in history at a particular place on a map of the place, or an illustration of word frequency in a literary work with the words ranged in size according to frequency.

The most relevant essay in the site for present purposes, however, is David L. Hoover's "Textual Analysis." This provides information on the variety of ways in which computers can be used in textual analysis. Some of the possibilities available are listed by Hoover, and include the following:

- Searching an electronic text for a word, phrase, or scene
- How large is the vocabulary of a particular work? How does it compare to other works by the same or different authors?
- Stylistic analysis of various sorts (do different characters in a novel speak in different ways? Do changes in style occur within a novel, or throughout an author's writing career?)
- Following the history of a particular word (in one work; in a number of works by the same author; over a long historical period)
- Investigating whether gender or class background affects vocabulary and other stylistic matters (for characters in a work, or comparing different works by the same or different authors)

Hoover has much sound advice on selecting or generating an electronic text for analysis; he provides important information about copyright (scanning a book that is in copyright may land you in legal difficulties); and he provides a neat example of what digital analysis can achieve through a "cluster analysis" of works by two Victorian authors.

"Reading Squared" (<http://www.readingsquared.com/about/>) is another interesting site. It presents the project "TextRays: ReadingSquared," which "focuses on one hundred canonical Anglophone novels written between 1719–1997." It presents computer-extracted information from these novels in graphic form, making it easy to see the variations in the hundred novels with regard to, for example, "body intensity" (comparative analysis of references to the human body). Other graphics represent key "semantic zones," such as the relationship between "food, clothing and shelter," or "the named body, the motor body, and the neurological body." These and other examples display patterns revealed by digital searches for word frequencies and relationships—the sorts of patterns of which a reader may be unaware but by which he or she is probably influenced.

What's free and what's not

What's free

If more and more is available on the internet, not all of it is free. There are some very useful free resources and programs. I have mentioned the Calibre program above; another open-access (i.e., free) program is Juxta (<http://www.juxtasoftware.org/>) which allows you to compare multiple versions of the same text, isolate variations, and print out a concordance. A facility only available in beta at the time of writing is "Juxta Commons," which is "an online space powered by the Juxta Web Service that lets you collate sets and share visualizations with your peers."

Then there is Google Books, with the associated Google Scholar. If you come across a strange word or phrase in a novel that you cannot find in a dictionary, then Google Books will help you find out if any other author has used it, and where. Google Books is also valuable as a way to check quotations. A critic in book A cites a passage from book B and you wonder if the citation is accurate: a quick search through Google Books can often isolate the quotation in the original, and because the text is reproduced in scanned form you can be sure that no errors of transmission have taken place. Google Scholar, as its own blurb states, "provides a simple way to broadly search for scholarly literature." Compared to, say, the criticism search using Literature Online, it is less sophisticated but more comprehensive.

What's not

Many of the electronic services that are aimed at individual student subscribers need to be either avoided completely or treated with great circumspection. In the "not to be touched at any cost" category are the straightforwardly dishonest—companies that sell either pre-written or written-to-order essays for cash. Your institution will certainly have a regulation forbidding plagiarism, and using such companies will risk contravening this regulation. Remember that academics and university administrators are getting clever at detecting web plagiarism and cheating, and there are now programs that will help your teachers to find out if you have cheated—although most of the plagiarism I have uncovered has been detected by reading rather than computer skills. Remember that your teachers have been trained to analyze texts, and can apply these skills to the texts you produce.

Then there are those companies that, for a few pounds (or, more usually, dollars), will sell you a text that gives you a plot summary of a novel, with commentary on characters, narrative technique, historical background, and so on. If you do not actually reproduce material in unacknowledged form from these, you may escape being accused of cheating, but it is clear that such material is designed to enable you to avoid reading and thinking about the text in question, so that admitting that you have used it will not improve your teachers' opinion of you.

Some of the most useful legitimate tools—for example, databases like Literature Online, now owned by ProQuest—are expensive to subscribe to and generally beyond the pockets of individual student subscribers. So your first step should be to find out exactly what your college or university library (and also your public library, if you live in a large town or city) does subscribe to. If you can access a database like Literature Online, it is well worth learning how to exploit what it has to offer; there is no doubt that such tools, sensibly used, are enormously useful. It is worth listing the different electronic resources available to you in local libraries, and learning how to use the ones that look relevant. In some cases, if you are a registered student, you can access these resources on a personal computer, normally by use of a password and sometimes in consort with a VPN facility.

Using your computer as a study tool

I list below some of the different ways in which you can use your computer as a study tool. All of these require an internet connection, although after you have downloaded material, you can then use it on a computer without such a connection.

1 Many of the novels and short stories you study can be downloaded as complete texts and saved on the hard disk of your own computer. A simple web-search along the lines of <nostromo + electronic> will soon establish whether there is an available and downloadable electronic text of Conrad's novel (there is). Remember that if the work was first published, or its author died, fewer than seventy years ago, then the work will probably be in copyright and you will be unlikely to be able legally to download a free electronic text of it, although copyright rules vary from Europe to the United States—and some texts that are in copyright in these areas are out of copyright in Australia.

But beware! The texts that you can download free from the internet are often not what textual scholars term "reliable." In other words, they may contain errors or disputed readings that paper editions published by reputable publishers have corrected or discussed—in a nutshell, what you read is not what the author wanted to be read. To stick to the example of *Nostromo*, chapter 11 in Part 3 of the novel ends with the character Mrs Gould stammering out aimlessly the words "Material interest." Or so you would think if you relied upon the text available from Project Gutenberg (<https://www.gutenberg.org/>). As the term "material interests" appears repeatedly in this novel—a total of eighteen times, in fact—you might be tempted to discuss why Conrad suddenly changes "interests" to "interest" at this point. The problem is that he doesn't: the singular form here is a mistake, one that descends from a text published in the 1920s as part of the Sun-Dial edition published by the American publisher Doubleday. Some recent editions—for example, the 1984 Oxford World's Classics one—correct this error; some other more recent ones do not (a recent date of publication is no guarantee of reliability). Your lecturer's advice on which text you should use should thus be heeded: a text downloaded free from the internet may be reliable, but it may well not. (See too the discussion of different versions of the same work on p. 183.)

However, even an unreliable electronic text can be a useful complement to a reliable printed one—my information that "material interests" appears eighteen times in *Nostromo* is based on a preliminary search of the version available from Project Gutenberg. Once you have the text of all or part of a novel in even a standard word-processing program, you can, for example, find all examples of a particular word or phrase, or compare—say—the average sentence length in two short stories by the same or two different authors. Because novels are generally longer than poems or plays, this facility is particularly useful for the student of the novel. If, for example, you think that you remember (as I once did) that Chablis wine is described as "straw-coloured" in Henry James's *The Ambassadors*, then the computer can locate the reference in seconds (I had searched for hours in the printed text, but had been looking in the wrong place). The location took me longer than seconds, alas, because the electronic text used a different code for hyphens than did my search-text. Remember that an electronic text that uses hard hyphens to divide words at the ends of lines may cause search problems.

Imagine that you are struck by the phrase "paradise of snakes" in *Nostromo*. Does this betoken a concern to link the development of the silver mine in that novel with the expulsion of Adam and Eve from the Garden of Eden? In a matter of a very few minutes you can electronically search through the text looking for words such as "Eden," "fall," "snake," "serpent," "Adam," "Eve," "Satan," "Devil," "tree," "forbidden," "fruit," and so on. Whatever you do, don't think that you can just list the results of such searches in an essay! You need to think about what such searches uncover, and relate the results to your reading of the work as a whole and to what critics have written about it. You can count how many times a word or phrase occurs in a text just by using search-and-replace for the same word or phrase; the program will tell you how many replacements it has made. Why bother? Well, Joseph Conrad's novel *Under Western Eyes* is a novel that foregrounds a concern with speech and language. But by means of such simple searches in an electronic text of the novel I discovered that although the words "language" and "languages" occur only 13 times, cognates of the word "word" occur an impressive 165 times. That forced me to consider what particular perspective on language Conrad has in this novel.

Google Books (<http://books.google.com>) allows you to enter a word or phrase and find a page reference to where this word or phrase appears in an edition that Google has scanned. This is a useful tool in the case of texts that cannot be downloaded electronically. Google Scholar (<http://scholar. google.co.uk> [the American site has US instead of UK]) allows you to search through published scholarly material. Both of these resources should be used as stepping-stones: they indicate where you will find fuller and more contextualized information.

2   I mentioned above ProQuest's Literature Online database. This is mostly what is known as a full-text database, meaning that it will allow you to search—for instance—for the word "photograph" in a very large number of—again, for instance—nineteenth-century novels. Its coverage of fiction is at present less comprehensive than of poetry and drama, but it is a very good place to start looking for criticism. If you search for <author: Fielding> and <keyword: picaresque>, it throws up a list of 147 articles, all but one of which can be downloaded in full-text format. With a more open search you can get a good sense of the critical issues associated with a particular text. Thus a search for <author: Ford, Ford Madox> and <keyword: good soldier> throws up the titles of 1,092 items ranging from reviews through articles to books. Just looking at the titles of these items will give you a sense of the different emphases in criticism of this novel over the past four decades, and many of the articles listed can again be immediately downloaded free in full-text form.

More specialist databases are available. To take a representative example, ECCO—Eighteenth Century Collections Online—offers at present "26 million pages of text from more than 136,291 titles (155,010 volumes)" with "full-search capabilities." In preparing each new edition of this book, I find that the number of hits in these examples has jumped up significantly, so the statistics quoted here will certainly be out of date by the time you read this.

The British Modern Humanities Research Association (MHRA) publishes a range of specialist bibliographies and also ABELL: *The Annual Bibliography of English Language & Literature*, published annually in electronic and printed form, which "aims to list annually all scholarly articles, books and reviews concerning English language and literature and related topics published anywhere in the world, and in any language." The American Modern Library Association (MLA) also produces an authoritative annual bibliography. Most academic libraries should be able to provide online access to these databases.

Literature Online gives you two ways of downloading texts: either as "full text" or as "page image." The latter option gives you a result like a photocopy, paginated exactly as it is in the printed version, so references can be given precisely as they would for an article consulted in a printed journal. "Full text" downloads make it easier to copy and paste quotations, but you need to reference the fact that the pagination quoted is for an electronic download.

3 What about Wikipedia? Like fire, Wikipedia is a good servant but a bad master. I use it myself very often when I want a quick information fix. It certainly has the merit of allowing for extremely fast updating, but although on occasions an entry may be written by a (or even the) world expert on a subject, you are very likely to get a more profound, reliable, and nuanced account of a topic in a specialist book or journal that has been subjected to what is called peer-review: reported on by (normally two) anonymous experts.

So if you are sitting at your computer writing an essay and you want quickly to confirm that you have remembered correctly the year in which *The Good Soldier* was published, by all means zip over to Wikipedia. And if you want an initial overview of the work of—say—Gérard Genette, then read what Wikipedia has to say. But my strong advice would be to move then to a source that includes more conventionally peer-reviewed material—an academic book published by a respectable academic publisher, or a good academic journal. The best entries in Wikipedia contain information about such sources. A student essay that ends with a bibliography citing only entries in Wikipedia will depress rather than impress your lecturer.

4 Electronic discussion groups on e-mail or (more usually nowadays) the internet allow you to follow debates between other students and specialists all over the world about a particular novel or novelist, and to make your own contributions. The International Virginia Woolf Society, for example, has run an e-mail discussion group about the author since 1996; the society's webpage provides details of how to subscribe. Remember that although you can submit questions to such discussion groups, if participants think that you are trying to get them to write your essay for you, you will get the cold shoulder. Specialist questions can often get useful replies: if you want tips on essays dealing with a relatively specialist topic, sometimes a discussion group can help where a scholarly bibliography cannot.

5 Even the general "search" function in an internet search engine (such as Google) can throw up useful leads. One Sunday, when my academic library was closed, I found very useful scholarly material on Thomas Hardy's short story "An Imaginative Woman" merely by Googling <Hardy + Imaginative> on my computer. You may well be able to access useful material put out for students in other universities. It is absolutely acceptable to use such material in an essay *provided you acknowledge where you got it from and furnish a webpage reference.*

If you want more detailed information about using the internet which covers such topics as the different ways to refine web searches, how to assess the academic reliability of webpages, and how to reference web material, you can consult the second section of Paul Goring, Jeremy Hawthorn, and Domhnall Mitchell, *Studying Literature: The Essential Companion* (2010) entitled "Guide to the Use of Electronic Media."

Revision/review

"Revision" is what American readers will know as "review." It involves refreshing your memory of what might have been studied months earlier.

You may take an examination requiring knowledge of a number of novels up to a year after you have read some of them. Full rereading is impossible, and some elements will certainly have slipped your memory. Do not try to skip-read the whole work again, but concentrate upon reading selected passages with care. These should always include the opening and closing pages of the work—beginnings and endings of novels are almost invariably revealing. Is the opening dramatic or descriptive? Does it plunge the reader into the middle of things, or carefully establish a scene? Does it set a dominant tone, and establish the narrative perspective or personality of the narrator? Is the reader addressed directly, and are we given an indication of what sort of reader (or reading) the narrative invites or appears to assume? Is the ending happy or sad? Why does the author choose to make it so? Does it tie up all the loose ends or leave many questions unanswered? With what effect?

Apart from opening and closing pages, you should pick some key passages—either those that have seemed important to you, or those which critics have found of great interest. Pick a couple of passages at random, preferably ones that seem unfamiliar on leafing through the work. Analyze these in detail.

If it makes you feel easier, construct a list of names (just the main characters and places) for each work prior to an examination. If you forget a name in an examination, do not panic; just leave a blank and go on writing. If the name does not come to you by the end of the examination, then asterisk the gap and write in a footnote explaining that you have forgotten it, and indicating the character or place by other means such as relationships to other characters or what happened there.

So far as critics are concerned, it is useful to be able to situate their arguments and positions—both in the context of critical debate about the work in question, and also in the context of the critic's own principles and theoretical allegiances (see my comments on p. 211).

Essays and examinations

Some rules concerning the writing of essays are not specific to study of the novel. There are various textbooks that will advise you on such matters, and you should find out which, if any, of these your lecturers recommend. But the best way to learn how to write an essay is to read articles in respected academic journals and note the conventions that they follow. The tips below are not necessarily specific to essays or examination answers on the novel, and you may find them irritatingly basic. But if you have not previously been aware of their importance, you should pay careful attention to them.

- If you are using a computer, you should *never* submit an essay without spell-checking it. It takes very little time, and reduces the risk that an irritated teacher will mark you down for careless spelling. But remember that spell-checkers can make mistakes: an essay that I once set included a passage from Joyce that contained the word "sottish." Students who spell-checked their essays in Word were recommended to replace this with "Scottish." Alas many did.
- I am much less enthusiastic about the grammar-checkers contained in basic word-processing programs. But if you know that you regularly make basic grammatical mistakes, then the grammar-check facility can help you to guard against them. But *never* accept any recommendation that such a program makes without thinking about it. If you want to amuse yourself, run the opening page of Charles Dickens's *Bleak House* through Word's grammar checker …
- I am a strong believer in the use of subheadings. This is partly because they help whoever reads your work to find his or her way through your argument, but also because they may reveal to you that a particular section or paragraph in an essay would be better placed elsewhere. Similarly, remember to use paragraphs sensibly. If you are not sure about the conventions governing paragraphing, consult a more specialist book on the writing of essays.
- Try to use an appealing layout. Heed your teachers' advice on such things as font, line spacing, reference systems, bibliographies.
- Always start your essay or examination answer by making it clear which question or topic you are addressing (but unless instructed to do so, do not copy the whole question out on the first page).

When it comes to writing essays and examination answers, there is no substitute for practice: the more that you write, and have your writing commented upon, the more clearly and easily you will come to write. The following advice, in my experience, indicates the most common sorts of weakness in essays and examination answers dealing with the novel, but it is important to listen to the advice of your teachers.

Be relevant

You will be responding to a specific question or topic. Do not just pick out a couple of words from it and proceed to write all you know about the text(s) mentioned. Remember that an essay or answer is like a meal: selection, preparation, and order are necessary if the result is to be pleasing. Use colored pens and underline key words in the question. If the question has several points, then *number* these. After every second page you write, look back to make sure that what you are writing is of relevance to the topic or question.

Argue a case

A question requires an answer, not just a response. You will be expected to take up a position in relation to what has been asked, and to argue your position as logically as possible. Do not be afraid to express a personal opinion, but, if you do, say that it is a personal opinion and justify it (see below). If you refer to the opinion of others (critics, for example), say whether or not you agree with them, and why. If the question or topic includes a quotation that asserts a claim, remember that you may disagree with the opinion of the person quoted. (Very often the person who has written the question expects you to do this.) Remember, however, that if you are to argue successfully, you need to …

Plan your answer

If you only have a very short amount of time, you may have to restrict this to a five-minute sketch of what you intend to say, but if you are writing an essay in your own time, then you should plan more carefully. With an essay, you can afford to restructure what you have written for its final presentation, such that the introduction and conclusion can be added on at the end in case your argument has become modified or more complex in the course of writing. Because essays are now almost always written on a computer you may get used to moving material around on screen. Remember that you cannot do this in a handwritten time-test examination, which means that examination answers need to be more carefully planned. In an examination, you may find as you write that your answer is moving in a rather different way from that laid out in your introductory paragraph. If so, the best thing is to admit to this change of direction, and even to explain why.

A good essay or examination answer should have an introduction which explains what attitude you are taking to the question asked, and how you are going to answer it. This need only be half a page long at most. You should then provide, in as ordered a way as possible, evidence to substantiate the position you have taken up. At any stage in an essay or examination answer, the person reading it should know (i) what you are trying to argue, and (ii) how this argument fits into your general thesis or response to the question. Anyone who has marked examinations knows that a sure sign that there is something wrong is when you have to flip back to page 1 to check exactly which question the script is supposed to be answering. See below for some further suggestions on how to make a positive impression with the opening sentences of your essay or answer.

Back up your arguments with evidence

There are different sorts of evidence that can be adduced in an essay or an examination answer. Unless the question specifically focuses on extratextual matters, the most important evidence that you can bring forward is likely to be *textual*. The general rule about textual evidence is that it should be *detailed* and it should be *analytical*. In an essay you should quote enough to make your point, and you should *never* assume that a quotation speaks for itself. Every time you quote from a novel or a short story in an essay you should explain what it is in the quotation that is important—pointing to *particular* words, *particular* phrases, *particular* techniques (such as those outlined in my suggested checklist on p. 162).

Examinations may present a different problem. Generally speaking, examinations have to be written without access to the novel or short-story texts on which they are based. I do not recommend that you spend hours learning selected passages by heart. Not only is this extremely time-consuming, but there is also a tendency for those who have shed blood learning long quotations to insist on demonstrating the fact in the examination room, and the quotations that have been learned may well not be relevant to the question asked. Even if you cannot quote at length from a novel, though, you can still be detailed in your reference to it. Refer to particular *scenes*, isolate the operative *events*, *actions* and *utterances* (you do not have to quote to do this), draw attention to relevant aspects of *narrative technique*, and comment upon such things as *symbolism* and *imagery* if they play a significant role. If you can refer to particular words and phrases used, all the better.

In addition to textual evidence, there are various forms of extratextual evidence that can be incorporated in an answer: comments and opinions from critics, statements from or about the work's author, parallels with other works either by the same author or by others, information of the sort mentioned in my brief discussion of "the sociology of literature" (p. 225), information about social, historical, and cultural events or states of affairs. In all of these, two issues should be borne in mind: *influence* and *relevance*. You may reproduce a lot of accurate facts, but did they have any influence on the writing (or the reading) of the work? Are they relevant to the question asked?

Do not tell the story

I suppose I ought to concede here that it is possible that one day you might encounter an essay topic or examination question which starts, "Tell the story of *Wuthering Heights* and then proceed to comment on …," but 99.9 percent of essay topics and essay questions do not require you to open with an obligatory three-page précis of what happens in the novel in question. You have to assume that the person marking the essay or answer has read the work and knows what happens: he or she will be irritated, and not impressed, by such a plot summary.

Remember that the characters are not "real people"

Although it is quite legitimate at times to discuss the characters and actions in a novel as we discuss the people we know in real life (almost all critics do this at some time or another, even those who say that they don't), you should also indicate clearly that you are aware that what we read are words that have been created and crafted by an author. Peter Lamarque has suggested that the reader of fiction needs to be able to combine the imaginative involvement of an internal perspective with the awareness of artifice of an external perspective (1996, 14), and you should make sure that the person reading your essay knows you are aware of this difference.

Arouse your reader's curiosity

Compare the following selection of opening passages for an essay on Virginia Woolf's novel *Mrs Dalloway*:

1 Virginia Woolf was born Virginia Stephen in 1882. Her father was Sir Leslie Stephen, famous for founding, and contributing significantly to, *The Dictionary of National Biography*. She had periods of mental disturbance all her life; the first in 1913 and the final one associated with her suicide in 1941. She was a member of the so-called Bloomsbury Group, and is credited with being one of the most important forces behind the modernist novel in England.

2 Toward the end of Virginia Woolf's novel *Mrs Dalloway*, we follow Clarissa Dalloway's thoughts as she considers Sir William Bradshaw, "a great doctor, but to her obscurely evil, without sex or lust, extremely polite to women, but capable of some indescribable outrage—forcing your soul, that was it." The words take the reader aback: it is as if being without lust is presented as a negative quality. What lies behind this attitude?

3 The very brief opening scene of Marleen Gorris's 1998 film *Mrs Dalloway* shows Septimus on the battlefield in Italy in 1918. He shouts "Evans! Don't jump!," but a massive explosion and his look of horror reveal that he has shouted in vain. The scene is not to be found in Virginia Woolf's novel, which opens with the words, "Mrs Dalloway said that she would buy the flowers herself" in the novel's "present" of June, 1923. The filmmaker's instinct that in Woolf's novel the past is always there, influencing the present, is however perceptive.

4 *Mrs Dalloway* is the first novel by Virginia Woolf that I have read. I had been looking forward to reading this novel because I had heard that Woolf was a fighter for women's rights and a major influence on feminist thinkers during the twentieth century. My first reading of the novel came as something of a shock: how could feminists respect a writer capable of producing such a negative, stereotyped portrayal of a lesbian character as Woolf does with Miss Kilman?

I venture to suggest that any teacher who has pulled the first of 30 (or 130) essays off a pile to be marked and has read opening number 1 will feel his or her heart dropping. This is not because there is anything wrong, or even irrelevant, about the information it contains, but because it suggests very strongly that it has been copied straight out of a reference book by someone who does not have a burning desire to propose an original response to whatever question has been asked.

In contrast to opening number 1, openings 2, 3, and 4 all suggest that the writer does have something interesting and original to say. Moreover, they all raise issues, problems, questions that stimulate the reader's curiosity. We want to read on to find out how the writer deals with the problem that he or she has outlined. We are hooked. Consider the different techniques involved: (2) raising a textual or interpretive problem; (3) using a film adaptation of a work to illuminate aspects of the original; (4) starting with a report of a strong personal reaction that you then use to lead into an issue relating to the text or its critical history.

Now care is needed here, because if there is one standard failing for which essays and examination answers are marked down in literary studies, it is that of failing to answer the question. So that immediately after an opening along the lines of alternatives 2 to 4 the writer needs to establish that he or she is indeed going to tie in a resolution of the problem raised with a relevant response to the chosen question.

Topics for discussion

- "Lecturers say they want our personal responses, but then they tell us our personal responses are wrong." Is there such a thing as a "wrong" response to a novel?
- What is the best way to refresh our memory of a long novel that was read six months ago?
- How does writing an essay with access to text and notes help prepare us to write exams with access to neither?
- Is it useful to "learn quotes"?
- What is the best way to prevent "exam panic"?

7

Versions, Adaptations, Translations

Preview

This chapter deals with:
- The difference between a version and an adaptation of a novel
- Gains and losses in film and television adaptations
- Studying fiction in translation

Versions

It is only occasionally that the attention of the casual reader is drawn to the fact that there are textual issues associated with novels. Recent editions of Charles Dickens's *Great Expectations* generally print both of the endings that Dickens wrote for this novel, and the influential *Norton Anthology of American Literature* included quite significantly different versions of Mark Twain's "The Celebrated Jumping Frog of Calaveras County" in successive editions. Generally speaking, though, we discuss novels and short stories as if their titles denoted unambiguously single texts. But the reality is rather more complex than this, and I would like to illustrate this by means of a representative example, taking Joseph Conrad's *The Secret Agent* as my text.

If you consult the scholarly "critical" edition of *The Secret Agent* published by Cambridge University Press in 1990, you will find in it a dense ninety-two-page discussion of the novel's textual history. From this, you can determine not only that prior to its first English book edition in

1907 the novel was published in a considerably shorter periodical version, in installments, but also that it was published in separate book editions in Britain and America. Of later book editions, one—the 1921 Doubleday "Sun-Dial"—was used for what was for many years the standard edition of Conrad's works, the Dent Collected Edition, published in the 1940s. Alas, this edition is not a reliable one, and contains many variants that almost certainly are not Conrad's. Behind these published editions, a web of manuscripts, typescripts, and copyedited proofs has been uncovered by the editors of the Cambridge edition, a web so complex that it is represented in their discussion by a sequence of graphic representations resembling a map of the London underground system. Establishing who made changes to these various texts, and when, is often difficult, as later printings of the first edition seem on occasions to reintroduce earlier formulations that Conrad had altered.

In November 1922, just over fifteen years after *The Secret Agent* was first published in book form, an adaptation of the novel for the stage written by Conrad himself opened in London at the Ambassador's Theatre. Not only did this dramatization remove many scenes present in the novel, in transforming the work from a *printed narrative intended to be read silently* to a *play written for performance*, it also completely removed the non-character narrator along with his ironic perspective on the events recounted— perhaps the most radical change that transformation from printed novel to performed play entailed. It also changed some aspects of the story, so that the character Winnie Verloc does not commit suicide but instead goes mad at the end of the work.

The play was not a great success, and ran for only a week. But in the audience for one of the few performances sat a young man named Alfred Hitchcock, who was shortly to begin a career in the film industry (see Spoto 1983, 62). Fourteen years later, after having directed a film entitled *The Secret Agent* that had nothing to do with Conrad, Hitchcock directed a film entitled *Sabotage* that included the acknowledgment "From the novel 'The Secret Agent' by Joseph Conrad" in the opening credits, but that transposed the action to the present day and made very significant alterations to the setting and story of both Conrad's novel and his stage adaptation. Sixty years after Hitchcock's film was first shown, a new film entitled *The Secret Agent*, written and directed by Christopher Hampton and starring Bob Hoskins and Patricia Arquette, was released in the United States. Both Conrad's own dramatization of his novel and Hampton's screenplay have been published and can be consulted.

By convention these varied texts are divided into separate categories. All of the variants and versions associated with Conrad's writing of the novel are usually deemed to be the preserve of the textual editor. Unless you are writing an advanced thesis on *The Secret Agent*, you will not be expected to pore over periodical and book versions of the novel in their British and American editions, nor to sit in front of a microfilm reader or computer deciphering the handwriting of Conrad's manuscript. Nor is it likely that you will be expected to read the novel in a full critical edition such as the Cambridge edition mentioned above. But you may—and in my opinion should—be expected to read the novel in a modern edition with a text that incorporates the results of recent scholarship, including that contained in the Cambridge edition. Such an edition will draw your attention to substantial variations in the text of the novel, and it should also allow you to ponder the significance of some of Conrad's own textual revisions. Recent editions of classic novels published by reputable firms such as Norton, Penguin, and Oxford World's Classics will almost certainly be reliable—that is to say they will not give you texts that repeat mistakes or changes unauthorized by the writer long after these have been pointed out by scholars, and they will contain information about the textual history of the work and about important textual variants.

Adaptations

But what about those later versions that we generally refer to as adaptations? And what is the difference between a version and an adaptation? Although the two terms overlap, generally speaking, we call a rewriting of a novel or short story an adaptation when it does not seek to *replace* a known work ("known," typically, because it has been published or performed), but to be treated as a new work, one that it is hoped will have a life of its own *alongside* that of the work of which it is an adaptation. It is usual for an adaptation to involve some generic change—from prose fiction to play or film, for example—so that we may find that a play that is based on another play is termed "a modern-dress version" rather than "a modern-dress adaptation." Conrad did not want people to stop reading *The Secret Agent* once he had dramatized it, and neither we assume did Alfred Hitchcock after he had made his film *Sabotage*.

Some introductory questions

There are many different issues to consider when a novel or short story is adapted. Here are some to consider.

1 *How great an involvement or presence in the adaptation does the author of the source text have?*

If for example the author writes a one-person monologue based on a short story and then directs him- or herself in a performance of this monologue, the involvement is very considerable. If the adaptation is written and performed after the author's death by someone with only the original story or novel as basis, there is no such involvement.

2 *How different are the medium and genre for which the adaptation is produced from those of the source text?*

Although a play is written to be performed, its reliance upon language is generally greater than is the case for a film, and the collective nature of film production inevitably reduces the importance of the writer's role when set against the writer's dominating importance for a novel. Remember that a basic issue such as the length of time available for a dramatization will vary between a film and a television series. Adapting John Galsworthy's *The Forsyte Saga* for a two-hour film would be a very different task from adapting it for a television series of many installments. See below for more detailed comments on such issues.

3 *How long a time is there between the writing and publication of the source text and the writing and publication or performing of the adaptation?*

A director who wishes to film *Hamlet* today must contend with issues of cultural change that do not arise in the case of the filming of a postmodern novel such as Don DeLillo's *Cosmopolis*. A similar point applies to the production of an adaptation in a different culture from the one to which the source text belongs, even if there is a small gap in time between the writing of source and of adaptation. *The Seven Samurai* and *The Magnificent Seven* are not so far removed in time or in medium and genre, but the cultures within which these two films were produced, and the cultures that they depict, are radically different. The term "reculturation" has been applied to such adaptations. Remember that this issue arises even if an author adapts their own work: *The Secret Agent* was performed as a play sixteen years after Conrad's novel was published, in a very different England and world from those in which the novel was written and first read.

4 *How well known is the source text?*

Anyone adapting *Hamlet* for a new film cannot ignore the fact that almost everyone who sees the film will have *some* idea of what Shakespeare's play is about. But behind many films based on relatively unknown literary works lies an assumption that most of those who see the film will not have read the source text beforehand, and will probably not read it afterwards either. A director may choose to satisfy or challenge an audience's expectations but he or she cannot ignore them completely. No director could make a film of Tolstoy's *Anna Karenina* which ended with Anna marrying Vronsky and settling down to a blissful married life without taking into account that a very significant number of those who saw the film would be aware that this ending is quite different from the ending of Tolstoy's novel. But when Conrad changed the ending of *The Secret Agent* in adapting it for the stage, he may well have assumed that the plot of his novel would not be familiar to many in his London theater audience. And when Beeban Kidron filmed Conrad's much less well-known short story "Amy Foster" as *Swept from the Sea* in 1997, she almost certainly assumed that only a very few members of her film's audience would know anything of the source text.

5 *Does the adaptation display or conceal its relationship with the source text?*

Clearly the starting point here is the title, followed shortly afterwards by character names. A change of title (from *The Turn of the Screw* to *The Innocents*, for example) may signal a desire on the part of writer, director, or producer to establish greater distance between the film and Henry James's novella than might have been implied by retaining his title for the film adaptation.

6 *What sort of adaptation are we dealing with?*

There are many ways of categorizing adaptations; one of the most influential has been Dudley Andrew's distinction between adaptations that "borrow," "intersect with," and "transform" their sources (see Andrew 1992, 422–3). Andrew glosses these terms as follows:

> *Borrowing*: Andrew describes this as "the most frequent mode of adaptation." "Here the artist employs ... the material, idea, or form of an earlier, generally successful text." Citing Richard Strauss's *Don Quixote*, Andrew comments that there is "no question of replication of the original," but instead "the audience is expected to enjoy basking in a certain pre-established presence and to call up new or especially powerful aspects of a cherished work."

> *Intersecting*: Andrew notes that "here the uniqueness of the original text is preserved to such an extent that it is intentionally left unassimilated in adaptation." An adaptation in the intersecting mode tends to "present the otherness and distinctiveness of the original text," thus initiating a dialectical interplay of literary and cinematic forms. An example of this ambitious form of adaptation is Francis Ford Coppola's *Apocalypse Now*, although as Jakob Lothe points out, this film—which did not on first release acknowledge its debt to Joseph Conrad's *Heart of Darkness*—"could be seen as an example of borrowing as well as intersecting" (Lothe 2000, 88).

> *Transformation*: "Here it is assumed that the task of adaptation is the reproduction in cinema of something essential about an original text." Andrew finds that as transformations tend to be faithful to the literary text, they may "become a scenario written in typical scenario form," yet it does not follow that this kind of adaptation is artistically inferior to the two other variants. An example of a successful adaptation in the fidelity and transformation mode is John Huston's 1987 film *The Dead*, which closely follows the plot of James Joyce's short story.

The economy of Andrew's tripartite distinction stands in sharp contrast to Robert Stam's mention of "a well-stocked archive of tropes and concepts to account for the mutation of forms across media: adaptation as reading, rewriting, critique, translation, transmutation, metamorphosis, recreation, transvocalization, signifying, performance, dialogization, cannibalization, reinvisioning, incarnation, or reaccentuation" (Stam 2005, 25). Indeed, in his concluding comments, Stam adds yet more terms when he proposes that "source-novel hypotexts are transformed by a complex series of operations: selection, amplification, concretization, actualization, critique, extrapolation, popularization, reaccentuation, transculturization" (2005, 45). ("Hypotext" in this context means the underlying, or foundational text that is the basis for later adaptations or transformations.) If the issue of fidelity, of how much of the source text the adapter wishes to preserve—ranging from "little" through "to some extent" to "something essential"—is central to Andrew's tripartite distinction, a much greater range of other issues is introduced by Stam's extended lists.

A good starting point is to ask very generally what has been omitted, added, and "concretized" in the transition from novel to film. The most obvious omissions will probably relate to excisions from the plot and from the cast of characters—especially if we are dealing with a narrative film that is based on a longish novel. By convention, films are not normally more than about three hours long, and even adaptations for television have less space for long complex plots and large character casts than do novels. While noting this fact it might be worth pausing a moment to ask why this is so. Why are we prepared to extend our reading of a long novel over several weeks if necessary, while anything over three hours in a cinema feels excessive? A simple answer to this involves the fundamental point that we have control over our private reading of a book in a way that we do not have over a film: we can pause, flick back to refresh our memory of earlier scenes, increase or decrease the speed of our reading—or even stop and think about what we have read or talk about it with a friend—so that we can pace ourselves as we read and adjust our reading to our mental state. But this is only part of the story, since electronic versions of films and television adaptations have enabled us to do much the same with a film, although with somewhat less ease than we do with a printed source. It might have been expected that as more and more people gained access to films on tablets and computers, films would start to extend in length and to take as long to watch as it takes to read a novel, but this seems not to have happened. Computer games can require a player to sit many hours or even days in front of a screen, but films remain much the same length that they have always been.

It is rather the case that such innovations in viewing technology have led to the ever-extended film sequence, what we can term the "*Game of Thrones* syndrome." Different fictional media each seem to settle down to an optimum length for stories, so that Samuel Richardson's *Clarissa* and Marcel Proust's *Remembrance of Things Past* remain as much exceptions in the history of the novel as Andy Warhol's 1967 film *Imitation of Christ* (480 minutes in the uncut version) does in the history of the cinema. Longer films are typically divided into parts for viewing, whether in public performance or private enjoyment. Even long television adaptations are typically shown in installments rather than in, say, a continuous six-hour session, and this suggests that there is something fundamentally different in the way that we experience a silently read novel and a dramatization or a performance, and that this is one of the factors that lies behind the issue of length. Another is that nowadays books are nearly always read privately, by individuals, whereas a film shown on a tablet may well be watched by a couple of people—or more if the tablet is linked to a TV.

Whatever the reason, a filmed or televised version of a novel is likely to involve significant abridgment, and a first point of interest in the study of adaptation has to be the following: "What has been cut?" Why have the screenwriter or director chosen to cut this rather than that scene, this rather than that character? What effect do such cuts have?

Abridgment need not involve elements of the plot or characters—it can also involve aspects of a novel that are integral to its narrative. In discussing Free Indirect Discourse, for example, I noted how the examples I chose (from Katherine Mansfield's "The Voyage," Virginia Woolf's *Mrs Dalloway*, and D.H. Lawrence's "Fanny and Annie") managed to present a particular scene in such a way as to combine what a narrator tells us and what a character is thinking. Turn back to page 121 and read once again the first two paragraphs of Lawrence's short story "Fanny and Annie" that I quote there.

How could one film this scene? Clearly a skilled filmmaker could depict Fanny's irritation as Harry fails to see her, and could reproduce some of the effects of flame and shadow that the passage presents. But how could a filmed adaptation of this scene convey the fact that "the nostalgia, the doom of home-coming went through her veins like a drug," when we are not even sure that Fanny herself is aware of what is happening to her? How could the filmmaker convey her sense of his unchangingness ("His eternal face"; "Always the same") without the crudity of a voice-over? In his introduction to *Aren't You Rather Young to Be Writing Your Memoirs?* (1973), the novelist B.S. Johnson commented with regard to film that it "is an excellent medium for showing things, but it is very poor at taking an audience inside characters' minds, at telling it what people are thinking" (Bradbury 1990, 166).

What about additions? Some of these may well be straightforward: added scenes or new characters to plump up the plot of a short story. Thus Andrew Haigh's 2015 film *45 Years*, which is based on "In Another Country," a short story by David Constantine, adds much to what is a quite short short story, including the concluding scene of a wedding anniversary party that is not present in Constantine's original work. Some additional elements, however, can be the result of the inevitable "concretization" that film involves. Here is critic Robert Stam again, considering exactly this issue in a discussion of John Ford's realist adaptation of Steinbeck's novel *The Grapes of Wrath*, released in 1940, the year after the novel was published. Stam comments in detail on a passage in which the character Ma Joad contemplates her memorabilia just before leaving her Oklahoma home for California. The passage in Steinbeck's novel reads as follows:

> She sat down and opened the box. Inside were letters, clippings, photographs, a pair of earrings, a little gold signet ring, and a watch chain braided of hair and tipped with gold swivels. She touched the letters with her fingers, touched them lightly, and she smoothed a newspaper clipping on which there was an account of Tom's trial.

Stam comments as follows:

> In the film version of this passage we do indeed see Ma Joad sit down, open the box, and look at letters, clippings, photographs, and so forth. But even here the "cinematization" generates an inevitable supplement. Where Steinbeck writes "photographs," Ford has to choose specific photographs. The mention of "earrings" in the novel, does not dictate Ford's choice of having Ma Joad try them on. The newspaper account of Tom's trial requires the choice of a specific newspaper, specific headlines, illustrations, fonts, none of which is spelled out in the original. (Stam 2005, 18)

Let us pause at this point just to absorb the force of some of Stam's discussion. We may be tempted to suggest that it is almost as if with Steinbeck's text we have a "script" on the basis of which each reader can mentally perform the scene in question, whereas with Ford's film we have a single performance of the scene.

I would not want to reject such a view entirely, but what is questionable about it is the assumption that every detail that is concretized in the film is also given a sort of mental concretization in the mind of the reader as he or she reads the scene in Steinbeck's novel—and this seems to me unlikely. Imagine reading the passage from Steinbeck's novel, then having someone snatch the book away and demand, "Describe the earrings!" I suggest that we would not be able to do so if asked, and neither would we have imagined the wording of the newspaper clippings. The filmed version of this scene *has* to add detail that is not present in the written text and is not even "performed in" by a reader. Concretization requires addition. One of the important things to note here is that the writer of prose fiction can ensure that only that which is relevant to his or her artistic intention is conveyed to the reader. The writer can state, "He sat down." But the filmmaker has to decide on what sort of chair, with what sort of movement he sat down. The economy of prose fiction contributes fundamentally to its artistic focus.

Stam also reminds us that there are other necessary additions in any filmed version of this scene.

> Thus nothing in the novel prepares us for the idea that Ma Joad will look at the memorabilia by the light of a fire, the reflections of which will flicker over her face. Nothing dictates the point-of-view editing which alternates close shots of Ma Joad's face with what she sees, within a contemplative rhythm of shot/reverse shot. Nor does the Steinbeck passage mention music, yet the Ford version features a melancholy accordion version of the song "Red River Valley." Even if the text *had* mentioned "Red River Valley" that would still have been quite different from our actually hearing it performed. And even if the passage *had* mentioned both the music and the firelight, and the light's flickering over Ma Joad's face, that would still not have been anything like our seeing her face and hearing the music *at the same time.* (18)

Stam notes that although critics writing about adaptation from novel to film tend "to emphasize the cinema's impairments and disabilities vis-à-vis the novel ... yet, on almost any plane one might mention, cinematic adaptation brings, whether for good or ill, not an impoverishment but rather a *multiplication* of registers" (20). We are used to metaphorical accounts of novels, or of our experience of them, as "rich," of their "complex texture," and so on. These metaphors are not inaccurate, as we build up a sense of varied patterns and impressions in the course of our reading, and these different elements do combine in rich and complex ways. But if we exclude for the time being the issue of illustrations, the traditional novel is "single-track" in the sense that everything that we experience in our reading of a novel comes from words and the arrangement of words. A film, in contrast, has many "tracks"—moving pictures, music, speech, and noises, for example.

A brief case study: Henry James's *The Turn of the Screw*

Henry James's *The Turn of the Screw* is a much-adapted work. In addition to Benjamin Britten's opera and a number of less well-known adaptations for the stage, there are at least ten film or television-film adaptations of the work. Not all of these are readily available; among the lost adaptations is a 1959 live television play with Ingrid Bergman playing James's unnamed governess. Even so, anyone prepared to scour the internet should be able to find five or six adaptations of the tale for the small or the large screen, along with a 1972 "prequel" starring Marlon Brando as the living Quint entitled *The Nightcomers*. Two adaptations of the story have been released with different titles: *The Innocents* (1961) and *The Haunting of Helen Walker* (1995).

Culture, convention, and adaptation

In a straightforward sense, a film adaptation can accommodate a story to a new culture by changing its setting. Thus Rusty Lemorande's 1992 version of *The Turn of the Screw*, which sets it in the 1960s and has a female narrator (played by Marianne Faithfull) tell her story to a woman's therapy group, clearly "reculturizes" the story. But an adaptation does not have to change the setting of a story to reculturize it. Adaptations are like forgeries and translations: they always seem to bear traces of the cultures from which they have emerged. So far as James's novella is concerned, what seems in particular to have interested many filmmakers during the past four or five decades is its underlying suggestion of sexual corruption. It is hard to imagine that so many adaptations would have been made had the Freudian interpretations of the novella—which, broadly described, see the ghosts as hallucinations produced by a sexually frustrated governess—not drawn attention to hints of sexual frustration and also of pedophilia, homosexuality, and extramarital sex in James's text. James's text is also full of religious elements and suggestions, and some adaptations do try to do justice to these, but the relative weight accorded to these two aspects of the novella in many recent adaptations reflects the cultures of the adapters rather than the cultures in which James lived and about which he wrote.

By common consent, one of the best film adaptations of the novella is the 1961 *The Innocents*, directed by Jack Clayton and based on William Archibald's stage adaptation of James's story—thus making it an adaptation of an adaptation. According to Lawrence Raw, "The screen play for *The Innocents* went through several drafts, with many different people—including Archibald, Clayton, and the writers John Mortimer, Nigel Neill, Rhys Adrian, and Truman Capote—contributing to it" (Raw 2006, 60), although not all of these are mentioned in the film's credits. In its own way, the film is a splendid example of successful adaptation, and a number of the terms suggested by Robert Stam could be appropriated to describe it, including perhaps "selection, amplification, concretization, actualization, critique, extrapolation, popularization, reaccentuation, transculturization."

The Innocents stars Deborah Kerr as the governess, and (again by common consent) one of the most shocking moments in the film is when the young boy Miles kisses the governess goodnight on the lips, but extends the kiss in what is unambiguously a sexual manner. It seems clear that this element in the film comes from the culture of the 1960s and not of 1898 when the novella was first published. It is not that the novella contains no hints that the young pre-adolescent children have had some sort of sexual relationship with adults, but that the explicit manner in which this element is presented in the film bears the mark of a culture later than James's. Lawrence Raw reminds us of the importance of the film's "conditions of production."

> Much had changed in Hollywood in the decade separating *I'll Never Forget You* from *The Innocents*. Censorship had been relaxed; in December, 1956, the Production Code was rewritten to allow references to previously forbidden subjects such as drug addiction, abortion, prostitution, and miscegenation, although topics like sexual perversion were banned. (57)

Two other significant factors concerning the film—the age of the lead actress and the decision to use monochrome film—need also to be understood in light of cultural attitudes in the Britain of the early 1960s.

At the time Deborah Kerr made the film she was about forty years old, whereas the governess in James's story is, we are told, twenty years old at the time of the events she reports in her narrative. Laurence Raw notes that it had become something of a tradition for the role of the governess to be played by older actresses. "Beatrice Straight was thirty-four and Flora Robson was fifty when they starred in *The Innocents* on Broadway and in London; in two of the television adaptations, the leading role was played by Sarah Churchill (forty-three) and Ingrid Bergman (forty-four)" (59). Why should this be?

One of our culture's most lasting stereotypes during the time since James's story was published is that a "frustrated, hysterical, unmarried governess" would be more likely to be older than just twenty years old. The one-sentence summary of the film given in the 1999 edition of Leslie Halliwell's *Film and Video Guide* reads, "In Victorian times, a spinster governess in a lonely house finds her young charges possessed by evil demons of servants now dead." The word "spinster" is used neither in the film nor in James's tale. Laurence Raw suggests that director Jack Clayton wished "to challenge the prevailing view of spinsters as witches or people suffering from mental problems" (63), and that this is why he contrived to make the governess remain something of an enigma. Assuming that Clayton did indeed have such an aim, it is a moot point whether or not he achieved it in the film.

Filming *The Innocents* in black and white would have been more obviously a "decision" in 1961 than it may appear today. Films were still being made in black and white at this time, and *The Naked Edge* in which Kerr also starred in 1961 was also made in monochrome. But the five films in which Kerr starred before these two films were in color, and by 1961 to make a film in black and white bespoke either a desire to save money or a decision that monochrome was somehow fitting. I suspect that the conventional associations of monochrome were deemed appropriate to the filming of a ghost story designed to scare the viewer. Alfred Hitchcock's *Psycho*, released a year earlier in 1960, was also filmed in monochrome: because black and white images were looked on as old fashioned by the 1960s, the monochrome film helps to evoke a sense of "the past."

Narrating vs enacting

The case of *The Turn of the Screw* is particularly useful in illustrating some of the crucial differences between a verbal narrative such as James's novella and a performance such as one of the film adaptations of the work. This is because the fact of narrative in *The Turn of the Screw* is so central to its artistic effect.

In the opening pages of the novella, an unnamed "outer" narrator reports on a scene (set, we presume, in the present day of the time at which it was published—1898) in which a group of adults exchange ghost stories on Christmas Eve. One of these adults, a man named Douglas, mentions a story concerning two children who witness some ghostly apparition. He agrees to tell the story, which he explains was told to him forty years earlier, by the governess of the story, who had subsequently become his own governess. Some days later, her written account is delivered, and he reads this story over several evenings to those assembled. The frame narrator explains that what the reader will then be given is a transcription of the governess's written account which Douglas passed on to him, but this is preceded by the frame narrator's summary of Douglas's introductory comments, which describe a meeting in London between the governess and her employer-to-be, the uncle of the two children in the story.

It is worth pointing out that although the reader is told that Douglas reads the governess's account to the assembled group, the narrative does not render this reading, but rather reproduces the governess's manuscript. In contrast, in Conrad's *Heart of Darkness*, the text gives the reader a purported transcription of Marlow's oral telling, complete with interactions with his listeners.

The foregoing account may strike you as long-winded, but even it compresses and simplifies the chain of connections necessary for the narrative to be delivered to Douglas's listeners and to the reader of James's tale. What is interesting is that film adaptations of the story typically simplify this chain of transmission. In *The Innocents*, for example, the Christmas Eve ghost-story session is missing completely—which means of course that the "outer" narrator and Douglas, and their exchanges and comments, are also absent. The film's opening credits actually run alongside an image of a woman's hands clasped in prayer. After a while a new shot reveals that the hands belong to the character who we later learn is the governess, played by Deborah Kerr. She changes the position of her hands from "clasped in prayer" to "clasped anxiously." On the soundtrack, a sort of sobbing, accompanied by birds twittering, can be heard. The shot changes from profile to full-face, and the woman says, "All I want to do is save the children, not destroy them. More than anything I love the children. More than anything." The scene then fades into the governess's interview with the uncle. At the end of this interview, the governess agrees to accept the position on the difficult conditions specified, and the film then moves to the governess's arrival at Bly, where the main action takes place.

What difference do these changes make? Perhaps their most important effect is, I think, to remove that combination of distance and claustrophobic imprisonment that James's original gives the reader. The distance comes from the fact that when we *read* the account of the governess's experiences, we seem to be at the end of a long chain of narrative transmissions. The governess told her story—which took place forty years before the opening of the tale—to Douglas, who repeats it to the gathered guests after the governess's death. The frame narrator receives the governess's written account from Douglas shortly before the latter's death. We are cut off from the source of the narrative by time and two deaths. We have only the words, written ostensibly by the governess. Neither she nor Douglas is alive to explicate them. In the first few pages of the novella, the reader learns that the governess is dead; at the start of *The Innocents* she is very much alive, there, in front of us. In the film, there is one "present time"; in the novella there are many. In the novella, everything we read after the frame narrator's introductory pages comes from the governess, and is given in her words. We are imprisoned in her account, in her way of seeing things. We can no more see her from the outside than we can see ourselves.

In the film, our sense that what we are seeing is *the governess's version* is more or less impossible to retain. Right from the start we look *at* as well as *with* her. The short opening scene of her praying and agonizing about the children raises an issue of which the first-time reader of James's novella becomes aware only toward the end of the tale: that in trying to protect the children she may actually destroy them. In the subsequent scene with the uncle, there is no suggestion that what we see may not actually have occurred—there it is, taking place before our eyes. But in James's novella, we learn of this scene through Douglas's report and not as part of the governess's account, even though, logically, Douglas can have had his information only from the governess. What the reader gets is Douglas's report of what the governess remembered about her interview with the uncle (or conceivably, what she invented). What the film viewer gets is the interview itself. The tale gives us a report of a report, a version of a version, while the film gives us the scene itself, however much the use of camera angle, cutting, and so on may encourage us to perceive the scene in a particular manner.

Because film *enacts* rather than *tells*, in other words, the governess is shown as a character along with other characters, and not as the source of all our knowledge about characters and events. It is true that by means of a variety of technical and artistic methods, a good filmmaker can cause us to sympathize with the governess and to adopt her point of view, but we never actually see things through her eyes and understanding in the way that we do when reading James's story. (There is even a scene in the film in which we observe the governess while she is asleep.)

The director of *The Innocents* does manage to keep the viewer in a certain doubt as to whether the ghosts are really there or are a product of the governess's imagination. But it is much more difficult for a filmmaker than for a writer to sow doubt as to whether something "really happened." Alfred Hitchcock has a nice comment in an interview in which he admits that in his film *Stage Fright* he made a mistake in putting in a flashback that was a lie. His comment draws attention to a key difference between films and written stories:

> Strangely enough, in movies, people never object if a man is shown telling a
> lie. And it's also acceptable, when a character tells a story about the past, for

the flashback to show it as if it were taking place in the present. So why is it
that we can't tell a lie through a flashback? (Truffaut 1986, 275)

This brief comment isolates a crucial difference: a lie can be *told* but it
is very difficult for it to be *shown*. When the real crime documentaries
shown on TV dramatize accounts told by suspects, they very often have
the word "re-enactment" superimposed on the screen so as to prevent
the viewer from making the automatic assumption that if we see it, then
it really happened. When we do see things happening on screen it is very
hard, and often impossible, for us to perceive them as someone's report, or
memory, or hallucination. Films concretize. Even in the age of digital image
manipulation, our senses still tell us that the camera cannot lie.

In James's novella the reader learns that the previous governess, Miss
Jessel, has died. The cause of her death is never given, even though—
tantalizingly—when asked in the opening pages what she died of, Douglas
replies, "That will come out." But it does not. In the course of her narrative,
the governess (who has just learned that the housekeeper, Mrs. Grose, does
not share Douglas's view of the previous governess's respectability) asks the
housekeeper about her death:

> "Poor woman—she paid for it!"
> "Then you do know what she died of?" I asked.
> "No—I know nothing. I wanted not to know; I was glad enough I did n't;
> and I thanked heaven she was well out of this!"
> "Yet you had then your idea—"
> "Of her real reason for leaving? Oh yes—as to that. She could n't have
> stayed. Fancy it here—for a governess! And afterward I imagined—and I still
> imagine. And what I imagine is dreadful."
> "Not so dreadful as what *I* do," I replied; on which I must have shown
> her—as I was indeed but too conscious—a front of miserable defeat. (James
> 1999, 32)

What seems obvious here—and this is amply confirmed by Henry James's
own comments about his strategy in this tale (from which I quote briefly on
p. 46)—is that James's aim is to get the reader to *imagine* why the previous
governess had to leave and how she died. An unwanted pregnancy, suicide—
these are possibilities that probably spring to the reader's mind. But in James's
text these imaginings are never confirmed, and they have to be set against
Douglas's statement in the opening pages of the tale that Miss Jessel "had
done for them [the children] quite beautifully—she was a most respectable
person—till her death." Note too that the reader has to guess not just what

happened to Miss Jessel, but also what both Mrs Grose and the governess *imagine* happened to her.

In *The Innocents* all of this indeterminacy is lost. Mrs. Grose tells the governess, "Miss Jessel put an end to herself; she was found in the lake." In the film Mrs. Grose also tells the governess that after Peter Quint died, Miss Jessel went into the blackest mourning, and that she "died of a broken heart," although in James's tale it is never made clear whether Quint or Jessel dies first. A later film version of James's novella—Ben Bolt's 1999 television film *The Turn of the Screw*—actually opens with a shot of Miss Jessel committing suicide by jumping into water. Accordingly when we see the ghost of Miss Jessel in this later adaptation we have already seen her in life. As the "ghost" is obviously the same as the person we saw committing suicide, a person who in life has *not* been seen by the governess, the viewer must assume that there really is a ghost and that it really is Miss Jessel.

My emphasis up to this point has been on what can be achieved in prose fiction that is beyond the ordinary scope of film. Clearly there is another tale to be told, and those interested in reading it will find an excellent starting point in Robert Stam's article, from which I have quoted a number of comments in this chapter. Film can do much—enormously much—that is beyond the scope of the printed page. Just the ability to combine moving pictures, sound, and language opens up for complex effects of potentially great artistic significance. The way in which the soundtrack at the start of *The Innocents* combines speech, the sound of sobbing and the twittering of birds establishes complex associations that are subtly developed as the film proceeds. We can see and hear Miles playing the piano, and piano music can later be used to suggest his presence even when he is off-screen. Film is certainly no less subtle a medium than prose fiction, but its subtleties are of a different order. In comparing an adaptation such as *The Innocents* with its source in a work of prose fiction we can learn to appreciate the unique potentialities of two different media, two related but independent artistic traditions.

Translations

This section should be read in conjunction with the section on World Literature (p. 237). It is clear that without a class full of super-polyglot students able to read many languages, World Literature courses must offer many texts in translation. Indeed, in a 2013 study, the title of which displays considerable skepticism toward the project of World Literature (*Against World Literature*), Emily Apter invokes the concept of "untranslatability." Such pessimism notwithstanding, in the present section I assume that all of us, and not just students on World Literature courses, will sometimes want or need to read a work of fiction written in a language in which they are not fluent. What follows, considers some of the issues involved in reading such works in translation, accepting that something is inevitably lost when a work is translated from one language to another, but asserting that a reader of a translated work may, by bringing a new perspective to it, discover elements hidden from native-speaker readers.

To start with, a personal anecdote. In 1983, two years after moving from England to Norway, I got married. My wife is Norwegian, and has two daughters, the younger of whom was at the time a teenager and an admirer of the pop group Pink Floyd. Spotting a copy of the group's first album *The Piper at the Gates of Dawn* in her possession, I told her that the album title was taken from a chapter in Kenneth Grahame's children's book *The Wind in the Willows*. She then pulled a copy of the Norwegian translation of the book off the shelf, and told me that I was wrong. I examined the book and discovered, to my dismay, that the chapter I remembered was indeed not there, and that my street cred was badly damaged. This was in the days before the internet, so it took me some time to check a copy of the original text of the novel—and there was the missing chapter, just as I remembered it. The Norwegian translation from 1949 was by Zinken Hopp, and contained no information that the translation omits a chapter from the original English edition.

The chapter in question (number 7) has the main characters in the novel joined by a mysterious, pipe-playing figure who clearly represents Pan, the pagan Greek God of wild nature, shepherds and shepherdesses, and rustic music. Why had this chapter been omitted from the translation? Perhaps because it adds nothing to the action of the story: it is indeed sometimes missing from abridged versions of the novel in English. But perhaps, too, because the publisher or translator feared that the open celebration of a pagan god would offend the Christian sensibilities of Norwegians in 1949, when the translation was first published, and especially because this was a book that would be read by and to children: universally seen as more vulnerable to corruption from books than adults. When the translation was reissued in 1973, the missing chapter was reinserted.

Discussion of literary translation generally concerns itself most with the problems of rendering specific words in a source text into specific words in another language so as to create a text that is "faithful" to the original, and I will have more to say about such issues below. But this example reminds us that both writers and translators have to negotiate social and cultural pressures and restrictions in their work.

And of course, so too do readers. Even when reading a work of fiction in one's own language, cultural differences can stand in the way of understanding. An English academic who taught for a while in Australia told me that he could not understand why his students all assumed that the family in James Joyce's short story "The Sisters" were very poor, until they explained that in Australia only the very poor would eat mutton (rather than lamb). Reading a translation, an extra layer of possible contamination has to be confronted: if the same word in English has different associations in the England of 2016 and 1716, or in present-day Britain and Australia, what of the associations of an English word and its translated equivalent in French, or Hindi, or Arabic? It is generally assumed that narratives such as novels and short stories "translate better" than poems, especially lyric poems, and there is something in this. Flow and process are so central to narrative that readers have less time or incentive to examine and absorb the cultural and semantic complexities of individual words than they do when reading a short lyric. Nonetheless, a single word can have a crucial force even in a very long novel, and the knowledge that this word has not been chosen by an author, but chosen by a translator to represent a word chosen by an author, should always be present at the back of a reader's mind during the act of reading a translated text.

I would like now to look at one specific example of the "translated life" of a particular novel, again sticking to the non-English language and culture with which I am most familiar: Norwegian. I will consider the tangled history of a translation not from English to Norwegian, but from Norwegian to English.

Case study: Knut Hamsun's *Hunger*

Knut Hamsun's first published novel, *Hunger* (in Norwegian, *Sult*), was issued in its full form in 1890, in Copenhagen. (At this time, written Norwegian and written Danish were more or less identical.) The novel has rightly been called proto-modernist: told in the first person, it plots the wanderings of an isolated and alienated individual in Christiania (sometimes spelled Kristiania, and now Oslo), trying to earn a living from his writing, but becoming increasingly affected by starvation and physical privation.

Read today, in light of what we now know about the fiction that would follow in the twentieth century, written by authors such as James Joyce, Virginia Woolf, and Franz Kafka, *Hunger* is an astonishingly prophetic work. Hamsun's alienated character-narrator is a sort of missing link between Fyodor Dostoyevsky's Raskolnikov (from *Crime and Punishment*) and Kafka's K (from *The Castle*). (In an important essay Jakob Lothe compares aspects of the modernism of these writers, and contrasts the opening of *Hunger* with that of Thomas Hardy's *Tess of the D'Urbervilles*. See Lothe 2002.) The narrator's outbursts against conventional norms and the divinity, his generally antisocial behavior (punctuated by acts of generosity), his contempt for the solid bourgeois individuals he meets in the course of the novel, and his inconclusive and abortive encounters with the young woman he names Ylajali—all of these elements are now familiar to us as typical of early modernism. The narrator's starvation produces effects in his mind that are part-hallucinatory, part what later became known as forms of defamiliarization, in which familiar things are "made strange" and perceived without the benefit of the knowledge that allows us to avoid looking closely at that which we take to be familiar. On a technical level, too, the author's use of Free Indirect Discourse (see p. 122) and of shifts backwards and forwards between the past and the present tense are also very much in line with later experiments by better-known modernist writers.

> Discouraged at not being able to prepare my article, I stuck my papers in my pocket again and leaned back on the bench. At this moment my head is so clear that I can think the most subtle thoughts without tiring. As I lie there in this position, letting my eyes wander down my breast and legs, I notice the twitching motion made by my foot at each beat of my pulse. I sit up halfway and look down at my feet, and at this moment I experience a fantastic, alien state I'd never felt before; a delicate, mysterious thrill spreads through my nerves, as though they were flooded by surges of light. When I looked at my shoes, it was as though I had met a good friend or got back a torn-off part of me: a feeling of recognition trembles through all my senses, tears spring to my eyes, and I perceive my shoes as a softly murmuring tune coming toward me. (Hamsun 2011 (Lyngstad), 21–22)

This is from the most recent translation of the novel by Sverre Lyngstad, published in 1996. *Hunger* was first translated by an Irishwoman named

Mary Chavelita Dunne, who used the pen name George Egerton. Her translation, published in 1899, renders this same passage as follows:

> Despondent at not being able to put my article together, I replaced the paper in my pocket, and leant back in the seat. At this instant my head is so clear that I can follow the most delicate train of thought without tiring. As I lie in this position, and let my eyes glide down my breast and along my legs, I notice the jerking movement my foot makes each time my pulse beats. I half rise and look down at my feet, and I experience at this moment a fantastic and singular feeling that I have never felt before—a delicate, wonderful shock through my nerves, as if sparks of cold light quivered through them—it was as if catching sight of my shoes I had met with a kind old acquaintance, or got back a part of myself that had been riven loose. A feeling of recognition trembles through my senses; the tears well up in my eyes, and I have a feeling as if my shoes are a soft, murmuring strain rising towards me. (Hamsun 2003 (Egerton), 13)

The passages are very close, and yet there are differences between them. Lyngstad's "good friend" and "surges of light" have a different ring from Egerton's "kind old acquaintance" and "sparks of cold light." So far as the second phrase is concerned, there is a simple explanation: Egerton's translation is based on the first, 1890, edition of the novel, whereas Lyngstad's is based on the version approved by Hamsun for the 1953 edition—the fourth edition to contain changes made by the author. In the former, the Norwegian word "koldt" (cold) appears; in the latter it does not. But so far as the first phrase is concerned, in both cases the Norwegian is "god bekjent"—a familiar acquaintance. While Egerton's version can be faulted for adding the word "old" here, Lyngstad's "friend" is less accurate than Egerton's "acquaintance."

One other detail deserves comment: where Egerton has "a fantastic and singular feeling," Lyngstad's version reads "a fantastic, alien state." The Norwegian "fremmed" can mean either "strange" or "foreign," so that both translations can be defended, but it is hard to avoid the suspicion that Lyngstad's version is influenced by twentieth-century theories of alienation, theories that have often used modernist literary texts as illustration. Nonetheless, "alien" is a better choice here, as the word contains the range of meanings from "strange" to "foreign" that the Norwegian word also encompasses.

Lyngstad's translation, when first published, contained comments on two translations of *Hunger* that preceded his own. Of Egerton's translation, he concedes that it is readable and that it contains few mistakes. But he claims that it "is not faithful to the original, since she felt compelled to expurgate the text of all explicitly erotic content. The most she allowed to slip through the Victorian censor that must have been operating at the back of her mind was a kiss or an embrace" (Hamsun 2011, xi). This criticism has made the rounds in English-language discussion of *Hunger*. It is repeated, for example, in *The Oxford Guide to Literature in English Translation* (France 2000, 573). And yet it is quite wrong. Egerton's translation was republished in the United States in 1920, and it was the American publisher, not Egerton, that then censored the text. The error is silently corrected in the edition of Lyngstad's translation reissued in 2011. Indeed, as critic Tore Rem has pointed out:

> Egerton's edition is in fact more explicit than the later editions that most Norwegian readers would encounter. Not only that, but it is, paradoxically, arguably more radical than Lyngstad's own translation. In Hamsun's 1890 edition, and therefore in Egerton's of 1899, the hero, for instance, gives Ylajali the command: "Off with that petticoat!," a line nowhere to be found in the 1907 edition or in the 1953 edition which Lyngstad primarily bases his translation on. The hero's famous blasphemous speech is substantially longer in Egerton than in later editions, and it is not qualified by the narrator's ironic tag sentence about it being "Alas, ... nothing but rhetoric and literature." (Rem 2002, 69)

Lyngstad is on surer ground, however, when he criticizes Robert Bly's 1967 translation. Bly might have seemed to be in a good position to translate Hamsun. His parents were of Norwegian ancestry, and in 1956 he received a Fulbright Grant to travel to Norway and translate Norwegian poetry into English. And yet a little knowledge—sometimes quite a bit of knowledge—can be a dangerous thing. Lyngstad lists errors in Bly's translation in a short essay and a 12-page appendix, errors that range from straightforward howlers, through over-literal renderings, to what he dubs examples of "reduced concreteness." One example must suffice to illustrate the extent of these weaknesses. In the third section of the novel, the narrator goes home with Ylajali, and makes sexual advances of a sort that can legitimately be classified as attempted rape. Here is a complete paragraph from this scene as translated first by Lyngstad and then by Bly:

> "Well, I never!" I blurted out. "Just you wait and see!" And I flung my arms lustily around her shoulders. Was the girl out of her mind? Did she take me for a complete innocent? Haw-haw, wouldn't I, though, by the living ... No one should say about me that I was backward on that score. What a little devil! If it was just a matter of pushing on, then ... (Hamsun 2011 (Lyngstad), 163; ellipses in original)

"Oh, you little fox!" I burst out. "All right, you'll see then." And I threw my arms firmly around her shoulders. Girl at a distance, beware! So she took me for an inexperienced boy. By the Lord, she would change her tune … No one should say about me that I couldn't keep up in *this* game. By the living Jesus, if all I had to do was to stay with it … (Hamsun 1967 (Bly), 175; ellipses in original)

Here there is no issue with different source texts; both translations are based on the same, final, 1953 Norwegian edition. The opening words of the paragraph in Norwegian are, "Nei men du store min"—a set idiom that means something like "Good gracious" or, as Lyngstad suggests, "Well, I never!" Bly wrongly takes the "du" (the intimate form of "you") to refer to Ylajali, and then has to create a descriptive term for her to mirror the narrator's irritation, thus leading to "you little fox!"—a characterization of Ylajali that has no place in Hamsun's original. (Is the English "minx" perhaps influencing him here?) Worse is to come: where the Norwegian has "Var piken fra forstanden!," Bly appears to have confused "forstand" (literally, "sense" or "understanding") with "avstand" ("distance"). Lyngstad's "Was the girl out of her mind?" is a reasonably correct rendering: Bly's "Girl at a distance, beware!" is ludicrously wrong.

What general lessons does this short account provide for the student having to choose between different translations? The most important one, I think, is to be aware that there are good and bad translations. Take note of advice you get from your lecturer; he or she has most likely investigated the strengths and weaknesses of those available in print and online. If you are in doubt, just try Googling "Best translation of X?" and see what different critics, reviewers, and bloggers have to say. More recent translations may not be better than older ones: Egerton's translation of *Hunger* is better than Bly's. And remember that sometimes small publishers publish good translations, and large, well-respected publishers publish bad ones. Translations that include notes or an essay from the translator are more likely to be reliable than those that do not. Where only one translation of a text is available, see if you can find commentary on its accuracy: the internet is a good place to start looking.

Second, bear in mind that different translations may not be easy to rank: each may have its strengths and weaknesses. Sverre Lyngstad's translation of *Hunger* may be more accurate than George Egerton's, but if you want to see what the novel looked like before Hamsun edited out some of the erotic and allegedly blasphemous material in the work, then Egerton's rendering is to be preferred.

Third, remember that all translations bear the marks of their time and culture. The fact that Egerton knew Hamsun (and was probably in love with him—about which you can read in Fjågesund, 2002), and translated *Hunger* not so very long after it was first published in Norwegian, means that it may catch the "spirit of the age" of the original better than later translations. As I have noted, a good edition of a translated novel will often contain notes on the translation, and sometimes an essay by the translator. Such an edition should make it clear what the source text is, if there are different editions with claims to be authoritative; it should explain terms that have a specific cultural significance; and it should draw attention to elements in the translation that have a significance that the reader may easily miss. For example, the French language distinguishes between two forms of the past tense, the *passé composé* and the *passé simple*. It is usual for novels in French to be written in the *passé simple*, but Albert Camus's *The Stranger* (*L'Étranger*) is written throughout in the *passé composé*, with only half a dozen occasions on which the *passé simple* is used. This was so unusual at the time the novel was first published in 1942 that it had something of a shock effect. It is impossible to convey this aspect of the novel in an English translation, and a good edition of the novel in translation will draw attention to this in an explanatory note or essay.

A final warning. Whatever you do, don't just go on to the internet and order the cheapest printed translation, or download the first electronic translation, that you find. While preparing this brief survey I looked for translations of Hamsun's novel on the internet and, in addition to the three print translations that I compared above, I found a fourth, "translated by W. W. Worster," and published in book form by Digireads.com in 2008. I knew that Worster had translated some works by Hamsun, but I was unaware that he had translated *Hunger*. However, when I received this book I discovered that although the title page does indeed state that the translation is by Worster, and furthermore claims "This edition copyright © 2008," the text is actually that of Egerton's translation—but not the complete one, rather the censored, American edition of 1920. I wrote to the publisher pointing this out, but received no reply. Likewise, if you download the free translation of *Hunger* available online from Project Gutenberg at <www.gutenberg.org> you will also get the censored version of Egerton's translation. However it is possible to download the full, uncensored version of Egerton's translation legally, from <https://archive.org/>, again for free.

So to misquote Robert Bly, my advice when it comes to choosing a translation is: girl or boy at a distance: beware!

Topics for discussion

- "Short stories make better films than do novels." Do they? If so, why?

- "A translator should try to be faithful to the original; a filmmaker adapting a novel should not." Do you agree? What is the difference between translating a novel, and adapting it for the screen?

- Do you agree that the biggest problem a filmmaker faces is that in a film private experience cannot be shown, and the public life cannot be hidden?

8

Critical Approaches to Fiction

Preview

This chapter deals with:

- Academic courses and critical approaches
- Classifying criticism into schools and approaches
- Structuralist and rhetorical narratology
- Literary critical traditions and approaches to the novel
- Textual, contextual, and ideological approaches

This chapter is not meant to substitute for a more detailed and comprehensive introduction to different literary theories and approaches. It is rather designed to help you to recognize these theories and approaches in the books and articles you consult while providing some information concerning their particular relevance to the study of the novel and shorter fiction. I start with some discussion of the ways in which courses of study may encourage (or discourage) specific critical approaches to fictional texts.

Courses and approaches

Discussion of critical approaches to fiction typically makes reference to schools of criticism as a means of categorizing these approaches, and, as in previous editions of this book, I do just this in what follows. For this edition, however, I add some comment on the ways in which different academic courses may encourage or even to some extent require a particular treatment of set texts.

A given novel can be adopted as a set text in a selection of quite different academic courses. I have myself lectured on Joseph Conrad's novella *Heart of Darkness* in courses with titles such as "The British Novel," "Realism and Modernism," "Nineteenth-Century British Literature," "The Fiction of Joseph Conrad," "Narratology," "Literature and Colonialism," "Travel Literature," "The Short Story and the Novella," and "Europe and Africa." The last-named course was offered by a department of Social Anthropology; the other courses by departments of English, Comparative Literature, and European Studies.

Just from the names of these courses it will be apparent that students will be encouraged to approach Conrad's novella in ways that are suggested by these titles, even if there will (indeed, should) be some shared aspects to the ways in which the text is read and studied. The set texts on some of these courses will all be works of fiction; on others they will all be literary works, but works belonging to different genres. And on some of these courses, literary and non-literary texts (historical accounts, non-fictional travel memoirs, non-fictional writings by a literary author) will together make up the syllabus. Some of these courses clearly direct attention toward matters formal and technical: "Narratology" and "The Short Story and the Novella," for example. Others direct attention toward political and historical contexts—either from which the text emerged, or which it can in some sense be said to be "about": "Literature and Colonialism" and "Europe and Africa," for example. Reading *Heart of Darkness* as one of a number of set texts on a course entitled "The Fiction of Joseph Conrad" a student would be expected to look at relations with Conrad's life and experiences, and with his other novels and short fictions.

We are talking here of matters of emphasis, not of mutually exclusive approaches. An understanding of the complexities of Conrad's narrative technique in the novella and of the work's combination of realist and modernist elements are certainly not irrelevant to studying *Heart of Darkness* on courses with titles such as "Literature and Colonialism" and "Europe and Africa." Conversely, studying the same work as a set text on a course entitled "Narratology" does not mean that some knowledge of Belgian imperialism or Conrad's experience in the Congo is irrelevant—far from it. Indeed, being able to bring some such information into an essay or a seminar discussion if you do it with tact and accuracy is absolutely to be recommended.

Categorizing criticism

Critical books and essays, unlike chocolate bars, are not required by law to contain a list of ingredients. In some cases the titles chosen by critics are helpful: "A Postcolonial Reading of *Jane Eyre*" or *Queer Henry James* leave little doubt as to the critical approach and theoretical allegiance of the writer (do not search for these books as I have invented them, but you will find many similar titles in bibliographies). If you are looking for criticism of *Jane Eyre* or of James's *The Turn of the Screw* that has a lot to say about narrative method, then these titles are not too promising—although of course you cannot rule out stumbling across some striking insights about narrative technique in a book or an article with a similar title. A title such as "The Personified Narrator in Charlotte Brontë and Henry James" is likely to indicate a work of much more use to you.

This much is relatively simple. If you can pull a book off the library or the bookshop shelf, then a skim through the contents list, the index, and a few pages will help you to decide if it is worth more serious reading. (You can often do this online, as publishers more and more frequently post previews of books that give you access to selected sections.) What students often find more difficult is the process of using a *categorization* of a particular critic's approach as a basis to *assess the force* of that critic's comments on a particular work.

Let me give a particular example, again using *Heart of Darkness*. The second edition of the Norton Critical Edition of Joseph Conrad's novella includes an extract from a book on Conrad by Robert F. Haugh to which the Norton editor gives the title "*Heart of Darkness*: Problem for Critics" (the essay is omitted in more recent editions of this textbook). Haugh pours scorn on the argument that Conrad's novella is a critique of Belgian imperialism, suggesting that this reveals a superficial understanding of the work, and concludes by arguing that the Conradian hero (such as Kurtz in *Heart of Darkness*) "in his remarkable actions … defines the mortal condition, and in his last moment of vision … sees all the scheme of the universe; and we share it in a moment of tragic exaltation" (Conrad 1971, 167).

Let us imagine that you are writing an essay on *Heart of Darkness*, and in the course of your argument you state that Conrad's novella is not primarily a critique of imperialism, Belgian or other, but rather represents a tragic view of the mortal condition, and you quote from Haugh's text to back up your argument. What is problematic about this is that it does not assess

Haugh's contentions in context: his book was published in the United States at a time (1957) when, because of the dominance of New Critical ideas, it was extremely fashionable to play down the extent to which works of literature engaged with specific sociopolitical situations or events, but it was more common to argue that "great" literature draws our attention rather to the human condition in general. This does not mean that we can just dismiss Haugh's arguments out of hand. It does, however, mean that they have to be assessed in light of Haugh's apparent critical beliefs and of the time at which he wrote. If you want to strengthen the force of your argument that Conrad's novella is about the human condition in general rather than an attack on a specific phase of imperialism, then you need other substantiating material: informed rebuttal of the views of critics who have taken a different view of *Heart of Darkness*, quotations from Conrad himself and from contemporary responses to the work, and renewed analytical attention to the literary text itself. Being able to categorize critical approaches should not mean that one prejudges the worth or the relevance of a book or an article, but it offers help in assessing the force of a given critic's argument.

In what follows in this chapter I divide critical approaches up into five main categories and a number of sub-categories. You should remember that a critical book or essay is unlikely to fit neatly into just one of these categories, but is likely to straddle two or more. In like manner, you too when writing an essay or taking an examination should be prepared to take what you find useful and relevant from the methods and theories associated with different approaches.

I find it convenient to start with one of the newer approaches that you may encounter.

Narratology: Structuralist and rhetorical

According to one account, the term "narratology" was coined as late as in 1969, and was subsequently popularized in the 1970s by structuralist writers, who applied the general principles of structuralist theory to the analysis of various examples of narrative. What distinguishes narratology as an academic discipline is that it has as its object of study *all* examples of narrative, literary and non-literary, fictional and non-fictional. However, because some of the most important and most highly valued narratives in our culture—and in other cultures—are works of literary prose fiction, narratologists have had much to say about novels, novellas, and short stories. And such has been the impact and influence of narratology that a good many of the concepts and terms that its practitioners have developed have been imported into literary criticism and into the study of literary narratives. It is no exaggeration to say that the development of narratology has revolutionized the study of prose fiction, and it has done this in a remarkably short time. Several of the terms that I list in the Glossary at the end of this book, for example, were coined by narratologists and adopted by literary critics in the course of a brief period of about a couple of decades. And behind the new terms were new concepts, or significant refinements of old concepts. Moreover, if literary criticism took much from narratology, it gave much, too. The foundational work of modern narratology—Gérard Genette's *Narrative Discourse* (first published in French as *Figures III* in 1972 and in English translation in 1980)—in its attempt to chart the system governing all narratives, pays detailed analytical attention to Marcel Proust's *A la recherche du temps perdu* (1913–27).

Structuralist narratology

Narratology is a rapidly expanding and multifaceted field of study, but in the course of its brief but influential life two distinct phases or types can be discerned: *structuralist narratology* and the more recent *rhetorical narratology*. The origins of structuralism as a body of theory are generally dated to Ferdinand de Saussure's *Course in General Linguistics* which was compiled from notes taken from his lectures by Saussure's students after his death, and first published in French in 1916. Saussure's most influential move in this work was to distinguish between what he terms "static" and "evolutionary" linguistics. Nowadays, the terms "synchronic" (or structuralist) linguistics and "diachronic" (or historical) linguistics are generally used to make the same distinction in English.

Saussure pointed out that language could either be studied in the way that, at the time he wrote, was traditional: by charting its development over time, or, alternatively, by looking at a given language as a functioning system at a particular moment of time without any concern for how it got to be that way. Saussure, incidentally, believed that these two approaches were complementary, although it is common to read claims that he wished to replace historical linguistics with synchronic linguistics. Those narratologists who used Saussure as their theoretical starting point adopted his synchronic approach to the study of language as a model (or "paradigm"—hence "the linguistic paradigm") for the study of narrative, and they attempted to construct a "grammar" of different systems of meaning in narratives in the way in which Saussure had written of the construction of a synchronic grammar of language.

Accordingly, early structuralist narratologists adopted some of the terms used by structuralist linguisticians. Gérard Genette, for example, takes his terms "mood" and "voice" from the structuralist analysis of language, and applies them to his own analysis of narrative methods. In my discussion of rhetorical narratology below, I will summarize some of the problems attached to the use of such terms by narratologists, and the reasons that may lie behind a stubborn Anglo-Saxon reluctance to adopt some of them. Certain of these terms have, however, indubitably caught on: for example, one of the most fruitful appropriations of a term and its related concept from structuralist grammar by narratologists involves the concept of "frequency," which I discuss on p. 137.

Central to structuralist linguistics is a concern for an abstract form of analysis that is not concerned with the particular meaning of a single sentence, but in the underlying system that makes meaning possible—its *grammar*. Structuralist narratologists share a comparable concern, although they have differed as to whether they are looking for the grammar of a particular narrative text, a set of texts, or of narrative in general. Thus the Russian folklorist Vladimir Propp (mentioned on p. 130) was interested not in any particular folktale, but in the underlying system or grammar that enabled the generation of large number of seemingly different folktales. Just as one grammar allows the generation of an enormously large number of grammatical sentences in English so too, the argument goes, one "grammar" of the folktale could be discerned behind any given folktale in a particular cultural or generic tradition.

Structuralist narratology in its purer form, accordingly, focuses far less on the detail of individual works than on the manner whereby they exemplify a set of possibilities open to the genre as a whole. Like the variant of linguistics upon which they are based, literary-critical structuralisms tend to be ahistorical, concentrating upon systems as they operate at a given moment of time rather than on their modification over time.

What structuralist narratology has given the student of the novel and of shorter prose fiction, then, is a set of concepts and their related terms that denote aspects of the underlying "grammar" of narratives. In some cases, this has involved refining and sharpening existing terms and concepts—thus the older term "point of view" has been refined by modern narratologists so as to enable a distinction between "perspective" and "voice" (see p. 113). Another example involves a narratological appropriation of the terms "diegesis" and "mimesis," used in the third book of Plato's *Republic* to distinguish between cases where the poet himself is the speaker (diegesis) and cases where the poet creates the illusion that speeches should not be attributed to him personally (mimesis). Gerald Prince's *Dictionary of Narratology* (1988) defines "diegesis" rather differently, as either the fictional world in which events occur in a narrative, or "telling" as against "showing" (see p. 131).

Structuralist narratologists have made several other important contributions to the analysis of literary narrative. Perhaps the most important of these has been the refinement of the distinction between "story" and "plot" (see p. 134). But many other theoretical advances in the study of literary narrative have been powered by the work of structuralist narratologists—important work on key techniques such as Free Indirect Discourse (see p. 122), for example. Attempts to apply some other concepts appropriate to the study of language—such as that between *langue* and *parole*—to narratives, have been less successful, and this has inspired some narratologists to look for an alternative model for narrative than that provided by structuralist linguistics. This search is one of the forces that has powered the shift from the linguistic paradigm to the rhetorical paradigm. Instead of the model being that of the grammar of a language as it exists in the heads of native speakers at a given time, the model is that of the persuasive delivery by one person of an utterance to another person or persons—known from antiquity as the art of rhetoric.

Rhetorical narratology

A commonly perceived problem with structuralist narratology has involved the terminology that it imports from structuralist linguistics. The rhetorical narratologist James Phelan makes the following comment in relation to a term that he himself has proposed.

> I want to explain why I use the term "character narration" rather than the more common "first-person narration" or narratology's more specialized "homodiegetic narration." "First-person narration" is, as Genette points out, insufficiently precise because any narrator, regardless of the grammatical person used to refer to the protagonist, can say "I." But Genette's more precise terms have not caught on beyond the field of narratology; they have simply

proven to be infelicitous coinages for most other contemporary critics in the United States. (Phelan 2005, xi)

Other structuralist-narratological terms, such as "tense" and "mode," have never enjoyed general acceptance in English because they are already used to express different meanings. The critic Robert Burden, writing about Joseph Conrad's *Heart of Darkness*, has, while making a set of absolutely correct and important distinctions, displayed something of the off-putting nature of the terminology of structuralist narratology.

> the first [frame] narrator is *extra-diegetic* but also *homo-diegetic* (located outside the main story as narrator, while participating in it as narratee). Marlow ... is ... *intra-diegetic* and also *auto-diegetic* (located in the main story as narrator while participating in it as its central character or protagonist). (1991, 54)

The presence of the explanatory notes in parentheses doubtless acknowledges the writer's awareness that his readers are in need of help at this point, but if use of the terms requires such glosses, then one must ask whether one might not dispense with the terms altogether and use just the glosses.

However, the rise of a rhetorical narratology that, while recognizing and incorporating many of the insights and conceptual tools of structuralist narratology, has moved to supplant some of these and to build on others is not just a matter of terminology. Richard Walsh has suggested that, in many respects, "the structuralist enterprise is now as much a part of the history of literary theory as Russian Formalism: narratology's figuration of narrative as a language (in accordance with structuralism's linguistic paradigm) has proved unsustainable ..." (Walsh 2007, 54). The title of the book from which this comment is taken—*The Rhetoric of Fictionality: Narrative Theory and the Idea of Fiction* (2007)—makes Walsh's affiliations with a rhetorical approach clear. Walsh's funeral oration over structuralist narratology may be premature, but there is no doubt that the rise of rhetorical narratology has exposed some of the shortcomings and limitations of structuralist narratology.

So what is rhetorical narratology? At bottom, one can say that whereas structuralist narratology can be understood as a *textual* approach to narrative, rhetorical narratology is a *communicative* approach to the same topic. Whereas the structuralist narratologist homes in on the text, and analyzes it with little or no direct reference to the writer, the reader, or the different social and cultural contexts in which these individuals have lived, written, and read, the rhetorical narratologist sees the text in terms of its *mediating function*—that is to say, in terms of the ways in which it forms a link in contact between human beings living in different times and places.

In his book *Narrative as Rhetoric: Technique, Audiences, Ethics, Ideology* (1996), James Phelan asks the (rhetorical!) question, "What does it mean to treat narrative as rhetoric?" (1). He answers this question by taking a short fiction (Katherine Anne Porter's "Magic" [1928]) that is itself "a narrative of rhetoric, that is, a narrative whose central event is the telling of a story" (1). He then draws attention to parallel acts: a character in the story, a maid, tells a story. As he comments, she is telling "*a particular story to a particular audience in a particular situation for, presumably, a particular purpose*" (4). But so too, he reminds us, is Katherine Anne Porter. After an extended discussion of the story and of its different levels of rhetoric, Phelan provides a summarizing comment. "[T]he phrase 'narrative as rhetoric' means something more than that narrative uses rhetoric or has a rhetorical dimension. It means instead that narrative is not just story but also action, *the telling of a story by someone on some occasion to someone for some purpose*" (7–8). Narratives are designed to have an effect on readers, and readers are indeed affected by the narratives they read. Moreover, writers' purposes and readers' responses are not independent of "occasions"—when a work is written and read, and in what situation broadly understood.

The Canadian poet and novelist Margaret Atwood has an amusing prose poem entitled "Murder in the Dark" in which she reminds us of the fact that authors have designs on their readers (Atwood 1984, 29). Her title refers to the game in which a group of people are dealt out pieces of paper. All but two of these are blank, but one has a black spot on it indicating "murderer," while another has an "X" written on it indicating "detective." The lights are turned out, the players mill around, then the murderer puts his or her hands round a victim's neck and the victim screams. At this point, everyone must stand still except the murderer, who can reposition him- or herself. The lights are then switched on and the detective must, by questioning people, find out who the murderer is. Everyone must tell the truth except the murderer.

Atwood suggests a number of ways to relate this game to books, writers, and readers. In one version, the murderer is the writer, the detective is the reader, and the victim is the book. In another, more worrying, version, the murderer is the writer, the detective is the critic, and the victim is the reader. It is this latter pattern that clearly appeals to Atwood, who proceeds to portray herself (the author) as hiding in the dark, with designs on the reader and with her hands reaching for the reader's neck. And she reminds her own, present, reader, that when questioned, the murderer must always lie.

"Murder in the Dark" is amusing and thought provoking, and its perspective has a lot in common with that of the rhetorical narratologist, who is always reminding us that authors and their narrators are not necessarily friendly, transparent, innocent collaborators with the reader, but are often pretending to be what they are not, misleading the reader about their motives, and never switching the lights on but forcing the reader to stumble about in the dark. Rhetorical narratologists remind us that just as a structuralist linguist is uninterested in meaning but is concerned with the system that makes meaning possible, so too a structuralist narratology may tell us something about the formal tools available to the writer of fiction but little or nothing about how and why these are used in a particular case, and with what effects on the reader.

How different are the results—the readings—that a rhetorical narratological approach generates from those enabled by other approaches? Let me take one example, again from James Phelan's book *Narrative as Rhetoric: Technique, Audiences, Ethics, Ideology*. In a chapter of this book on Joseph Conrad's novella *The Secret Sharer* (1910), Phelan discusses what he calls "the homosexual secret" of (or in) this story. Conrad's tale ostensibly gives a first-person narrator's account of how, in his first voyage as a sea captain, he rescued and hid a fugitive murderer, and finally helped him to escape. In recent years, a number of critics, including Phelan, have considered the possibility that the tale hints at a homoerotic or even homosexual relationship between narrator-captain and fugitive. Phelan admits that Conrad's relation to this homosexual secret is "hard to pin down," and he comments as follows:

> If we opt for the understanding of the captain as in control of his narrative, we will also see Conrad as carefully in control behind the captain. If, however, we see the captain's revelation as unwitting, we may decide that Conrad has planned it that way or that Conrad himself is not fully aware of the homosexual subtext. In fact, articulating the secret and specifying the evidence for it helps to illuminate one of the fault lines in rhetorical reader response: the one running between the authorial and the flesh-and-blood audiences. On the one hand, the evidence points to a design on Conrad's part that the authorial audience needs to discern; indeed, without such a pattern of evidence, I would not suggest that this secret is a plausible one. On the other hand, I can't help wondering how much my perception of this secret is a consequence of my historical moment, in particular, the way in which the gay studies movement has made me and numerous other academic readers especially attuned to representations of same-sex desire. (Phelan 1996, 127–8)

Note here that Phelan's approach does not abandon close attention to Conrad's text; his skills as a close reader would satisfy the most rigorous of old-fashioned "words-on-the-page" critics. But he extends his concern from Conrad's captain-narrator to Conrad as author, wondering about both Conrad's conscious control over what lies under the surface of his text (its "subtext"). Moreover, these three instances—author, narrator, and text—are interrelated: change your view of the level of control exerted by the author, and you may need to change your understanding of the narrator's control over *his* (or *her*) story.

Then there is the reader and his or her "moment." Phelan asks himself whether what he as reader detects in Conrad's tale is partly or wholly the product of his own historical circumstances, including the ways in which his awareness of the possibility of "representations of same-sex desire" has led him to detect just such a representation here. In this case, we have come to what, in his earlier formulation, he uses the term "occasion" to denote: here the occasion of his own reading of Conrad's tale.

But there is yet another step to be taken, and perhaps here the most challenging aspects of a rhetorical narratology become apparent. The above-quoted passage continues as follows:

> Is the secret constructed by the implied Conrad or the flesh-and-blood critic? I don't fully know. Furthermore, there is a sense in which, within the rhetorical approach, it is not all that important to know. When the situated subjectivity of the reader encounters the otherness of the text, the analyst cannot always definitively locate the boundaries that mark off flesh-and-blood and authorial audiences—or more generally, reader, text, and author—from each other. The synergy among these different elements of the rhetorical transaction is precisely what the rhetorical approach wants to acknowledge. (128)

It is at this point that those I have termed "old-fashioned 'words-on-the-page' critics" would undoubtedly throw up their hands in horror. For here the "old-fashioned" view that a single text may be complex and resistant but can nonetheless be analyzed correctly or incorrectly gives way to the text as a component in a complex chain of mediated and creative relationships. "Creative," because a reading now does not just respond to what is already "in" the text, but may involve the creation of meaning via the interaction between text and reader in a particular context on a specific occasion. Whether an element is already "in" the text—put there by the author—or whether it is created through interaction between text and critic or reader frequently cannot be known for sure. Not only that, but as Phelan declares, "it is not all that important to know."

The student reader may be forgiven for responding that it may be very important "to know" (or to pretend to know) such things in certain specific contexts: writing an examination answer, for example. The rhetorical narratologist may respond that novels and short stories are not composed in order that they should be written about in examinations, but for the pleasure and enlightenment of readers. And if the usage for which they are intended causes problems for those sitting, or grading, examinations, then this should serve to remind us that writers and readers have different goals from examiners and examinees.

The literary critical tradition

Narratology is a recent development in terms of the history of the novel and prose fiction, although those who have interested themselves in what Henry James termed "the art of fiction" have always taken an interest in many of prose fiction's technical and formal characteristics. A concern with narrators, point of view, plot, chronology, characterization, and so on did not first emerge with the development of modern narratology.

There is a sense, however, in which the differences between structuralist and rhetorical narratology can be compared to a major division in more traditional approaches to prose fiction—that between textual and contextual approaches. This is a crude distinction, but it serves as a useful starting point for considering differences in the ways that prose fiction and, to some extent, other literary genres have been studied by literary critics.

Textual approaches

Textual critics concentrate on the actual words of the novel or short story that they are studying, and pay less, or no, explicit attention to biographical information about the author (including other writings by him or her), information about the author's society and historical period, the history of readers' responses to the novel, and so on. Critics known as *formalists* take a particularly exclusivist attitude to the text. A formalist critic is one who pays great attention to the *form* of a literary work, but the term has been applied mostly to three groups of critics: the Russian and Czech formalists whose most influential work was written in the second two decades of the twentieth century, and the Anglo-American New Critics who flourished in the 1940s and 1950s. Because the Czech formalists (often referred to as the "Prague School") were influenced by the work of Ferdinand de Saussure, there are important connections between formalism and structuralist narratology.

Russian and Czech formalism

Russian formalism developed during the First World War and lasted into the 1920s, but by 1930 antagonism from Soviet authorities had forced its most prominent members into exile. One Russian formalist, Roman Jakobson, moved first to Czechoslovakia and then to the United States, and René Wellek's migration from Prague to the United States established important lines of indirect influence from Russian and Czech formalism through to the Anglo-American New Criticism.

The importance of Russian formalism for critics of the novel is that members of this critical and theoretical grouping paid serious attention to the novel, and developed an analytical terminology which has remained important. It is the Russian formalists we have to thank for the distinction between *fabula* and *sjužet* (story and plot in my terminology, see p. 134).

The Czech formalists of the "Prague School" flourished from the late 1920s through to the German invasion of Czechoslovakia, and had less to say about prose fiction than their Russian predecessors. However, they further developed certain concepts of the Russian formalists such as that of *defamiliarization*, producing their own concept of *foregrounding*, which has played a useful role in criticism of prose fiction.

New Criticism

The New Critics—to oversimplify somewhat—at least in principle rejected what they termed "external" or "extrinsic" information more or less *in toto*, preferring to concentrate upon "the work itself" in relative isolation. In certain ways, New Critical approaches resemble structuralist-narratological approaches: they pay little or no attention to extrinsic factors, and consider either "literature" or a genre such as the novel as a self-enclosed system that can be studied in terms of itself. Thus, just as the New Critics argued against "The Intentional Fallacy" of granting extratextual statements of intent any prioritized weight in interpreting that text, so too structuralist critics have followed Roland Barthes in agreeing to announce "The Death of the Author" (see Glossary) so far as the interpretation of his or her text is concerned. In terms of method, the New Critics typically use what has been called *close reading*—taking a small section of a novel or a recurrent verbal feature and analyzing this in exhaustive detail, drawing attention to the sort of issues that I outlined in the checklist in Chapter 6 (p. 162). The poet T.S. Eliot, in a lecture delivered in 1956 and entitled "The Frontiers of Criticism," referred disparagingly to the New Criticism as "the lemon squeezer school of criticism," and this put-down does sum up something about close reading as practiced by the New Critics. Because the New Critics (unlike the Russian formalists) developed their critical ideas and practices mainly in connection with the interpretation and analysis of poetry, they tended to bring to the criticism of the novel a new concern with such matters as linguistic detail, paradox, tension, irony, and symbolism. The title of an essay written by the New Critic Robert Heilman and first published in 1948, "'The Turn of the Screw' as Poem," can be seen to announce a representative critical trajectory.

Such critics have, by common consent, contributed enormously to our understanding of the complexity and subtlety of great works of fiction, moving us away from merely discursive discussion of plots and characters and demonstrating that the novel is as receptive to detailed analysis as is poetry. Chapter 5 in the present book, "Analyzing Fiction," could not have been written without the work of such critics. The analytical methods of structuralist narratologists also owe a considerable debt to the New Critics. Jonathan Culler summed up this debt in 1981 when he admitted that "[w]hatever critical affiliations we may proclaim, we are all New Critics, in that it requires a strenuous effort to escape notions of the autonomy of the literary work, the importance of demonstrating its unity, and the requirement of 'close reading'" (1981, 3).

Post-structuralism and deconstruction

For the purpose of a brief survey such as this, "post-structuralism" and "deconstruction" will be treated as synonymous. However, certain usages distinguish between the two terms in important ways and make post-structuralism a more general position of which deconstruction represents one possible variant.

Again, to simplify, we can say that post-structuralism extends and even universalizes the structuralist assumption that no element in a system of meaning has significance in and for itself but only as part of the system. There should, accordingly, be no elements in any text whose fixity of meaning can be used as a foundation stone or interpretative bedrock. Jacques Derrida, the French high-priest of deconstruction, calls such a desired point of stability in the swirl of meanings generated by the play between the different components of the system a *transcendental signified*, in other words, an element that has meaning in and for itself rather than a meaning that is defined by relations to other elements. For Derrida, meaning is always relational, and thus when he famously (or infamously) declared that there was nothing outside of the text, he was arguing that there was no such fixed, extratextual point by reference to which the meaning of a text could be plotted and fixed.

Deconstructionists are accordingly committed to the unweaving of apparently firm and solid interpretations through a display of the way in which such interpretations rely upon such a transcendental signified. Examples of such transcendental signifieds in the criticism of the novel would be such things as "the intended meaning of the author," "how contemporary readers read the work," and "what the work means to a competent reader." In practice, deconstructionist readings very often involve dispensing with such traditional critical points of reference as these, and responding to the work in a way that is unconstrained by them.

At an early stage in undergraduate study, such post-structuralist readings are either terrifying or exhilarating or both. The terror can be reduced by noting that post-structuralist readings often rely upon relatively simple processes of de- or recontextualization of a work or an element in a work, playing with the interpretations that can be generated once the work or the passage is unhooked from a fixed textual or other context that restricts its possible meanings. The exhilaration can be eye-opening, revealing how our readings and responses are often channeled into familiar paths by reliance upon familiar but unregarded anchor-points.

Contextual approaches

If the most valuable aspect of the work of textual critics has been their development of methods of critical analysis, the aspect of their work which has gone least unchallenged by others has been their rejection or playing down of "extrinsic" information as an adjunct to the reading and criticism of literature.

Socio-historical approaches

Sociological and historical critics have placed great stress upon the need to understand the context of the author's own society and his or her position within it, both as an individual (a member of a particular social group or class) and as an author (a member of a literary group, relying on certain publishers, libraries, readers, and so on).

Let us return to Joseph Conrad's *Heart of Darkness*. Recent critics have suggested that the novella can only be fully appreciated in the context of what European powers were doing in Africa in the last part of the nineteenth century, and in particular in the context of statements made by prominent Belgians—including King Leopold II—concerning the Belgian exploitation of the Congo (where Conrad himself had worked). Thus some of Leopold's statements concerning the (extremely brutal) Belgian exploitation of the Congo make claims about opening to civilization the only part of our globe where Christianity has not penetrated, and piercing "the darkness which envelops the entire population." Conrad's ironic use of words such as "civilization" and "darkness" in the novella, it has been argued, can only fully be appreciated in light of his aim to mock and expose statements such as Leopold's.

Some contextual critics argue that more than this is needed. The narrative indirection in the novella—Marlow's inability to tell the truth to Kurtz's "Intended" and his feeling that he cannot make himself understood to his auditors—mirrors a situation in which comfortable Europeans who had never witnessed colonial brutality firsthand in Africa were unable to hear the truth spoken by such as Marlow. This argument raises some problems in its turn. Conrad deliberately left out localizing information such as the name of the European country or the part of Africa in which the novella was set, and with regard to his short story "Youth," he made it clear that he very much objected to having such information reinserted (Davies and Stape 2005, 457). Novelists themselves tend, like Conrad, to be suspicious of critics who fill in background information claimed to be relevant to their works. Asked whether it was important to know the history of Czechoslovakia to understand his novels, Milan Kundera replied, "No. Whatever needs to be known of it the novel itself tells" (Kundera 1988, 39). Key issues to be confronted are: Does the information point to material that had a *determining* effect on the writing of the work? What information does the reader *need*, or benefit from?

Sociological critics have also drawn attention to the important influence that factors referred to collectively as the "sociology of literature" can have on the creation of works of literature: publishers, patronage (see Glossary), literacy rates, readership profiles, libraries, booksellers, and so on. It is clear that if only a part of society is literate and thus able to read novels, then this will affect the sort of novels that are written—as was the case in eighteenth-century England. If the habit of listening to novels read aloud by a friend or family member becomes customary in a society, this will alter the importance of the fact that many members of that society are illiterate. If success as a novelist depends upon having your work accepted by the circulating libraries, and these do not accept anything that does not conform to a set of rigidly moralistic views, then the reader should know this before expressing dissatisfaction with the portrayal of sexual relationships in a novel—and should also be on the lookout for concealed hints and suggestions! Some of these concerns have been pursued in the field of study known as "World Literature," which I discuss in the next chapter.

Cultural materialism and New Historicism

Cultural materialist and New Historicist critics allow some of the insights (or claims) of post-structuralism concerning the difficulty or impossibility of confronting or interrogating reality other than through texts of some sort, while retaining a degree of what we can call a realist commitment—a belief that reality is not just texts or closed systems of meaning. New Historicists typically juxtapose literary and non-literary texts in ways that produce unexpected and frequently highly illuminating flashes of insight. Cultural materialists are especially interested in following the life of literary works through successive ages and varied cultures, and often responses to and interpretations of a literary work are as much of interest to them as is "the work itself." It has to be said, however, that up to now these critics have paid less attention to the novel than to other literary genres.

Postcolonial theory

The field of postcolonial theory is fashionable, fast growing, and riven with debates. At its best, it has confronted readers and critics with the hidden or unstated implications of colonial and imperialist relations between lands and people for the reading and interpretation of literary works. Thus my discussion of the way in which Jean Rhys's *Wide Sargasso Sea* interrogates Charlotte Brontë's *Jane Eyre* (in Chapter 9, p. 242) owes much to the new perspectives brought to literary and cultural criticism by postcolonialism. A key text is Edward Said's *Orientalism* (1978), which attempted to describe how Western domination of subject lands required not just physical force but also a discourse, a system of ideas by which European culture was able to manage and even to produce "the Orient."

Following Said's example, many writers have attempted to use the vantage point of a period after colonialism ("post" colonialism) to interrogate literature written both during and after the classic forms of colonialism, and also to draw attention to the silenced voices of those who wrote from the standpoint of the oppressed. Postcolonialism has played an important role in the development of the field of "World Literature," and I discuss this in the next chapter.

Generic approaches

A genre is a type or kind of literature, and we often refer to prose fiction itself as one of the three main literary genres, along with poetry and drama. There are many different ways to classify literature generically, and the novel has been divided into a number of sub-genres by various critics—for example, the gothic novel, the epistolary novel, the postmodernist novel (see the Glossary). Note that these generic divisions involve different sorts of category: there is no single set of principles that are available for dividing novels into sub-genres, and as a result a single novel can usually be classified in more than one way.

A generic approach to prose fiction insists that we cannot begin to read or understand a novel until we are clear as to what sort of novel it is. This typically means getting clear about the author's intentions with regard to his or her work, although it can also involve seeing how successive generations of readers have classified a work. Thus—the argument goes—unless we understand the picaresque tradition (see the Glossary) within which Defoe's *Moll Flanders* is written, we will run the danger of misreading and misunderstanding this novel.

I list this under "Contextual approaches" because a genre is a sort of context: it helps us to understand the aims of a writer and the expectations of readers, to recognize conventional elements as well as divergences from what is conventional. Obtaining a better understanding of a work's generic associations can often be one of the most useful benefits of reading critics.

Biographical approaches

A writer's life is also a sort of context. The more books by the same novelist that we read, the more we become conscious of common or similar elements in them (as well as of contrasts, new directions, surprise variations), and the more we begin to build up a picture of the man or woman behind the printed text, constructing an idea of his or her values, interests and attitudes. We can, in short, start to use the life as a sort of explanatory context for the work.

Such an interest in an author can make us want to know more about the person in question in his or her own right, and then we may start to read the novels in light of what we have learned about the author—even in terms of what he or she has said about them explicitly. Such a biographical approach to the study of the novel—reading fictional works with explicit reference to the life, personality, and opinions of the author—seems straightforward enough, yet it is fraught with problems and has involved many sharp debates. In a piece entitled "The Spirit of Place," D.H. Lawrence advised, "Never trust the artist. Trust the tale" (Beale 1961, 297), and generations of critics have pointed out that novelists can be very bad guides to their own work.

Why should this be so? We can isolate a number of possible explanations. First, there is the issue of *inspiration*. The writer seems often not to use the conscious and rational part of his or her mind for literary composition—something that has been appreciated since the days of antiquity when a term equivalent to "inspiration" was first used. As a result, secrets of the created work may not be accessible to the rational, enquiring mind in the same way that details of other actions and utterances are. Second, the author may want actually to *conceal* something: a real-life model, a confessional element in the work, or whatever. Third, the author may comment on his or her work a very long time after writing it. Fourth, the very fact that an author creates a "secondary world" in a novel (see p. 19) means that his or her primary world may not always be the best model to understand the work.

When it is a matter of relating a novelist's work to his or her life, similar problems may emerge. How do we know which experiences in a writer's life were reflected (or transformed) in his or her work? Experiences which seem minor to us may have been crucial to the person who had them—but, even so, they may not have influenced the writing of a given work.

If all this sounds like a counsel of despair, I should add that it is not meant to be. Biographical information can be of great help in enabling us to respond more fully to a novel or a short story. However, we should be fully aware of the problems involved in such critical procedures, and we need always to be sensitive to what the work itself can tell us.

Take D.H. Lawrence's novel *Women in Love*. It seems very likely that Lawrence's experiences in the period of the First World War had a crucial effect on the writing of this novel even though the war is not mentioned at all in it (and although it was written in the middle of these experiences). Lawrence was medically unfit for service in the war, and came under suspicion from the authorities for his anti-war views and because his wife Frieda (*née* von Richthofen) was the cousin of "the Red Baron"—a man notorious for shooting down scores of British airplanes. Lawrence and Frieda were even forced to leave their cottage on the Cornish coast, allegedly because they were suspected of signaling to German U-boats. Now although none of this is directly referred to in *Women in Love*, it is arguable that much of the tone of that novel—in particular its dismissive remarks about England—can only be fully understood in light of these experiences. Moreover, the comments in the novel by Birkin about the destructiveness of the "mechanical principle" have, too, to be seen in the context of Lawrence's complex responses to the slaughter of the war—a slaughter that is not mentioned directly in the novel at all.

Psychological and psychoanalytic approaches

In broad terms, the distinction between psychology and psychoanalysis is that between theories of how the mind functions and theories of how the secrets of the mind can be unlocked through analysis. The question is then, which mind—the author's, the reader's, or a character's? Let us return to Henry James's novella *The Turn of the Screw*. A succession of critics has attempted to psychoanalyze the governess in this tale, finding evidence of mental instability of a sort that leads her to hallucinate and to imagine the ghosts that she reports on to the reader. But given James's clearly reported intention to make the reader "think the evil" in this tale, it is possible to concentrate on the way in which readers and critics have responded to and interpreted the work, and to thus use the *work* as a way of analyzing *readers*. (Compare the way in which the Rorschach "ink-blot test" is used; the interpretive responses of different individuals to the same "blot" are used to tell us something about these individuals rather than anything about the blot itself, which is normally possessed of an appropriately Jamesian ambiguity.)

Finally, it is possible to use James's novella as a way of psychoanalyzing James himself, and there is no shortage of critics who have attempted to do just this.

Certain short stories and novellas have been much used by psychological and psychoanalytic critics: Sigmund Freud wrote an influential essay on E.T.A. Hoffmann's "uncanny" tale "The Sandman," while Marie Bonaparte's study of the tales of Edgar Allan Poe remains much-quoted. More recently, Jacques Lacan's analysis of Poe's "The Purloined Letter" has confirmed the American writer's work as a richly seamed mine waiting for psychoanalytical excavation.

Children's literature, fairy tales, and folktales have also provided material for analysis by writers such as Bruno Bettelheim. Generally speaking, though, psychological and psychoanalytical criticism has had most impact on criticism of the longer novel through incorporation in other approaches, such as those of feminism and deconstruction.

Ideological approaches

I choose the word "ideological" for want of a better one, but I recognize that the problem with it is that it has a pejorative ring, suggesting narrow-mindedness and a lack of impartiality. These suggestions are not intended: all that I want to imply by my choice of this word is that certain critical schools and approaches carry with them an overt and conscious commitment to ideas, values, systems of belief that generally have a wider scope than the purely literary. Putting the matter crudely, knowing that a critic is a narratologist or a psychoanalytic critic does not help us to work out how they would vote or whether they are in favor of equal rights for men and women, whereas knowing that a critic calls him- or herself a feminist does give us information that may be relevant to an enquiry into such questions.

"Ideological" schools and approaches are often accused of imposing beliefs and positions onto innocent and resisting literary works, and there is no doubt that such accusations are sometimes justified. On the other hand, an ideologically committed critical approach may just as well illuminate something in a novel or a short story that has gone unnoticed by more seemingly impartial critics. In my personal opinion, for example, much criticism that can loosely be associated with Queer Theory (see p. 233) has indubitably revealed aspects of the work of well-known writers that has lain undiscovered for many years, and the same is true of feminist criticism.

Marxist approaches

Like sociological critics, Marxist critics are interested in relating literary works to the societies in which they were written. Marxism is a materialist philosophy, one which insists upon the primacy of material living conditions and the secondary nature of the ideas or beliefs that arise out of these conditions. It sees history as, in Marx's words, "the history of class struggle"—the history of struggle for control of the material conditions upon which life rests. It is on the basis of these material conditions, and in response to the struggle for them, that ideas, philosophies, mental pictures of the world develop—as secondary phenomena. These secondary phenomena may provide human beings with an accurate picture of reality, including themselves and their situation, but they may not. Ideologies are related to class positions and thus, in turn, to material conditions and the struggle for their control, but this is not to say that they provide a reliable picture of these. Traditional Marxists have laid great stress upon the distinction between base (or basis) and superstructure, seeing the social base as essentially economic in nature, and the superstructure as constituting the world of mental activities—ideas, beliefs, philosophies, and (in the opinion of some but not all Marxists) art and literature.

Marxists have been particularly interested in the novel because the novel can be argued to have emerged in response to a changed social situation and to the needs of an emergent class—the bourgeoisie in the capitalism that replaces feudalism. The Hungarian Marxist Georg Lukács, who remains an important critic of the novel, clearly also values the novel because of its association with realism, an association that holds out the promise of finding accurate rather than distorted analyses of social structures within realist (or "classical") novels. More generally, it seems clear that the novel typically (although not inevitably) raises issues concerning the relationship between the individual and society in a more historically detailed and concrete way than do poetry or drama.

Feminist approaches

Over eighty years ago, Virginia Woolf's *A Room of One's Own* (1929) startled readers by claiming that they lived in a patriarchy (a society ruled by men) and that this fact conditioned the ways in which novels were written (or not written) and read. In more recent years, a growing number of feminist critics have offered challenging alternative readings of the novel in general and of particular novels. Feminist critics have argued that not only have women had to overcome severe difficulties to become writers, but also that once they have produced novels, these have consistently been read in dismissive ways by male readers. Thus, once a woman had managed to become literate (no easy matter in the past), she had to overcome all sorts of male prejudices in the reception accorded to her work. As Virginia Woolf expresses it in *A Room of One's Own*, "This is an important book, the critic assumes, because it deals with war. This is an insignificant book because it deals with the feelings of women in a drawing-room" (Woolf 1998, 96). Moreover, as Woolf points out, it may be difficult for a woman to write about such things as war because of the domestic role to which she has been confined, and she declares that a woman could not have written *War and Peace*.

Feminist critics have also done much to show the ways in which male views of reality have dominated much fiction—especially, of course, that by men, and especially their views of women. Women are typically portrayed *in relation to men*, and are often seen in certain stereotyped ways—as passive, hysterical, emotional, "bitch" or "goddess." One of the works which introduced the new wave of feminist literary criticism was Kate Millett's *Sexual Politics*, first published in 1970. Millett's book is divided into three connected sections: "Sexual Politics," giving a theoretical basis for what follows; a section on the historical background detailing the movements toward female emancipation and those seeking to reverse their effects; and finally a section entitled "The Literary Reflection." In this final section, Millett looks at the work of D.H. Lawrence, Henry Miller, Norman Mailer, and Jean Genet. In the writing of all of these, she detects what we now familiarly refer to as patriarchal ideas—frequently linked to portrayals that debase, ridicule, and humiliate women. The following comments on Lawrence's *Lady Chatterley's Lover* are representative:

> In *Lady Chatterley*, as throughout his final period, Lawrence uses the word "sexual" and "phallic" interchangeably, so that the celebration of sexual passion for which the book is so renowned is largely a celebration of the penis of Oliver Mellors, gamekeeper and social prophet. While insisting his mission is the noble and necessary task of freeing sexual behavior of perverse inhibition, purging the fiction which describes it of prurient or prudish euphemism, Lawrence is really the evangelist of quite another cause— "phallic consciousness." This is far less a matter of "the resurrection of the body," "natural love," or other slogans under which it has been advertised,

than the transformation of masculine ascendancy into a mystical religion, international, possibly institutionalized. (Millett 1971, 238)

Millett's book is a fine piece of polemic, and one which jolted both men and women into reconsidering various well-known authors and characters from previously unconsidered perspectives.

A variety of feminist criticism which believes "gendering" to take place at a fundamental level concerns itself with what, using a French term, is called *écriture féminine*—"feminine writing." Theorists of *écriture féminine* believe that men and women use language in fundamentally different ways, and that the task of the feminist critic is to give women writers the self-confidence to write as their femaleness requires, and not to ape the writing habits and style of men. As the term suggests, the concept in its modern form has originated in France, especially in the writing of Hélène Cixous. It has, however, antecedents and parallels outside France, and it is interesting in this context to see how many of the recent formulations about "writing and the body" have parallels in Virginia Woolf's essay "Professions for Women" (1942).

A further task undertaken by feminist critics has been that of the "rediscovery" or reinstatement of a number of (mainly women) writers whose works have been undervalued or forgotten.

Ecocriticism

A relatively new development, ecocriticism is less than half a century old. As the name suggests, its concern is with the relationship between literature and our changing physical environment. This concern includes, most obviously, depictions of the physical environment in literature. But it also includes the ways in which ideas of nature are preserved and disseminated in and by literary works. The tradition of portraying a nature that has been ravaged by human beings is not just a recent one; Richard Jefferies's *After London, or Wild England* (1886) is a strikingly modern-seeming account of a London that has been abandoned by man following some unspecified catastrophe and that is being recolonized by nature. Behind Jefferies's portrayal, of course, is a polemic against what human beings have done to nature and, indirectly, to themselves.

Much literature, of course, has used comparisons and contracts involving humanity and nature to make points about humanity; the new force of ecocriticism is that while it clearly includes the condition and fate of humanity in its agenda, it is also interested in the fate and condition of nature for its own sake.

Queer Theory

If Marxist criticism has sought to expose hidden links with class or economic interests in novels and short stories, Queer Theory attempts to expose different sorts of concealed or disguised elements in literary works. Although "queer" was originally used as a term of abuse to stereotype homosexuals, it has now been reclaimed by gay men and women and used to express pride in their sexual identity.

Since the legalization of homosexuality in Britain, the United States, and many other societies, it has been possible to write far more openly about issues of sexual orientation. This, combined with the fact that many writers in the past have not enjoyed this freedom, has meant that criticism aimed at exposing gay sub-texts in the works of "canonical" writers has flourished in the course of recent decades. When I was an undergraduate studying English in the 1960s, no one mentioned the fact that E.M. Forster was homosexual, and no one considered whether this might have a bearing on the novels that he wrote. Today this is a factor that it is hard not to take into account in reading and responding to Forster's novels.

On a rather more sophisticated level, Queer Theorists have done much to challenge our sense of the fixity of gender divisions—partly by drawing attention to the sort of gender destabilization that can be traced in important novels and short stories. Much very important recent work on the fiction of Henry James is of this sort, and goes far beyond the treatment of James's tales and novels as a sort of homoerotic *roman à clef* (see the Glossary). Instead, the binary gender divisions fixed by social convention are seen to match up very imperfectly with the personal gender preferences and identities of James's characters, while the interplay of gender, class, and culture can be traced in the convolutions of Jamesian narrative. Here, for example, is a passage from James's short story "The Death of the Lion" (1894). In this story, the narrator discovers that a newspaper journalist named Guy Walsingham is actually a woman, while one named Dora Forbes is referred to as "he."

> I was bewildered: it sounded somehow as if there were three sexes. My interlocutor's pencil was poised, my private responsibility great. I simply sat staring, none the less, and only found presence of mind to say: "Is this Miss Forbes a gentleman?"

> Mr Morrow had a subtle smile. "It would n't be 'Miss'—there's a wife!"
> "I mean is she a man?"
> "The wife?"—Mr Morrow was for a moment as confused as myself. But when I explained that I alluded to Dora Forbes in person he informed me, with visible amusement at my being so out of it, that this was the "pen-name" of an indubitable male—he had a big red moustache. (James 1970, 115–16)

While not rejecting a more traditional reading that sees this and comparable passages as examples of James's whimsical humor, Queer Theorists have shown how effectively (and, I think, deliberately) they chip away at a conventional sense that the sexual diversity of the human race can be neatly divided into two standard genders.

Cognitive criticism

The label "cognitive criticism" is something of an umbrella term. Some cognitive critics attempt to link developments in cognitive neuroscience to the study of literature: the title of Paul Armstrong's book *How Literature Plays with the Brain: The Neuroscience of Reading and Art* (2013) associates it with such attempts. Armstrong's book is accessible and thought-provoking, but as he admits, "it is not likely that neuroscience will provide us with new interpretations of literary texts" or tell us "whether there are actually ghosts in *The Turn of the Screw*" (2013, 3). Less "hard science" in its orientation, Lisa Zunshine's book *Why We Read Fiction: Theory of Mind and the Novel* (2006) does focus on specific novels, and she has much of interest to say about Virginia Woolf's *Mrs Dalloway*, Samuel Richardson's *Clarissa*, and Vladimir Nabokov's *Lolita*. The book focuses on the way in which readers use socially acquired skills to read the minds of fictional characters. Zunshine links such skills to particular socio-historical developments, arguing that the advent of print culture and literacy actually makes possible what she terms "theory-of-mind-intense" fictional narratives. (See pp. 22 and 23 for a discussion of the importance of literacy and printing for the rise of the novel, and pp. 28 for a mention of theorists who argue that early fiction lacking in displays of characters' inner lives confirms that such skills are not universal.)

Thing theory

Thing theory focuses on the way in which (normally physical) "objects" become "things"—in other words, when they assume a meaning for human beings that is not intrinsic but acquired, not universal but social and cultural. In novels, such things may be natural or created—from the leaves that Marianne rhapsodizes about in Jane Austen's *Sense and Sensibility* to Henry James's golden bowl. Although he does not associate his study with this particular approach, Thomas J. Otten's *A Superficial Reading of Henry James: Preoccupations with the Material World* (2006) shares many of its preoccupations. For Otten, "there is in James a powerful account of the material world, a deeply formative ontology that is continually overwritten and obscured by James's epistemological concerns" (3). Put simply, James's "powerful account" of what things are, is "overwritten and obscured" by "how we know about things." The material objects in his novels are thus pumped full of meanings by the attempts characters make to know them—both for these characters and for readers.

Topics for discussion

- Are the most useful critics the ones who share your own beliefs and opinions?
- "If I want to quote a critic, should I say something about his or her theoretical position? How do I find out what it is?"
- When two critics disagree about a novel, how are we expected to decide who is right?
- Is "close reading" an unnatural way to deal with a novel or short story?
- Should we ignore an author's political or religious views when studying one of his or her fictional works? When are such views relevant to reading and understanding a novel?

World Literature and Fiction

Preview

This chapter deals with:

- Studying fiction in the context of World Literature
- Centers and peripheries: the novel and cultural imperialism
- The fiction of atrocity as World Literature
- A peripheral case study: Knut Hamsun's *Hunger*

World Literature

World Literature courses are becoming increasingly common in a range of undergraduate programs. The title does not specify a particular critical theory or approach, but as I noted in the previous chapter, specific course-titles carry with them implications about critical approaches, theories, and methodologies, and World Literature is no exception.

"World Literature" is both an old and a recent term. It is old in the sense that the term has been used (in different language forms) for about two centuries by writers from Johann Wolfgang von Goethe onwards. It is new to the extent that courses in World Literature are now more and more replacing courses in "Comparative literature," "General literature," "The Western canon," "Literature in translation," and—a standard designation in the United States—"Great Works 101." All these terms are genre-inclusive, and the syllabus attached to any such course may include poems and plays in addition to works of prose fiction, but because novels are perceived to be more "translatable" than poems (see p. 101), World Literature courses are often fiction-heavy. But what distinguishes such courses from the alternatives listed above? And what implications do such courses have for how students are expected to approach individual novels or short stories?

Given that a course in World Literature in the English-speaking world may, and normally does, include works written in English, it is not hard to see how a World Literature course differs from one entitled "Literature in translation." And given that the world is larger than the West (however one defines this problematic term), much the same may be said about "The Western canon." But what about courses with titles such as "Comparative literature," "General literature," and "Great works?" The editors of *World Literature: A Reader* suggest that "comparative literature … had difficulties living up to the ambition of being sufficiently inclusive to the literatures of the world," and displayed a lack of interest in so-called "minor, and particularly non-Western literatures" (D'haen et al. 2013, x). This suggests a close link between World Literature and post-colonialism, and Emily Apter, the title of whose book *Against World Literature* indicates a skepticism regarding the growth of the category and the courses, argues that between 1991 and 1997 "the journal *World Literature Today* cast World Literature as a hosting ground to literary postcolonialism" (Apter 2013, 1). Courses in World Literature have mushroomed at much the same time that traditional language courses such as French and German have been disappearing from universities all over the English-speaking world, and some of those unable to teach Thomas Mann or Albert Camus in the original language have been able to continue teaching them in translation on World Literature courses.

Mads Rosendahl Thomsen concedes that the "concept of world literature is notoriously difficult to define," and notes facetiously that it excludes literature by Martians, but allows that the term may imply "that world literature is the best of the world's literature" (Thomsen 2008, 2). This emphasis on quality can also be found seventy years earlier in Albert Guérard's 1940 essay "What is World Literature?": "A selection there must be; but the basis of our selection should be excellence. It is far more important for us to know world masterpieces than to clutter up our minds with the names of local mediocrities" (Guérard 2013, 51). This lurches in the direction of "Great Works" courses, offers a very different emphasis from that of post-colonialism, and runs the risk that judgments about quality may reflect the cultural preferences and blindnesses of "our" (European or North-American) situation (a common objection to "Great Works" and "The Western canon").

Franco Moretti has also displayed skepticism about the term. Writing in 2013, he states:

> Although the term "world literature" has been around for almost two centuries, we don't yet have a genuine theory of the object—however loosely defined—to which it refers. We have no set of concepts, no hypotheses to organize the immense quantity of data that constitutes world literature. We do not *know* what world literature is. (Moretti 2013b, 123)

Moretti's own writings focus particular attention on to the processes of distribution and circulation of literature, and his method of "distant reading," which tries to see how the form of the novel in particular moves from "centers" of political and cultural dominance to "peripheries" lacking power and influence, is one that many World Literature courses pay particular attention to, and I will return to it below.

Many attempts to define World Literature link it to processes of globalization. From this perspective, World Literature is not so much a category created by educational systems, but more a matter of developments in the larger world, and the literature in part produced by such developments, to which educational systems respond. We can trace this view back at least a couple of centuries. In a much-quoted comment in *The Communist Manifesto* (1848), Karl Marx and Friedrich Engels reveal a more positive attitude to cultural globalization than is prevalent today:

> And as in material, so also in intellectual production. The intellectual creations of individual nations become common property. National one-sidedness and narrow-mindedness become more and more impossible, and from the numerous national and local literatures, there arises a world literature. (Quoted in D'haen et al. 2013, 17)

In a similar vein, Emily Apter quotes with approval Simon During's view that the "interest in world literature obviously follows the recent rapid extension of cross-border flows of tourists and cultural goods around the world, including literary fiction" (Apter 2013, 2). Note how different commentators imply that the concept of World Literature arose in their own times—times spanning more than two centuries.

For other commentators, World Literature is the product not so much of peaceful activities such as tourism, but of more traumatic experiences. Indeed Goethe, who may well be the originator of the term, writes in his introduction to Thomas Carlyle's *Life of Schiller* (1830):

> There has been talk for some time of a general world literature, and indeed not without justice. For the nations, after they had been shaken into confusion and mutual conflict by the terrible wars, could not return to their separate and independent life again without noticing that they had learned many

foreign ideas and ways, which they had unconsciously adopted, and had come to feel here and there previously unrecognized spiritual and intellectual needs. (Quoted in D'haen et al. 2013, 15)

Some commentators have developed an alternative term—"cosmopolitan writing"—to capture what they see as a new internationalism in writing. For Jessica Berman (2001), this cosmopolitan impulse is already to be found in modernism with its imagined cosmopolitan communities, while for others such as Berthold Schoene (2009), cosmopolitanism is an aspect of globalization, seen most clearly in an economic system and the threats of terror that are not and cannot be restricted to national borders.

At this point, I would like to turn from the theorists of World Literature to some examples of the ways in which their ideas may help us to look at certain novels and short stories in a different way. Let us first focus on the novel's association with travel and movement in the world from the point of its emergence.

The international life of the novel: The novel and travel

The novel has always been associated with movement and travel—with *mobility*, both geographical and social. In the passages I quote in Chapter 2 from *Moll Flanders* and *Oliver Twist* we are reminded how important being able to move from place to place was for Moll and for Oliver, but we should remember, too, that for both characters *geographical* movement is closely linked to a desire for *social* movement or advance.

This stress upon mobility is one of the points at which the socio-historical conditions of the novel's emergence, and the social tensions which contribute to its birth, are transposed into generic and formal features. The very name "novel" directs our attention to what is new, and we typically discover the new by changing our location and by seeing either new things, or old and familiar things from an unusual perspective. Peter Burke has suggested that travel is one of the factors which can help to explain the emergence of what he refers to as "the autobiographical habit" in the sixteenth century. As he reminds us, this "was the age not only of the rise of the autobiography or journal but also of fictional narratives in the first-person story, such as the picaresque novel in Spain or the sonnet-sequences of Sidney, Shakespeare and others." He proposes three likely reasons for this development: first, the fact that this is the age in which print becomes a part of everyday life, which means that the diffusion of printed models can create a new or sharper sense of self; second, urbanization, because the alternative styles of life offered by the city encourage a sense of individual choice; third, travel, because travel "encourages self-consciousness by cutting off the individual from his or her community" (Burke 1997, 22). While we remain in familiar surroundings we receive more regular confirmation of our identity from those who expect us to continue to be what we have been in the past, but in a strange situation, surrounded by people we do not know, we become aware that to a certain extent we are able to choose who we are, and indeed it is easier to *change* who we are: character and individuality are no longer givens.

In the mainstream novel, as the line of prose snakes its way ahead from page to page, pressing on in the direction our culture calls "forward" and always moving away from its point of birth to that last line where it will stop for ever, it constantly reminds us not just of the individual human life journeying from birth to death but also of the typical fictional hero or heroine: progressing ever forward, continually encountering new blank pages untouched by the pen of experience.

There is, then, a relationship of mutual dependency between the novel's concern with the new, its questioning of laws and conventions, its curiosity about the strange and unusual, and its stress on geographical mobility. From its birth, the novel conceives the whole world as its territory, as a page to be written on.

Imperialism and gender

When people move around the world they meet and interact with other people with whom they may have a range of different sorts of relationship: collaborative, subservient, antagonistic, competitive, or exploitative. The travel experiences of a tourist are not those of a refugee; those of a soldier are not those of an ambassador. The modern novel emerged in a world in which relationships between peoples were certainly not of an exclusively collaborative or equal type; by the end of the seventeenth century, Europe was already some way into those processes of exploitation and repression which we know as colonialism and imperialism.

Firdous Azim has pointed out that from the moment of its birth the novel enjoyed an "imperialist heritage," one which is visible both in its themes and also in the problematic nature of its status: "[t]he novel becomes a form dealing with adventures in far-off lands, Oroonoko and Robinson Crusoe on the one hand, and the sexual adventures of bold and courageous women at home—Zara, Rivella, Moll Flanders and Roxana, on the other" (Azim 1993, 21). We can add that Moll Flanders's adventures are not just "at home": she also travels to America, where a significant portion of Defoe's novel takes place.

"Imperialist heritage" may sound somewhat tendentious, but it is nevertheless a fact that the modern novel emerged in Western Europe at a time when this part of the world was in the early stages of a long process of imposing its will and influence—by both peaceful and non-peaceful means—on other peoples. Thus the master–slave relationship in *Robinson Crusoe* has to be seen as more than just an interesting plot detail or method of exploring character. Defoe's hero explores his own individuality in a number of ways, but one that is of defining importance to this novel, as well as to the experience of its author and his or her fellow citizens, is the imposition of an individual and collective will on the inhabitants of other lands. Crusoe discovers who he is—*makes* his identity—in part by establishing Friday's subordination to himself.

In her book *The Ballistic Bard: Postcolonial Fictions* (1995), Judie Newman considers Jean Rhys's novel *Wide Sargasso Sea* (1966) and its attempted settling of accounts with Charlotte Brontë's *Jane Eyre* (1847), and in so doing shows how closely imperialism is knitted in to the very substance of this novel, including its treatment of gender. Jean Rhys's interest in the Caribbean aspect of Brontë's novel was doubtless related to her own problematic upbringing in Dominica and even more problematic travel to England, but her taking what had generally been experienced as a marginal or peripheral element in Brontë's novel and making it a central issue in her own intertextual reworking of *Jane Eyre* has had the effect of allowing modern readers to approach the earlier work from a revealingly different perspective. Newman points out that Charlotte Brontë's portrayal of Bertha is designed to obliterate all sympathy for her:

> [Bertha] is described ... in terms which appeal to both racial and sexual prejudices. Her hereditary madness, which is supposedly accelerated by sexual excess, clearly reflects Victorian syphilophobia. (The nineteenth century had shifted the point of origin of syphilis to Africa.) Brontë's Bertha has "a discoloured face," "a savage face" with "fearful blackened inflation" of the features: "the lips were swelled and dark." Successively described as a demon, a witch, a vampire, a beast, a hyena, and even an Indian Messalina, Bertha unites in one person all the available pejorative stereotypes. (Newman 1995, 14)

Newman draws attention to the description by (Brontë's) Rochester of Jamaica as "hell," its sounds and scenery those of "the bottomless pit." She also notes that when Rochester contemplates suicide he is saved by a "wind fresh from Europe," and she reminds us that "Penny Boumelha has observed that in *Jane Eyre* all the money comes from colonial exploitation" and that "Jane herself gains her financial independence as a result of a legacy from an uncle in Madeira who is connected to the same firm which Mr. Mason, Bertha's brother, represents in Jamaica." Finally, Newman, quoting again from Penny Boumelha, provides us with a phrase very similar to one already taken from Firdous Azim. For Boumelha, Rhys's vindication of Brontë's "madwoman" serves to display and to criticize "the legacy of imperialism concealed in the heart of every English gentleman's castle" (14; for Penny Boumelha's comments, see Boumelha 1988, 111–22).

Rhys's novel, in other words, helps us to see *Jane Eyre* as more than an English novel. It is that, of course, but it is also a novel that reflects and comments upon a network of connections that spans the world. The "madwoman in the attic" is the return of England's repressed self; she is imperialism's victim come home to haunt her oppressor.

Cultural imperialism and the novel

There is another, rather different, way in which the novel can be seen as an "imperialist" genre. William B. Warner has noted that, as the producer of the greatest number and variety of fictions, "France of the seventeenth and early eighteenth centuries is positioned as something of a 'Hollywood' for romances and novels." In like manner, as the novel conquered European culture in the late eighteenth and nineteenth centuries, so too did ideas, attitudes—ideologies—associated not now solely with France but with England, too, succeed in influencing and even dominating the cultures of Europe. Franco Moretti puts it thus:

> [I]n the crucial century between 1750 and 1850 the consequence of centralization is that in most European countries the majority of novels are, quite simply, *foreign* books. Hungarian, Italian, Danish, Greek readers familiarize themselves with the new form through French and English novels: and so, inevitably, French and English novels become *models to be imitated.* (Moretti 1998, 187)

In his *Atlas of the European Novel 1800–1900* (1998), Moretti provides powerful evidence in support of the thesis that by the nineteenth century the novel had consolidated a cultural dominance based in the centers of political and economic power in Europe—France and Britain. Not only does the novel come to dominate the bookshelf both in the private house and the public library from the late eighteenth century onwards (to the dismay, as Moretti reports, of nineteenth-century library committees), but novels set in, and emanating from, the powerful urban centers of major European powers—especially France and England—tend to dominate that increasingly large amount of shelving set aside for fiction. Moretti comments:

> Be it mid eighteenth-century Britain … or mid nineteenth-century Italy … the message is the same: the novel is *the most centralized of all literary genres*. And its centralization increases with the passage of time …
>
> Because, first, the novel closes European literature to all external influences: it strengthens, and perhaps it even establishes its *Europeanness*. But then this most European of forms proceeds to deprive most of Europe of all creative autonomy: two cities, London and Paris, rule the entire continent for over a century, publishing half (if not more) of all European novels. It's a ruthless, unprecedented *centralization* of European literature. (Moretti 1998, 165, 186)

Moretti develops some of these points in his 2000 essay "Conjectures on world literature," in which, focusing on the novel, he reminds us that our syllabus lists with perhaps ten titles provide us with a minuscule selection from the total number of novels written: "there are thirty thousand nineteenth-century British novels out there, forty, fifty, sixty thousand—no one really knows, no one has read them, no one ever will. And then there are French novels, Chinese, Argentinian, American" (Moretti 2013a, 161). What is more, this immense pool of fictional works is divided and circulated in ways that reflect international divisions of power and authority. David Damrosch cites Lawrence Venuti's observation that in 1987 "Brazilian publishers brought out over fifteen hundred translations of English-language books, while only *fourteen* translations of Brazilian literature were issued in England or the United States" (Damrosch 2003, 113).

Moretti further notes that the reliance of literary studies on tiny selections from this bewildering immensity is symbiotically related to an academic valorization of "close reading." Put simply, you cannot base the study of novels on a close and detailed verbal analysis of them if your target selection consists of ten thousand novels (Moretti 2013a, 162). Thus, a small canon facilitates close reading, and close reading returns the compliment by confirming the special value of those works chosen (for "canon," see the Glossary; for close reading, see p. 221). Moretti's way of breaking out of this closed circle is encapsulated in the title of his recent (2013b) book *Distant Reading*. As the title's play on the term "close reading" suggests, what Moretti argues for in this book is an approach that, rather than investigating a small number of texts, zooms back and looks at more general movements of large numbers of texts, often over extended periods of time, and on a world scale.

Center and periphery

One very influential conceptualization of Moretti's involves a distinction between "center" and "periphery," with London and Paris the classic centers from the eighteenth century onwards, to be joined in the twentieth century by New York. Where one society controls another because it is stronger militarily or economically, it is likely also to exert control ideologically and culturally.

But beyond this, we must remember that the novel requires a quite complex social and industrial machine for it to emerge as a dominant cultural force. Until very recently, most works of fiction were still read in printed form, and although this situation is changing, many of the points following apply as much to electronic as to printed texts. Indeed, access to printed books often presents far fewer problems to the very poor than does access to electronic texts. Printing involves not just the technical and economic means to produce and circulate books—a printing industry—but also a universal or at least widespread literacy that comes from an effective system of public education. Generally speaking, where literacy is not universal in a culture, more men than women are taught how to read and write. In those countries that have recently emerged from colonial rule not only may education be closed to many, but much of the publishing business may be controlled by foreign, often multinational, companies. Even when high levels of literacy are established in post-colonial countries, education systems have frequently been built up by colonial or imperialist powers and modeled upon European or North American lines. Given these facts, it is not surprising that little of the literature read by the student of English in many newly independent African countries was actually written by Africans, and it has taken time to alter this situation.

In his 2003 essay "More conjectures," Moretti asserts that:

> hardly any forms "of consequence" don't move at all; that movement from one periphery to another (without passing through the centre) is almost unheard of; that movement from the periphery to the centre is less rare, but

still quite unusual, while that from the centre to the periphery is by far the most frequent. (Moretti 2013c, 171)

This generalization has to be taken together with Moretti's case that "when a culture starts moving towards the modern novel, it's always as a compromise between foreign form and local materials" (Moretti 2013b, 52). By "form" Moretti seems to mean something akin to "sub-genre"; thus early in *Distant Reading* he writes:

> In twenty years, with a striking rapidity, all the forms that will dominate Western narrative for over a century find their masterpiece. *The Mysteries of Udolpho*, 1794, for the Gothic; *Wilhelm Meister's Apprenticeship*, 1796, for the *Bildungsroman*; *Elective Affinities*, 1809, for the novel of adultery; *Waverley*, 1814, for the historical novel. In another fifteen years, with Austen and Stendhal, Mary Shelley and Pushkin, Balzac and Manzoni, almost all the main variations on the basic forms are also in place. (Moretti 2013b, 19)

It is these elemental forms that, according to him, circulate from and through centers to peripheries, getting plumped out with local content as they emerge in local variants.

For whom does the novel speak today?

Moretti's view of centers and peripheries almost inevitably leads to reflections about whether the dominance of a few "centers" actually seeps in to the very fabric of the form, making the novel a genre that has not just conquered the world, but has conquered the world on behalf of its European masters. Is the novel essentially a non-collective, "Western," and masculinist genre, used as a weapon of ideological propaganda or control by those cultures within which it emerged and from which it allegedly took its defining characteristics?

It seems to me that it is quite wrong to treat a novel written today in Africa or India as no more than a European import. As a starting point, consider the following words by the Indian novelist Mulk Raj Anand. They compose part of his introduction to a collection of Indian fairy tales:

> The stories contained in this volume were told me by my mother and my aunts during my childhood. The primary inspiration to retell them, therefore, came from the nostalgic memories of the hour when "once upon a time" began and when one's eyes closed long before the story had ended.

But I also had in mind the fact that in the old stories of our country lay the only links with our broken tradition. I fancied that only by going back to the form of these stories, told by mother to son, and son to son, could we evolve a new pattern for the contemporary short story. Of course, the modern short story is a highly developed folk tale if it is a folk tale at all. But a revival of the short story form … seemed a fit occasion to relate it to its more primitive antecedents which, surprisingly enough, seem to lie in the sources of the sheaf of tales which I have gleaned. At any rate, I must confess that although I have taken in much new psychology into my own writing of the short story, I have always tried to approximate to the technique of the folk tale, and the influence of these fairy stories has always been very deep on my own fiction.

These fairy stories can, therefore, be read not only by children, but by those adults who have not forgotten the child in them. And, however foreign they may seem to non-Indians, in their atmosphere and effect, I offer them here, not as something completely alien to the Western peoples, but as familiar and well known themes to set beside the fairy tales which they have read in their childhoods, because there has been much international traffic in folk lore between India and the West through traders, travellers, gypsies, craftsmen and crusaders, and many of the stories current abroad have their source in the same springs in which these stories have their origin. (Anand 1946, 7–8)

The comments are interesting for a number of reasons. First, because they remind us that just as a tradition of fictional tales emerged and established itself in Europe before literacy became widespread, so too can comparable traditions be found in those cultures and societies which were on the receiving end of colonialism and imperialism. Second, because, as Anand points out, the stories with which he is concerned strike non-Indian readers as both foreign and familiar. Oral prose fiction traditions may often share common or familial features, but they almost always possess culture-specific elements. Third, because, as Anand also points out, "there has been much international traffic in folk lore," and although the emerging novel may reflect the inequalities and injustices of its mother-culture, it is also the resting place for many perspectives which are critical of that mother-culture and its dominant values. Indeed, as the phrase "dominant values" may remind us, the societies from which the early novel emerged were by no means monolithic; they contained minority views, "faultlines," oppositions, and contradictions. And finally, Anand's comments can be set alongside Albert Guérard's claim that "*World Literature begins, not in the graduate school, but in the nursery. Our children are told immemorial tales, the fairy lore of all ages and climes*" (Guérard 2013, 51).

Anand's collection of fairy tales was published in 1946, in the dying years of British India. (Indian readers of the collection probably picked up straightaway what the discreet term "broken tradition" referred to.) Anand knew as well as anyone what imperialism and colonialism were capable of, but he also knew that in addition to the crusaders and the traders there were also travelers and craftsmen moving from country to country, and that the commerce was not all one way. The Roma people (formerly called gypsies because they were believed to originate in Egypt) came originally from India, and were certainly part of Western European culture by the eighteenth century, although of course neither a dominant nor a privileged part.

In short, not only can a novelist writing in newly independent lands incorporate powerful elements of native storytelling tradition into his or her work, but in important senses the European tradition of the novel is itself by no means exclusively European.

Where does this leave us in our quest to determine the extent to which the genre of the novel is or is not value-neutral? It seems to me to be arguable that the novel is probably less well suited to the expression of collective or communal experiences and beliefs than are some other forms such as orally delivered poetry or drama. Not only do such performance arts involve a direct contact between artist-performer and audience, thus allowing both for collective response and also collective feedback from audience to creator, but the drama also allows for the dramatized presentation of distinctive voices—often simultaneously. Now the skilled novelist can resist the individualistic and monologic tendencies of the genre, and in my comments on the narrative technique used by Lewis Grassic Gibbon in his *A Scots Quair* (see p. 154), I suggest that this technique is designed to help us to experience a working-class collectivity and that it largely succeeds. Nevertheless, it is arguable that the representation of such collectivity is more difficult for the novelist than it is for the dramatist. What is more, a culture whose vital life is more closely associated with oral expression and an oral tradition than with written expression and a written tradition may find more natural expression in the drama or poetic recital than in the printed pages of a book.

Having said all this it seems to me that, if we are asking the crude question "Is the novel essentially a bourgeois, individualist and 'Western' (or imperialist) genre?," it is perhaps more productive to look at issues of tradition and economic control than of innate generic identity—in other words, to focus more upon differences of culture and on socioeconomic issues than on the inherent formal or technical qualities of the genre. Indeed, so far as the latter are concerned, I should repeat that although the novel does seem to be generically predisposed in the direction of representing individual experience, especially when that experience is that of a socially and geographically mobile individual, it is also the case that the novel is a genre which seems to survive by permanently revolutionizing itself, in light of which fact it is dangerous to talk of what the novel cannot do because of any innate generic identity.

Snatching the pen

If we turn to the issues of tradition and economic control, we do, I think, see how particular values and perspectives may be associated with the genre. To explore this issue, I would like to take two novels by the Kenyan novelist Ngũgĩ Wa Thiong'o: his first published novel, *Weep Not, Child*, which appeared in 1964, and *Devil on the Cross*, which was published first in Gĩkũyũ in 1980 and then in the author's own English translation in 1982. In fact, when *Weep Not, Child* was first published, its author's name was given as "James Ngugi."

Weep Not, Child is a wonderful first novel and was welcomed as such on its initial publication. Re-read today from the perspective of Ngũgĩ's later work, the novel nonetheless gives the sense of a writer having to adapt to the requirements of a tradition and a publishing situation which are partly alien to him and which restrict his freedom of movement. Take the following short passage from the opening pages of the novel:

> There was only one road that ran right across the land. It was long and broad and shone with black tar, and when you travelled along it on hot days you saw little lakes ahead of you. But when you went near, the lakes vanished, to appear again a little farther ahead. Some people called them the devil's waters because they deceived you and made you more thirsty if your throat was already dry. And the road which ran across the land and was long and broad had no beginning and no end. At least, few people knew of its origin. Only if you followed it it would take you to the big city and leave you there while it went beyond to the unknown, perhaps joining the sea. Who made the road? Rumour had that it came with the white men and some said that it was rebuilt by the Italian prisoners during the Big War that was fought away from here. (Ngugi 1972, 5–6)

It seems clear that this passage attempts to present the reader both with the consciousness of Njoroge, the main character of the novel, and also with a sense of the, as it were, collective consciousness of Njoroge's people, as well as of the immediate history of his land and culture. Such multiple perspectives are not uncommon in the novel, especially in novels which deal with "suppressed" or oppressed groups whose lives and experiences are sharply different from those of the writer's intended or expected readers. (Again, my comments on Lewis Grassic Gibbon's narrative technique on p. 154 are relevant to the present discussion, not least with regard to both writers' use of the collective "you" to affirm and represent shared and communal knowledge.) What the passage gives us is a statement of what, because it is shared cultural knowledge, is actually unlikely ever to be *stated* unless an outsider asks the right questions, and so putting it in Njoroge's unspoken but verbalized thoughts is slightly jarring.

Who is the "implied reader" (see the Glossary)? Ngũgĩ seems very conscious of the fact that many of the first readers of this novel would know little about Kenya or Kenyans, or about the history or culture of this part of Africa. Passages such as the one which I have quoted seem in part designed to impart knowledge to such individuals. Writing a novel, in English, for what was then a British publisher, Ngũgĩ must have felt the pressure of his potential readers' ignorance in a way in which a middle-class European of his age and generation would not have done. This may help to explain a stiffness at certain points of the narrative of *Weep Not, Child*.

> Ngotho often wondered if he had really done well by his sons. If he and his generation had failed, he was ready to suffer for it … But whatever Ngotho had been prepared to do to redeem himself in the eyes of his children, he would not be ordered by a son to take an oath. Not that he objected to it in principle. After all, oath-taking as a means of binding a person to a promise was a normal feature of tribal life. But to be given by a son! That would have violated against his standing as a father. (Ngugi 1972, 83–4)

In this passage, it seems to me that the sentence "After all, oath-taking as a means of binding a person to a promise was a normal feature of tribal life" also jars somewhat: it is sandwiched by sentences which are in Free Indirect Discourse, specifically in represented thought (see p. 122), but it cannot itself be read in this way. This is an authorial interpolation, an explanatory detail provided for the benefit of the reader who is not familiar with the "tribal life" in question. Writing about that part of Charles Dickens's novel *Bleak House* which is narrated by Esther Summerson, E.M. Forster comments in his *Aspects of the Novel* (first published in 1927) that even when Esther is ostensibly telling the story Dickens may snatch the pen from her and take notes himself (Forster 1962, 86). I have a sense of something similar happening in Ngũgĩ's first novel.

By the time of Ngũgĩ's *Devil on the Cross* (1982) we feel that this writer is possessed of much greater self-confidence. It is neither accidental nor irrelevant to the argument in hand that this is a novel that is thematically very much concerned with the issues of cultural independence and cultural subservience. In the author's own English translation, words which appeared in English in the original Gĩkũyũ version of the novel are italicized, so that the text of the novel gives a sense of cultural struggle, as the author's very language is invaded by English words and phrases. One of the characters—Gatuĩria—actually finds it hard to speak in Gĩkũyũ without peppering his speech with English words: ironically enough he is a "junior research fellow in African culture," and to double the irony he uses English in order to describe his post.

This is a novel in which we feel that the novelist's technical assurance is directly related to his sense of who he is writing for and why. Where culture-specific details have to be provided for European readers they are given in footnotes rather than being smuggled into the thoughts or speech of the characters. The novel speaks freely from within a culture to those sharing the culture: its dedication "To all Kenyans struggling against the neo-colonial stage of imperialism" provides convincing evidence concerning the readers for whom Ngũgĩ intended the work. The whole theme of cultural imperialism is foregrounded in the novel, and this allows Ngũgĩ the freedom to use the resources of his own culture without self-consciousness or a concern that this might not be proper or understood. For all that he is presented as a victim of cultural imperialism, Gatuĩria is aware of the process that is oppressing him and he bemoans the loss of an indigenous cultural tradition: "Our stories, our riddles, our songs, our customs, our traditions, everything about our national heritage has been lost to us" (Ngũgĩ 1982, 59).

Devil on the Cross does not just propose such a case in abstract terms: by incorporating the force and vitality of such indigenous cultural and narrative traditions into its own telling, the novel also enacts a process of cultural self-assertion and revolt. It is very difficult to illustrate this by means of selective quotation, because the shifts between more traditional realism and the fantastic, which are mediated through a range of narrative techniques including "standard" third-person narrative, riddles and sayings, dance-songs and verses, and other forms unfamiliar to European readers such as that of the "verse-chanting competition," have a cumulative effect which is lost in brief extracts. The result is to revolutionize the genre within which Ngũgĩ is working and to open the novel to traditions which are certainly "un-Western," collective rather than individualistic, holistic rather than fragmented. What the novel is today it is partly because of its enrichment by writers such as Ngũgĩ.

Fiction, truth, and (recent) history

Mads Rosendahl Thomsen has noted that writing "that addresses some of the worst horrors and crimes of humankind, genocide and war, has a particular position in world literature" (Thomsen 2008, 103). Taking this as a starting point I would like to discuss briefly, and with some hesitation, one aspect of a moment of history characterized by some of the worst of these "horrors and crimes," so far as it impinges on the function and responsibilities of the writer of fiction. To do this, I will look at two short narratives, "The Death of Schillinger" by Tadeusz Borowski and "Revenge of a Dancer" by Sara Nomberg-Przytyk. These two very short stories have much in common: both are set in the Auschwitz concentration camp during the Second World War, and both recount a similar event. Among a group of prisoners destined for the gas chamber is a young woman who manages to snatch a revolver from an SS guard and kill him.

What these stories also have in common is that each of them is authored by an individual who themself survived imprisonment in the Auschwitz concentration camp in the closing years of the Second World War, and both stories appear in a collection of tales or stories that are either set in Auschwitz or that involve those who survived Auschwitz. Borowski's story appears in *This Way for the Gas, Ladies and Gentlemen*, which contains stories written in Polish between the end of the war and the author's suicide in 1951, and which was first published in English in 1976; Nomberg-Przytyk's story is to be found in *Auschwitz: True Tales from a Grotesque Land*, the Polish typescript of which is dated 1966 but which was first published in English in 1985.

Formally speaking, the two accounts also have certain features in common. Both are framed narratives, with the "I" narrator reporting what a firsthand witness of the event had seen and has told him. This is how Borowski's story opens.

> Until 1943, First Sergeant Schillinger performed the duties of Lagerführer, or chief commanding officer of labour sector "D" at Birkenau, which was part of the enormous complex of large and small concentration camps, centrally administered from Auschwitz, but scattered throughout Upper Silesia.

Schillinger was a short, stocky man. He had a full, round face and very light blond hair, brushed flat against his head. His eyes were blue, always slightly narrowed, his lips tight, and his face was usually set in an impatient grimace. He cared little about personal appearance, and I have never heard of an incident involving his being bribed by any of the camp "bigwigs." (Borowski 1976, 143)

After having described Schillinger and his actions, Borowski's narrator goes on to report that in August 1943 "we heard the news that Schillinger had died suddenly in unusual circumstances," and he then recounts the story told to him by the "*Sonderkommando* foreman" who was in charge of getting the female victims undressed and into the gas chamber. According to this man, Schillinger drew his revolver, then walked up to one of the women and took her hand. She bent down, scooped up some gravel and threw it in Schillinger's eyes, at which he cried out in pain and dropped his revolver. She then picked up this revolver and shot Schillinger several times in the chest, then also shooting the chief. At this, the *Sonderkommando* men drove the victims into the gas chamber with clubs, and called on the SS to release the poison gas.

Borowski's story does not end there. The foreman concludes his account by describing the men of the *Sonderkommando* carrying the dying Schillinger ("not too gently," as he puts it) out to a car.

"On the way he kept groaning through clenched teeth: "*O Gott, mein Gott, was hab' ich getan, dass ich so leiden muss?*", which means—O God, my God, what have I done to deserve such suffering?"

"That man didn't understand even to the very end," I said, shaking my head. "What strange irony of fate." (Borowski, 146)

In the final paragraph of the story, the "I" narrator reports that later, shortly before the evacuation of the camp, the same *Sonderkommando* attempted to escape but were all machine-gunned by the SS guards.

In Borowski's story, then, the act of desperate and doomed defiance on the part of the woman serves as a backdrop to the main focus of the story, on an overwhelmingly bleak double irony. Even when Schillinger is given the chance to experience something of what it is like to be on the receiving end of violence, and even when he is contemplating his own imminent death, he is utterly unable to learn anything from this shift of perspective and he betrays no sense of sympathy for those he has murdered or any sense of having merited his fate. The woman and her fellow victims die, Schillinger dies, and the men of the *Sonderkommando* die—and none of these deaths is reported to have led to any understanding on the part of those who die, or to any sense of having established any sense of worth through their death.

This is how Nomberg-Przytyk's story opens.

> During the summer of 1944 the transports used to arrive at Auschwitz at night as well as in the daytime. We often woke up because of the shouting of the SS men, the barking of dogs, the whistling of trainmen, the stamping of hundreds of feet, and the cries of desperation in different languages. At night the atrocities combined with our sleeplessness to give us a very real sense of existing in a factory of death. And yet, it all appeared unreal.
>
> This particular July night it was the shouting of the SS men and the barking of the dogs that awakened me. (Nomberg-Przytyk 1985, 107)

The I narrator of the story—in this case a woman prisoner—is summoned by a friend to the infirmary, where they find a very frightened young girl, who eventually tells them her story. She and her fellow female prisoners had arrived at Auschwitz the previous evening. They were wearing bathing suits because of the extreme heat. They believed that they were going to be put to work and did not respond to warnings that they were heading for death. One of her fellow prisoners was "an unusually beautiful woman," a young dancer from Paris.

On arrival at Auschwitz they are told to take off the clothes they have and are treated brutally by the SS men. The dancer refuses, and is approached by an SS man who is apparently the commandant of the guards.

> "Beautiful girl, take off your suit," he said quietly, coming closer and closer to her. Then, all of a sudden, with a rapid movement, she grabbed the pistol out of his holster and shot straight at him. After that, she took three steps backward and shot at the SS men who were running all over the place. She saved the last bullet for herself. (109)

The young girl who tells the story to the narrator is thrown a dress by a German soldier and, in the confusion, pulled behind a gate and taken to the infirmary, where she is subsequently able to assume the identity of a French girl who has died in the camp. One of the listeners to her story comments on the action of the dancer: "'That's how you're supposed to die,' said Magda" (109).

Speaking very generally we can say that a comparison of these two stories can serve to show how comparable events can be presented in different narratives in ways that lead the reader to utterly different conclusions. In Nomberg-Przytyk's narrative, the act of rebellion asserts certain recognizable human qualities: independence, resistance to oppression, courage, activity rather than passivity. In the most extreme circumstances, the young dancer asserts her independent humanity and reminds her listeners (and the readers of Nomberg-Przytyk's story) of ours. In Borowski's story no such positives are apparent. In this story, as in others by Borowski, the message is that both perpetrators and victims are corrupted and morally destroyed by the degradation of Auschwitz. There is no assertion of a shared humanity, no uplifting message for the listeners, no reported final insight on the part of Schillinger, the young woman, the *Sonderkommando*, the framed narrator, or his listeners.

Fiction, fact, truth

At this point I want to discuss something that I have deliberately avoided commenting on up to now—the actual generic status of these two stories. The collection in which Borowski's story is gathered in English translation is categorized on its back cover as "fiction," and the translator's note that prefaces the stories describes them as "stories inspired by his [Borowski's] concentration-camp experiences" (9). The edition of Nomberg-Przytyk's stories at no point describes them as fictional, and indeed the volume title describes them as "true tales," although there is no unambiguous statement in the volume confirming that this title was chosen by Nomberg-Przytyk herself. The translator's note refers to the original manuscript as "a readable, dramatically compelling account, not simply of the author's consciousness, but of the people in the camp" (ix). The assumption, then, is that the "I" of these stories is Nomberg-Przytyk herself rather than a fictional narrator, and that although they can accurately be described as *stories*, they are not *works of fiction* but "accounts"—reports of real people and actual events. Indeed, other accounts of this event have been published, including one brief one in the memoirs of Auschwitz commandant Rudolf Höss written shortly before his execution in 1947. Another account, by Auschwitz survivor Wieslaw Kielar in his memoir *Anus Mundi: Five Years in Auschwitz*, was first published in Polish in 1972. A further one by Buchenwald survivor Eugen Kogon in his *The Theory and Practice of Hell: The German Concentration Camps and the System Behind Them* (2006) was first published in German in 1946. Kielar reports that there are different versions of what happened, but indicates which version he finds most likely to be accurate. A document in the U.S. National Archives and Record Administration, declassified only in 2010, reads as follows: "INCIDENTS: 48. Informant remembers that in Nov 43 there occurred the celebrated incident when a notorious S.S. SCHARFUEHRER, SCHILLINGER, one of the worst murderers and henchmen in Birkenau, was shot dead with his own revolver by a French Jewish actress who had already been stripped naked and was about to be gassed." The existence of these accounts prompts a difficult question: why should one read a fictional account of a terrible event when there are non-fictional accounts available?

To write fictional accounts of the horrors of the Holocaust, even when the writer is him- or herself a Holocaust survivor, is a very contentious activity. During, immediately following, and long after the events of the Holocaust many commentators have insisted that only the truth will do, that fictional accounts of these terrible events betray the writer's duty to give true testimony and may play into the hands of those who deny all or part of the reality of the sufferings and murders inflicted on the victims. However, the editors of Nomberg-Przytyk's stories, Eli Pfefferkorn and David H. Hirsch, note that "even [Eli] Wiesel has recognized that sometimes it is only fiction that can make the truth credible," and they quote from his imagined conversation with a Rabbi: "Things are not that simple, Rebbe. Some events do take place but are not true; others are, although they never occurred" (166). The narrator of another work of fiction dealing with Holocaust experiences—Anne Michaels's novel *Fugitive Pieces*—comments, "Never trust biographies. Too many events in a man's life are invisible" (141). Such events may be invisible to the historian, but some may be exposed by the writer of fiction. Such fictional exposures are sometimes referred to by the generic term "faction" (see the Glossary). Faction is associated very much with postmodernism, and we may wonder whether certain of the characteristics that strike us now as postmodernist may have emerged in experiences that in some cases could be represented fully—even truly—only in fiction.

It may be something of a seven-league leap to link this perceived similarity with the postmodern tendency to reject Henry James's view that the fictional world that a novelist creates, and the real world that he or she inhabits, should never be confused, but I think that the thought is worth some consideration. The historical moment of postmodernism is one at which we have become more conscious of the puzzling fact that not only can fictional accounts open up to our scrutiny aspects of experience that are closed to the gaze of the historian, but also that the accounts of the historian contain artifices and arrangements that are shared with the writer of fiction. Remember that in Chapter 1, I quoted Dorrit Cohn's claim that only in fiction can narrators enter the consciousnesses of individuals other than themselves. One implication of this is that the only form of narrative that can present the reader with the inner experiences of those who cannot bear testimony to their own sufferings is fiction.

Wieslaw Kielar's account of the incident has one significant point of interest. He reports that when the story became known, "[t]he news spread through the camp like wildfire and was greeted everywhere with rejoicing" (Kielar 1982, 178). Kielar further comments:

> The incident passed on from mouth to mouth and embellished in various ways grew into a legend. Without doubt this heroic deed by a weak woman, in the face of certain death, gave moral support to every prisoner.
>
> …
>
> Reaction came swiftly; prisoners straightened up, hope grew once more. (178, 179)

"Embellished accounts," legends—*fictions*—even if based on a fundamentally factual and true core, are one of the means whereby people discover their own potentialities and alter their behavior in the real world.

A case study: Knut Hamsun's *Hunger*

Let me now return to Franco's Moretti's distinction between "centers" and "peripheries." To illustrate some of the issues raised by these and other concepts I will focus on the same example that I discuss in the section on reading and studying novels in translation on p. 201: Knut Hamsun's 1890 novel *Hunger* (in Norwegian, *Sult*). In Moretti's terms, this is clearly a novel that emerges from the periphery. Scandinavia as a whole had a peripheral importance so far as European literary culture was concerned at this time, but in addition Norway in 1890 was not an independent country but was then still under Danish rule. In my discussion of translation I claim that, read in the light of what we know of the modernist fiction by Joyce, Woolf, and Kafka that would follow the publication in Norwegian of Hamsun's *Hunger* in 1890, it is an "astonishingly prophetic work" (see p. 202). And yet in the context of World Literature *Hunger* has remained very much a marginal work, known about more than known, although on publication it established Hamsun's reputation in Norway. Why should this be? Why is Kafka, for example, much more familiar to readers in English than Hamsun? Is this exclusively a matter of the quality of their respective fictions?

To start with, we can note that while the three novelists I mention above can all be described as alienated from a dominant culture, each retains a significant present in this culture. Joyce belongs to an Ireland struggling for independence from Britain, an Ireland from which Joyce feels in many ways alienated. Yet he writes in English and his early work is published in England, while *Ulysses* is first serialized in an American journal then published in Paris (one of Moretti's "centers"). Woolf made it clear in non-fictional works such as *A Room of One's Own* and *Three Guineas* that she rejected the patriarchy and militarism of Britain—and yet she too was published in English by British publishers, latterly in her writing career by a publisher owned by herself and her husband, and she belonged to a rich network of central figures in English culture. Kafka experienced the isolation of being a German-speaking Jew in Prague; however, he wrote not in Czech but in the language of a "center": German.

Hamsun had no such connection with any such "center." He wrote in Dano-Norwegian, *Hunger* was first published in Copenhagen, and it had to wait nine years to be published in English. As I note in my discussion of *Hunger* in the section on translation, Hamsun was fortunate in his first English translator, George Egerton, who produced a readable and relatively accurate translation of his first novel. But she had difficulty finding a publisher for her translation; it was rejected by John Lane in 1896 and by Egerton's own new publisher, Grant Richards, in 1898 (Fjågesund 2009, 66). It was finally accepted by a publisher named Leonard Smithers, and published in 1899. Critic Tore Rem writes that after the trial and imprisonment of Oscar Wilde, "the most radical of the writers on [John] Lane's list had left for Smithers, a publisher notorious for his business in rare editions of erotic books" (Rem 2002, 65). Rem further reports, "In the same year that *Hunger* was published, for instance, Yeats told one correspondent that Smithers was a person 'of so immoral a life that people like [Arthur] Symons and [George] Moore despise him.' The publisher's private life seems to have been too much even for the decadents" (66). The year after *Hunger* was published in English, in 1900, Smithers went bankrupt. He was to live only seven more years, dying in 1907 on his forty-sixth birthday, surrounded by empty bottles of "Dr J. Collis Browne's Chlorodyne"—a patent medicine that at that time contained opium. Smithers published *Hunger* with a jacket illustration by William T. Horton which firmly linked the book to "decadent" writers such as Wilde and Aubrey Beardsley and which was disturbing in its own right. Alas for Hamsun, since the mid-1890s, as Tore Rem notes, the influence of the decadents had been waning.

As Rem concludes, the publication context of the English translation of *Hunger* "was, arguably, more important than the quality of the translated text itself, since it so radically shaped the premises for the reception of Hamsun's book" (Rem 2002, 62). *Hunger* disappeared very much without trace in the English-speaking world, attaining a certain amount of new attention only in 1920, when Hamsun was awarded the Nobel Prize in literature. But by this time Hamsun was writing a very different sort of fiction from his first novel, and *Hunger* was often treated as an odd piece of juvenalia by those who admired his later, more national-romantic fictions. Moreover, by the 1930s, Hamsun's anti-British prejudices, which he had held since his youth, developed into a full-scale sympathy for Nazism and Hitler. In 1943, during the German occupation of Norway, Hamsun traveled to Germany and met both Adolf Hitler and Joseph Goebbels; on his return to Norway, Hamsun sent Goebbels his Nobel medal as a mark of admiration. On May 7, 1945, just one day before the end of the war in Europe, Hamsun published a short obituary of Hitler in the Norwegian newspaper *Aftenposten*, which reads in full:

> I am not worthy to raise my voice for Adolf Hitler, and his life and actions do not invite outbursts of sentimentality.
> Hitler was a warrior, a warrior for humanity and a preacher of the gospel of justice for all nations. He was a reformer of the highest order, and his historical fate was that he acted during a time of unparalleled brutality, which in the end defeated him.
> It is thus that we ordinary west-Europeans are permitted to perceive Adolf Hitler. And we, his close followers, now bow our heads on the occasion of his death. (My translation, JH)

This was on the front page of the newspaper, whose Nazi-sympathizing staff considered it prudent to have as the main news item the death and blinding of several individuals in Stavanger consequent on drinking illegal methanol alcohol rather than anything about the war. Any chance that Hamsun's work—late or early—might enjoy renewed interest in the world post-1945 was effectively destroyed by such extremely offensive (and absurd) political posturing. Two new translations of *Hunger*—in 1967 and 1996—have done something to bring the novel before a new English-speaking readership, but the political baggage that any work by Hamsun brings with it have, rightly or wrongly, made the gaining of acceptability for the work outside Norway something that is located on a continuum from difficult to unattainable.

There seems little doubt that had Egerton's translation of *Hunger* been published by leading British and American publishers soon after its Norwegian publication, and had these publishers worked to publicize and market the novel, the book would have had a good chance of attaining a significant international readership soon after its original publication. And had Hamsun moved in a different direction politically in the first half of the twentieth century, such a "canonical" status might have been confirmed. Such counterfactual suppositions have, note, nothing to do with the text itself: they concern the associations of its appearance in English translation, and the reputation of its author after its publication.

An illuminating contrast with a key moment in the writing career of Joseph Conrad can be drawn here. Born in 1857, Conrad came late to his career as professional writer, publishing his first novel in 1895. From *Lord Jim* (1899) on and up to 1911 he published a succession of fictional works now recognized as masterpieces, and yet his sales were relatively modest and he fell deeper and deeper into massive debt. In 1912, his novel *Chance* was serialized in the women's pages of the Sunday Magazine section of the *New York Herald*, following a very active marketing campaign that stressed Conrad's intention to write for women (he had previously been perceived as very much of a "man's novelist"). Unusually, for Conrad, the novel's main character is a young woman, and it clearly engages with discussion and debates about the place of women in society inspired by the Suffragette movement. The novel was Conrad's biggest sales success in Britain and, especially, the United States, where the young Alfred Knopf marketed the novel with skill and vigor. For the past half century, *Chance* has been considered as one of Conrad's less successful works, even to the extent of being categorized as the first in the period of Conrad's "decline." But it brought Conrad's name into the limelight, solved his financial problems, and established him as a writer of world importance. Who knows: had *Hunger* been published in English by a major publisher who marketed it as well as Alfred Knopf marketed *Chance*, might it not too have achieved that "canonical" status that it never quite achieved in the English-speaking world, even after its author was awarded the Nobel Prize?

***

At this point, it is worth pausing to note some very different conceptions of "World Literature" that we have encountered in this section.

- A new way of organizing the academic approach to literature, one that involves a wider, transnational selection of texts and a different approach to their study (often an approach informed by postcolonial theory that seeks to revise the canon [see the Glossary] or to reject the whole notion of a canon)

- An academic approach to the study of literature that puts a premium on literary quality rather than national or cultural origin
- A response to the emergence of a World Literature that has already taken place—not within universities and colleges, but out in the real world, as an integral part of more general processes of internationalization and globalization, and especially processes associated with crimes and suffering

These are not mutually exclusive conceptions, and indeed many courses on World Literature are premised on a commitment to approaching the study of literary works from a less insular, more comprehensive perspective, one informed by the insights and values of postcolonialist theory, while also attempting to expose and explore processes of international influence in the writing and reading of fiction.

Emily Apter suggests that we should be wary of endorsing two quite different positions when reading works from unfamiliar cultures. The first is that of "cultural equivalence and substitutability"—in other words the assumption that all cultures are basically similar and any differences are only variants on the surface of a shared human nature—so that any intelligent reader can recognize common human experiences and issues in any work of literature. The second position involves "the celebration of nationally and ethnically branded 'differences' that have been niche-marketed as commercialized 'identities'" (Apter 2013, 2). Put another way, in this second simplification, cultural difference is recognized, but unfamiliar cultures are categorized in crude and stereotyped ways that erase their complexities. David Damrosch expresses it thus: "Worse yet, non-Western traditions may be almost impossible for Westerners to assess without falling into neocolonial patterns of projection and downright appropriation" (Damrosch 2003, 113). However, as Damrosch also notes, striking a more optimistic note, "works of literature take on a new life as they move into the world at large" (2003, 24), and this new life is in part generated by the new interpretative and responsive perspectives provided by readers from different cultures. Reading novels from other cultures, whether in translation or in their original language, can be a rich and rewarding experience, and as readers we may actually profit from such reading in ways that those who read the same texts in their original language do not, but we should neither ignore nor simplify the cultural divide that separates us from the original.

What does all this mean if you are studying a novel as part of a World Literature course, rather than, say, as a prescribed text for a course on the nineteenth-century British novel? The answer to this question would need to be adjusted with regard to different courses, but some general points can be made:

- First, you are very likely to find yourself reading some works in translation, and so you should read what I write on p. 199 regarding the issues that are thrown up when the words you read have been transposed from one language to another by someone other than the original author. This is particularly important when you need to choose one from a number of available translations.

- Second, because the works you read will come from different cultures, and probably also from different language communities and moments of history, it will be impossible to provide or expect the same level of detailed knowledge of the national, linguistic, and historical contexts from which a given work arises. This means that choosing good editions of the works you study that provide some of this missing knowledge is particularly important. It also means that you should be prepared to read more secondary and theoretical material that provides and discusses the relevance of such contextual information.

- Third, and for the same reason, relations of influence from individual author to individual author and work to work are likely to be more tenuous on a World Literature course—if they can be traced at all. But on the other hand, many World Literature courses typically pay more attention to the sorts of political and economic forces impacting on those processes of circulation and dissemination that are discussed by Franco Moretti than do, say, courses in Comparative Literature or "Great Works."

- Fourth, a World Literature course that uses "quality" as its only criterion for selection of texts may well make little or no attempt to contextualize works, or to consider processes of circulation and dissemination.

- But fifth, and on a more positive note, the study of novels and short stories from cultures other than the dominant European and North American ones will provide a new perspective on histories shared by first- and third-world cultures.

- And sixth, the ability to study works of fiction from different times, language communities, and cultures also provides a wider and usefully comparative perspective on formal and technical innovations.

Topics for discussion

- Should the study of World Literature avoid a concern with well-known works, and rather focus attention on those that have not been much read and studied, from cultures that are unfamiliar to us?

- On p. 224 you can read the Czech writer Milan Kundera's claim that whatever the reader needs to know about the history of Czechoslovakia can be found in his novels. Does this mean that reading fiction written in cultures with which we are unfamiliar, we do not need any "background" information?

- Are some historical events too terrible to be represented in fiction?

- "We should not see the strangeness of fiction from unknown cultures as a problem: it is one reason it is exciting." Do you agree?

Timeline of the Novel

The following list includes the dates of birth and death of major figures connected to the novel. It also lists key works of fiction, key critical studies, and significant public events. Titles of novels are those by which they are commonly known. Unless otherwise stated, publication dates are for first book publication in the original language. The list is inevitably selective, and to a certain extent anglocentric. It is included to provide readers with a general sense of "what was happening" and "who was active" from year to year. Those looking for more detailed biographical or encyclopedic information should consult specialist sources.

c. 1494	François Rabelais born
1508	*Amadis de Gaula* (first known printed edition published in Zaragoza)
1532	François Rabelais, *Pantagruel* (followed in 1534 by *Gargantua*)
1547	Miguel de Cervantes (Miguel de Cervantes Saavedra) born
1553	François Rabelais dies
1594	Thomas Nashe, *The Unfortunate Traveller*
1597	Thomas Deloney, *Jack of Newberry*
1605	Miguel de Cervantes, *Don Quixote* (Part 1; Part 2 followed in 1615)
1616	Miguel de Cervantes dies
1628	John Bunyan born
1640	Aphra Behn born (date not confirmed)
1678	John Bunyan, *The Pilgrim's Progress* (Part 1; Part 2 followed in 1684)
1688	John Bunyan dies; Aphra Behn, *Oroonoko, or The Royal Slave*
1689	Samuel Richardson born; Ahra Behn dies
1703	Daniel Defoe sentenced to stand in the pillory, largely because of his ironic pamphlet "The Shortest Way with the Dissenters"

1707	Henry Fielding born
1713	Laurence Sterne born
1715	Alain-René Lesage, *Gil Blas*
1719	Daniel Defoe, *Robinson Crusoe*
1721	Tobias Smollett born
1722	Daniel Defoe, *Moll Flanders*
1726	Jonathan Swift, *Gulliver's Travels*
1731	L'Abbé Prévost, *Manon Lescaut*
1740	Samuel Richardson, *Pamela*
1742	Henry Fielding, *Joseph Andrews*
1748	Samuel Richardson, *Clarissa Harlowe*; Tobias Smollett, *Roderick Random*
1749	Johann Wolfgang von Goethe born; Henry Fielding, *Tom Jones*
1750	Samuel Johnson's *Rambler* essay number 4 on the "works of fiction, with which the present generation seems more particularly delighted"
1752	Frances Burney born
1754	Henry Fielding dies
1760–7	Laurence Sterne, *Tristram Shandy*
1761	Samuel Richardson dies
1768	Laurence Sterne dies
1771	(Sir) Walter Scott born; Tobias Smollett dies
1774	Johann von Goethe, *The Sorrows of Young Werther*
1775	Jane Austen born
1782	Frances Burney, *Cecilia*
1794	Ann Radcliffe, *The Mysteries of Udolpho*
1804	Nathaniel Hawthorne (Hathorne) born
1812	Charles Dickens born
1813	Jane Austen, *Pride and Prejudice* (the title of which Austen most likely took from a passage toward the end of Frances Burney's *Cecilia*)

1816	Charlotte Brontë born
1817	Jane Austen dies
1818	Emily Brontë born; Mary Shelley, *Frankenstein*
1819	George Eliot (Mary Ann, or Marian, Evans) born
1820	Sir Walter Scott, *Ivanhoe*
1821	Fyodor Mikhaylovich Dostoyevsky born
1830	Stendhal (Henri-Marie Beyle), *The Red and the Black*
1832	Sir Walter Scott dies
1835	Mark Twain (Samuel Langhorne Clemens) born
1837	Charles Dickens, *The Pickwick Papers*
1839	Edgar Allen Poe, "The Fall of the House of Usher"
1840	Frances Burney dies; Thomas Hardy born
1842	Johann Wolfgang von Goethe dies; Nicolai Gogol, *Dead Souls*; Alessandro Manzoni, *The Betrothed*. A London bookshop opened by Charles Edward Mudie in 1840 starts to lend rather than sell books, and "Mudie's Lending Library" is born
1843	Henry James born
1846	Herman Melville, *Typee*
1847	Emily Brontë, *Wuthering Heights*, Anne Brontë, *Agnes Grey*, and Charlotte Brontë, *Jane Eyre* are all published pseudonymously (Ellis Bell, Currer Bell, and Acton Bell)
1847–8	William Makepeace Thackeray, *Vanity Fair*
1849	Emily Brontë dies
1850	Robert Louis Stevenson born; Nathaniel Hawthorne, *The Scarlet Letter*; Charles Dickens, *David Copperfield*
1851	Herman Melville, *Moby Dick*
1855	Charlotte Brontë dies
1857	Joseph Conrad (Józef Teodor Konrad Nalecz Korzeniowski) born; Gustave Flaubert, *Madame Bovary*; unsuccessfully prosecuted in France, for obscenity.
1859	Charles Darwin, *On the Origin of Species*
1860	George Eliot, *The Mill on the Floss*

1860–1	Charles Dickens, *Great Expectations*
1864	Nathaniel Hawthorne dies
1861–5	American Civil War
1865	Lewis Carroll, *Alice's Adventures in Wonderland*
1865–72	Leo Tolstoy, *War and Peace*
1866	Fyodor Dostoyevsky, *Crime and Punishment*
1870	Charles Dickens dies; Jules Verne, *Twenty Thousand Leagues Under the Sea*
1872	George Eliot, *Middlemarch*; Thomas Hardy, *Under the Greenwood Tree*
1873	Ford Madox Ford (Ford Hermann Hueffer) born
1874	Thomas Hardy, *Far from the Madding Crowd*
1875–6	Leo Tolstoy, *Anna Karenina*
1876	Mark Twain, *The Adventures of Tom Sawyer*
1879	E.M. Forster born
1880	Fyodor Dostoyevsky, *The Brothers Karamazov*
1881	Fyodor Dostoyevsky dies; Henry James, *The Portrait of a Lady*
1882	James Joyce born; Virginia Woolf born
1883	Franz Kafka born; Robert Louis Stevenson, *Treasure Island*
1884	Henry James, "The Art of Fiction"; Mark Twain (Samuel Longhorne Clemens), *Huckleberry Finn*
1885	D.H. Lawrence born; Guy de Maupassant, *Bel-Ami*
1888	Katherine Mansfield (Kathleen Mansfield Beauchamp) born
1890	Jean Rhys (Ella Gwendolyn Rees Williams) born; George Eliot dies; Knut Hamsun, *Hunger*
1891	Thomas Hardy, *Tess of the D'Urbervilles*
1892	Arthur Conan Doyle, *The Adventures of Sherlock Holmes*
1894	Robert Louis Stevenson dies; Stephen Crane, *The Red Badge of Courage*
1895	Mikhail Mikhailovich Bakhtin born; H.G. Wells, *The Time Machine*
1896	F. Scott Fitzgerald born

1897	William Faulkner born
1898	Henry James, *The Turn of the Screw*
1899	Ernest Miller Hemingway and Vladimir Nabokov born
1900	Joseph Conrad, *Lord Jim*
1901	Lewis Grassic Gibbon (James Leslie Mitchell) born
1902	Joseph Conrad, *Heart of Darkness*
1905	Edith Wharton, *The House of Mirth*
1910	Mark Twain dies
1913	D.H. Lawrence, *Sons and Lovers*
1913–27	Marcel Proust, *A la recherche du temps perdu*
1914–18	First World War
1914	James Joyce, *Dubliners*
1914	Robert Tressell (Robert Noonan), *The Ragged Trousered Philanthropists* published in expurgated form; first complete edition 1955
1915	Franz Kafka, "The Metamorphosis"
1915	D.H. Lawrence, *The Rainbow*, published then seized by the police and banned by court order. Unavailable in Britain for the following 11 years.
1916	Henry James dies
1917	Russian revolution
1919	Virginia Woolf, "Modern Novels" published in the *Times Literary Supplement*. Published in revised form as "Modern Fiction" in 1925
1920	The New York Society for the Suppression of Vice initiates a prosecution of a literary magazine for publishing the "Nausicaa" section of James Joyce's *Ulysses*. The book is banned in USA until 1933.
1920	Georg Lukács, *Theory of the Novel*, published in German; English translation 1971
1921	Percy Lubbock, *The Craft of Fiction*
1922	James Joyce, *Ulysses*; Kurt Vonnegut born
1923	Katherine Mansfield dies; Joseph Heller born

1924	Franz Kafka dies; Joseph Conrad dies; Virginia Woolf, "Mr Bennett and Mrs Brown" read as a paper at Cambridge
1924	E.M. Forster, *A Passage to India*
1925	Franz Kafka, *The Trial*
1925	Virginia Woolf, *Mrs. Dalloway*
1927	E.M. Forster, *Aspects of the Novel*; Jean Rhys, *The Left Bank and Other Stories*
1928	Thomas Hardy dies
1929	William Faulkner, *The Sound and the Fury*
1930	D.H. Lawrence dies
1933	U.S. Customs seize copies of James Joyce's *Ulysses* that the publisher Random House is attempting to import. In a subsequent trial, the novel is found not to contravene the obscenity laws and can be published in USA.
1935	Lewis Grassic Gibbon dies; Christopher Isherwood, *Mr Norris Changes Trains*
1936	Walter Benjamin, "The Storyteller: Reflections on the Works of Nikolei Leskov"; Don DeLillo born
1937	Georg Lukács, *The Historical Novel*, published in Russian 1937. English translation 1962.
1938	Ngũgĩ wa Thiong'o (James Ngugi) born
1939	Ford Madox Ford dies; James Joyce, *Finnegans Wake*
1939–45	Second World War
1940	F. Scott Fitzgerald dies; Angela Carter born; Richard Wright, *Native Son*; Ernest Hemingway, *For Whom the Bell Tolls*
1941	James Joyce dies; Virginia Woolf dies
1942	Albert Camus, *The Outsider* (also translated as *The Stranger*)
1945	George Orwell, *Animal Farm*
1947	Ahmed Salman Rushdie born
1948	Ian McEwan born; F.R. Leavis, *The Great Tradition*. Included in Leavis's great tradition are Jane Austen, George Eliot, Henry James, and Joseph Conrad; excluded are Sterne, Hardy, and Dickens, although Dickens is granted belated

recognition in *Dickens the Novelist* (1970), co-written with his wife Q.D. Leavis.

1949	George Orwell, *1984*
1951	Hanif Kureishi born
1954	Louise Erdrich born
1955	Alain Robbe-Grillet, *The Voyeur*; Vladimir Nabokov, *Lolita*
1957	Ian Watt, *The Rise of the Novel*
1958	Chinua Achebe, *Things Fall Apart*
1959	Jeanette Winterson born
1959	Vassily Grossman, *Life and Fate* completed; first published in the West in 1980
1960	Trial of Penguin Books for having published D.H. Lawrence's *Lady Chatterley's Lover*. The "not guilty" verdict allows the book to be published legally in Britain for the first time since its Italian publication in 1928, and heralds a relaxation of the laws governing obscenity.
1961	Ernest Hemingway dies; Wayne C. Booth, *The Rhetoric of Fiction*; Joseph Heller, *Catch-22*
1962	William Faulkner dies
1966	Jean Rhys, *Wide Sargasso Sea*
1967	Jonathan Littell born
1969	Maya Angelou, *I Know Why the Caged Bird Sings*; Philip Roth, *Portnoy's Complaint*
1969	American astronauts land on the moon, three hundred and seven years after Cyrano de Bergerac's *Voyages to the Moon and the Sun* (1662); Kurt Vonnegut, *Slaughterhouse 5*
1970	E.M. Forster dies
1975	Mikhail Bakhtin dies
1977	Vladimir Nabokov dies
1979	Jean Rhys dies; Sandra M. Gilbert and Susan Gubar, *The Madwoman in the Attic*
1980	Gérard Genette, *Narrative Discourse: An Essay in Method* published in English (first published in French as a part of *Figures III* in 1972)

1981	Mikhail Bakhtin's *The Dialogic Imagination*, containing four essays, introduces Bakhtin's idea on the novel to the English-speaking world
1981	Salman Rushdie, *Midnight's Children*
1982	Ann Banfield, *Unspeakable Sentences: Narration and Representation in the Language of Fiction*
1983	Alice Walker, *The Color Purple*
1984	Louise Erdrich, *Love Medicine* (revised 1993 and 2009)
1987	Toni Morrison, *Beloved*
1988	Salman Rushdie, *The Satanic Verses*
1989	(14 February) "Fatwah" demanding Salman Rushdie's death proclaimed on Radio Tehran by Ayatollah Ruhollah Khomeini, the spiritual leader of Iran, in response to the "blasphemous" *The Satanic Verses*
1992	Angela Carter dies
1997	J.K. Rowling, *Harry Potter and the Philosopher's Stone*
1999	J.M. Coetzee, *Disgrace*; Joseph Heller dies
2001	W.G. Sebald, *Austerlitz*
2006	Jonathan Littell, *The Kindly Ones*
2007	Don DeLillo, *Falling Man*; Kurt Vonnegut dies
2014	Nadine Gordimer dies

Glossary of Terms

Where terms have been defined and discussed in earlier chapters, I limit entries to a brief comment and a cross-reference to the relevant page(s). Cross-references within the Glossary are indicated by the use of small capitals. To avoid repetition, terms such as "novel," "short story," and "fiction" are not cross-referenced.

ACHRONICITY/ACHRONY Achronicity is a state in which temporal relationships cannot be established; applied to a NARRATIVE it implies the impossibility of establishing an accurate chronology of EVENTS. An achrony is an event in a narrative which cannot be located on a precise time scale, and cannot be temporally related to other events in the narrative.

ANACHRONY Also, following Bal (1985), *chronological deviation*. Any lack of fit between the order in which EVENTS are presented in the PLOT or *sjužet*, and that in which they are reported in the story or *fabula*, is termed an "anachrony." Both analepsis and prolepsis are examples of anachrony. See also STORY AND PLOT.

Bal isolates two sorts of anachrony: *punctual anachrony*, when only one instant from the past or future is evoked, and *durative anachrony*, when a longer span of time or a more general situation is evoked.

ANALEPSIS AND PROLEPSIS Both terms denote a divergence from strict chronological sequence in a NARRATIVE. An analepsis (otherwise flashback) moves out of the present of STORY-time to describe or evoke something from the "past" of the story being told. A prolepsis (or anticipation, or flashforward) moves out of the present of story-time to describe or evoke something from the "future" of the story being told.

ANISOCHRONY See ISOCHRONY.

ANTI-NOVEL A now outdated term used in the mid-twentieth century to describe experimental fiction that frustrated reader expectations by refusing to conform to accepted conventions—often by containing self-contradictions which could not be resolved by the reader. Compare *nouveau roman*.

Bildungsroman The German term *Bildungsroman* is now generally used in English to denote a novel that concentrates upon one CHARACTER's development from early youth to some sort of maturity. Goethe's *Wilhelm Meister's Apprenticeship* (1795–6), Dickens's *David Copperfield* (1849–50), and James Joyce's *Portrait of the Artist as a Young Man* (1916) can all be described as examples of the *Bildungsroman*.

This type of novel clearly attracts the writer interested in depicting the close relationship between early influences and later character development, and its emergence can be related to the growing interest in the THEME that "the child is father to the man" that accompanies the late eighteenth- and nineteenth-century interest in the young.

CAMPUS NOVEL A novel which takes place within a university or college, or which involves CHARACTERS drawn from such an academic milieu.

CANON The term originates in debate within the Christian Church about the authenticity of the Hebrew Bible and books of the New Testament. That which was termed "canonical" was accepted as having divine authority within the Church, while writing of no, or doubtful, authority was termed "apocryphal." In literary-critical usage the term came to be applied (i) to works which could indisputably be ascribed to a particular author, and (ii) to a list of works set apart from other works by virtue of their literary quality and importance, and which accordingly could appropriately be put on academic reading lists.

Although for much of the twentieth century there were arguments about which works were canonical, in the last few decades the very idea of a canon has been a matter of debate—leading to "canon wars." Critics have argued that although canonical status was allegedly related purely to literary quality, in reality it reflected ideological commitments and prejudices, so that works written by women, people of color, overtly gay authors, or members of subordinate or "peripheral" groups and cultures were excluded from it. In the present edition of this book although I have moved to place words such as "canonical" in quotation marks to alert readers to the fact that this is a contested term, I continue to use the term to reflect the fact that certainly for the first sixty years of the twentieth century what got on to academic reading lists, and what did not, did not vary that much in European and American universities.

CHARACTER An actor in a literary NARRATIVE. If this seems like stating the obvious, it should be pointed out that genres such as science fiction provide borderline cases of entities which from a narrative point of view function as characters (they initiate actions, engage in communication or even speech, and form relationships), but are non-human in other ways.

E.M. Forster's *Aspects of the Novel* provides the now-familiar distinction between the round and the flat character; the former having depth, complexity, and unpredictability, and the latter being reduced almost to a single quality. Flat characters are often compared to *types*. See the extended discussion on p. 130.

A *chorus character* is a character used by a writer to comment authoritatively on EVENTS; for *cancelled* or *erased character* see p. 127. For *synonymous character* see p. 130. A character narrator is a narrator who is also a character in the story he or she tells, living in the same reality as the other characters.

CHARACTER ZONE A term coined by Mikhail Bakhtin to describe the way in which a fictional CHARACTER is surrounded by various verbal and stylistic elements which create a "zone" that is "the range of action of the character's voice, intermingling in one way or another with the author's voice" (Quoted in Todorov 1984, 73).

CHRONOTOPE Coined by Mikhail Bakhtin to designate "the distinctive features of time and space within each literary genre" (Todorov 1984, 83).

CLOSURE That sense of satisfying or reassuring finality that accompanies the end of a traditional REALIST novel, when no problems remain to be solved. It is typical of MODERNIST and POSTMODERNIST novels that they postpone or frustrate closure by giving their works *open endings*.

COGNITIVE CRITICISM See p. 234.

COLORING The modification of the language of (say) a NARRATOR by the linguistic characteristics of (say) a CHARACTER. Also referred to as the "Uncle Charles Principle," after a sentence in James Joyce's *A Portrait of the Artist as a Young Man*: "Uncle Charles repaired to the outhouse," in which the word "repaired," which is typical of Uncle Charles's usage, "colors" the narrator's description. See also the discussion on p. 125.

CONTE The *conte* was originally distinguished from the novel by its (often quirky) wit, its more FANTASTIC, less REALISTIC nature, and by a strongly didactic element normally focused in a moral point or use of allegory. Typical examples are two works both first published in 1759: Samuel Johnson's *Rasselas* (first published as *The Prince of Abissinia. A Tale*) and Voltaire's *Candide*. For the past century or so, however, the term in English has become roughly synonymous with "short story," although Frank O'Connor (whose views on the short story are discussed in Chapter 3) categorizes Robert Browning's poem "My Last Duchess" (1842) and Ernest Hemingway's "Hills Like White Elephants" (1927) as *conte*s (O'Connor 1963, 26).

COVERT PLOT See SUBPLOT.

CYBERPUNK/CYBERFICTION From "cybernetics," a coinage by Norbert Wiener, whose book *Cybernetics: or Control and Communication in the Animal and the Machine* was first published in 1949. "Cyber" comes from the Greek word for "steersman," and Wiener's book was particularly concerned with what are known as feedback systems. The yoking together of animals and machines in Wiener's title may be one reason why "cyber" has been hooked on to "punk" and "fiction" to refer to recent examples of SCIENCE FICTION that involve various graftings of the inorganic on to the human or organic. According to Austin Booth and Mary Flanagan, cyberfiction is "writing that explores the relationship between people and virtual technologies" (Booth and Flanagan 2002, 1), but some works defined as cyberfiction, especially earlier ones, are concerned with technology rather than virtual technology.

So far as cyberpunk is concerned, the second part of the term focuses attention on to the "young male outlaws who hack and crack computer networks to steal, manipulate, or erase the information they find" (Booth and Flanagan 2002, 7). Such works are generally set in the desolate urban spaces of technologically advanced but culturally and morally decayed societies of the future, and they implicitly draw critical attention to what are seen as negative trends in today's world, in which large impersonal corporations control more and more of human life. Fredric Jameson has suggested that cyberpunk "is fully as much an expression of transnational corporate realities as it is of global paranoia" (Jameson 1991, 38).

The term "cyberpunk" seems first to have been used by Bruce Bethke, who published a story of this name in the magazine *Amazing* in 1983 (Butler 2000, 9). The most influential early cyberpunk author, however, is generally agreed to be William Gibson. Cyberpunk has moved from being the preserve of a small band of enthusiasts to a generic term more widely known as a result of the very successful filming of certain key cyberpunk texts. Philip K. Dick's 1968 novel *Do Androids Dream of Electric Sheep?* was made into the blockbuster film *Blade Runner* (1982, directed by Ridley Scott).

Cyberpunk has attracted the attention of women writers, who see in its concern with bodily modification and gender adaptation possibilities for feminist development. Again in the words of Booth and Flanagan, "[w]omen writers are appropriating the cyberpunk aesthetic—metaphors of jacking in, figures of outlaws and outsiders, and film noir rhetoric—for their own ends" (2002, 2). The work of writer Donna Haraway is often seen as forging a bridge between cyberfiction ("cyberfeminism") and postmodernism. Haraway has fixed on the concept of the cyborg—part human, part machine—as a figure that uses technology to break down divisive binaries, especially those connected with gender. It is interesting to note that the work that can claim to have had a founding function so far as the concept of the cyborg is concerned—Mary Shelley's *Frankenstein* (1818)—was written by a woman. Haraway's optimism has not been shared by all: others have suggested that bodily modification is today more testimony to the control of women's bodies by patriarchal forces than evidence of a potential liberation.

DEATH OF THE AUTHOR A term taken from an essay by Roland Barthes, "The Death of the Author" (1977, in French 1968). One commentator (Carlier, 2000) has suggested that Barthes's essay had a satirical intention, but it continues to be taken as a serious argument advocating that the author be relieved of any authority over his or her work once it has been published, and that it is language, rather than the author, that speaks in a work. Barthes's arguments are often associated with those of his fellow countryman Michel Foucault, whose essay "What Is an Author?" was also published in English in 1977.

DEFAMILIARIZATION From the Russian meaning "to make strange," the term originates with the Russian Formalists and, in particular, the theories of Viktor Shklovsky. In his essay "Art as Technique," Shklovsky argues that perception becomes automatic once it has become habitual, and that the function of art is to challenge automization and habitualization, and return a direct grasp on things to the individual perception. Of interest to students of the novel is that the Russian Formalists exemplified defamiliarization by reference to the work of novelists such as Tolstoy, and Boris Tomashevsky, one of Shklovsky's fellow Russian Formalists, refers to Swift's defamiliarizing techniques in *Gulliver's Travels* in his essay "Thematics" (the scene in which the Lilliputians discover Gulliver's watch and describe it without understanding what it is—thus encouraging the reader to see something familiar as if it were strange).

DEIXIS Those features of language which fasten utterances temporally or spatially: "here" and "now," for example. Deictics, or deictic elements (deictic can perform as either noun or adjective) play an important role in NARRATIVE; they constitute an important token of Free Indirect Discourse, for example.

DELAYED DECODING A term coined by Ian Watt in his *Conrad in the Nineteenth Century* (1980) to describe a particular impressionist technique used by Joseph Conrad by means of which the experiences of a CHARACTER who understands what is happening to him or her only while these experiences are taking place (or afterwards) are recreated in the reader. Thus in Conrad's *Heart of Darkness* we share Marlow's belief that lots of little sticks are dropping on the ship, up to the point when Marlow realizes that the "sticks" are in fact arrows, and that the ship is being attacked.

DIALOGUE The standard meaning of this term with regard to prose fiction concerns the representation of the speech of CHARACTERS, either interactively between two or more individuals, or monologically addressed by one person to him- or herself. See the extended discussion on p. 150, and compare also INTERNAL/ INTERIOR DIALOGUE.

The writings of Mikhail Bakhtin have helped to make the term fashionable by suggesting that language itself is naturally dialogic, and that all use of language involves interaction with those others who have left traces on the words and phrases they have used.

DIEGESIS AND MIMESIS These are terms that present a number of problems of usage, as the meanings attached to them have changed since their appearance in the third book of Plato's *Republic*, in which Socrates uses them to distinguish between two ways of presenting speech. For Socrates, diegesis stands for those cases where the poet himself is the speaker and does not wish to suggest otherwise, and mimesis stands for those cases in which the poet attempts to create the illusion that it is not he who is speaking. Recent usage among critics and theorists of prose fiction is rather different: diegesis is commonly used to denote "the world of the story." Thus in *Wuthering Heights* we can describe Lockwood and Nelly Dean as intradiegetic NARRATORS, because they are also CHARACTERS occupying the same reality as Heathcliff and Cathy. The narrator of Fielding's *Tom Jones*, in contrast, clearly belongs to a reality that represents the STORY he tells as fictional, and thus he is described as an extradiegetic narrator.

In like manner, mimesis has come to be used to describe the more general capacity of literature to imitate reality, and has on occasions accumulated a somewhat polemical edge as a result of its use by those wishing to establish imitation as central or essential to art.

For *extradiegetic*, *autodiegetic* and *homodiegetic*, see p. 105.

DISTANCE A term used in a number of different ways to suggest varying levels of involvement (emotional, intellectual, ideological) with what goes on in a STORY on the part *either* of a NARRATOR *or* a reader. See also p. 118.

DURATION In NARRATIVE theory, the relation between the time covered by the STORY or part of it (such as an EVENT), and the "time" allotted to it by the text (story-time and text-time). Thus three years of story-time may be covered by three pages of text, while further on in the same text one hour of story-time may occupy fifty pages. Unfortunately "pages" do not give a particularly reliable measure: some readers read more quickly than others and the same reader will read more or less quickly depending upon textual complexity, reader involvement and tension, and so on. As a result many writers on narrative find *speed* or *tempo* more fruitful concepts.

See also p. 136, and compare ISOCHRONY.

ECOCRITICISM See p. 232

ELLIPSIS A gap in the information provided for the reader, which may be permanent (we never learn what Heathcliff did after he left Wuthering Heights and before he returned) or temporary (as with most detective stories, when the missing details about the crime are provided in the book's concluding pages). Ellipses can be marked or unmarked—that is to say the attention of the reader may or may not be drawn to the gap. See also p. 135.

EPIC Traditionally a long NARRATIVE poem presenting a heroic subject in an elevated style. Among the earliest epics are the *Odyssey* and the *Iliad*, although earlier examples exist. Some commentators distinguish between primary and secondary epics, where secondary epics have a single author rather than a collective origin, and are written within a literate culture rather than sung or recited in an oral culture. The novel has been approached as a modern epic, and some authors have attempted to give their works something of an epic status, although Mikhail Bakhtin (see p. 5) has argued for a sharp dividing line between epic and novel.

EPISTOLARY NOVEL An epistolary novel is told through letters ("epistles") exchanged between different CHARACTERS. The form flourished in the English novel in the eighteenth century. Samuel Richardson's *Pamela* (1740) and *Clarissa* (1747–8), Tobias Smollett's *Humphry Clinker* (1771), and Frances Burney's *Evelina* (1778) are classic epistolary novels. Writers in subsequent periods have made sporadic attempts to adapt the technique to their own needs, and one of the most successful examples of a recent epistolary novel is Alice Walker's *The Color Purple* (1982).

In his novel *Clarissa* Samuel Richardson gives a comment to his character Mr Belford, writing to Lovelace about Clarissa, which helps to explain why Richardson (and his readers) favored the technique:

> Such a sweetness of temper, so much patience and resignation, as she seems to be mistress of; yet writing of and in the midst of *present* distresses! How much more lively and affecting, for that reason, must her style be, than all that can be read in the dry, narrative, unanimated style of persons relating difficulties and dangers surmounted! The minds of such not labouring in suspense, not tortured by the pangs of uncertainty about events still hidden by the womb of fate; but on the contrary perfectly at ease; the relater unmoved by his own story, how then able to move the hearer or reader? (Italics in original). (Richardson 1985, 1178)

Clearly the personal insight, self-display, and dramatic effectiveness of the epistolary technique are what appeal to Richardson. On the negative side, a novel told exclusively through letters (Richardson allows himself the occasional authorial footnote and square-bracketed interpolation!) can be unwieldy and inflexible. The characters have to be kept apart (otherwise they have no reason to write to one another), and sometimes this involves artificiality: Richardson's heroines are banished to locked rooms with disturbing regularity. When they actually meet their loved ones, Richardson has somehow to arrange for someone else to write a letter about the encounter. Moreover, whatever else the characters do they must always have access to pen and paper. As Clarissa on one occasion writes to Miss Howe: "And indeed, my dear, I know not how to forbear writing. I have now no other employment or diversion. I must write on, although I were not to send it to anybody" (483). It was this element in Richardson's *Pamela* that was so cruelly but effectively satirized by Henry Fielding in his parody *An Apology for the Life of Miss Shamela Andrews* (1741), in which the heroine continues to write a letter while the man who is assaulting her virtue climbs into bed with her.

If the "pure" epistolary novel is rare after the eighteenth century, the technique taught novelists how very useful letters could be as an element within the NARRATIVE variety of a novel. Two good examples are Isabella's long letter about her marriage to Heathcliff in Emily Brontë's *Wuthering Heights*, and Helen's letters to her sister in E.M. Forster's *Howards End*.

EPITEXT See Chapter 4, p. 75.

EVENT and EXISTENT The two are distinguished by NARRATOLOGISTS. "Events" are those things that are "done" or that "occur" in a narrative, while "existents" are those things in a narrative that "are." The distinction is thus roughly analogous to that between a verb and a noun.

FABLIAU A short medieval tale in verse, usually humorous and satirical and often bawdy. Geoffrey Chaucer's "The Miller's Tale" from the late fourteenth century is frequently cited as a typical example of the form.

FABULA AND SJUŽET See STORY AND PLOT.

FABULATION and SURFICTION These two terms are used relatively interchangeably. Both imply an aggressive and playful luxuriation in the non-representational, in which the writer takes delight in the artifice of writing rather than attempting to describe or make contact with a perceived extra-fictional reality. The terms are normally used in connection with relatively recent fiction.

FACTION The term comes from the American author Truman Capote and is a portmanteau word (= fact + fiction) which describes novels such as his own *In Cold Blood* (1966). In this work, primarily novelistic techniques are used to bring actual historical EVENTS to life for the reader. The term has thus come to denote a work that is on the borderline between fact and fiction, concerned primarily with a real event or persons, but using imagined detail to increase dramatic impact and verisimilitude. See also p. 256.

FANTASTIC Characteristic of the fantastic is that it *hints* at a supernatural explanation without actually confirming that the supernatural has been involved in the EVENTS and experiences described. It thus constitutes one of the more recent movements away from a view associating the novel with classic realism. According to some theorists—especially those influenced by Tzvetan Todorov—to be classified as a genuine example of the fantastic, a novel or short story must retain a sense of ambiguity to the end, never allowing the reader finally to establish that the depicted events can only be accounted for by natural or, alternatively, by supernatural explanations. From this perspective there are few pure examples of the fantastic; according to some (but not all) accounts one would be Henry James's *The Turn of the Screw*. Recent interest in the fantastic has been encouraged by feminist writers and critics interested in exploring alternative "realities" in which the gender conventions of past and existing societies are challenged or held up to scrutiny. I discuss the ways in which the new electronic media have developed more traditional forms of the fantastic in Chapter 4. See also MARVELLOUS.

FICELLE From the French meaning "string," the term is used by Henry James to denote a minor CHARACTER in a novel whose FUNCTION is that of helping the reader with information, as an anchor-point, and so on.

FICTION See the first two sections of Chapter 1.

FLAT CHARACTER See CHARACTER.

FOCALIZATION A term used by structuralist NARRATOLOGISTS to specify what used to be known as "point of view." See PERSPECTIVE AND VOICE.

FRAME Used within NARRATIVE theory to describe the way in which certain works present the reader with "narratives within narratives," or *framed* or *nested* narratives. Thus Marlow's telling in Conrad's *Heart of Darkness* is framed by introductory, interjected and concluding comments from an unnamed "frame NARRATOR."

FREE INDIRECT DISCOURSE The term denotes a NARRATIVE technique for providing the reader with a CHARACTER's speech, thoughts, or even unconsidered attitudes without the use of direct attribution by tag-phrase ("she thought," "he said") or even quotation marks. Discussed in more detail on p. 122. Often abbreviated to FID.

FREQUENCY The numerical relationship between "EVENTS in a PLOT" and "events in a STORY." See p. 137.

FUNCTION According to Vladimir Propp, "an act of a character, defined from the point of view of its significance for the course of the action." See p. 130.

GOTHIC NOVEL Also *Roman noir*. A type of fiction that was ushered in by Horace Walpole's *The Castle of Otranto* (1764). Walpole was much influenced by the revival of interest in the gothic that occurred in the later eighteenth century, a revival that can be seen as a precursor to aspects of Romanticism in its predilection for the wild, the uncanny, and the horrific—all of which were associated by the pre-Romantics with the medieval period. The gothic novel introduced stock CHARACTERS, situations and SETTINGS that still survive in the modern horror film: gloomy medieval settings, ancient castles with secret rooms and passages ruled over by a sinister nobleman tortured by a guilty secret, and strong hints of the supernatural. The gothic novel proper flourished for a limited period, and was more or less a thing of the past by the early nineteenth century, but gothic elements survive up to the present day and are enjoying a new lease of life in various fantasy forms in films and electronic games as well as in the novel. Jane Austen parodies aspects of the gothic novel in *Northanger Abbey* (begun in 1798 and published in 1816). The term "gothic" has been applied to the works of Mervyn Peake much more recently, and present-day "Goths" can trace their fashion and lifestyle preferences back to this sub-genre.

The work of certain recent women writers such as Angela Carter has been claimed to contain gothic elements, and a revival of interest in the gothic has been encouraged by a feminist interest in the way in which gothic formulae can be seen both to encapsulate certain stereotypical masculine fears about women and also to allow women the space to explore hidden aspects of gender formation.

HISTORICAL NOVEL As its name suggests, the historical novel sets its EVENTS and CHARACTERS in a well-defined historical context, and it may include both fictional and real characters. It is often distinguished (in its more respectable forms) by convincing detailed description of the manners, buildings, institutions and scenery of its chosen SETTING, and generally attempts to convey a sense of historical verisimilitude. Its most respected practitioner in Britain has been Sir Walter Scott.

In its more recent popular, "pulp," and electronic forms it tends to abandon verisimilitude for fantasy, and in some ways can be seen as the present-day version of the ROMANCE.

IMAGE AND IMAGERY Terms with a range of meanings in literary critical discussion, but generally implying the use of language to evoke sensuous (often visual) experiences in the reader. More loosely, any examples of figurative language, especially those with a repetitive or cumulative effect in a work. See the discussion on p. 149.

IMPLIED AUTHOR/READER Terms coined by the American critic Wayne C. Booth. The term "implied author" is used to refer to that sense of the creating author behind a literary work that a reader builds up solely on the basis of a reading of that work. The term "implied reader" is used to refer to that image of the reader that the author (or the work) appears to want—again based solely on "internal information," that is on the reader who seems to be implied by a sympathetic reading of a work.

In medias res From the Latin meaning "in the middle of things," the term is generally applied to beginnings (of works, chapters, or sections) that plunge the reader into a scene without any explanatory or introductory material.

INSTALLMENT, Publication by: see PERIODICAL PUBLICATION.

INTERNAL/INTERIOR DIALOGUE Generally used to refer to a DIALOGUE between two well-defined voices within the single consciousness of a literary CHARACTER (or, in a wider usage, of a real human being), and the NARRATIVE representation of this process. Interior dialogue involves more than the representation of a character's verbalized thought processes in which questions are asked and answered. To count as genuine interior dialogue the questions and answers must stem from two recognizably different voices that may represent varying or even opposed and *personified* attitudes, beliefs, or characteristics. A good example occurs toward the beginning of the tenth chapter of Charlotte Brontë's *Jane Eyre*, in which we have represented a long dialogue between different and personified aspects of Jane Eyre's personality or identity.

INTERNAL/INTERIOR MONOLOGUE A NARRATIVE technique for representing the unexpressed thoughts of a CHARACTER. Strictly speaking interior monologue, unlike the broader term STREAM OF CONSCIOUSNESS, applies when the words used to express the thoughts are those that the character is assumed to be using for thinking. The term is often used more loosely, however, as a synonym for stream of consciousness. See also p. 120.

INTERTEXTUALITY A relation between two or more texts which has an effect upon the way in which the *intertext* (that is, the text within which other texts reside or echo their presence) is read. In some usages the term *transtextuality* is reserved for more overt relations between specific texts, or between two particular texts, while intertextuality is reserved to indicate a more diffuse penetration of the individual text by memories, echoes, transformations, of other texts. Gérard Genette uses his coinages *hypertext* and *hypotext* such that the relationship between James Joyce's *Ulysses* and Homer's *Odyssey* is that of hypertext to hypotext.

INTRUSIVE NARRATOR A NARRATOR who is generally situated outside the world of the action, and who intrudes his or her own thoughts, opinions, comments about a CHARACTER or a situation. Compare METALEPSIS. See p. 115.

ISOCHRONY Borrowed by recent NARRATIVE theorists from a term used to describe poetic rhythm, isochrony denotes an *unvarying* or an *equal* relationship between narrating-time and STORY-time. The two are not the same: if a story covers three hours and each hour is narrated by means of five thousand words, then the relationship between narrating-time and story-time is unvarying. If a story covers three hours and each hour of the story takes approximately an hour to read, then the relationship between narrating-time and story-time can be said to be equal. The opposite of isochrony is *anisochrony:* either a varying or an unequal relationship between narrating-time and story-time—normally the former. Compare DURATION.

ITERATIVE See FREQUENCY.

KÜNSTLERROMAN From the German meaning "a novel about an artist." A *BILDUNGSROMAN* which has an artist as its hero or heroine, and which often contains a concealed or partly concealed autobiographical element, can be described as a *Künstlerroman*. A good modern example of the *Künstlerroman* would be Philip Roth's *The Ghost Writer* (1979).

LOCAL COLOR Realistic detail, often concerned with such matters as dress, scenery, customs, which has no THEMATIC significance but which is there to give the reader a greater sense of verisimilitude.

MAGIC REALISM A blending of the FANTASTIC or fantasy with realism, which today is particularly associated with certain Central and South Ameri=can novelists such as Gabriel García Márquez and Isabel Allende but which has also been applied to some of the later work of the Kenyan novelist Ngũgĩ Wa Thiong'o and to various European novelists including the German Günther Grass and the British Angela Carter—and even retrospectively to a novel such as Virginia Woolf's *Orlando* (1928) and to the female GOTHIC NOVEL. In Europe the term is particularly associated with certain recent female and feminist novelists. "Blending" is perhaps misleading; magic realism seems typically to involve the sudden incursion of fantastic elements into an otherwise realistic PLOT and SETTING.

MARVELLOUS A MODE in which the non-realistic and other-worldly is presented in such a way as to exclude any possible realistic or rational explanation. See also FANTASTIC.

METAFICTION Literally, fiction about fiction—normally denoting the sort of novel or short story which deliberately breaks fictive illusions and comments directly upon its own fictive nature or process of composition. The English father-figure of metafiction is Laurence Sterne, in whose *Tristram Shandy* (1759–67) the NARRATOR jokes with and teases the reader in various ways—advising him or her to turn back several pages to read a passage afresh, for example (see p. 136). Metafictional techniques are common to much MODERNIST and, especially, POSTMODERNIST writing.

METALEPSIS According to Gérard Genette, any transgressing of NARRATIVE levels, such as when Laurence Sterne (or his NARRATOR) implores the reader of *Tristram Shandy* to help the CHARACTER Mr Shandy get back to his bed. Compare INTRUSIVE NARRATOR.

MODE A term that is used in a confusing variety of ways. It is commonly used in a loose sense to denote a manner of writing characterized by a particular tone or attitude, as in "the ironic mode." It can also refer to a specific type of "fictional world," such as the ROMANCE or the FANTASTIC. Structuralist narratologists, however, use it as a rough way of categorizing different sorts of DISTANCE, and Gerald Prince names TELLING AND SHOWING as two different modes (1988, 54). See also p. 215.

MODERNISM See Chapter 4, p. 59.

MOOD Apart from being used as a rough synonym for "atmosphere," mood is a term adapted by STRUCTURALIST NARRATOLOGISTS from its grammatical sense, which distinguishes between grammatical moods such as the subjective or the indicative. In this usage, mood is roughly equivalent to the old-fashioned "point of view" (see PERSPECTIVE AND VOICE).

MOTIF In discussion of prose fiction "motif" is often used as a synonym for the German *leitmotif*, to refer to recurrent elements that are not quite SYMBOLS or THEMES, but that have a cumulative effect on the reader. Thus in his Penguin edition of Joseph Conrad's *Lord Jim*, Cedric Watts provides the reader with a useful list of *leitmotifs*: "butterflies and beetles"; "dream, dreams"; "glimpse (of Jim's character) through mist or fog"; "in the ranks"; "jump, leap"; "nothing can touch me"; "one of us"; "romance, romantic"; "under a cloud"; "veiled opportunity."

NARRATEE According to Gerald Prince, "The one who is narrated to, as inscribed in the text" (1988, 57). Thus if an author addresses a particular person in a dedication, this person would not be the narratee of the work because he or she is (i) not "inscribed in the text" (a dedication is strictly speaking not part of the text of a novel or short story), and (ii) not addressed by the NARRATOR of the work but by the author. Prince further claims that the narratee must be "located at the same diegetic level" as the narrator, and many take this to mean that if the narrator exists within the fictional rather than the real world, then so too must the narratee. This would mean that if a fictional work were narrated by a fictional narrator to, say, Napoleon, then Napoleon would not be the narratee because he is a real-world person. Not all critics accept this requirement, and would in this imagined case be happy to define Napoleon as the narratee. A work can have more than one narratee; in an EPISTOLARY NOVEL, for example, each recipient of one of the letters forming the work is a narratee. Shlomith Rimmon-Kenan (1983, 89) disagrees with Seymour Chatman's view that there can be narratives without narratees, but concedes that the narratee may be implicit rather than explicit.

NARRATIVE See Chapter 1, p. 6.

NARRATIVE SITUATION Defined according to the NARRATOR's relationship to the narrative and the STORY. Is the narrator diegetic or extradiegetic (see DIEGESIS AND MIMESIS)? Is the NARRATIVE ostensibly spoken or written? See p. 113.

NARRATOLOGY Used to refer (i) to the structuralist inspired theory (or theories) of NARRATIVES that have flourished in the past four or five decades, and (ii) to the rhetorical narratology that is a more recent development. The term is also used more loosely to describe any body of theory concerned with the analysis of narratives, literary or other. See the extended discussion in Chapter 8, p. 212.

NARRATOR The person, voice, or language-source that tells the STORY. This awkward formulation stems from the fact that some novels and short stories have no clearly personified or human teller, but it is still conventional to refer to their having a narrator. Some recent theorists have however argued that the term should be reserved for human or personified tellers. See also INTRUSIVE NARRATOR. See p. 102.

NATURALISM Naturalism is a variety of realism, and the term is used in much the same way but with a narrower focus. Strictly speaking, naturalism should be restricted to a description of those literary works which were written according to a method founded upon the belief that there is a natural (rather than supernatural or spiritual) explanation for everything that exists or occurs. Naturalist novelists include the Goncourt brothers, Émile Zola, George Moore, the German Gerhard Hauptmann, and Americans such as Theodore Dreiser and Stephen Crane.

NOUVEAU ROMAN (French for "new novel") In the *nouveau roman* the accepted conventions of fictional composition are deliberately distorted or flouted in order to disorient the reader and to foreground certain processes of artistic illusion or NARRATIVE convention. As such it can be seen as a post-Second World War development of MODERNISM and precursor of POSTMODERNISM. It is associated particularly with France.

The best-known exponents of the *nouveau roman* are Alain Robbe-Grillet (whose book *Pour un Nouveau Roman* [1963] originated the term), Michel Butor, and Nathalie Sarraute. Compare ANTI-NOVEL.

Nouvelle A *nouvelle* is characterized by a concern with a single episode or state of affairs, although its treatment of this (which conventionally moves to a surprise ending of one sort or another) may cover many pages. The genre is generally agreed to achieve a recognized form in the middle of the sixteenth century, with the publication of *Nouvelles Récréations et Joyeux Devis*, a collection ascribed to Des Périers. The term can be a little treacherous as in some usages it has come to be seen as synonymous with *conte*, while in others it is used interchangeably with NOVELLA. See Dieter Meindl's comments on this term on p. 107.

NOVEL, NOVELLA, SHORT STORY The problems involved in defining these three terms are discussed at length in Chapters 1, 2, and 3. Apart from the characteristics of prose, and fictionality, all three forms are generally restricted to works with CHARACTERS, action, and a PLOT. The terms are conventionally distinguished by reference to their length, and in Chapter 3 I quote Mary Doyle Springer's proposal that a work of fiction of between 15,000 and 50,000 words be categorized as a novella. More than 50,000 words and we have a novel; fewer than 15,000 and we have a short story. Remember however that these are arbitrary and by no means universally accepted distinctions.

NOVELLA See NOVEL, NOVELLA, SHORT STORY.

OBSTINATION The reader's tendency to continue to FRAME a passage of NARRATIVE in a consistent manner (e.g. as Free Indirect Discourse) unless prompted by textual or contextual features to shift to a new FRAME.

OCCASION The situation in which a narrative is delivered and by which it is influenced. See p. 115.

OMNISCIENCE All-embracing, godlike knowledge. Often applied to the NARRATORS of classical realist novels for whom there are no secrets within the created world of the novel. Dorrit Cohn has however cited Gérard Genette's objection to the term, which is that it is absurd because the author has nothing to know because he or she "invents" everything (Cohn 1999, 175).

PARABLE A short NARRATIVE intended to convey a moral or other lesson. Best known from Christ's Biblical parables, but more widespread than is often appreciated. Many modern novelists and (especially) short-story writers have written parable-like works.

PARALEPSIS Presenting more information in a NARRATIVE than is strictly or logically speaking justified by the ostensible NARRATOR and his or her situation. Thus in Joseph Conrad's novel *Under Western Eyes* the narrator (the "Teacher of Languages") claims to base his account on the written report of the CHARACTER, Razumov. Yet after Razumov has finished this report and has wrapped it up, the Teacher of Languages continues to describe Razumov's actions and experiences.

PARALIPSIS The omission of certain information relevant to the story being told that the NARRATOR should in "real world" terms be aware of.

PARATEXT and PERITEXT See Chapter 4, p. 75.

PATRONAGE The specific meaning of this term within the study of literature involves a particular method of financing authorship. Rather than relying upon royalties, or payments from a publisher, an author is supported by a patron, who is rewarded by having his or her name in the eventual book, and perhaps by having his or her person or politics supported within the book. It is generally accepted that an important element in "the rise of the novel" was the freedom from patronage that the market (i.e. publishers' fees or royalties) gave writers.

PERIODICAL PUBLICATION Normally initial publication of a longer work in installments in a periodical or magazine. An important source of finance for writers in the nineteenth and early twentieth centuries (periodicals paid well), the constraints of periodical publication (censorship, division into sections, writing against the clock) did have some negative effects on works and writers.

It is useful to be able to read Henry James's *The Turn of the Screw* (1898) in an edition that marks the division between the installments of its first published version, as we can then note that James attempts to end each separate installment at a point of increased tension or dramatic surprise (much like the old film serials for children, each episode of which typically ended with a "cliff-hanging" finale).

PERSPECTIVE AND VOICE Gérard Genette has drawn attention to the importance of a long-neglected distinction between *who sees?* and *who speaks?* I exemplify this distinction by reference to Katherine Mansfield's "The Voyage" on p. 113. In Genette's terminology the distinction between *who sees?* and *who speaks?* is expressed in terms of the opposition between MOOD and VOICE (1980, 30). According to him, *mood* operates at the level of connections between STORY and narrative, while *voice* designates connections both between narrating and narrative, and narrating and story (1980, 32). Others following Genette have preferred to replace *mood* by *perspective*, as the pair "perspective and voice" matches up more neatly with "who sees/who speaks." If "who sees" = perspective and "who speaks" = voice, then a single narrative passage may combine the voice of one character or position and the perspective of another character or position.

The matched terms perspective and voice thus provide a more fine-tuned way of investigating what was known as "point of view" in the days prior to the emergence of modern NARRATOLOGY.

PICARESQUE NOVEL A "picaro" in Spanish is a rogue, and the picaresque novel is built on the tradition of the sixteenth-century Spanish picaresque NARRATIVE, which typically portrayed a sharp-witted rogue living off his wits while traveling through a variety of usually low-life SETTINGS. The picaro typically lives by begging or by minor theft, he is cynical in his attitude to the softer emotions, especially love, and through witty and satirical comments questions established beliefs and customs. Critics frequently relate the emergence of the picaro to the break-up of the feudal world, and his open-minded, self-interested, geographical, and intellectual wandering and questing are seen by many to merge into the spirit of possessive individualism that is ushered in with the growth of capitalist social relations.

The picaresque novel is typically *episodic*, lacking both a sophisticated PLOT, and psychologically complex—or developing—CHARACTERS.

Daniel Defoe's novel *Moll Flanders* is by no means a pure picaresque novel; quite apart from anything else the fact that its main character is a woman represents a significant divergence from previous picaresque novels. It is nonetheless possessed of many typical characteristics of the picaresque novel. It is constructed around a sequence of short "episodes" none of which is longer than two or three pages, and it has little real development of character.

Part of the appeal of the picaresque lies in its concern with the ordinary and the trivial, a concern which sets the picaresque apart from the ROMANCE, and which explains the historical importance accorded the picaresque in the history of the novel's emergence and development.

See the discussion of CYBERPUNK/CYBERFICTION above for comment on picaresque elements in a recent sub-genre.

PLOT See STORY AND PLOT.

POINT OF VIEW See PERSPECTIVE AND VOICE.

POSTMODERNIST NOVEL During the last two or three decades it has become clear that "postmodernism" has emerged as the umbrella term which is most frequently used to describe a range of formal and technical experiments that are linked to theories about reality in general and the modern world in particular. In his *Postmodernist Fiction*, Brian McHale distinguishes postmodernism from MODERNISM by differentiating between a poetics (or systematized theory of literature) dominated by ontological issues (meaning a concern with the nature of reality in general), and a poetics dominated by epistemological issues (meaning how and if we know the world or "the real") (1987, xii). Postmodernism is seen by many to involve (among other things) the taking of certain modernist techniques to an extreme, and the more extended consideration of modernism and postmodernism in Chapter 4 should be consulted for a fuller discussion.

POST-STRUCTURALISM See the discussion in Chapter 8, p. 222.

PROLEPSIS See ANALEPSIS AND PROLEPSIS.

QUEER THEORY See the discussion in Chapter 8, p. 233.

REALISM See Chapter 4, p. 54.

REGIONAL NOVEL The regional novel involves a focus on the life of a particular, well-defined geographical region. Traditionally the region in question will be rural rather than urban (thus it would be distinctly odd to refer to Charles Dickens as a regional novelist, in spite of the fact that so many of his novels explore London life in such intimate detail). Very often, a "regional novelist" will write a number of books all involving the same territory or place—as with Thomas Hardy's "Wessex" and William Faulkner's "Yoknapatawpha County." Both of these "regions" are closely modeled on particular areas of England and the United States.

RHETORICAL NARRATOLOGY See p. 215.

ROMAN À CLEF (French: "novel with a key") The *roman à clef* is the sort of novel that can be "unlocked" given the right "key"—in other words one which refers to real people, places or EVENTS in disguised form so that once one realizes what the work is about the hidden references all become apparent. Thomas Love Peacock wrote several humorous novels in the early nineteenth century in which thinly disguised portrayals of contemporary individuals such as Shelley and Coleridge appeared.

ROMAN À THÈSE/TENDENZROMAN The *roman à thèse* has, as the term suggests, a particular thesis or argument underlying it. It is typically a novel concerned to encourage social reform, or the correction of a particular abuse or wrong. Central to the definition is the idea of a *dominant* and usually a simple and uncomplicated thesis. (See p. 145 for the distinction between "thesis" and "theme.") Harriet Beecher Stowe's *Uncle Tom's Cabin* (1852), which is structured around an attack upon the institution of slavery in the United States, is a classic *roman à thèse*. A novel like Thomas Hardy's *Jude the Obscure* (1896) in contrast, although it undeniably involves an attack upon certain social conventions which are seen as repressive and although in a sense it clearly "calls for" a change in society so that women and working people have greater opportunities for self-development and for education, is too complex and involved a novel to be termed a *roman à thèse*.

ROMANCE The medieval romance is discussed in Chapter 2. The modern use of the term denotes a type of formulaic prose fiction aimed at women readers and focused on courtship and marriage seen from a woman's point of view. Although very different in many ways, there are arguably lines of continuity linking the medieval romance with its modern namesake.

ROMAN FEUILLETON A novel published in installments in unabridged form by a daily newspaper. The method of publication is unusual today for a novel, but flourished in the nineteenth century.

ROMAN-FLEUVE This term denotes a series of sequence of novels which can be read and appreciated individually but which deal with recurring CHARACTERS and/or common EVENTS and which form a sequence or which complement one another. Perhaps the best-known example is Balzac's *La Comedie Humaine*, but Anthony Powell's *A Dance to the Music of Time* (1951–75) is a more recent example. The *roman-fleuve* is closely related to what is called the *saga novel*—a series of novels about a large family each of which concentrates upon different branches of the family or different events in which it is implicated. Thomas Mann's tetralogy *Joseph and His Brothers* (1933–43) is one twentieth-century example; John Galsworthy's *Forsyte Saga* (1906–35) is another. Many of Louise Erdrich's novels also focus on the same Native-American communities and characters.

ROMAN NOIR See GOTHIC NOVEL

ROUND CHARACTER See CHARACTER.

SAGA NOVEL See *ROMAN-FLEUVE*.

SATIRICAL NOVEL Satire does not have to be either in prose or fictional, although there is a sense in which the exaggeration upon which it typically depends necessarily involves a certain amount of fictive imagining. There is a tradition of satire which is independent of the novel and which stretches back to antiquity, and aspects of this tradition have been important influences upon the novel. Satire attacks alleged vices and stupidities—either of individuals or of whole communities or groups—and its tools are those of ridicule, exaggeration, and contempt.

Jonathan Swift's satirical writings—and especially his *Gulliver's Travels* (1726)—are extremely important staging-posts for the novel, although most commentators have been unwilling to allow that any themselves merit the title "novel." If we think of Mark Twain's *The Adventures of Huckleberry Finn* (1884), we can see how the mature novel of the nineteenth century was able to incorporate important satirical techniques from earlier writers within a much more realistic framework than Swift, for example, provides. The use of a naïve NARRATOR traveling among people whose strange ways he describes innocently while at the same time conveying his creator's biting satire of what they stand for is one element which unites Swift's and Twain's best-known works.

The satirist is by definition more concerned to draw our attention to what he or she is attacking than to create characters, situations, and EVENTS that are believable in and for themselves. A novelist may however include satirical elements in works that do not, overall, merit the term "satirical novel" (and indeed most novelists do). Thus E.M. Forster's *Howards End* is not usually categorized as a satirical novel, but it does include a distinctively satirical vein in its treatment of various characters. Take the following passage from the end of the first paragraph of Chapter 3 of the novel. Mrs Munt is considering her responsibilities toward the two Schlegel sisters, Helen and Margaret:

> Sooner or later the girls would enter on the process known as throwing themselves away, and if they had delayed hitherto it was only that they

might throw themselves more vehemently in the future. They saw too many people at Wickham Place—unshaven musicians, an actress even, German cousins (one knows what foreigners are), acquaintances picked up at continental hotels (one knows what they are too). It was interesting, and down at Swanage no one appreciated culture more than Mrs Munt; but it was dangerous, and disaster was bound to come.

The passage is clearly satirical: it attempts to diminish a set of beliefs by making it appear ridiculous. Although the passage is ostensibly related to us from the viewpoint of Forster's narrator it mimics Mrs Munt and makes her views seem absurd by pretending to adopt them. (Forster makes delicate use of Free Indirect Discourse here—see p. 122.)

If we compare *Howards End* with Joseph Heller's *Catch-22* (1961) we will appreciate that the latter can more properly be termed a "satirical novel" than the former. Heller's dominating concern is clearly to diminish war and the military in our eyes by making them appear ridiculous and vain; his major aim in the novel is, in other words, satirical.

SCIENCE FICTION Some definitions link science fiction with FANTASTIC literature, and the two are clearly closely related. The fantastic normally invokes the strong possibility (but not certainty) of supernatural agencies, however, while science fiction does not generally do this. Science fiction is rather characterized by SETTINGS involving interplanetary travel and advanced technology, and its plots typically unfold in the future. In contrast to fantasy literature its settings and EVENTS are conceivable but not actual.

Jules Verne and H.G. Wells are often granted the joint title of the fathers of science fiction (its most celebrated authors tend to be male), and its best-known practitioners today are Ray Bradbury, Arthur C. Clarke, and Isaac Asimov.

It is possible to relate science fiction to a work such as Swift's *Gulliver's Travels*, and clearly science fiction can have a "pastoral" element: commenting upon one society or community under the pretext of describing another, imagined one. Often abbreviated to SF, the tradition is an important source of CYBERPUNK and of various forms of electronic fiction (see p. 82).

SETTING See p. 143.

SHORT STORY See NOVEL, NOVELLA, SHORT STORY.

SILVER FORK NOVEL A now archaic term used to refer to a particular sub-genre of the novel, popular in the early years of the nineteenth century, that focused on the lives and preoccupations of high society and that included much LOCAL COLOR of the "silver fork" variety. The novels of Benjamin Disraeli are sometimes so categorized. Compare the dismissive "white telephone film," from the Italian "telefoni bianchi," a term coined to denote Hollywood-imitating Italian films of the 1930s that featured luxurious settings in which all the telephones were white (a sign of luxury at this time).

S*KAZ* A MODE or technique of narration that mirrors oral NARRATIVE. The term comes from the Russian, as Russian Formalist theorists were the first to tackle the issues raised by *skaz*, but there are many non-Russian examples. For example, from a technical point of view much of Joseph Conrad's *Heart of Darkness* can be described as *skaz*, as most of what we read represents the CHARACTER Marlow's oral address to listeners. The technique allows for the depiction of such things as hesitation, tone of voice, slips of the tongue, self-correction, and interaction with a depicted intradiegetic (see DIEGESIS AND MIMESIS) audience.

STORY AND PLOT A distinction related to that made by the Russian formalists between fabula (story) and sjužet (plot). "Story" is used to refer to the events of a NARRATIVE in the order in which they happened (or in an order determined by cause-and-effect), while "plot" is used to refer to the events of a narrative as they are ordered and presented artistically, in the work. See Chapter 5, p. 134.

STREAM OF CONSCIOUSNESS The representation in words of a succession of thoughts in a CHARACTER's mind, typically when the character is alone and is allowing thought to succeed thought without external prompting. Strictly speaking stream of consciousness is the umbrella term within which internal (or interior) monologue (which requires that the words used be those that the character thinks by means of) is a subordinate category. The two terms are however often used as synonyms. See the discussion on p. 120.

STRUCTURALISM and STRUCTURALIST NARRATOLOGY See Chapter 8, p. 213.

SUBPLOT The term is more commonly applied to classical drama, as in a Shakespearian tragedy for example, where it denotes a "second and subordinate story" which accompanies or runs alongside the main STORY of the fall of a person of high estate. It is sometimes applied to fiction, although, because the novel often involves very many PLOT "threads," it is less appropriate to this genre.

Cedric Watts has coined the term "covert plot" to describe those subplots that are concealed and apparent only after having been teased out during a second or subsequent reading.

SUBSCRIPTION A method of financing publication which requires prospective buyers of the work to purchase a subscription, which the writer redeems by providing subscribers with a copy of the work once it is published. Along with PATRONAGE, this is a method of financing authors which was largely replaced by publishers' fees and royalties ("the market") in the course of the eighteenth century. Like patronage, of which it can be seen to be a variant, subscription freed the author from the need to sell lots of copies of a work and it provided income while the work was being written (like an "advance on royalties"), but it required the author to stay on good terms with the source of his or her income.

SYLLEPSIS In traditional usage, another term for "zeugma," or the use of a single word to modify two other words in very different ways in a single phrase, as in Pope's "Or stain her honour, or her new brocade." In NARRATOLOGY, a cluster or gathering (of EVENTS, circumstances, experiences, and so on) ordered according to some principle other than temporal unity or sequence. Thus "John told her all the things that had happened in his mother's house" is a syllepsis based on situational coherence.

SYMBOL A unit (linguistic or otherwise) which either conventionally or naturally represents something apart from itself. See the extended discussion on p. 146.

TELLING AND SHOWING A term used to distinguish two ways of providing the reader with relevant information. Telling is seen as the cruder technique, involving overt statement on the part of NARRATOR or CHARACTER. Showing is more subtle and indirect, presenting scenes of DIALOGUE, thought, or action and allowing the reader to draw certain conclusions him- or herself. See also p. 6 and the longer discussion on p. 131.

THEME See the discussion on p. 145, and the entry for MOTIF.

THING THEORY See p. 234.

THIRD PERSON See FOCALIZATION.

THREE-DECKER During the Victorian period, publication of a novel in book form (rather than in instalments in a periodical) commonly involved three volumes. Such three-deckers were generally borrowed from one of the circulating libraries such as Mudie's. Publication aimed at personal sales usually followed three-decker publication, and was normally in the form of a single volume. Because circulating libraries exercised forms of censorship on authors, it is important to know if a novel was first published in this form.

TONE The sense of an author's or narrator's attitude to his or her character, situation, or subject, as conveyed by the words he or she chooses. Sometimes used in a wider sense to describe the mood engendered in a reader by a particular work. See the discussion on p. 125.

UNCLE CHARLES PRINCIPLE See COLORING.

UNNATURAL NARRATOR See p. 107.

VOICE See PERSPECTIVE AND VOICE, and the discussion in Chapter 5, p. 113.

WORLD LITERATURE See the extended discussion in Chapter 9.

Bibliography

Anand, Mulk Raj (1946), *Indian Fairy Tales*. Bombay: Kotub Publishers.

Andermahr, Sonya (2009), *Jeanette Winterson*. Houndmills: Palgrave.

Andrew, Dudley (1992), "Adaptation." First published in Dudley Andrew, *Concepts in Film Theory* (Oxford: Oxford University Press, 1984). Reprinted in Gerald Mast, Marshall Cohen and Leo Braudy (eds) (1992), *Film Theory and Criticism* (New York and Oxford: Oxford University Press), 420–8.

Apter, Emily (2013), *Against World Literature*. London: Verso.

Armstrong, Paul (2013), *How Literature Plays with the Brain: The Neuroscience of Reading and Art*. Baltimore: Johns Hopkins University Press.

Atkins, Barry (2003), *More than a Game: The Computer Game as Fictional Form*. Manchester and New York: Manchester University Press.

Atwood, Margaret (1984), *Murder in the Dark: Short Fictions and Prose Poems*. London: Jonathan Cape.

Atwood, Margaret (1991), "Weight." In *Wilderness Tips* (London: Bloomsbury), 177–93.

Azim, Firdous (1993), *The Colonial Rise of the Novel*. London: Routledge.

Bakhtin, M.M. (1981), *The Dialogic Imagination: Four Essays*. Trans. Caryl Emerson and Michael Holquist. Austin: University of Texas Press.
Bakhtin's work has been very influential in European and North American academic circles since it started to appear in translation. This volume makes available a key collection of essays: "Epic and Novel," "From the Prehistory of Novelistic Discourse," "Forms of Time and Chronotope in the Novel," and "Discourse in the Novel."

Bal, Mieke (1985), *Narratology: Introduction to the Theory of Narrative*. Trans. Christine van Boheemen. Toronto and London: University of Toronto Press.
Now available in a revised, second edn (1997; paperback 1998). This and Shlomith Rimmon-Kenan's Narrative Fiction: Contemporary Poetics (see below) are recommended as accessible but sophisticated introductions to narrative theory.

Banfield, Ann (1982), *Unspeakable Sentences: Narration and Representation in the Language of Fiction*. London: Routledge.
An advanced and often difficult book that has been very influential in the development of debate around the topic of Free Indirect Discourse. Banfield is concerned with FID as a technique that can be used to present information that is, paradoxically, "unspeakable." See my comments on p. 111.

Barnes, Julian (1985), *Flaubert's Parrot*. First published, 1984. Picador edn. London: Pan Books.

Barthes, Roland (1974), *The Pleasure of the Text*. Trans. Richard Miller. New York: Hill and Wang.

Beale, Antony (ed.) (1961), *Selected Literary Criticism: D.H. Lawrence*. London: Mercury Books.

Beckett, Samuel (1957), *Murphy*. First published, 1938. New York: Grove Press.

Berman, Jessica (2001), *Modernist Fiction, Cosmopolitanism, and the Politics of Community*. Cambridge: Cambridge University Press.

Blewett, David (ed.) (2000), *Reconsidering the Rise of the Novel*. Special issue of *Eighteenth-century Fiction*, 12(2–3).
    A very valuable collection of essays engaging with the arguments of Ian Watt's influential. The Rise of the Novel.

Booth, Austin and Mary Flanagan (eds) (2002), *Reload: Rethinking Women + Cyberculture*. With an Introduction by the editors. Cambridge, MA and London: MIT Press.

Booth, Wayne C. (1961), *The Rhetoric of Fiction*. Chicago: University of Chicago Press.
    A study that really initiated the new wave of interest in narrative technique in the English-speaking world. Booth is a stimulating and accessible critic, and his book has been enormously influential. The second edition contains a useful "Afterword."

Borowski, Tadeusz (1976), *This Way for the Gas, Ladies and Gentlemen*. Selected and Trans. Barbara Vedder. First published in Polish, 1959, and in English, 1967. London: Penguin.

Boumelha, Penny (1988), "Jane Eyre, Jamaica and the Gentleman's House," *Southern Review*, 21(2), July, 111–22.

Bowen, Elizabeth (1949), *Encounters*. First published, 1923. London: Sidgwick & Jackson.

Bowen, Elizabeth (1976), Introduction to *The Faber Book of Modern Short Stories*. First published, 1936. Reprinted in May 1976, 152–8.

Bradbury, Malcolm (ed.) (1990), *The Novel Today: Contemporary Writers on Modern Fiction*. Revised edn. Glasgow: Fontana.
    A very useful collection of essays by practicing novelists writing about their own, and others', fiction. Essential for any student interested in modernism and postmodernism in the novel. The 1990 edition includes a new introduction, a new piece by Italo Calvino, and an interview with Milan Kundera by Ian McEwan.

Brecht, Bertolt (1977), "Against Georg Lukács." This consists of four pieces written by Brecht in the late 1930s. Trans. Stuart Hood. In Bloch, Ernst and Georg Lukács, Bertolt Brecht, Walter Benjamin and Theodor Adorno (eds), *Aesthetics and Politics* (London: New Left Books), 68–85.

Brontë, Emily (2003), *Wuthering Heights*. First published, 1847. Edited by Linda H. Peterson. Boston: Bedford/St Martin's.

Brooke-Rose, Christine (1981), *A Rhetoric of the Unreal: Studies in Narrative and Structure, Especially of the Fantastic*. Cambridge: Cambridge University Press.

Burden, Robert (1991), *Heart of Darkness*. Houndmills: Macmillan.

Burke, Peter (1997), "Representations of the Self from Petrarch to Descartes." In Porter, Roy (ed.), *Rewriting the Self: Histories from the Renaissance to the Present* (London: Routledge), 17–28.

Butler, Andrew M. (2000), *Cyberpunk*. Harpenden: Pocket Essentials.

Butte, George (2004), *I Know That You Know I Know: Narrating Subjects from Moll Flanders to Marnie*. Columbus: Ohio State University Press.

Camus, Albert (1983), *The Outsider*. Trans. Joseph Laredo. First published in French, 1942. London: Penguin.

Carey, Charles Stokes (ed.) (1912), *Letters Written by Lord Chesterfield to His Son*. Volume 1. London: Wm. Reeves.

Carlier, J.C. (2000), "Roland Barthes's Resurrection of the Author and Redemption of Biography." Trans. from the French by C.T. Watts. *The Cambridge Quarterly*, 29(4), 386–93.

Chatman, Seymour (1990), *Story and Discourse: Narrative Structure in Fiction and Film*. Ithaca and London: Cornell University Press.

Cohn, Dorrit (1999), *The Distinction of Fiction*. Baltimore and London: Johns Hopkins University Press.
  Cohn argues strongly for literary fiction as a distinct category, one that must be distinguished from narrative in general. The final chapter, "Optics and Power in the Novel," takes up a determined opposition to recent attempts to see fictional narrators in terms of Michel Foucault's extension of Jeremy Bentham's idea of the "Panopticon."

Common, Jack (1951), *Kiddar's Luck*. London: Turnstile Press.

Conrad, Joseph (1971), *Heart of Darkness*, Edited by Robert Kimbrough. Norton Critical Edn. Second edn. New York and London: W.W. Norton. (The fourth edition of the Norton edition of this text, edited by Paul B. Armstrong, was published in 2005).

Cornwell, Neil (1990), *The Literary Fantastic: From Gothic to Postmodernism*. Hemel Hempstead: Harvester Wheatsheaf.

Culler, Jonathan (1981), *The Pursuit of Signs: Semiotics, Literature, Deconstruction*. London: Routledge.

D'haen, Theo, César Domínguez and Mads Rosendahl Thomsen (eds) (2013), *World Literature: A Reader*. Milton Park, Abingdon: Routledge.

Damrosch, David (2003), *What Is World Literature?* Princeton, NJ: Princeton University Press.

Davies, Laurence and J.H. Stape (eds) (2005), *The Collected Letters of Joseph Conrad*, vol. 7, 1920–1922. Cambridge: Cambridge University Press.

Day, Geoffrey (1987), *From Fiction to the Novel*. London: Routledge.

Defoe, Daniel (1971), *Moll Flanders*, G.A. Starr (ed.). First published, 1722. Oxford: Oxford University Press.

DeLillo, Don (2004), *Cosmopolis*. First published, 2003. London: Picador.

Dickens, Charles (1953), *Little Dorrit*. First published, 1857. Oxford: Oxford University Press.

Dickens, Charles (1965), *Great Expectations*. First published, 1861. Edited by Angus Calder. Harmondsworth: Penguin.

Dickens, Charles (1966), *Oliver Twist*. First published, 1837–9. London: Penguin.

Dickens, Charles (1971), *Bleak House*. First published, 1853. Edited by Norman Page. Harmondsworth: Penguin.

Doody, Margaret Anne (1996), *The True Story of the Novel*. New Brunswick, NJ: Rutgers University Press.

Dostoyevsky, Fyodor (2009), *Notes from Underground* and *The Double*. Trans. Ronald Wilks. London: Penguin.

Downie, J.A. (2000), "Mary Davy's 'Probable Feign'd Stories' and Critical Shibboleths about the Rise of the Novel." In *Reconsidering the Rise of the Novel*. Special issue of *Eighteenth-Century Fiction*, 12(2–3), January–April, 309–26.

Doyle, Sir Arthur Conan (1974), *The Memoirs of Sherlock Holmes*. First published, 1893. London: John Murray and Jonathan Cape.

Edel, Leon (ed.) (1964), *The Complete Tales of Henry James*. Volume 11, 1900–1903. London: Rupert Hart-Davies.

Ferguson, Suzanne (1989), "The Rise of the Short Story in the Hierarchy of Genres." In Lohafer and Clarey 1989, 176–92.

Fjågesund, Peter (2002), "Knut Hamsun and George Egerton: Factual and Fictional Encounters." In Bjørn Tysdahl, Mats Jansson, Jakob Lothe, and Steen Klitgård Povlson (eds), *English and Nordic Modernisms* (Norwich: Norvik Press), 41–59.

Fjågesund, Peter (2009), "'A Cool Reception': Hamsun in Britain." In Peter Fjågesund (ed.), *Knut Hamsun Abroad: International Reception* (London: Norvik Press), 65–77.

Fludernik, Monika (1993), *The Fictions of Language and the Languages of Fiction*. London: Routledge.
Along with Ann Banfield's Unspeakable Sentences *(see above and also p. 111), on which it builds but with which it takes issue on a number of points, probably the most exhaustive and demanding study of Free Indirect Discourse available. Not recommended as an introductory text, but very rewarding for the reader prepared to grapple with its difficulties.*

Fludernik, Monika (2009), *An Introduction to Narratology*. London: Routledge.
*A very student-friendly text by an expert in the field, making good use of
illustrations to present complex ideas.*

Forster, E.M. (1962), *Aspects of the Novel*. First published, 1927.
Harmondsworth: Penguin.
*In spite of its chatty tone and of the fact that criticism of the novel has refined
and expanded its repertoire of terms and concepts since 1927, this is a study
that is still worth reading. Full of shrewd insights and illuminating asides on
particular novels.*

Forster, E.M. (1975), *Howards End*. First published, 1910. Harmondsworth:
Penguin.

Fox, Ralph (1979), *The Novel and the People*. First published, 1937. London:
Lawrence & Wishart.

France, Peter (ed.) (2000), *The Oxford Guide to Literature in English
Translation*. Oxford: Oxford University Press.

Friedman, Norman (1976), "What Makes a Short Story Short?" First published,
1958. Reprinted in May 1976, 131–46.

Friedman, Norman (1989), "Recent Short Story Theories: Problems in
Definition." In Lohafer and Clarey 1989, 13–31.

Frow, John (1997), *Time and Commodity Culture: Essays in Cultural Theory and
Postmodernity*. Oxford: Oxford University Press.

Genette, Gérard (1980), *Narrative Discourse: An Essay in Method*. Trans. Jane
E. Lewin. First published in French, 1972. Ithaca, NY: Cornell University
Press.
*Perhaps the most influential of the first wave of structuralist studies of
narrative. There are more accessible introductions, and sometimes Genette's
use of the linguistic paradigm (or analogy) makes for difficulties of
terminology and comprehension, but this is a book rich in local insights and
conceptual innovations.*

Genette, Gérard (1997), *Paratexts: Thresholds of Interpretation* (*Literature,
Culture, Theory*, 20). Trans. Jane E. Lewin. First published in French, 1987.
Cambridge: Cambridge University Press.
*A fascinating account of such things as titles, prefaces, forewords, and so on,
and their effect upon the works they penetrate and surround.*

Gibbon, Lewis Grassic (1986), *A Scots Quair* (the third story in the trilogy,
Grey Granite, first published in 1934). Harmondsworth: Penguin.

Gilbert, Susan M. and Susan Gubar (1979), *The Madwoman in the Attic: The
Woman Writer and the Nineteenth-century Literary Imagination*. New Haven,
CT: Yale University Press.
*An extremely influential account of recurrent themes and stereotypes of
women as represented in nineteenth-century literature. Gilbert and Gubar
devote considerable attention to prose fiction.*

Gombrich, Ernst (1960), *Art and Illusion*. New York: Pantheon.

Good, Graham (1994), "Notes on the Novella." First published, 1977. In May (1994), 147–64.

Goring, Paul, Jeremy Hawthorn and Domhnall Mitchell (2010), *Studying Literature. The Essential Companion*, second edn. London: Bloomsbury Academic.

Graves, Richard (1967), *The Spiritual Quixote or The Summer's Ramble of Mr. Geoffry Wildgoose. A Comic Romance*, Clarence Tracy (ed.). First published, 1773. London: Oxford University Press.

Guérard, Albert (2013), "What Is World Literature?" First published, 1940. In D'haen 2013, 51–7.

Hamsun, Knut (1967), *Hunger*. Trans. from the Norwegian by Robert Bly, New York: Farrar, Straus and Giroux.

Hamsun, Knut (2003), *Hunger*. Trans. from the Norwegian by George Egerton. Translation first published 1899. Mineola, NY: Dover Publications.

Hamsun, Knut (2011), *Hunger*. Trans. from the Norwegian by Sverre Lyngstad. Translation first published, 1996. Edinburgh: Canongate Books. With an essay ("Translator's trap: Knut Hamsun's *Hunger* in English") and an Appendix, by the translator.

Harvey, David (1989), *The Condition of Postmodernity*. Oxford: Blackwell.

Hassan, Ihab (1985), "The Culture of Postmodernism," *Theory Culture and Society* 2(3), 119–31.

Hawthorn, Jeremy (1998), "Repetitions and Revolutions: Conrad's Use of the Pseudo-iterative in *Nostromo*." In *Joseph Conrad 1*, special Conrad issue of *La revue des lettres modernes* (Paris: Editions Minard), 125–49.

Hunter, J. Paul (1990), *Before Novels: The Cultural Contexts of Eighteenth-century English Fiction*. New York: W.W. Norton.
I refer repeatedly to this book in Chapter 2. It contains a wealth of detailed information about social and literary contexts within which the modern novel emerged.

Huyssen, Andreas (1988), *After the Great Divide: Modernism, Mass Culture and Postmodernism*. London: Macmillan.

James, Henry (1970), *The Lesson of the Master, The Death of the Lion, The Next Time, and Other Tales*. New York Edition of the Novels and Tales of Henry James, vol, XV. New York: Augustus M. Kelley.

James, Henry (1984), *Literary Criticism: Essays on Literature; American Writers; English Writers*. Selected and with Notes by Leon Edel. New York: The Library of America.

James, Henry (1999), *The Turn of the Screw*. Edited by Deborah Esch and Jonathan Warren. Norton Critical Edn. Second edn. New York and London: W.W. Norton.

Jameson, Fredric (1991), *Postmodernism, or, The Cultural Logic of Late Capitalism*. Durham, NC: Duke University Press.

Johnson, B.S. (1973), *Aren't You Rather Young to Be Writing Your Memoirs?* First published, 1973. In Bradbury (1990), 151–68.

Johnson, Samuel (1958), *Rasselas, Poems, and Selected Prose*. Bertrand H. Bronson (ed.). New York: Holt, Rinehart and Winston.

Joyce, James (1993), *Ulysses*. First published, 1922. Jeri Johnson (ed.). Oxford: Oxford University Press.

Joyce, James (2000), *Dubliners*. First published, 1914. With an Introduction and Notes by Terence Brown. London: Penguin.

Karl, Frederick and Laurence Davies (eds) (1986), *The Collected Letters of Joseph Conrad*. Volume 2, 1898–1902. Cambridge: Cambridge University Press.

Kettle, Arnold (1967), *An Introduction to the English Novel*, second edn. Volume 1. London: Hutchinson.

Kielar, Wieslaw (1982), *Anus Mundi: Five Years in Auschwitz*. Trans. from the German by Susanne Flatauer. First published in Polish, 1972. Harmondsworth: Penguin.

Kogon, Eugen (2006), *The Theory and Practice of Hell: The German Concentration Camps and the System behind Them*. Trans. Heinz Norden. Revised edn. First published in German, 1946. New York: Farrar, Straus and Giroux.

Kundera, Milan (1988), *The Art of the Novel*. Trans. Linda Asher. First published in French, 1986. London and Boston: Faber.

Lamarque, Peter (1996), *Fictional Points of View*. Ithaca: Cornell University Press.

Lamarque, Peter and Stein Haugom Olsen (1994), *Truth, Fiction, and Literature: A Philosophical Perspective*. Oxford: Clarendon Press.

Landow, George (1992), *Hypertext: The Convergence of Contemporary Critical Thought and Technology*. Baltimore, MD: Johns Hopkins University Press.

Larkin, Philip (1975), *Jill: A Novel*. First published, 1946. London: Faber and Faber.

Lawrence, D.H. (1994), *Collected Stories*. Everyman's Library. London: David Campbell Publishers.

Lawrence, James Cooper (1976), "A Theory of the Short Story." First published, 1917. In May 1976, 60–71.

Leitch, Thomas M. (1989), "The Debunking Rhythm of the American Short Story." In Lohafer and Clarey 1989, 130–47.

Levenson, Michael (1991), *Modernism and the Fate of Individuality: Character and Novelistic Form from Conrad to Woolf*. Cambridge: Cambridge University Press.

Levi, Primo (1996), *Survival in Auschwitz: The Nazi Assault on Humanity*. First published in English as *If This Is a Man*. Trans. from the Italian by Stuart Woolf. First published in Italian, 1958. New York: Simon & Schuster.

Little, T.E. (1984), *The Fantasts*. Avebury: Amersham.

Lodge, David (1992), *The Art of Fiction*, Harmondsworth: Penguin.
A collection of short articles originally published in The Independent on Sunday, *offering both accessible and authoritative accounts of fifty different terms and concepts ranging from "Beginning" to "Ending" and taking in others such as suspense, stream of consciousness, defamiliarization, repetition, showing and telling, symbolism, allegory, epiphany, metafiction, aporia, and the Uncanny. All are illustrated with extracts from either classic or modern texts.*

Lohafer, Susan and Jo Ellyn Clarey (eds) (1989), *Short Story Theory at a Crossroads*. Baton Rouge and London: Louisiana State University Press.
A most useful collection of extracts and articles concerned to define and discuss the short story. Updates and extends May (1976) (see below).

Lothe, Jakob (1989), *Conrad's Narrative Method*. Oxford: Clarendon Press.

Lothe, Jakob (2000), *Narrative in Fiction and Film: An Introduction*. Oxford: Oxford University Press.
A very readable and stimulating introduction to the differences between narrative in prose fiction and in film. Detailed and rewarding discussion of theoretical issues and of film adaptations of Kafka's The Trial, *James Joyce's* "The Dead," *Joseph Conrad's* Heart of Darkness, *Francis Ford Coppola's* Apocalypse Now, *and Virginia Woolf's* To the Lighthouse.

Lothe, Jakob (2002), "Openings: Thomas Hardy's *Tess of the D'Urbervilles* and Knut Hamsun's *Hunger*." In Bjørn Tysdahl, Mats Jansson, Jakob Lothe and Steen Klitgård Povlsen (eds), *English and Nordic Modernisms* (Norwich: Norvik Press), 77–101.

Lubbock, Percy (1921), *The Craft of Fiction*. London: Jonathan Cape.

Lugowski, Clemens (1990), *Form, Individuality and the Novel*. Trans. John Dixon. Revised edn. First published in German, 1932 (revised edn 1976). Cambridge: Polity Press.

Lukács, Georg (1969), *The Historical Novel*. Trans. Stanley and Hannah Mitchell. First published in Russian, 1937, and in English, 1962. Harmondsworth: Penguin.

Luria, A.R. (1976), *Cognitive Development*. Trans. Martin Lopez-Morillas and Lynn Solotaroff. First published in Russian, 1974. Cambridge, MA: Harvard University Press.

Mansfield, Katherine (1951), *The Garden Party and Other Stories*. First published, 1922. Harmondsworth: Penguin.

March-Russell, Paul (2009), *The Short Story: An Introduction*. Edinburgh: Edinburgh University Press.

An excellent introduction to the short story; wide-ranging in its scope, up-to date with recent developments, and very readable.

Margolies, David (1985), *Novel and Society in Elizabethan England.* Beckenham: Croom Helm.

Marías, Javier (1997), *Tomorrow in the Battle Think on Me.* Trans. from the Spanish by Margaret Jull Costa. First published in Spanish, 1994 and in English, 1996. New York: New Directions.

Martin, W., with D. Hinrichs and S. Baker (2006), *The Art of the Short Story.* Boston and New York: Houghton Mifflin.

Maupassant, Guy de (1975), *Bel-Ami.* First published in French, 1885. Trans. Douglas Parmée. Harmondsworth: Penguin.

May, Charles E. (ed.) (1976), *Short Story Theories.* Athens: Ohio University Press.
Along with Lohafer and Clarey's collection (see above), this provides a most useful collection of extracts and articles concerned with theories of the short story.

May, Charles E. (ed.) (1994), *The New Short Story Theories.* Athens: Ohio University Press.

McGann, Jerome J. (1991), *The Textual Condition.* Princeton: Princeton University Press.

McHale, Brian (1978), "Free Indirect Discourse: A Survey of Recent Accounts," *Poetics and Theory of Literature*, 3, 249–87.

McHale, Brian (1987), *Postmodernist Fiction.* London: Methuen.
McHale's study is extremely wide-ranging, including authors and texts from several continents, and theoretically penetrating and insightful. The author is very well versed in modern narrative theory, but he brings other theoretical perspectives to bear on his analyses.

McKeon, Michael (1987), *The Origins of the English Novel 1600–1740.* Baltimore: Johns Hopkins University Press.
In common with J. Paul Hunter's study (see above), this is an indispensable inquiry into the sources of the English novel. Contains many thought-provoking arguments about such things as the relationship between the novel's linear order and "quasi-Calvinist" view of the linear life of the hard-working middle classes.

Meek, James (2004), "Get a Life," *Guardian*, 3. August. Accessed on <http://www.guardian.co.uk/online/story/0,3605,1274808,00.html>, August 30, 2004.

Meindl, Dieter (2008), "Henry James's Turn-of-the-Century Nouvelles: Centers of Consciousness and Unlived Lives." In Jakob Lothe, Hans H. Skei and Per Winther (eds), *Less Is More: Short Fiction Theory and Analysis* (Oslo: Novus Press), 30–44.

Michaels, Anne (1998), *Fugitive Pieces*. First published, 1996. London: Bloomsbury.

Millett, Kate (1971), *Sexual Politics*. First published, 1970. London: Sphere Books.

Milligan, Spike (1980), *Mussolini: His Part in My Downfall*. First published, 1978. Harmondsworth: Penguin.

Montfort, Nick (2003), *Twisty Little Passages: An Approach to Interactive Fiction*. Cambridge, MA and London: MIT Press.

Moretti, Franco (1998), *Atlas of the European Novel 1800–1900*. London and New York: Verso.
   Contains answers to questions such as: Which places and geographical areas are referred to by novelists, and do they change over time? Where are books published? Which books do people have in their homes? What percentage of library books are novels—and what did nineteenth-century librarians think of this?

Moretti, Franco (2013a), "Conjectures on World Literature." First published, 2000. In D'haen *et al* 2013, 161–70.

Moretti, Franco (2013b), *Distant Reading*. London and New York: Verso.

Moretti, Franco (2013c), "More Conjectures." First published, 2003. In D'haen *et al* 2013, 170–75.

Newman, Judie (1995), *The Ballistic Bard: Postcolonial Fictions*. London: Arnold.

Ngugi, James (1972), *Weep Not, Child*. First published, 1964. London: Heinemann Educational.

Nomberg-Przytyk, Sara (1985), *Auschwitz: True Tales from a Grotesque Land*. Trans. Roslyn Hirsch. David Pfefferkorn and David H. Hirsch (eds). Chapel Hill and London: University of North Carolina Press.

Novak, Maximilian E. (1991), "Review of J. Paul Hunter," *Before Novels: The Cultural Contexts of Eighteenth-century English Fiction, Times Literary Supplement*, no. 4582, January 25, 8.

O'Connor, Frank (1963), *The Lonely Voice: A Study of the Short Story*. London: Macmillan.
   A quirky but insightful account of the short story, written by one of its leading practitioners.

O'Faolain, Sean (1972), *The Short Story*. First published, 1948. Cork: The Mercier Press.

O'Rourke, William (1989), "Morphological Metaphors for the Short Story: Matters of Production, Reproduction, and Consumption." In Lohafer and Clarey 1989, 193–205.

Otten, Thomas J. (2006), *A Superficial Reading of Henry James: Preoccupations with the Material World*. Columbus: Ohio State University Press.

Phelan, James (1996), *Narrative as Rhetoric: Technique, Audiences, Ethics, Ideology.* Columbus: Ohio State University Press.

Phelan, James (2005), *Living to Tell about It: A Rhetoric and Ethics of Character Narration.* Ithaca and London: Cornell University Press.
If you want to learn about rhetorical narratology, this is the place to start.

Phelan, James (2007), *Experiencing Fiction: Judgments, Progressions, and the Rhetorical Theory of Narrative.* Columbus: Ohio State University Press.
A development of Phelan's "rhetorical narratological" approach to fiction, this time focusing on the "character narrator." Includes chapters on Kazuo Ishiguro's The Remains of the Day *and Vladimir Nabokov's* Lolita. *Phelan is very good at showing how the ethical questions such works raise for readers cannot be separated from their rhetorical techniques and performances.*

Price, Leah (2000), *The Anthology and the Rise of the Novel: From Richardson to George Eliot.* Cambridge: Cambridge University Press.

Prince, Gerald (1988), *A Dictionary of Narratology.* First published, 1987. Aldershot: Scolar Press.

Propp, Vladimir (1968), *Morphology of the Folktale.* Trans. Laurence Scott. Revised edn. Austin: University of Texas Press.

Raw, Lawrence (2006), *Adapting Henry James to the Screen: Gender, Fiction, and Film.* Lanham, MD: Scarecrow Press.

Rem, Tore (2002), "The Englishing of *Hunger*: Knut Hamsun, George Egerton and Leonard Smithers." In Bjørn Tysdahl, Mats Jansson, Jakob Lothe and Steen Klitgård Povlsen (eds), *English and Nordic Modernisms* (Norwich: Norvik Press), 61–76.

Rhys, Jean (1969), *Good Morning, Midnight.* First published, 1939. Harmondsworth: Penguin.

Rhys, Jean (1971), *After Leaving Mr Mackenzie.* First published, 1930. Harmondsworth, Penguin.

Richardson, Brian (2006), *Unnatural Voices: Extreme Narration in Modern and Contemporary Fiction.* Columbus: Ohio State University Press.

Richardson, Samuel (1985), *Clarissa or the History of a Young Lady.* First published, 1747–8. Edited by Angus Ross. London: Penguin.

Rimmon-Kenan, Shlomith (1983), *Narrative Fiction: Contemporary Poetics.* London: Methuen.
Still probably the best place to start for those requiring an introduction to structuralist-influenced theories of narrative. Clearly and concisely written, and very fully illustrated with examples from a range of texts.

Rohrberger, Mary (2004), "Origins, Development, Substance, and Design of the Short Story. How I Got Hooked on the Short Story and Where It Led Me." In Per Winther, Jakob Lothe and Hans H. Skei (eds), *The Art of Brevity: Excursions in Short Fiction Theory and Analysis* (Columbia: University of South Carolina Press), 1–13.

Ryan, Marie-Laure (2001), *Narrative as Virtual Reality: Immersion and Activity in Literature and Electronic Media*. Baltimore and London: Johns Hopkins University Press.

Saussure, Ferdinand de (1974), *Course in General Linguistics*. Trans. Wade Buskin. Charles Bally and Albert Sechehaye (eds). Revised edn. London: Peter Owen.

Schoene, Berthold (2009), *The Cosmopolitan Novel*. Edinburgh: Edinburgh University Press.

Sebald, W.G. (2001), *Austerlitz*. Trans. Anthea Bell. First published in German, 2001. London: Penguin.

Seidel, Michael (2000), "The Man Who Came to Dinner: Ian Watt and the Theory of Formal Realism." *Reconsidering the Rise of the Novel*. Special issue of *Eighteenth-Century Fiction*, 12(2–3), January–April 2000, 193–212.

Seymour-Smith, Martin (1973), *Guide to Modern World Literature*. London: Wolfe Publishing.

Shaw, Valerie (1983), *The Short Story: A Critical Introduction*. London and New York: Longman.

Skinner, John (2001), *An Introduction to Eighteenth-century Fiction: Raising the Novel*. Houndmills: Palgrave.
A very useful study that opens with a discussion of theoretical and critical issues, the formation of a canon, and the issue of gender, and then devotes chapters to the work of a range of canonical and less well known novelists, ending with Jane Austen.

Skvorecky, Joseph (1985), *The Engineer of Human Souls*. Trans. Paul Wilson. First published in Czech, 1977. London: Chatto and Windus/The Hogarth Press.

Spoto, Donald (1983), *The Dark Side of Genius: The Life of Alfred Hitchcock*. Boston: Little, Brown and Company.

Springer, Mary Doyle (1975), *Forms of the Modern Novella*. Chicago and London: University of Chicago Press.

Stam, Robert (2005), *Literature and Film: A Guide to the Theory and Practice of Film Adaptation*. Oxford: Blackwell.

Thomas, Brook (1991), *The New Historicism: And Other Old-fashioned Topics*. Princeton: Princeton University Press.

Thomsen, Mads Rosendahl (2008), *Mapping World Literature: International Canonization and Transnational Literatures*. London: Continuum.

Todorov, Tzvetan (1984), *Mikhail Bakhtin: The Dialogical Principle*. Minneapolis: University of Minnesota Press.
An excellent introduction to the work and ideas of a writer who has had a profound influence on our ideas about the novel.

Toker, Leona (1993), *Eloquent Reticence: Withholding Information in Fictional Narrative*. Lexington: University Press of Kentucky.
   A must for anyone interested in how the creative powers of readers contribute to the experience of reading novels. Toker takes a number of examples in which the reader has to "fill in" missing or delayed information. There are excellent chapters on The Sound and the Fury, Nostromo, Bleak House, Emma, Tom Jones, A Passage to India, *and* Absalom, Absalom!

Truffaut, François (1986), With the collaboration of Helen G. Scott. *Hitchcock*. Revised edn. First published, 1968. London: Paladin.

Various authors (1956), *Did It Happen? Stories*. London: Oldbourne Press.

Vonnegut Jr, Kurt (1972), *Slaughterhouse 5*. First published, 1969. Frogmore, St Albans: Granada Publishing. (Some editions also render the title as *Slaughterhouse-Five or The Children's Crusade A Duty-Dance with Death*.)

Walsh, Richard (2007), *The Rhetoric of Fictionality. Narrative Theory and the Idea of Fiction*. Columbus: The Ohio State University Press.
   A difficult but original and challenging book. Walsh writes from within the perspective of rhetorical narratology, and argues that the distinctiveness of fiction "consists in the recognizably distinct rhetorical set invoked" by a particular use of language. Contains a fresh and iconoclastic view of the concepts of fabula and sjužet [story and plot] in discussion of literary fiction.

Warner, William B. (1998), *Licensing Entertainment: The Elevation of Novel Reading in Britain, 1694–1750*. Berkeley: University of California Press.

Wa Thiong'o, Ngũgĩ (1982), *Devil on the Cross*. First published in Gĩkũyũ, 1980, and in the author's English translation, 1982. London: Heinemann Educational.

Watt, Ian (1963), *The Rise of the Novel*. First published, 1957. Harmondsworth: Penguin.
   In spite of repeated attempts to qualify, rebuff, or supersede Watt's arguments (see for example Reconsidering the Rise of the Novel, *above) this is a book that continues to require and repay attention.*

Watt, Ian (1980), *Conrad in the Nineteenth Century*. London: Chatto & Windus.

Watts, Cedric (1984), *The Deceptive Text: An Introduction to Covert Plots*. Brighton: Harvester.

Winterson, Jeanette (2005), *Lighthousekeeping*. First published, 2004. London: Harper Perennial.

Wood, James (2009), *How Fiction Works*. London: Vintage.
   An accessible but sophisticated discussion of what the title promises. Very useful chapters on "character" and "language," as well as helpful material on such topics as Free Indirect Discourse and "thisness."

Woolf, Leonard (ed.) (1972), *A Writer's Diary: Beings Extracts from the Diary of Virginia Woolf.* London: Hogarth Press.

Woolf, Virginia (1966a), *Collected Essays.* Volume 1. London: Hogarth Press.

Woolf, Virginia (1966b), *Collected Essays.* Volume 2. London: Hogarth Press.

Woolf, Virginia (1992), *Mrs Dalloway.* First published, 1925. Edited by Stella McNichol. London: Penguin.

Woolf, Virginia (1998), *A Room of One's Own.* Edited by Morag Shiach. First published, 1929. Oxford: Oxford University Press.

Wyndham, Francis and Diana Melly (eds) (1984), *Jean Rhys: Letters 1931–1966.* London: André Deutsch.

Zunshine, Lisa (2006), *Why We Read Fiction: Theory of Mind and the Novel.* Columbus: Ohio State University Press.

Index

Terms defined in the Glossary generally include cross-references to previous discussion in the body of the book, and are not included in the index.